A
FINGERTIP GUIDE
TO
CRIMINAL LAW

A FINGERTIP GUIDE TO CRIMINAL LAW

J Ross Harper
Peter Hamilton
with
Paul McGuigan

Fourth edition

Butterworths
Law Society of Scotland

Edinburgh   1999

Butterworths

United Kingdom	Butterworths, a Division of Reed Elsevier (UK) Ltd, 4 Hill Street, EDINBURGH EH2 3JZ and Halsbury House, 35 Chancery Lane, LONDON WC2A 1EL
Australia	Butterworths, a Division of Reed International Books Australia Pty Ltd, CHATSWOOD, New South Wales
Canada	Butterworths Canada Ltd, MARKHAM, Ontario
Hong Kong	Butterworths Asia (Hong Kong), HONG KONG
India	Butterworths India, NEW DELHI
Ireland	Butterworth (Ireland) Ltd, DUBLIN
Malaysia	Malayan Law Journal Sdn Bhd, KUALA LUMPUR
New Zealand	Butterworths of New Zealand Ltd, WELLINGTON
Singapore	Butterworths Asia, SINGAPORE
South Africa	Butterworths Publishers (Pty) Ltd, DURBAN
USA	Lexis Law Publishing, CHARLOTTESVILLE, Virginia

Law Society of Scotland
26 Drumsheugh Gardens, EDINBURGH EH3 7YR

A CIP Catalogue record for this book is available from the British Library.

First published 1986

ISBN 0 406 98259 7

Typeset by Phoenix Photosetting, Chatham, Kent
Printed by Thomson Litho Ltd, East Kilbride

Visit us at our website: http://www.butterworthsscotland.com

Preface

When this book first appeared, with its aim of providing access at his or her fingertips for the criminal court practitioner to the statute and case law, the authors would have been surprised to learn that it would one day be necessary to pen a preface to its fourth edition.

There is no falling-off, however, in consolidation and in new legislation in the field of criminal law (the novel Human Rights provisions being the most recent example) and the text seeks to take account of this.

Of equal importance is the need to ensure as best we can that the references to case law allow the user to find the up-to-date authority which sets out present judicial views on any particular topic. As the case reports amply demonstrate, traditions of pragmatic flexibility and vitality remain vigorous in the day-to-day activities of the Scottish criminal courts.

It is important to remind the users of this book that its purpose is to provide the practitioner with a starting point for fuller, more detailed research on salient points in issue in the conducting of a case.

We have taken this opportunity to set out the contents in what seems to us a more conveniently arranged way. The format in the sentencing section now accords with the other sections of the book.

We have enjoyed good fortune in the help provided with earlier editions by those who have worked with us. The task this time was particularly daunting and onerous, because of the volume of statute and case law which required to be updated. Paul McGuigan steadfastly refused to be daunted, and shouldered lightly the burdens it presented. Our gratitude to him, and to our patient publishers, is profound.

The law is stated as at 31 December 1998.

J Ross Harper
Peter Hamilton
June 1999

Contents

Table of Statutes

Table of Statutory Instruments

Table of Cases

Table of Cases

Table of Cases

PAGE

PAGE

SUBSTANTIVE LAW

OFFENCES OF DISHONESTY

THEFT

Definition

Theft is the **felonious taking** or **appropriation** of the **property of another** without the consent of the owner and **with intent to deprive** him of that property.

COMMENTARY	CASE LAW	STATUTE LAW
Felonious taking Amotio: taking property from its place. Place: (a) Container—property must be taken out of container before amotio occurs. Movement inside the container may be attempt to steal only.	*Peter Anderson* 1800 Hume I 72 Taking something out of a till.	
(b) Room, etc—amotio occurs if property taken out of room *or* moved in a way indicating intention to steal. (c) Open spaces—any movement of the property probably sufficient for amotio (Gordon, p 464).	*Cornelius O'Neil* (1845) 2 Broun 394 O'N raised window from outside. With a stick he moved some clothing in the room from original position to a place nearer the window. *Held* theft completed.	
Appropriation By dealing with goods as if they were one's own property,	*Dewar v HMA* 1945 JC 5 Manager of crematorium convicted of theft of two coffins and the lids of others which had been received for cremation. Sold them for use as coffee tables. *Herron v Diack* 1973 SLT (Sh Ct) 27 Manager of firm of funeral directors convicted of theft for dishonest appropriation of a steel casket intended for sea burial. *Black v Carmichael* 1992 SCCR 709 Wheel clamping. Car clamped in a private car park, notice attached demanding payment for release. Sheriff said it could be theft but not extortion. Appeal. *Held* that it was theft and extortion. Extortion to seek to enforce a debt otherwise than by legal process even if legitimate. The appropriation necessary for theft existed in the immobilising of the car and the mens rea in deliberately so appropriating. Intention to deprive temporarily would suffice. Theft by appropriation in the car park, detaining the motor car against the owner's will. But see:	

Mackenzie v Maclean 1981 SLT (Sh Ct) 40
Bar manager told to dispose of damaged cans of beer. Sold cans to passers-by at rubbish tip.
Held that abandoned cans were the property of the Crown, but found not guilty due to lack of intent to steal.

or by finding.
Finding property of another and appropriating it, is theft.

John Smith (1838) 2 Swin 28
Found a wallet and appropriated it. Convicted of theft.

Burgh Police (Scotland) Act 1892, s 412. It is an offence for a finder of property to fail to hand it into a police station within 48 hours.

Lawson v Heatley 1962 SLT 53
L received £1 from son which she knew must have been lost. Made no attempt to find owner and appropriated it for her own use. Convicted of theft.

MacMillan v Lowe 1991 SCCR 113
M found with chequebooks, said he had found them four hours earlier. Convicted on the grounds that he had not tried to hand them in and tried to conceal them from the police. Upheld on appeal.

Repealed by Civic Government (Scotland) Act 1982, s 67. Duty of finder of property to take reasonable care of it and to hand it to a police constable or official mentioned in subsection (3).

Kane v Friel 1997 SCCR 207
Appellant's conviction of theft by finding quashed on appeal, since no evidence inferring the appellant must have known the property (piping and sink on waste ground) were items someone intended to retain.

Under s 134 of CG(S)A 1982 the provisions of the Burgh Police (Scotland) Act 1892 remained in force until end of 1984. See also CG(S)A 1982, s 137(3).

CG(S)A 1982, s 73: no right of ownership conferred by finding.

Property
Anything which is the subject of public or private ownership can be stolen.

A *res nullius*, eg a wild animal, cannot be stolen until brought into ownership.

John Huie (1842) 1 Broun 383
Once fish are in a fisherman's net they are his property and can be stolen from him.

Animals which have escaped from captivity.

Valentine v Kennedy 1985 SCCR 89
Theft of rainbow trout which had escaped from 'stank' or enclosure.
Held that the enclosed trout were clearly owned by person who purchased them from fish farm and who subsequently enclosed them. If, despite adequate precautions, some trout escaped, they still were owned and could be stolen by another.
Per Sheriff Younger: '. . . if some of these rainbow trout escaped occasionally in spite of proper precautions from that enclosed water or stank I consider that they as escapers remain the property of that purchaser insofar as they can be identified as his property; accordingly, someone who catches trout which he knows to have escaped . . . is guilty of theft, if he does not return them to their rightful owner.'

Of another
A person cannot steal his own property (Hume I, 77).

Sandlan v HMA 1983 SCCR 71
S and K charged with theft of jewellery, money and sales records from company of which S was a director. K's defence was that he believed goods belonged to S personally. S convicted. K found not proven.

Hamilton v Wilson 1994 SLT 431
Accused convicted of theft of his illegitimate child. Upheld on appeal, given he did not have parental rights of custody and not necessary to deprive mother permanently.

If a person takes, believing what he is taking is his own, or that he has the owner's concurrence, he is not guilty of theft, but his belief must be reasonable and he must prove it (Macdonald, p 18).

Dewar v HMA 1945 SC 5
The belief in this case was totally unreasonable.

With intent to deprive
Generally, intention to deprive permanently required.

Kivlin v Milne 1979 SLT (Notes) 2
Theft of car. Abandoned where owner could not find it. Found by police.
Held, on appeal, that facts demonstrated that appellant had intention to deprive owner permanently of car.

Herron v Best 1976 SLT (Sh Ct) 80
Car mechanic removed van from its owner, without permission, in pursuit of unpaid repair bill. Intended to return it when bill was paid.
Held conditional intention to appropriate van not sufficient for theft. (Disapproved in *Milne v Tudhope* 1981 SC 53.)

Smith v Dewar 1977 SLT (Sh Ct) 75
Taking a moped with intention of having a 'shot'. Not guilty due to lack of theftuous intent.
Would, however, if charged be guilty of offence under Road Traffic Act 1988, s 178.

But in certain exceptional cases, intention to deprive temporarily may suffice where the accused's purpose is reprehensible.

Milne v Tudhope 1981 JC 53
Accused contracted to carry out work on cottage. Owner dissatisfied and accused refused to remedy work unless he received further payment. Removed and stripped house of various items to force owner to grant further payment. Convicted of theft.
Opinion of the court: 'We agree that in certain exceptional cases an intention to deprive temporarily will suffice and disagree that an intention to deprive permanently is essential.'

Sandlan v HMA 1983 SCCR 71
Goods taken for a nefarious purpose with intention of returning them later sufficient for conviction of theft.

Kidston v Annan 1984 SCCR 20
K received goods from owner for the purpose of estimating cost of repairs. He refused to return the goods unless owner paid for repairs.
Held guilty of theft.

Fowler v O'Brien 1994 SCCR 112
Intention to deprive indefinitely. Bicycle taken without permission but openly and not returned. Conviction upheld on appeal.
Held that it could not be said that the intention was to deprive permanently or temporarily, most accurate to say indefinitely. No need for theft to be clandestine.

Substantive law

Theft outside Scotland.

Criminal Procedure (Scotland) Act 1995, s 11(4). Every person who has in his possession in Scotland property which he has stolen in any other part of UK may be dealt with in Scotland in same way as if offence committed here, and any person who receives in Scotland property stolen in any other part of UK may also be dealt with in Scotland as if he had stolen it there.

Alternative verdicts.

When accused is charged with theft he can be convicted of reset but not vice versa: Sch 3, para 8(2) of CP(S)A 1995. When charged with robbery, fraud he may be convicted of theft: Sch 3, para 8(3). When charged with theft may be convicted of fraud, or may be convicted of theft although the circumstances in law amount to robbery: Sch 3, para 8(4).

Aggravation of theft

Theft may be aggravated by certain factors; in particular, **by opening lockfast places, by housebreaking** or **by violence**.

COMMENTARY	CASE LAW	STATUTE LAW
By opening lockfast places Applies to anything secured by a lock apart from buildings.	*Jas Gray* 1824 Alison I 296 Breaking open a chest in a stable loft by staving in the lid. *McLeod v Mason* 1981 SCCR 75 Lockfast car. Unnecessary to prove whether intent to steal car or contents or both, since in the circumstances theftuous intent could be presumed from the facts.	
The effraction of the lockfast place must precede the theft and be for the purpose of the theft.	*Jas Stuart and Alex Low* (1842) 1 Broun 260 Accused of stealing a lockfast chest and then forcing it open and stealing its contents. *Held*, that removing a container meant removing its contents, and aggravation of opening lockfast place was not relevantly charged.	
By housebreaking 'House' covers any roofed building.	*John Fraser* 1831 Bell's Notes 41 A henhouse.	
'Breaking': any means of surmounting the security of the building or by unusual entry.	*Alston and Forrest* (1837) 1 Swin 433 Improper use of a key to enter. *Jas Davidson* (1841) 2 Swin 630 Entry through a window was normal mode of access and did not constitute the aggravation of housebreaking. *Burns v Allan* 1987 SCCR 449 B charged with attempted housebreaking with intent to steal in that he disconnected the external burglar alarm of premises in question. *Held* that an alarm system is an integral part of the security of a building and to disconnect it is plainly an attempt to overcome that security and therefore constitutes attempted housebreaking with intent to steal.	
Housebreaking must precede and be for purpose of theft.	*Cornelius O'Neil* (1845) 2 Broun 394 Standing outside window O'N used a stick to remove handkerchief and socks in room, having overcome security by pushing up window. *Donaghy v Normand* 1991 SCCR 877 D convicted of housebreaking with intent to steal. D had entered house to rescue an intruder who had been discovered by the houseowner. On appeal *held* that there was no need for D to give explanation for his presence in the house but if he did not, court entitled to draw its own inference.	
Crime completed by gaining entry and stealing. Actual bodily entry not required. *Note:* The act of housebreaking without intent to steal does not of itself constitute a nominate crime (but see Malicious mischief, p 18, or could be Breach of the peace, p 48).	*McClung v McLeod* (1974) 38 JCL 221 Court held that the essential feature was the violation of the security of the premises, not the entry. Accused had broken the window of the premises but not actually entered them. Conviction of housebreaking with intent to steal upheld.	

Substantive law

By violence
If theft is followed by violence it may constitute the aggravated offence of theft and assault.

See also: Robbery, p 10.

Associated crimes.
Clandestinely taking possession of property.

Reid and Barnet (1844) 2 Broun 116
Struggle to retain a purse by its owner after accused had snatched it from him. Not robbery to use force to retain a stolen article.

Strathern v Seaforth 1926 JC 100
'Clandestinely taking possession of a motor-car, property of another, in the knowledge that permission to do so would be refused.'
Defence objected to relevancy of complaint. Sustained by sheriff, but High Court held complaint relevant under law of Scotland.

Murray v Robertson 1927 JC 1
Fish merchant charged with clandestinely taking possession of a number of fish boxes belonging to other merchants and using them to transport his own fish. Conviction quashed on basis that accused had used boxes openly.

Road Traffic Act 1988, s 178(1)(a): taking and driving a motor vehicle without consent or lawful authority.

References: Hume I, 57; Alison I, 250; Macdonald, 16; Gordon, 449; Gane and Stoddart, 548.

Civic Government (Scotland) Act 1982, ss 57, 58

Civic Government (Scotland) Act 1982, ss 57, 58.

Section 57(1). **Any person** who without lawful authority **is found** in or on **any building, premises, vehicle or vessel** in circumstances from which it may be reasonably inferred that he intended to commit theft there, shall be guilty of an offence.

Section 57(2). 'Theft' includes any aggravation, including robbery.

Section 58(1), (4). Any person with **two or more convictions for theft which are 'not spent'**, who has or has **recently** had in his possession any tool or object from which it may be reasonably inferred that he intended to commit theft or has committed theft, and is unable to demonstrate satisfactorily that his possession was not for this purpose, shall be guilty of an offence.

The maximum penalty under each section is level 4 fine or three months' imprisonment or both.

COMMENTARY	CASE LAW	STATUTE LAW
Any person Person no longer requires to have been a 'known thief'.		Civic Government (Scotland) Act 1982, s 57, replaces the provisions of the Prevention of Crimes Act 1871, s 7, and also the Burgh Police (Scotland) Act 1892, s 409.
Is found Must be actually present on the building, etc. Not sufficient to prove that he had been there or might have been there.	*Maclean v Paterson* 1968 JC 67 Convicted of having been found in a goods yard. Ample circumstantial evidence but no direct eye-witness evidence. *Held* could not be held to have been found! (Prosecution under Prevention of Crimes Act 1871, s 7.)	
Any building, premises, vehicle or vessel Defines more clearly the locus compared to the old provision of 'certain places'.	*McIntyre v Morton* (1912) 6 Adam 634 Found in entrance of hotel. Convicted. (Prosecution under Prevention of Crimes Act 1871.)	
	Fulton v Normand 1995 SCCR 629 Conviction upheld on appeal. Found that explanation that looking for friend in hotel (who was not a guest there) unconvincing, since he avoided reception and was found in corridors accessed by fire doors which were open.	Civic Government (Scotland) Act 1982, s 57(1).
	Moran v Jessop 1989 SCCR 205 M found on roof of office block undergoing renovation, which had been broken into by others. M argued that there was no case to answer as Crown had not proved that he had no lawful authority to be there. Defence evidence did not include any evidence of lawful authority and M convicted. *Held* on appeal that the circumstances were such as to support the inference of absence of lawful authority and appeal refused.	
	Frail v Lees 1997 SCCR 354 Conviction upheld on appeal. Reference to 'all the circumstances' includes circumstances which may have taken place some distance from locus but infer intention to commit crime at particular locus. Evidence led of suspicious actings at other places prior to being found in garden of house in circumstances set out in s 57(1).	Civic Government (Scotland) Act 1982, s 57(1).

Two or more convictions for theft which are 'not spent'

Re provision of Rehabilitation of Offenders Act 1974, s 1. After a set period certain convictions must be treated as 'spent' and convicted person treated as a rehabilitated person. Consult statute for definition of 'spent'.

Civic Government (Scotland) Act 1982, s 58, replaces reference to known thief or reputed thief and the offence no longer extends to possession of unexplained sums of money or articles, nor does the offence apply to 'associates of known thieves'.

Recently
Within fourteen days before the date of arrest without warrant, issue of warrant, or service of complaint against him alleging that he has committed the offence.

Section 58(2)

Possession of tools.

Section 58

Doherty v Normand 1996 SCCR 701
At trial appellant did not give evidence, on view that any explanation of possession of screwdriver would be too late in light of dictum in *Mathieson v Crowe* 1993 SCCR 1100. *Held*, by bench of 5 judges, that (1) no time limit on when explanation can be made as long as one which could have been made at time and whether explanation was satisfactory was to be determined at trial; (2) whether a caution should be administered is at discretion of police who cannot charge accused until given opportunity to explain; (3) but since reliance on *Mathieson v Crowe*, conviction quashed. *Mathieson v Crowe* disapproved: time to determine innocent possession was when found in possession. Observed by LJ-C that explanation put forward at trial too late.

Philips v Macleod 1995 SCCR 319
Appellant went down lane with what looked like bag of tools but emerged without them. Denied knowledge of them three hours later in interview. At trial accepted he had tools but argued required to be asked for explanation at time of offence (per *Mathieson v Crowe*). Conviction upheld on appeal: explanation only required before charge. *Mathieson v Crowe* distinguished.

THEFT

SENTENCING POLICY
Clark v Cardle 1989 SCCR 92—C, unemployed and dependent on state benefits, pleaded guilty to theft by housebreaking of nine jackets valued at over £4,000. Sentenced to six months' imprisonment and ordered to pay £500 compensation at £3 per week after release.
Held on appeal that in light of financial and family circumstances, it was unreasonable to impose order on top of maximum sentence and compensation order quashed.

Collins v Lowe 1990 SCCR 605—C convicted of theft by housebreaking, damage caused. Four months' imprisonment and compensation order to cover the damage, humiliation and distress. Upheld on appeal.

McQueeney v Carmichael 1991 SCCR 221—M and another caught stealing tiles worth £350. Fined £200 and van worth £1,500 used in theft ordered to be forfeited. Upheld on appeal. Criminals using vehicles do so at their own risk.

Downie v Normand 1992 SCCR 894—Security guard stealing £4,500 from employer, no money recovered. First offender. Three months' imprisonment upheld on appeal.

McCulloch v Friel 1993 SCCR 7—Plagium by 53-year-old, first offender with alcohol problem. Three months' imprisonment reduced to 200 hours' community service on appeal. Determination to beat the alcohol problem.

Holywood v Brown 1996 SCCR 64—17-year-old first offender, no previous convictions at time of offence, pleaded guilty to three charges of theft by housebreaking and one of housebreaking with intent to steal, premises in each case being private dwelling house. Three months upheld on appeal.
Per Lord Sutherland: 'It must be made abundantly clear that breaking into private dwelling houses is something of which the courts will take a serious view.'

Robertson v Maguire 1996 SCCR 58—Theft of mail (1,666 letters) by post office employee. He delivered important ones, but medical condition meant he could not carry a heavy sack. Theft not for personal gain. 60 days' imprisonment quashed on appeal and 200 hours' community service substituted, since exceptional case within type of exception set out in *Fleming-Scott v HMA* 1991 SCCR 748.

Wilson v Hamilton 1996 SCCR 193—Criminal Procedure (Scotland) Act 1975, s 436, sub para 71 Criminal Justice (Scotland) Act 1980: forfeiture of property in possession at time of arrest used to facilitate offence. Sheriff admonished naive driver but said in absence of compelling reasons to contrary the car would be forfeited.
Held, matter discretionary; sheriff used wrong approach; and £1,000 fine substituted.

ROBBERY

Robbery is **theft achieved by means** of **personal violence** or **intimidation**. Robbery may be further aggravated where it is preceded by a distinct **assault**.

COMMENTARY	CASE LAW	STATUTE LAW
Theft Must be completed for conviction of robbery. See Theft, p 1.	*O'Neill v HMA* 1934 JC 98 Knocked woman against a wall and took her handbag. *Purves and McIntosh* 1846 Ark 178 Pulled watch out of victim's pocket and then dropped it. *Held* amotio completed when watch taken out of pocket. Convicted of robbery.	
Achieved by means Violence used must precede or be contemporaneous with theft and be for the purpose of the theft.	*Reid and Barnet* (1844) 2 Broun 116 *Held* that it is not robbery to use force against an owner so as to retain an article one has just snatched from him. *A McGinnes* (1842) 1 Broun 231 Accused, who had been charged with assault and robbery, was found guilty of robbery alone since the assault had been committed 'entirely for the purpose of the plunder' and was held not to constitute a distinct assault.	
Personal violence Degree of violence necessary may vary according to the circumstances but must be more than that required for 'theft by surprise'.	*Jas Fegen* (1838) 2 Swin 25 Pulled victim's watch out of pocket by grabbing at chain. Victim fell and while he was falling accused broke the chain by another pull. Convicted of robbery. *Givan* 1846 Ark 9 Accused put his arms round the victim and gripped him while other stole his watch. Convicted of robbery.	
The violence used need not constitute an actual physical assault.	*O'Neill v HMA* 1934 JC 98 Per LJ-C Aitchison: 'It is enough if the degree of force used can reasonably be described as violence.' Convicted. *Cromar v HMA* 1988 SCCR 635. Accused pulled at bag held by complainer, who tried to hold it but handle snapped. Conviction of robbery upheld on appeal. Per LJ-C Ross: '... the theft had been accomplished by means of personal violence and ... accordingly this was a robbery and not a theft.' On appeal, sentence reduced from nine to six months. *Flynn v HMA* 1995 SCCR 590. F convicted of robbery under deletion of all averments of assault. *Held*, jury not entitled to find appellant guilty of robbery since appellant not found responsible as actor or art and part for any violence. Verdict of theft substituted. Observed, that a relevant charge of robbery may be made without specifying the violence used.	

Intimidation
Consists of any threat of immediate injury which induces the victim to hand over the property (Gordon, p 556).

Matthias Little 1830 Alison I 231
Convicted of robbery. Robbed woman of valuable property by threats of instant death. Condemned and executed.

Assault
Where there is a distinct assault preceding the violence involved in the actual act of taking there may be a charge of assault and robbery.

O'Neil v HMA 1976 SLT (Notes) 7
Armed robbery of station booking office. Convicted of assault and robbery.

MacKay v HMA 1997 SCCR 743. Charge of assault and robbery, jury convicting under deletion of 'you did assault' but without deleting the specification of assault. There was corroboration that article taken by threats or violence but no corroboration of assault. *Held*, sufficient evidence that ring taken by violence or intimidation and complainer's evidence as to precisely what happened was merely narrative and did not require corroboration, and appeal refused.

References: Hume I, 104; Alison I, 227; Macdonald, 39; Gordon, 550; Gane and Stoddart, 572.

SENTENCING POLICY

Davidson and Anr v HMA 1981 SCCR 371—Armed robbery. D convicted. Used sawn-off shotguns (one of which was loaded and operative) and bayonet. £4,500 stolen. D had long criminal record. Sentence of 14 years' imprisonment. Appealed. Sentence reduced to 11 years, but court upheld trial judge's view that in the public interest a very substantial sentence was merited.

McIntyre v HMA 1989 SCCR 34—Assault and robbery. M convicted of luring doctor to locus by making false telephone call, where he was threatened with sticks and forced to hand over his medical bags. Sentenced to seven years' imprisonment. On appeal *held* that sentence was the minimum which could properly be imposed.

HMA v Hodgson 1998 SCCR 320—Criminal Procedure (Scotland) Act 1995, s 108. Assault and robbery. Accused pleaded guilty. Went to ex girlfriend's flat but she no longer lived there and he assaulted and robbed occupants.
Held, on appeal, deferred sentence of one year unduly lenient as failed to take account of breach of probation and need for treatment. Probation for two years on conditions of alcohol counselling and treatment of mental condition substituted.

Graham v HMA 1996 SCCR 105—Two armed robberies with loaded pistol within period of two hours.
Held, 15 years outside range of sentences normally considered for such offences, and sentence reduced to 12 years.

Deeney v HMA 1997 SCCR 361—Assault and robbery in shop by threatening with knife and robbing persons of £117. 18-year-old had no significant record and was drug-free at time of plea, despite history of addiction.
Held, five-year detention excessive, since accused had co-operated with police and pleaded guilty at an early stage, and three years substituted.

FRAUD

By **false pretence,** the **achievement** of a **definite practical result.**

COMMENTARY	CASE LAW	STATUTE LAW
False pretence The false pretence must be an essential, not collateral, matter.	*Tapsell v Prentice* (1910) 6 Adam 354 T pretended that she would be buying considerable amounts of provisions from a shopkeeper who bought a rug from her 'in excess of its value'. Per Lord Ardwall: 'There can be no crime in such a sale unless the fraudulent misrepresentations relate directly to the articles to be sold.' Conviction quashed. *Strathern v Fogal* 1922 JC 73 Misrepresentation made in relation to leasing of a shop. Charge irrelevant. Per Lord Hunter: 'The misrepresentation if made did not in any real sense affect the subject of the bargain but was essentially collateral.' *Hood v Young* (1853) 1 Irv 236 Misrepresentation was that two horses being sold for a 'knocked down' price were only parted with because the owner was about to emigrate. Convicted.	
It may be explicit,	*Turnbull v Stuart* (1898) 25 R (J) 78 Misrepresentation was that a horse being sold had been owned by people well known for their expertise in matters relating to horses. Convicted.	
or by implication,	*Alex Bannatyne* 1847 Ark 361 Misrepresentation that a mixture of grains in chiding oats was pure oats. Nothing actually said but way mixture 'got up' implied it. Convicted. *Jas Paton* (1858) 3 Irv 208 Prizes won by cattle at a show by inflating their skins and putting false horns on them. Charge relevant—not proven. *Steuart v Macpherson* 1918 JC 96 Misrepresentation by two men intent on cheating a third at cards by acting as if they were strangers to each other. Convicted.	
or result from silence when there is a duty to furnish information.	*Strathern v Fogal* 1922 JC 73 Non-disclosure of grassum exacted from tenants for renewal of lease. Charge relevant. *Buchmann v Normand* 1994 SCCR 929 On an application form for private hire licence, appellant left blank space in section of form asking about previous convictions, of which he had several. Appellant convicted of recklessly making false statement. *HMA v Pattisons* (1901) 3 Adam 420 Non-disclosure of liabilities in balance sheets.	
The misrepresentation may be as to future conduct.	*Richards v HMA* 1971 JC 29	

Achievement
Unless it is as an outcome of the false pretence that the result is achieved, there is no fraud as there must be a causal connection between the two.

Mather v HMA (1914) 7 Adam 525; 1914 SC(J) 184
Cheque tendered *after* delivery of goods and subsequently dishonoured.
Held that the indictment did not contain a relevant charge of fraud. It did not set forth that the accused had obtained delivery of goods by reasons of worthless cheque.
Per LJ-G Strathclyde: 'Telling a falsehood simpliciter is not a crime by the law of Scotland', although observed 'if a person obtain goods or money by issuing a cheque, he having no funds in bank and knowing the cheque will not be honoured, he commits a fraud'.

Definite practical result
If the false pretence achieves something which would not otherwise have been achieved, that is fraud.

Adcock v Archibald 1925 JC 58
A misrepresented amount of coal which he had produced by substituting his own marker on fellow miner's batch of coal. A convicted of fraud even though he made no financial gain, because the company had to pay statutory minimum wage which was in excess of sum due even on misrepresented amount. Conviction upheld on appeal.
Per LJ-G Clyde: 'It is, however, a mistake to suppose that for the commission of a fraud it is necessary to prove an actual gain by the accused or an actual loss on the part of the person alleged to be defrauded. Any definite practical result achieved by the fraud is enough.'

McKenzie v HMA 1988 SCCR 153
Appellants charged with attempting to defraud a company in that they instructed solicitors to raise civil actions against the company based on false averments.
Held that dishonest representations had been made to solicitors which had a practical effect, ie the raising of an action, and that was sufficient to make relevant case of attempted fraud.

A person charged with fraud may be convicted of a different charge.

Criminal Procedure (Scotland) Act 1995, Sch 3, para 8. Where an accused is indicted for fraud he can be convicted of theft or reset.

Certain frauds are covered by statutory provisions and most frauds in connection with the sale and purchase of motor vehicles are prosecuted under statute.

Tarleton Engineering Co Ltd v Nattrass [1973] 3 All ER 699
Mileage shown on milometer amounts to a trade description.

Norman v Bennett [1974] 3 All ER 351
Unsuccessful attempt to use disclaimer to defeat protective provisions of the 1968 Act.
Held that to be effective such a disclaimer had to be made before goods supplied: to be as bold and compelling as the description of the goods itself and to be effectively brought to the buyer's attention.

Trade Descriptions Act 1968. Section 11 deals with false and misleading representations as to price. Section 13 deals with false representations concerning the supply of goods or services. Section 14 deals with false and misleading statements as to services.

Limited company can be charged with fraud

Purcell Meats (Scotland) Ltd v McLeod 1986 SCCR 672
Attempted fraud. Central issue is whether the facts show that the persons by whose hands the acts were performed were of such a status that the acts fell to be regarded as the acts of the company.
Tesco Supermarkets Ltd v Nattrass [1972] AC 153; [1971] 2 WLR 1166; [1971] 2 All ER 127 applied.

Criminal Law (Consolidation) (Scotland) Act 1995, Pt IV (ss 27–30), provides for investigating powers to be exercised by nominee of the Lord Advocate in the event of a direction being given by him when a suspected offence may involve serious or complex fraud.

References: Hume I, 172; Alison I, 362; Macdonald, 52; Gordon, 588; Gane and Stoddart, 401.

SENTENCING POLICY

Scott v Lowe 1990 SCCR 15—S and three others pleaded guilty to fraud. S earned £120 per week and was fined £600. Co-accused were fined varying sums amounting in each case to five weeks' income.
Held that sheriff had assessed fines in correct manner; and appeal refused.

Caldwell v Jessop 1991 SCCR 323—Community national, 16 charges of obtaining money by false hard luck stories. Three previous convictions for dishonesty. Sentenced to 60 days' imprisonment and deportation recommended. Upheld on appeal.

McLean v HMA 1991 SCCR 972—Seven charges of 'clocking cars', nine months' imprisonment. Upheld on appeal, public interest required effective deterrence against such offences and restitution would not meet that need.

RESET

Reset is taking **possession** of, or **being privy** to the **retention** of, property **dishonestly appropriated** by another, **knowing** it to have been so appropriated and **intending** that the owner be deprived of its recovery.

COMMENTARY	CASE LAW	STATUTE LAW
Possession is the control of the property and occurs as soon as there is **retention**.	*Robert Finlay* 1826 Alison I 333 Stolen property was thrown on bed by thieves and covered over by one of the accused who was convicted of reset. 'If he once acquiesce in the placing of the goods there under circumstances inferring his guilty knowledge, and still more if he lend any aid towards their concealment . . . his guilt is incurred.'	Criminal Procedure (Scotland) Act 1995, s 11(4)(b). Any person who, in Scotland, receives property stolen in any other part of the United Kingdom may be dealt with in like manner as if it had been stolen in Scotland.
	HMA v Browne (1903) 6 F(J) 24 B participated in arrangements for banking of stolen money. Per LJ-C Macdonald: 'Not necessary . . . that the property passed into the personal possession of the receiver.' Accused convicted.	Road Traffic Act 1988, s 178(1)(b): driving or allowing oneself to be carried in a motor vehicle taken away without lawful authority.
Privity Where the dishonestly acquired property has not been handled, it requires an overt positive act in connection with it to demonstrate privity or connivance.	*McCawley v HMA* (1959) SCCR Supp 3 McC a passenger in stolen car. *Held* thereby privy to its retention and convicted. *McNeil v HMA* 1968 JC 29 McN a passenger in car transporting stolen property and convicted. 'Reset consists of being privy to the retaining of property that has been dishonestly come by.' but compare: *Clark v HMA* 1965 SLT 250 C present at, but not participating in, negotiations for the sale of stolen cigarettes. *Held*, a misdirection that non-reporting of dealings in stolen property could constitute connivance in its retention. Per LJ-C Grant: 'It was a direction that connivance could be inferred from mere inactivity and I do not think it properly can.' *Girdwood v Houston* 1989 SCCR 578 G convicted of reset of number of articles. When police first questioned G, he denied all knowledge of theft. Subsequently made statement that he knew where articles were and knew who had stolen them. Took police to hiding place. *Held* that as reset could be committed by being privy to retention of stolen goods and in light of G's initial denial, sheriff correct in convicting.	
Dishonestly appropriated Reset was at first restricted to reset of theft, then extended to robbery and now by statute extends also to property appropriated by breach of trust and embezzlement, or by falsehood, fraud and wilful imposition.	*Isabella Cowan* (1845) 2 Broun 398 *Daniel Clark* (1867) 5 Irv 437	Criminal Procedure (Scotland) Act 1995, Sch 3, para 8(2). May be a conviction for reset where the property was obtained by robbery, theft, breach of trust and embezzlement, or by falsehood, fraud and wilful imposition.

Criminal Law (Consolidation) (Scotland) Act 1995, s 51. Criminal resetting of property shall not be limited to the receiving of property taken by theft or robbery, but shall extend to property appropriated by breach of trust and embezzlement and by falsehood, fraud and wilful imposition.

But the dishonest appropriation must be complete before reset can occur.

Robert and Agnes Black 1841 Bell's Notes 46
RB convicted of theft, not reset, because intention to appropriate pocket-book found by AB not formed until she had taken it home to him. RB could not reset property not yet stolen although physically in possession of AB. AB also convicted of theft.

Reset and theft are mutually exclusive.

Backhurst v MacNaughton 1981 SCCR 6
B charged with reset of a number of articles. Gave evidence admitting theft of some of the articles. Convicted of reset of them all.
Held, on the concession of the Crown, that person admitting to theft of articles cannot be guilty of resetting them. Conviction quashed quoad the articles admittedly stolen.

Druce v Friel 1994 SCCR 432
Appellant convicted of theft by house breaking of TV, chequebook and card and other items and reset of chequebook and card. On appeal verdict set aside and conviction of theft by housebreaking of chequebook and card returned, since criminative circumstances found in relation to chequebook and card but not TV.

Knowing
Guilty knowledge is the first of the two constituents of the mens rea of reset. If possession is innocent at first, there is no reset until the property is known to have been dishonestly appropriated.

Latta v Herron (1967) SCCR Supp 18
L, a solicitor, bought two guns at 11 pm at a price about one-third of their true value. The transaction was arranged by a former client of L. In the case stated for appeal, the sheriff, who convicted, found 'although I was inclined to believe that when [he] purchased the firearms he was not conscious of the fact that they had been stolen, after a reasonable time for reflection he must have come to realise that they had been dishonestly obtained'. Conviction upheld.

Friel v Docherty 1990 SCCR 351
F obtaining prima facie valid HGV MOT certificates by means other than standard procedure. Convicted on the grounds that he must have known them to be stolen. Appeal.
Held the sheriff was entitled to find as he did on the facts.

Forbes v HMA 1994 SCCR 471
Guilty knowledge. Lowry painting found in F's car sandwiched between sheets of cardboard, painting partly visible.
Held on appeal that given the possession and the awkward account given for the presence of the painting and the cardboard, sufficient for guilty knowledge.

See also:

Nisbet v HMA 1983 SCCR 13
Awkward explanation of acquisition of goods enough when corroborated by statement of the thief.

Davidson v Brown 1990 SCCR 304
McKellar v Normand 1992 SCCR 393
Murray v O'Brien 1993 SCCR 90
Hamilton v Friel 1994 SCCR 748

Intending

An intention to prevent the owner recovering his property is the second of the two constituents of the mens rea of reset. Therefore, if it is absent, there is no reset.

If the intention is present there need be no motive of personal profit from the possession of the property dishonestly appropriated.

Cook's Case 1917, unreported; Macdonald, p 67
C, a law agent, negotiated with a thief to buy stolen property from him. However, since he was doing so on behalf of the owner, who was his client, he was acquitted on a charge of reset.

Husband

A wife cannot be charged with reset for receiving or concealing stolen goods brought in by her husband, with the purpose of protecting him from detection or punishment, unless she made a trade of the crime and has taken part in disposing of the stolen goods (Alison I, 338).

Smith v Watson 1982 SCCR 15
Accused was wife of man sentenced and imprisoned for robbery. Received money from the robbery through the letter-box and retained it awaiting husband's release.
Held, sustaining an appeal by the Crown, that accused should be convicted, and that wife's exemption should be restricted to cases where (a) the property is brought into the matrimonial home by the husband and (b) the wife conceals it to protect her husband from detection.
Decision in *Clark v Mone* 1950 SLT (Sh Ct) 69 doubted.

References: Hume I, 113; Alison I, 328; Macdonald, 67; Gordon, 683; Gane and Stoddart, 612.

SENTENCING POLICY

Bennett v Tudhope 1987 SCCR 203   B, first offender, convicted of resetting shotgun and of possessing it without a firearms certificate. Sheriff took view that danger of shotguns getting into wrong hands was such that offender should be dealt with severely. Sentenced to three months' imprisonment, upheld on appeal.

Rankin v McGlennan 1990 SCCR 607—Convicted of resetting £200, sentenced to 240 hours' community service. Order breached and three months' detention substituted. Appeal.
Held that appellant could now pay a fine. £300 substituted.

OFFENCES AGAINST PROPERTY

MALICIOUS MISCHIEF

Malicious mischief is the **damaging** in part or in whole of **another's property.**

COMMENTARY	CASE LAW	STATUTE LAW
Damaging May be achieved intentionally,	*Forbes v Ross* (1898) 2 Adam 513 An appeal against conviction of having wilfully, maliciously and mischievously broken down a wall. Held, that since appellant caused the wall to be destroyed in the knowledge that it was not his property, conviction should be upheld, although it was not clear to whom the wall belonged, the wall was of little value and the appellant claimed the destruction was to vindicate a right of way.	
	But contrast: *Black v Laing* (1879) 4 Couper 276 Conviction quashed where removal of a fence which formed an obstruction to one of the entrances to the accused's property was not considered to warrant crime of malicious mischief, since in the circumstances the removal was justified as the gap was the only access to the garden and that question of rights was one to be determined by a civil court.	
	Clark v Syme 1957 JC 1 Farmer shot and killed sheep which strayed from adjoining land under mistaken belief that he was legally entitled to do so. *Held*, on appeal by Crown, that wilful disregard of the property rights of another was sufficient to make the destruction of that property an act of malicious mischief.	
or result from deliberate disregard of another's property rights and therefore cannot be caused accidentally or unwillingly.	*Ward v Robertson* 1938 JC 32 Trespassers crossed an unfenced field of growing grass, on foot. Conviction of causing malicious mischief to the crop of grass quashed on appeal. It is essential that the accused had or should have had knowledge that he was likely to cause damage.	
Damage need not be physical.	*HMA v Wilson* 1983 SCCR 420 W activated emergency stop button of power station generator, causing loss of electricity costing £147,000 to replace. Sheriff held that the indictment of malicious mischief was irrelevant in the absence of an averment of physical damage. Overturned on appeal. *Held* that an element of physical injury is not necessary. Malicious mischief may be constituted by any patrimonial injury. Indictment held relevant.	
	Bett v Hamilton 1997 SCCR 621 Appellant convicted of malicious mischief for moving position of bank's security cameras. *Held*, on appeal, malicious mischief requires intent to cause physical damage or patrimonial loss, and what was lost was benefit of security cameras performing proper function. This loss extended the concept of patrimonial too far: since there was no financial loss (because the cost of cameras running would have been incurred anyway), there was no patrimonial loss.	

Another's property
A belief that the goods are one's own is also a good defence provided it is not held recklessly.

Malicious mischief different from vandalism.

Black v Allan 1985 SCCR 11
Accused charged with vandalism contrary to s 78(1) of Criminal Justice (Scotland) Act 1980: breaking window as result of horseplay. Court of appeal made it plain that this statutory offence different from common-law crime of malicious mischief.
Opinion of the court: 'The statutory offence is an offence standing in its own language and is committed if the conduct in question resulting in damage to property is wilful or . . . reckless.'

Criminal Law (Consolidation) (Scotland) Act 1995, s 51(1). Any person who without reasonable excuse wilfully or recklessly destroys or damages any property belonging to another shall be guilty of the offence of vandalism, but fire raising is excluded (s 52(2)).

Note: Summary procedure is mandatory for vandalism, whereas malicious mischief can be taken on indictment.

References: Hume I, 122; Alison I, 448; Gordon, 711.

Substantive law

FIRE RAISING

Fire raising is the **wilful or reckless setting alight** of the **property of another.**

COMMENTARY	CASE LAW	STATUTE LAW
Wilful or reckless If the fire is not started deliberately the mens rea—that it must be started intentionally—will be found if it is started with a high enough degree of recklessness.	*HMA v Geo MacBean* 1847 Ark 262 MacB set fire to house by setting alight some straw and paper in a garret room with a lighted candle. Fire spread through his and neighbours' houses. *Held* that if fire is raised in such a state of reckless excitement, to show that the person raising it does not know or care what may result, the requisite degree is attained.	Criminal Law (Consolidation) (Scotland) Act 1995. Section 52(2). It shall not be competent to charge acts which constitute the offence of wilful fireraising as vandalism under this section.
But carelessness alone will not provide the necessary mens rea.	*Carr v HMA* 1994 SCCR 521 C setting fire to church hall into which he had broken. Sheriff directed the jury that if the fire was caused accidentally then the crime could not be wilful fire raising but could be culpable and reckless fire raising. Direction upheld on appeal in this regard but court said that in considering recklessness it was important to focus on whether C's actions showed complete disregard for any dangers which might result from what he was doing. *Thomson v HMA* 1995 SLT 827 Sheriff gave correct direction on recklessness, then mistakenly told jury that it would be reckless if a man lit his pipe and without thinking threw the match over his shoulder and it landed in a field and burned the crops. *Held*, the example was not a good one, but direction that recklessness involved a complete disregard of any potential danger which might result was correct, and appeal refused. Per LJ-C Ross: 'In a case of fire raising it is not the manner of doing an act which would otherwise be lawful which is in issue (as in reckless driving) but whether the accused had the necessary mens rea for the commission of the crime.' Dictum of LJ-G Hope in *Carr v HMA* 1994 SCCR 521 applied.	
Setting alight The fire must have taken hold, no matter how minimally,	*John Arthur* (1836) 1 Swin 124 Chemist tried to set shop alight by igniting various chemicals. However, fire was discovered when only a part of the door was alight. *Held* to be sufficient to constitute fire raising, if proved. *Peter Grieve* (1866) 5 Irv 263 Door of the premises found to be charred. Jury question as to whether that implied fire had actually taken hold. Convicted. However, court observed that charring of a door did not necessarily mean that it had been *set* on fire. *Alexander Pollock* (1869) 1 Couper 257 P set stock and materials alight. However, building itself did not seem to be on fire. Some time after extinction of the fire, smouldering joist discovered. Lord Ardmillan: 'To constitute fire raising, a portion of the fabric must actually have been on fire, through the act of the accused.'	

although it may not have been applied directly or initially to the property alight.

Margaret Anderson 1826 Hume I 130
Set fire to furniture in room from which the fire then spread through the house.

Janet Hamilton 1806 Hume I 129
H set fire to a cart-house adjoining a dwelling-house which was subsequently burned down.

Property
The nature of the property does not now determine whether the fire raising is wilful or reckless, although certain property is protected by statute.

Angus v HMA (1905) 4 Adam 640
Conviction of wilful fire raising of a haystack upheld in the circumstances although haystack is not heritable property.

Blane v HMA 1991 SCCR 576
Hostel going on fire after the accused set fire to his bedding. Sheriff convicted, sufficient if the premises burnt as a result of the bedding being set on fire. Appeal.
Held that there could be no transferred intent. Sheriff should have looked to the likely consequences, reckless indifference. Conviction for setting fire to bedding substituted.

Of another
It is not fire raising to set own property alight but may be the crime of fire raising with the intent to defraud insurers.

HMA v Paterson (1890) 2 White 496

Hannah McAtamney & Others (1867) 5 Irv 363
McA set alight stock in store in her shop, intending to claim insurance

In both the above cases it was made clear that the crime was fire raising to defraud insurers.

HMA v Bell 1966 SLT (Notes) 61
D charged with setting his hotel alight with the intent to defraud his insurers. Despite Crown's failure to libel alleged intimation by B of claim to insurance company, charge held relevant, but proceedings later withdrawn and B found not guilty.

It is probably also a crime to endanger life or property by setting fire to one's own property.

John Arthur (1836) 1 Swin 124

Setting fire to moorland or land covered with heath except during specified period is an offence. (Specified period usually 16th April–30th September.)

Hill Farming Act 1946, s 25

References: Hume I, 122; Alison I, 429; Gordon, 719.

SENTENCING POLICY

Donaldson v HMA 1983 SCCR 216—D convicted of seven charges of fire raising. Had a bad record. Life sentence in young offenders' institution imposed. Appeal refused. Sentence not excessive. Indeterminate life sentence different from determinate sentence of preventive detention.

OFFENCES AGAINST THE PERSON

HOMICIDE

Homicide, the killing of another, is murder when the perpetrator **intends to take life** or is **wickedly reckless** as to the consequence of those actions which result in death. Homicide is culpable homicide where either the perpetrator intends to kill but there are **mitigating factors** relating to the act or where the perpetrator did not intend to kill but has been **criminally negligent** as to his actions.
Homicide will not be criminal when **casual** or **justifiable.**

COMMENTARY	CASE LAW	STATUTE LAW
Homicide The destruction of a human life other than one's own.	*HMA v Scott* (1892) 3 White 240 Accused strangled child immediately on birth. Evidence that the child breathed. *Held*, could be culpable homicide. Did not matter that child not fully born at the time. *Jean McCallum* (1858) 3 Irv 187 LJ-C Inglis stating that child must have separate existence from its mother.	
Destruction of foetus not homicide.		Abortion Act 1961 Concealment of Birth (Scotland) Act 1809.
Injuries sustained in utero.	*McCluskey v HMA* 1989 SLT 175 Charge of causing death by reckless driving. Child in utero born but dying of injuries sustained in utero. *Held* on appeal, charge competent. Following Hume (I, 189) culpable homicide charge might be relevant in such circumstances. *Tess v HMA* 1994 SCCR 451 Victim dying 15 months after assault and three months after accused convicted of assault. Accused charged with culpable homicide. High Court upheld repelling of plea in bar of trial, since appellant was being charged with different crime. Observed, case of oppression could be made out if death occurred many years after the trial for assault.	
Wickedly reckless Involuntary murder.	*Cawthorne v HMA* 1968 JC 32 Attempted murder charge, C firing shots into a room containing four people. Per LJ-G Clyde: 'The mens rea which is essential to the establishment of such a common law crime may be established by satisfactory evidence of a deliberate intention to kill or by satisfactory evidence of such wicked recklessness as to imply a disposition depraved enough to be regardless of the consequences.'	
Shown by intention to do serious bodily harm (sometimes seen as a separate aspect of mens rea).	*Brennan v HMA* 1977 JC 38 Full bench. B killing father while in a state of self-induced intoxication. Murder conviction upheld. Intention to do serious injury sufficient for mens rea.	

Halliday v HMA 1998 SCCR 509
Murder. Deceased kicked by brothers, who left and returned to stamp on his head. They put him in recovery position and went home. They later returned and called ambulance. Convicted of murder.
Held, on appeal, evidence of what happened once attack over could cast light on attitude of appellants during attack. They were wickedly indifferent to consequences of attack (by failing to call ambulance immediately after attack). Trial judge correct not to direct jury to leave these matters out of account. Appeal refused.

See also:

Broadley v HMA 1991 SCCR 416

Lord Advocate's Reference (No 1 of 1994) 1995 SCCR 177
Supply of controlled drug on request. Trial judge upheld submission of no case to answer as decision voluntary. Reference point whether supplier in circumstances guilty of culpable homicide.
Held, (1) causal link not broken merely because voluntary act required to produce injurious consequences; (2) supply was equivalent of culpable and reckless conduct; (3) trial judge wrong to acquit X of charge of culpable homicide on basis that that verdict not open to jury.

Shown by the use of weapons.

HMA v McGuinness 1937 JC 37
Victim killed by knife.
Held that people using deadly weapons guilty of murder.

Homicide during the course of robbery.

Miller and Denovan v HMA (7 December 1960, unreported) C of CA
Blow to the head of victim with block of wood during robbery causing death.
Held, no room for culpable homicide. Homicide in course of robbery due to serious and reckless violence is murder.

Mitigating factors
Pleas of diminished responsibility and provocation may reduce a charge of murder to one of culpable homicide.

HMA v Blake 1986 SLT 661
Attempted murder, attack with an axe.
Held that diminished responsibility requires some sort of mental illness, that is '. . . unsoundness of the mind bordering on but not amounting to insanity.'

See also:

Connelly v HMA 1990 SCCR 358
LT v HMA 1990 SCCR 540
Martindale v HMA 1992 SCCR 700

Provocation: See Special defences (Self-defence) p 148.

Gray v HMA 1994 SCCR 225
Homicide committed by four people in concert: two convicted of murder and two convicted of culpable homicide on ground of provocation.
Held, jury entitled to reach verdict and appeal on this ground refused.

Williamson v HMA 1994 SCCR 358
Murder. Four psychiatrists gave evidence accused not suffering from mental illness but had personality disorder. Trial judge's withdrawal of diminished responsibility upheld on appeal.
Per LJ-C Ross: 'what the appellant was suffering from was ... an extreme form of personality disorder, and that is not sufficient to satisfy the recognised test.'

Criminally negligent
Involuntary homicide may be culpable where the person is deemed criminally negligent.

Homicide in the course of a lawful act.

Paton v HMA 1936 JC 19
Charge of culpable homicide by reckless driving.
Held that criminal negligence amounting to criminal indifference must be shown.

Homicide in the course of an unlawful act.

Mathieson v HMA 1981 SCCR 196
Culpable homicide by culpable and reckless fire raising.
Held that if the act causing death was unlawful, crime would be culpable homicide.

Sutherland v HMA (No 1) 1994 SCCR 80
A and B art and part in setting fire to A's house with intent to defraud insurers. B died in fire.
Held, B's consent to fire raising no defence to charge of culpable homicide, and conviction upheld on appeal.

Bird v HMA 1952 JC 23
Accused assaulting a woman who collapsed and died. Judge in charge including directions that death resulting from any assault would be culpable homicide. Attacker must take the victim as he finds him or her.

Casual

HMA v Rutherford 1947 JC 1
Per LJ-C Cooper quoting with approval from Alison I, 139: 'It is casual homicide where a person kills unintentionally, when lawfully employed and neither meaning harm to any one nor having failed in the due degree of care and circumspection for preventing mischief to his neighbour.'

Justifiable
'... committed in the necessary prosecution of that which the killer is bound or hath a right to do.'
Hume I, 195.

Armed forces.

HMA v Sheppard 1941 JC 67
Soldier shooting a prisoner he was escorting who tried to escape.
Held that if soldier acting in line of duty jury should acquit.

References: Hume I, 179; Alison I, 1; Macdonald, 87; Gordon, 727; Gane, 479; McCall Smith and Sheldon, 170.

SENTENCING POLICY

LT v HMA 1990 SCCR 540—Mother setting fire to home killing two children. Mentally disturbed but no diminished responsibility. Ten years' imprisonment upheld on appeal. No need for life sentence: sentence reflecting public outrage and the need for treatment of the accused.

RJK v HMA 1991 SCCR 703—Twelve-year-old convicted of culpable homicide of three-year-old. Sentenced to be detained 'without limit of time'.
Held on appeal that it was competent under s 206 of the Criminal Procedure (Scotland) Act 1975 and appropriate here where the child needed psychiatric assessment over several years.

Casey v HMA 1993 SCCR 453—Murder in the course of a violent robbery. Trial judge under s 205A of the 1975 Act ordering minimum recommended sentence of 20 years. Appeal.
Held that recommendations may be made where crime particularly brutal or where accused a danger to the public. No recommendations of less than 12 years and normally will be 15 to 30 years. Fifteen years appropriate here.

Beddie v HMA 1993 SCCR 970—Culpable homicide. B killing victim by driving his car at him causing him to fall on the bonnet then braking so he fell on the road and fractured his skull. Four years' imprisonment. Appeal.
Held that the culpability was slight: six months substituted.

Baillie v HMA 1993 SCCR 1084—Culpable homicide. Twenty-two-year-old assaulting and killing 20-month-old child of cohabitee. Sentenced to life imprisonment to protect the public. Appeal.
Held that there was no evidence that public needed such protection; 15 years substituted.

McLaren v HMA 1994 SCCR 855—Attempted murder. Accessory sentenced to same period, 15 years, as person who fired gun. Upheld on appeal.

Sutherland v HMA (No 2) 1994 SCCR 350—Culpable homicide and setting fire with intent to defraud insurers.
Held, five years not excessive, since trial judge rightly modified sentence because appellant had no intention of killing friend and may himself have been killed in explosion.

McGuire v HMA 1995 SCCR 776—Appellant convicted of murder of victim he twice threw out of bedroom window of flat and later abandoned on waste ground in wheelie bin. Recommendation of 15 years.
Held, trial judge had discretion to make recommendations, but the effect in this case was to tie the hands of the parole board and the Secretary of State to a degree not justified by circumstances, and recommendations set aside.

Murphy v HMA 1995 SCCR 55—Murder by shooting. Accused had previous convictions for firearm offences.
Held, judge entitled in exercise of discretion to make recommendation of 15 years.

Houston v HMA 1006 SCCR 851 Culpable homicide. Fifteen year sentence for placing objects on line derailing train, causing death of two persons.
Held, if punishment sole consideration there might have been room for leniency but not where court has duty to protect public and deter, and appeal refused.

Strathearn v HMA 1996 SCCR 100—Culpable homicide on grounds of diminished responsibility: appellant traumatised after deceased committed sexual offence against his son for which he received probation. Crown had deleted allegation of previous malice of appellant to deceased
Held, judge should not have regard to deleted allegation and eight years excessive and seven years' imprisonment substituted.

Walker v HMA 1996 SCCR 818—Appellant convicted of culpable homicide of cohabitee who had abused her for two years. She stabbed deceased then went to kitchen and returned later with larger knife and killed deceased.
Held, considerable leniency already shown by reduction of charge to culpable homicide and trial judge entitled to strike balance with six-year sentence.

HMA v Gordon 1996 SCCR 274—Culpable homicide. Death caused by one blow at end of drunken brawl started by deceased.
Held, three years not unduly lenient in circumstances.

HMA v McC 1996 SCCR 842—15- and 16-year-old males convicted of culpable homicide of 58-year-old man after attack involving multiple punching and kicking.
Held, 18 months unduly lenient and trial judge failed, inter alia, to recognise public condemnation, and sentences of six years' detention imposed.

HMA v Spiers 1997 SCCR 479—Culpable homicide. Death caused by stabbing with broken bottle under provocation.
Held, except in exceptional circumstances a custodial sentence was only appropriate disposal and previous conviction highly relevant, and four years' imprisonment imposed.

Burns v HMA 1998 SCCR 281—Appellant pleaded guilty to culpable homicide. Blow delivered with little force and only landed on right ear because deceased, who was very drunk, moved away.
Held, result not in contemplation of anyone who witnessed blow, and given appellant's remorse and fact charge hanging over him for eight months, two years excessive and 240 hours' community service substituted.

HMA v Wheldon 1998 SCCR 710—Culpable homicide by stamping on deceased's head.
Held, four years' detention not unduly lenient. Trial judge had not erred on basis of medical evidence (minimum force), and attack was not pre-meditated (forming part of pattern of casual violence).

ASSAULT

A **deliberate attack** on the person of another which may be **aggravated.** There may be **defences.**

COMMENTARY	CASE LAW	STATUTE LAW
Deliberate The mens rea of assault is the intention to injure. It is not a crime which can be committed through recklessness.	*David Keay* (1837) 1 Swin 543 K whipped and alarmed a pony which bolted and threw its rider. Per Lord Moncreiff: 'I cannot see what purpose the panel could have except to do him a direct injury or to put him in alarm . . . if a person throws a stone out of a window into the street [causing injury] done without intention to hurt anybody he could not be charged with assault.' *John Roy* (1839) Bell's Notes 88 R maliciously broke glass which hit the eye of a girl whom he did not know to be in the vicinity. Acquitted of assault. *HMA v Phipps* (1905) 4 Adam 616 P, to frighten off salmon poachers, fired a sporting gun in their direction. Some of the shot lodged in the eye of one of them. Accused maintained this was accidental. Per Lord Ardwall: 'Evil intent is the essence of the charge.' Acquitted. *Note:* But could be convicted of reckless conduct. But see: *Connor v Jessop* 1988 SCCR 624 C charged with assaulting S by throwing tumbler at her. Tumbler thrown at someone with whom C fighting earlier, but had missed and hit S. C convicted. *Held* on appeal that circumstances were such that what happened was likely to occur as result of what appellant did and appeal refused. *Roberts v Hamilton* 1989 SCCR 240 R charged with assaulting C by striking him with a stick. C was attempting to separate two other men who were fighting, one of whom R had intended to strike. R convicted of assault and appealed on ground that she lacked the necessary mens rea to assault C. *Held* that where A intends to assault B and strikes C instead he is guilty of assaulting C; and appeal refused. *Lord Advocate's Reference (No 2 of 1992)* 1992 SCCR 960 Accused entering shop with imitation gun, telling shopkeeper to empty the till, then saying 'I'm only kidding'. Acquitted. *Held* that evil intention is the essence of assault which cannot be committed recklessly. Accused was acting deliberately with necessary intent, motive irrelevant. See also: *Quinn v Lees* 1994 SCCR 159 *Gilmour v McGlennan* 1993 SCCR 837	

Attack

Attack must be physical in character but need not have a physical result.	*Stewart v PF Forfarshire* (1829) 2 SJ 32 S aimed a blow at someone but missed. Convicted.	
	Ewing v Earl of Mar (1851) 14 D 314 Accused rode horse at victim to alarm him. Convicted.	
	Kay v Allan (1978) SCCR Supp 188 K set dog on two young boys in garden. Assault constituted by establishing intention to use dog to frighten person. Fact that dog caused injury is aggravation of that assault.	
Uttering threats is a separate crime.	*James Miller* (1862) 4 Irv 238 Per LJ-C Inglis: 'The use of threats is in certain well-known cases a crime in the eye of the law of Scotland.'	
The attack need not be direct *qui facit per alium facit per se*.	*David Keay* (1837) 1 Swin 543	
Injury to the victim is unnecessary (Gordon, p 815).	*HMA v Jane Smith or Thom* (1876) 3 Couper 332	

Aggravated

An assault may be aggravated by various factors, eg, by the nature of the injury caused.	*Kay v Allan* (1978) SCCR Supp 188	
or by the identity of the person assaulted, eg officers of the law in the execution of their duty,	*Monk v Strathern* 1921 JC 4 M seriously injured a police constable returning home who prompted M and others to go home at a late hour of the night. The constable was in uniform. Conviction quashed on appeal on grounds that constable had left beat and was no longer on duty, although still in uniform. Accordingly, he was not assaulted in the execution of his duty.	Police (Scotland) Act 1967, s 41 Criminal Procedure (Scotland) Act 1995, Sch 3, para 14. If the evidence demonstrates that the police officer was not in the execution of his duty there can be a conviction for assault at common law.
	Smith v Hawkes (1980) SCCR Supp 261 A police officer who has reasonable grounds for making proper inquiries is acting in the execution of his duty.	
	Annan v Tait 1981 SCCR 326 Knowledge of fact that victim is a police officer is essential to the statutory charge.	
	Stocks v Hamilton 1990 SCCR 190 Assault on constable when accused attempting to leave a room in police station. *Held* on appeal that accused unlawfully detained, constable not in the exercise of his lawful duty so statutory charge not available.	
and by use of weapons,	*HMA v Fitchie* (1856) 2 Irv 485 By throwing acid on victim.	
	HMA v Morison (1842) 1 Broun 394 Assault, especially when committed by presenting a loaded firearm.	

although merely presenting a weapon at someone may or may not be an assault,	*Mackenzie v HMA* 1982 SCCR 499 Accused presented a knife onto which victim impaled himself in course of a scuffle. *Held* that the trial judge had misdirected the jury in withdrawing the defence of accident and verdict set aside but Crown given leave to raise fresh indictment. Per LJ-C Wheatley: 'I am not prepared to say that in every situation, irrespective of the facts, where a person presents a weapon at another with the intention of frightening him off from further violence, an assault is committed.'	
by circumstances of indecency,	*Sweeney v X* 1982 SCCR 509 Intercourse with drunken woman incapable of consent held to be an indecent assault.	Criminal Law (Consolidation) (Scotland) Act 1995, s 14
by intention, eg assault with intent to ravish,	*John Hosie* 1826 Alison I 186 Pursued woman into a pond where she had run to avoid his advances: assault with intent to ravish. *Robertson v HMA* 1998 SCCR 390 Appellant was charged with attempted rape and convicted of assault with intent to ravish. *Held*, in absence of compelling reasons, court would not extend rule that assault with intent to ravish not competent on charge of rape to cases of attempted rape. Appeal refused.	
or by the nature of the injury caused.	*HMA v Jane Smith or Thom* (1876) 3 Couper 332 Assault to the danger of life. Charged with throwing a child out of a railway train. Although child uninjured, held relevant to libel that the assault had been to danger of life. *Kerr v HMA* 1986 SCCR 91 K convicted of assault by stabbing to severe injury and the danger of life. Medical evidence that complainer's life had not in fact been endangered. K appealed on that ground against the retention of the aggravation of danger to life in the verdict. *Held*, following *HMA v Jane Smith or Thom* (1876) 3 Couper 332, that jury entitled to convict where the inference of danger to life had been drawn, even if the complainer's life was not in fact at risk.	
Defences Generally where there is evil intent to injure, consent is not a defence to assault.	*Smart v HMA* 1975 SLT 65 Victim accepted challenge to a 'square go'. *Held* that state of mind of victim irrelevant and that consent was not a defence where there was an evil intent to inflict injury. Opinion of the court: 'It is in the public interest that it should be decided and made known that consent to a "square go" is *not* a defence to a charge of assault based on that agreed combat.' *C v HMA* 1987 SCCR 104 C aged 14 charged with indecently assaulting girl aged 11. His defence was that she had consented, or at least that he believed she had so consented. *Held* that as an 11-year-old girl incapable in law of giving consent, C's state of mind as to conduct irrelevant.	
A physical attack may not be assault where it is so justified as to be protected by statute,	*Skinner v Robertson* 1980 SLT (Sh Ct) 43 Nurse in mental hospital charged with assaulting certain mentally handicapped children by throwing water over them, striking them on the face and head with his knuckles. *Held* that use of force reasonably required to control the children and in circumstances protected by s 107(1) of Mental Health (Scotland) Act 1960.	Mental Health (Scotland) Act 1960, s 107(1), now Mental Health (Scotland) Act 1984, s 122(1)

Compare:
Norman v Smith 1983 SCCR 100
Nurse at a mental hospital held to have exceeded the limits of reasonable restraint in relation to a patient.

or where it constitutes reasonable chastisement,

Stewart v Thain 1981 SLT (Notes) 2
Headmaster held *not* to have exceeded the limits of proper chastisement of a 'difficult and fractious' pupil.

Peebles v McPhail 1989 SCCR 410
P charged with assaulting her two-year-old son by slapping him on the face. Child having a temper tantrum and P became angry. The force of the slap knocked him off balance and left red mark on face. *Held* that to slap child aged two on face, knocking him over, is an act as remote from reasonable chastisement as one could imagine and conviction upheld.

or carried out in *self-defence*,

See Special defences, p 148.

or in exercise of citizen's right of arrest.

Codona v Cardle 1989 SCCR 287
Force used must not be excessive, and arrest by a private citizen only justifiable where the citizen has witnessed the crime or has 'information equivalent to personal observation'.

Bryans v Guild 1989 SCCR 569
B chased group of youths who had been throwing things at his house. B mistakenly took hold of a youth who had not been part of the group and twisted his arm up his back, bruising his arm. B convicted of assault and admonished. On appeal *held* (1) B had not witnessed offence committed by complainer and had no right of citizen's arrest but (2) sentence quashed and absolute discharge substituted.

Note:
Recklessness.
Culpable, reckless acts which may or do cause injury to others may incur criminal liability.

RHW v HMA 1982 SCCR 152
W charged with causing culpable and reckless injury by dropping a bottle from a fifteenth-floor flat. *Held* (1) mens rea required was total indifference to and disregard for public safety, and (2) appellant had shown recklessness so depraved as to be regardless of consequences.

MacPhail v Clark 1982 SCCR 395 (Sh Ct)
Culpably and recklessly endangering lieges. Farmer set fire to straw in field. Fire spread to verge of road. Smoke obscured visibility on road and collision resulted.
Held that to allow the fire to spread demonstrated reckless indifference to the consequences for the public and road users. Convicted.

Khaliq v HMA 1983 SCCR 483
Shopkeepers charged that they did culpably, recklessly and wilfully supply children with solvents in the knowledge of the intended use, that use being injurious to health and dangerous to lives. Convicted.
On appeal, sentence reduced (see *Khaliq v HMA* 1984 SCCR 212).

See also:

Ulhaq v HMA 1990 SCCR 593

Lord Advocate's Reference (No 1 1994) 1995 SCCR 177
Khaliq v HMA 1983 SCCR 483 and *Ulhaq v HMA* 1990 SCCR 593 applied.

Normand v Morrison 1993 SCCR 207 (Sh Ct)
Accused charged with culpably and recklessly denying there was an unprotected needle in her handbag, permitting police officer to place his hand in the bag, exposing him to risk of infection. Plea to relevancy repelled. Accused has total disregard for health and safety of the officer.

See also:

Kimmins v Normand 1993 SCCR 476
—relevancy of similar charge upheld on appeal.

Donaldson v Normand 1997 SCCR 351
Culpably and recklessly endangering lieges. Accused failed to tell police of unguarded needle in sock prior to search, having forgotten it was there as a result of taking drugs. Conviction upheld, since self-induced intoxication was no defence to a charge involving criminal recklessness. *Brennan v HMA* 1977 JC 38 followed.

HMA v Harris 1993 SCCR 559
Doorman pushing girl down stairs onto a road where she was struck by a car. Charged with assault or alternatively with culpably and recklessly causing injury. Plea to relevancy.
Held on appeal (five-judge bench) that conduct can be criminally reckless either where there is danger to the lieges or reckless conduct causing actual injury. To be distinguished from assault which must be deliberate and cannot be committed recklessly.

See also:

Normand v Robinson 1993 SCCR 1119

References: Macdonald, 115; Alison I, 175; Gordon, 815; Gane and Stoddart, 383.

SENTENCING POLICY

Brown v Normand 1988 SCCR 229—Assault resulting in permanent disfigurement. B sentenced to 240 hours of community service and ordered to pay £650 compensation. Appealed, submitting sentence excessive in light of fact that he was first offender and conduct of complainer. Appeal allowed: community service reduced to 100 hours, and as complainer's conduct would have prevented him from recovering compensation from CICB, compensation order quashed.

Stirling v Stewart 1988 SCCR 619—Appellants (aged 16) pleaded guilty to assaulting lone US serviceman at Dunoon pier. Sheriff imposed sentence of 30 days' detention as short, sharp shock and as deterrent to the frequency of such attacks. *Held* that appeal court could not interfere with sheriff's sentence.

Mays v Brown 1988 SCCR 549—M convicted of assaulting water bailiff in course of his duty by throwing lamp at him. Fined £250. On appeal against sentence fine increased to £500.

Dick v Jessop 1989 SCCR 258—D convicted of assault by kicking A on head. D, aged 25, in good employment, had no previous custodial sentences and no previous convictions for crimes of violence. Sheriff imposed a two months' custodial sentence. On appeal *held* that although the assault was serious, careful weight should be given to the fact that D would lose job if imprisoned; and appeal allowed with hesitation and fine of £500 substituted.

McCardle v Douglas 1989 SCCR 262—Similar facts to *Dick v Jessop* 1989 SCCR 258. McC was 17 years old. Sentence of 30 days' detention quashed, compensation order of £200 substituted.

Ferguson v Lowe 1989 SCCR 281—F (aged 17, in employment, no previous convictions, but convicted of minor assault and two breaches of peace after offence in question) convicted of assaulting bus driver by knocking him down and repeatedly punching and kicking him. Sheriff sentenced to 60 days' detention. On appeal *held* that sheriff had exercised discretion properly. Appeal refused.

Pearson v HMA 1990 SCCR 125—P, a first offender, pleaded guilty to three assaults on his wife, the first two involving only punching and kicking. The third was an assault with knife to injury and permanent disfigurement. Fined on first two charges and sentenced to 15 months' imprisonment on third charge.
Held that as it was a domestic issue, parties were now divorced, assault out of character and P a first offender, appropriate disposal was probation for 18 months in place of imprisonment.

Murchie v McGlennan 1990 SCCR 533—Assault with cricket bat and meat tenderiser. Victim alleged to have used lewd practices towards appellant's children. Three years' imprisonment on the basis that court could not tolerate people taking law into their own hands.

Galloway v Mackenzie 1991 SCCR 548—Careers officer admonished on minor assault on youth scaring his children. Job exempt from Rehabilitation of Offenders Act 1974, admonition a conviction. On appeal *held* that an absolute discharge would be more appropriate.

Leslie v HMA 1992 SCCR 880—Punching glass into the face of victim to his severe injury. Eighteen months' imprisonment. Appeal.
Held that custody appropriate but given accused's good background, no material previous convictions and six months served prior to appeal that sentence quashed. 240 hours' community service and £1,500 compensation order substituted.

McKay v HMA 1992 SCCR 584—Striking victim with glass to severe injury. Fifteen months' imprisonment *held* on appeal to be severe but not excessive. Alternatives looked to but not appropriate.

Modiak v HMA 1992 SCCR 572—Acid attack on wife to her permanent severe injury and loss of sight. Trial judge said it was hard to think of a more cowardly, wicked and premeditated crime. On appeal, no difficulty in upholding 20 years' imprisonment, devastating injuries.

Garrett v HMA 1993 SCCR 1044—G striking solicitor on face in the cells. Twelve months' detention upheld on appeal. Officers of court must be able to carry out their duties free from violence at hands of clients.

Andrews v HMA 1994 SCCR 191—Indecent assault on 13-year-old boy by 27-year-old intellectually impaired stepbrother. On appeal *held*, custodial sentence inevitable, serious assault by person in position of trust but sentence too long. Two years' imprisonment reduced to nine months.

McGowan v HMA 1994 SCCR 217—M assaulting 63-year-old shopkeeper, threatening her with a needle and AIDS, pushing her to ground, breaking her hip. Seven years' imprisonment upheld on appeal. Serious injury and public anxiety about such matters.

HMA v Heron 1998 SCCR 449—Accused pleaded guilty to assault of estranged wife with knife to her severe injury. Psychiatric reports said custody less likely to reduce risk to complainer than statutory supervision. Sentence of three years' probation order with condition respondent did not approach complainer during that period.
On appeal *held*, sentence not unduly lenient.

HMA v O'Donnell 1995 SCCR 745—Assault to severe injury and danger of life by repeated punching and kicking and stamping on head.
Held, on appeal, trial judge took too narrow a view of aggravation and on basis of film evidence the whole attack constituted danger to life. Four years unduly lenient and seven years substituted.

Henderson v Carmichael 1995 SCCR 126—60-day sentence for an assault to severe injury which took place in a rugby match where appellant headbutted opponent, fracturing his nose.
Held on appeal, sentence not excessive.

Ferguson v Normand 1995 SCCR 770—Assault by professional footballer on another player during match.
Held, three months not excessive, since appellant on probation at time and was a public figure and assault in public before large number of spectators.

Sim v Lockhart 1994 SCCR 243—Criminal Justice (Scotland) Act 1975, s 290. Six months for second or subsequent offence inferring personal violence.
Held, sheriff wrong to take account of earlier conviction which postdated the current offence, and three months substituted.

Turner v Scott 1995 SCCR 516—Indecent assault by police officer against 20-year-old nieces.
Held, three months excessive given appellant's loss of employment, and 150 hours' community service substituted.

McNamee v HMA 1996 SCCR 423—Nineteen-year-old appellant pleaded guilty to assault to severe injury and permanent disfigurement. Struck complainer on face with tumbler. Only explanation was that he was affected by mother's death two months earlier. He was employed as apprentice and looked after siblings.
Held, in circumstances 12 months' detention quashed, and 240 hours' community service and £750 compensation substituted.

HMA v Jamieson 1996 SCCR 836—Assault to severe injury and danger of life. Unprovoked attack with hammer causing depressed fracture of skull.
Held, £3,000 compensation order and 240 hours' community service unduly lenient, but since £2,200 already paid the appropriate course was to refuse the appeal. Observed, not appropriate for complainer to be asked to consider whether he should return the money so that the respondent might receive a more severe sentence.

HMA v McColl 1996 SCCR 523—Respondent pleaded guilty to assault to severe injury and permanent impairment and disfigurement. Trial judge sentenced co-accused to five years, but deferred sentence on respondent for six months on condition he should attend clinic for medical treatment.
Held, respondent could attend outside clinic while detained, and sentence of three years' detention substituted.

Substantive law

Young v Hamilton 1996 SCCR 66—First offender aged 16 convicted of assault to injury sentenced to 60 days' detention. Upheld on appeal, given gravity of offence.

Marr v HMA 1996 SCCR 696—Indecent assault by taxi driver on passenger. Six months' imprisonment not held to be excessive.

HMA v Fallon 1996 SCCR 80—Indecent assault on stranger in street at night. Trial judge deferred sentence for six months with a view to dealing with the case by some form of community-based disposal.
Held, unduly lenient and nine months' imprisonment imposed.
Observed, normally longer sentence appropriate for such offence but for delay in bringing case and appellant's good behaviour.

HMA v Donaldson 1997 SCCR 738—Assault with attempt to rape an elderly woman by first offender under the influence of alcohol and suffering from stress.
On appeal, *held* two years' imprisonment not unduly lenient.

Hewitt v Vannet 1997 SCCR 530—Assault on hospital staff. First offender sentenced to 60 days' detention.
On appeal, *held* trial judge's approach was wrong. Community service does not indicate the offence is less serious than if a custodial sentence had been imposed. Sentence quashed and community service imposed.

Robertson v HMA 1997 SCCR 534—Assault and abduction of seven-year-old girl with intent to commit sexual assault and to danger of her life. Accused described as danger to public.
Held, on appeal, life sentence with recommendation of minimum period of eight years not excessive, as appellant should be detained until doctors were satisfied he no longer presented a risk to young children and only appropriate that an indeterminate sentence be imposed.

HMA v Smith 1998 SCCR 637—Assault to danger of life and robbery of 83-year-old woman in home. Experts said non-custodial sentence to treat post traumatic stress disorder (from seeing friend commit suicide).
Held, not unduly lenient.

SEXUAL OFFENCES

HOMOSEXUAL OFFENCES

Homosexual offences are principally regulated by **statute** although they can also be dealt with at **common law**.

COMMENTARY	CASE LAW	STATUTE LAW
Statute	*McDonald v HMA* 1997 SCCR 408 Appellant convicted of homosexual offence when over 21 with persons aged 16. He took plea to competency on ground that press report (inaccurate anyway) that age of consent reduced to 16 by Crown Office. Prosecution policy not refuted by Crown. *Held*, Crown not bound by publication of untrue report. Observed, Lord Advocate can reconsider any policy statements.	Criminal Law (Consolidation) (Scotland) Act 1995 Section 13(1). Homosexual act not an offence if in private between two persons both over 21, and both parties consent. *Note*: Sexual Offences (Amendment) Bill, clause 1, reduces the age of consent for homosexual people from 18 to 16. *Note*: Sexual Offences (Amendment) Bill, clause 3, introduces a new offence of abuse of position of trust. Subject to certain exceptions, where A (over 18) is in a position of trust in relation to B (under 18), and engages in sexual activity with B, A thereby commits an offence. CL(C)(S)A 1995, s 13(2). 'Private' means not more than two people present and not in a public lavatory. Section 13(8). Defence if accused under 24 with no previous for like offence and had reasonable cause to believe other person over 21. Section 13(3). A male person suffering from a mental deficiency ... that he is incapable of living an independent life or of guarding himself against serious exploitation cannot in law give consent; but a person shall not be convicted of offence on account of incapacity of person to consent if he proves that he did not know and had no reason to suspect that person suffering from such mental deficiency. Section 13(4). In this section 'homosexual act' means sodomy or an act of gross indecency or shameless indecency by one male person with another male person.

Common law

Charges may relate to sodomy or acts short of sodomy.

M'Laughlan v Boyd 1934 JC 19

Lewd, indecent and libidinous charge arising out of incident involving boys whose ages were not proved.

Held on appeal, charge relevant even if boys not below the age of puberty.

INCEST

Under the Criminal Law (Consolidation) (Scotland) Act 1995, a person who has sexual intercourse with a person of the opposite sex who falls within one of the **specified categories** is guilty of an offence unless he can establish a relevant **defence. Step relations** are also covered.

COMMENTARY	CASE LAW	STATUTE LAW
Specified categories		Criminal Law (Consolidation) (Scotland) Act 1995
		Section 1. Specified categories eg mother, sister, niece etc (or male equivalents if female charged). Half blood is treated as equivalent to full blood.
		Defences: accused did not know and had no reason to suspect the person was related to him/her; did not consent to the sexual intercourse; married to the person within the specified category and the marriage is recognised as valid in Scotland.
Step relations	*McGregor v Haswell* 1983 SLT 626 'Member of same household' under the Social Work (Scotland) Act 1968 defined per LP Emslie as 'a group of persons held together by a particular kind of tie who normally live together . . . akin to a family unit.'	Section 2. Offence for a step parent or former step parent to have intercourse with a step child or former step child if the child under the age of 21 or at any time before 18 years old the child lived in the parent's household and was treated as a child of the family.
	McDade v HMA 1998 SLT 68 Consent is not a relevant sentencing factor. Appellant convicted of committing incest with 18-year-old niece. Trial judge, sentencing to four years' imprisonment, said he was left in no doubt girl did not consent. *Held*, issue of consent not in issue, appeal allowed and 30 months' imprisonment substituted (ie if no consent then Crown should charge rape).	Defences: accused —did not know child was a step child; —had reasonable cause to believe the child was over 21 years old; —did not consent to the sexual intercourse; —was married to the child and the marriage was recognised as valid in Scotland.
	Note: *R v HMA* 1988 SCCR 254 Any sexual relationship between a parent and child may also constitute shameless indecency.	
Time bar for summary proceedings		Section 4(2). Provides a period of six months from when sufficient evidence in the opinion of the Lord Advocate becomes available. A certificate by him of that date is conclusive.
		Section 136(3) of the Criminal Procedure (Scotland) Act 1995 provides that proceedings are deemed to commence when a warrant to cite or apprehend the accused is granted where the warrant is executed without undue delay.

RAPE

Rape occurs when **a man** has **sexual intercourse** with **a woman** by **intentionally or recklessly overcoming her will.**

COMMENTARY	CASE LAW	STATUTE LAW
A man Above the age of eight, question of proof in each case (Macdonald, 121),		
'Sex change.'	*R v Tan* [1983] QB 1053 Charge of living on the earnings of a prostitute. *Held* that a person who is biologically male, despite a 'sex change', still a male in law.	
A woman may only be guilty of rape art and part.	*Walker and McPherson* (1976, unreported)	
Sexual intercourse Penetration per vaginam by male genitals, extent of penetration unimportant.	*Alex Macrae* (1814) Bell's Notes 83	
No emission required.	*Arch Robertson* (1836) 1 Swin 93	
A woman A female of any age can be raped. Intercourse with a girl under 12 years of age is rape regardless of 'consent'.	*Jas Burtnay* (1822) Alison I, 214	
Mentally abnormal.	*Chas Sweenie* (1858) Alison I, 214 Charge of raping a sleeping woman. Charge held irrelevant. Dicta equating the position of the mentally abnormal with the position of children ie consent irrelevant.	
Wife.	*Stallard v HMA* 1989 SCCR 248 Husband charged with violent rape of wife while cohabiting with her in the matrimonial home. *Held* that Hume's statement of the husband's immunity (I, 306) no longer consistent with modern attitudes. Per LJ-G Hope, 'Nowadays it cannot be seriously maintained that by marriage a wife submits herself irrevocably to sexual intercourse in all circumstances.'	
Intentionally or recklessly Honest belief of consent may be a defence even if based on unreasonable grounds.	*Meek and Ors v HMA* 1982 SCCR 613 Gang rape. Trial judge refusing to give a direction that an honest belief even on unreasonable grounds would stop conviction. *Held* on appeal, absence of honest belief essential. Reasonableness of grounds will affect whether jury sees belief as honest. No direction necessary here where jury choosing between two completely contradictory accounts of the same incident. See also: *Jamieson v HMA* 1994 SCCR 181 *Doris v HMA* 1996 SCCR 854 Rape of wife's half-sister. Sentenced to 7 years. Trial judge did not direct that a genuine belief in consent was a defence. *Held*, a direction about honest belief in rape cases should be given only when raised in evidence, and appeal refused.	

McPhelim v HMA 1996 SCCR 647
Trial judge directed Crown had to establish appellant had reasonable grounds to believe complainer consenting.
Held, misdirection and conviction set aside and authority granted for new prosecution.

Geddes v HMA 1996 SCCR 687
Appellant convicted of rape of 12-year-old girl.
Held, on appeal, direction sound in law that honest belief in consent a defence was sound in law and appeal on this ground refused.

Robertson v HMA 1998 SCCR 390
Can return verdict of assault with intent to ravish on charge of attempted but not actual rape.

Overcoming her will
Victim's physical resistance not a pre-requisite, matter of proof.

Barbour v HMA 1982 SCCR 195
Charge of abduction, rape and indecent assault. Victim not consenting but not physically resisting.
Held that threats of violence may be enough to overcome will.
Per Lord Stewart: 'The important matter is not the amount of resistance put up but whether the woman remained an unwilling party throughout'.

Criminal Law (Consolidation) (Scotland) Act 1995.

Section 7(2)(a). Procuring sex by threats is an offence.

Section 7(2)(b). Procuring sex by false pretences is an offence.

Fraud.

Wm Fraser (1847) Ark 280
Charge of rape held not to be relevant where F had pretended to be the victim's husband.

Section 7(3). Sex by pretending to be victim's husband is rape.

Chas Sweenie (1985) Alison 1, 214
Sexual intercourse with a sleeping woman was a crime but not rape.

Victim intoxicated.

HMA v Grainger and Rae 1932 JC 40
Supplying alcohol to make victim insensible so as to have intercourse may be rape but taking advantage of victim voluntarily incapacitated by alcohol held to be the crime of clandestine injury on a woman.

Section 7(2)(c). It is an offence to administer a drug or any other matter with intent to obtain sex.

See also:
Quinn v HMA 1990 SCCR 254

Alternative verdicts

Section 14. If trial on indictment for rape or offence under s 5(1) and jury:
(a) are not satisfied accused guilty of charge or attempt; but
(b) are satisfied accused guilty of an offence under s 5(2)(3) or s 7(2)(3) of this Act, or an indecent assault, then jury may acquit him of charge in para (a) above and convict him of offence in para (b) or of an indecent assault.

References: Hume I, 301; Alison I, 209; Macdonald, 119; Gordon, 883; Gane and Stoddart, 479; McCall Smith and Sheldon, 191.

SENTENCING POLICY

HMA v MacPherson 1996 SCCR 802—Respondent pleaded guilty to attempted rape of four-year-old girl he was babysitting. Sentenced to four years' imprisonment. Crown appealed, arguing, under section 108 of the Criminal Procedure (Scotland) Act 1995, that sentence was unduly lenient. *Held*, four years not unduly lenient, since single brief incident and not a character disposed to such behaviour.

Substantive law

Clark v HMA 1997 SCCR 416—Abduction and rape. Trial judge imposed a sentence of life imprisonment and made an order under s 2 of the Prisoners and Criminal Proceedings (Scotland) Act 1993 specifying a period of 12 years. *Held*, on appeal, sentencing judge not entitled to take into account the appellant's dangerousness in determining the period under s 2(2) which related to the punishment of the offender rather than the protection of the public. Appeal against order under s 2(2) allowed and period of nine years substituted.

Robertson v HMA 1997 SCCR 534—Prisoners and Criminal Proceedings (Scotland) Act 1993, s 2. Assault and abduction of 7-year-old girl with intent to commit sexual assault and to danger of her life. Accused described as danger to the public. Life sentence imposed with recommendation of a minimum period of 12 years. Appeal refused.

SEXUAL OFFENCES AGAINST CHILDREN

Sexual offences against children are regulated at **common law** and by **statute**.

COMMENTARY	CASE LAW	STATUTE LAW
Common law Girl below the age of 12 incapable of consent. (Macdonald, 112)	*C v HMA* 1987 SCCR 104 Indecent assault by 14-year-old boy on 11-year-old girl. Defence that girl consented or that C believed that she consented. Conviction upheld on appeal. Girl below the age of 12 incapable of consenting so C's state of mind irrelevant. See also: Brothel keeping Shameless indecency Assault, indecency	
Statute Intercourse with: —girl under 13 years, —girl 13 to 16 years.		Criminal Law (Consolidation) (Scotland) Act 1995
	Mair v Russell 1996 SCCR 453 Appellant satisfied preconditions for statutory defence. Charged with having sexual intercourse with 13 year old girl. Evidence led she told him she was 16. Sheriff rejected defence on account of girl's appearance in witness box. On appeal conviction quashed: sheriff wrongly substituted his views for views appellant could reasonably have formed.	Section 5(1). Offence of strict liability. Section 5(2), (3). Offence. Section 5(5). Defence if man has either: (a) reasonable cause to believe the girl was his wife. (b) man under 24 years, no previous analogous convictions, reasonable cause to believe girl above 16 years.
Indecent behaviour to girl 12 to 16 years.	*Batty v HMA* 1995 SCCR 525 Appellant convicted of shameless indecency in respect of girls under 16 but over the age of puberty. He was 'house parent' in a residential school and slept in the girls' wing. Observed, per LJG Hope: the balance of authority is now in favour of view that the age of the complainer is not the essence of the crime of lewd practices.	Section 6. Offence if behaviour such as would be an offence if girl under 12 years ie lewd, indecent or libidinous practices. *Note*: under s 15, it is a defence to a charge of indecent assault of girl under 16 if reasonable cause to believe girl was his wife.
Abduction of girl under 18.		Section 8: Offence to abduct girl from the possession of her parents for purpose of unlawful sexual intercourse.
Abuse of position of trust—any child under 16 years, abuse by person over 16 years.	*HMA v RK* 1994 SCCR 499 Shameless indecency. RK had sexual intercourse with a girl aged over 16 years of age but who had been his foster daughter since the age of eight. Plea to the relevancy of the charge repelled. *Held* that the fact that under the Sexual Offences (Scotland) Act 1976, s 2C, a person is only guilty of an offence if the girl is under 16 years of age or the accused has no reasonable belief that she is over that age does not mean that intercourse such as charged cannot be a crime. Society would regard RK's behaviour as repugnant certainly as long as the fostering relationship continued. See also: Incest Homosexual offences	Section 3. Person in the same house and in a position of trust and authority to the child. Defences: accused —had reasonable cause to believe child was over 16 years old; —did not consent to the sexual intercourse; —was married to the child and the marriage was recognised as valid in Scotland.

Time limits		Section 5(4). No prosecution commenced under s 5(3) more than one year after the commission of the offence. This is time bar on indictment. Appearance on petition will prevent period running. Section 136 of the Criminal Procedure (Scotland) Act 1995 will apply the six-month time bar to offences triable only summarily.
		Note: maximum penalty on indictment for offence under s 5(2)(3) increased from 2 to 10 years by s 14(1) of the Crime and Punishment (Scotland) Act 1997.
Paedophile 'sex tourists'		See conspiracy notes for reference to the Criminal Law (Consolidation) (Scotland) Act 1995, s 16A: conspiracy or incitement to commit certain sexual acts outside UK-legislation targeted at paedophile 'sex tourists'. Also, s 8 of the Sex Offenders Act 1997 inserts s 16B, which enacts that the commission abroad by a UK citizen of an offence which if committed in Scotland would be a 'listed sexual offence' (see subsection (7)) shall be triable in Scottish courts.
Notification by sex offenders	*Lees, Petr* 1998 SCCR 401 Respondent pleaded guilty to indecent exposure in the presence of children aged 8 and 9. Sheriff declined to issue a certificate under s 5 of the Sex Offenders Act 1997, on the grounds that 'indecent exposure' was a nomen juris since introduction of statutory form of charge and therefore separate from shameless indecency. *Held*, indecent exposure in the presence of young children to which the respondent pleaded guilty amounted to shameless indecency.	Sex Offenders Act 1997 requires persons convicted of designated sexual offences, inter alia, to register their names and addresses, and any subsequent changes, with the police. See para 2(1) of Schedule 1 to SOA 1997 for the designated sexual offences and para 2(2)–(4) for the restriction on the application of some of those offences. The restrictions include situations where certain parties willing participants; where offender is near 16; where offender not sentenced to 30 months' imprisonment or more or subject to a restriction order and admitted to hospital.
		Note: under s 5 of SOA 1997 it is sufficient evidence of a conviction of a designated sexual offence for the judge to state in open court that the accused is being convicted of such offence and to certify it (see Form 20.3 AA for style).

References: Hume I, 309; Macdonald, 119; Gordon, 901; Gane and Stoddart, 672; McCall Smith and Sheldon, (204-6).

SENTENCING POLICY

HMA v McK 1996 SCCR 866—Respondent pleaded guilty to four charges of lewd conduct against two sisters over an eight-year period. Sentenced to three years' probation with 240 hours' community service. Crown appealed against sentence. *Held*, unduly lenient and concurrent sentences of two years' imprisonment imposed on each charge.

HMA v Ross 1996 SCCR 107—Lewd and libidinous practices towards niece aged between 4 and 12 on repeated occasions. Sentenced to one years' imprisonment on each charge to run concurrent. Crown appealed against sentence.
Held, not unduly lenient. Judge entitled to take account of fact that respondent had serious charge of raping young child hanging over him for some time for which Crown led no evidence.

HMA v Brough 1996 SCCR 377—Respondent pleaded guilty in December 1995 to charges of lewd practices committed in 1976 against adolescent girls who were his pupils. Sentenced to probation. Crown appealed against sentence.
Held, unduly lenient, but given mitigating circumstances (good conduct since crime), concurrent sentences of 12 months' imprisonment on each charge imposed.

M v HMA 1997 SCCR 365—Appellant pleaded guilty to lewd practices towards daughter and one instance of incest. She was 14 at the time. Sentenced to concurrent sentences of 18 months and 5 years respectively. At appeal, girl, now aged 17, said she suffered no harm and was shocked at sentences.
Held in light of this, sentence excessive and sentence of three years and six months' imprisonment with a supervised release order substituted.

Thomas v HMA 1997 SCCR 77—Appellants aged respectively a little over and just under 16 convicted of having unlawful intercourse with 14-year-old girl. Sheriff considered lack of consent as important under s 4 of the Sexual Offences (Scotland) Act 1976.
Held, on appeal, lack of consent not an issue and given ages custodial sentence not necessary and community service substituted.

HMA v Brand 1998 SCCR 71—65-year-old man convicted of lewd practices towards young girls (analogous previous conviction). Charge of attempted rape withdrawn.
Held, four years' imprisonment towards lower end of permissible range but not unduly lenient. Observed, reduction was factor judge entitled to take into account.

BROTHEL KEEPING

Criminal Law (Consolidation) (Scotland) Act 1995, s 11(5)
(a) The **keeping or management** or acting or assisting in the management of a **brothel.**
(b) A tenant, lessee, occupier or person in charge of any premises, **knowingly permitting** premises or part thereof to be used as a brothel or for the purposes of **habitual prostitution,** *or*
(c) The letting of premises or part of premises with the knowledge that such premises are to be used as a brothel *or* wilfully being a party to the continuing use of such premises as a brothel, by a lessor or landlord or the agent of a lessor or landlord of premises.

COMMENTARY	CASE LAW	STATUTE LAW
Keeping or management	*Vaughan v Smith* 1919 JC 9 Per LJ-G Strathclyde: 'One who assists in the management of a brothel manages a brothel only with aid, but he is none the less managing a brothel.'	Criminal Law (Consolidation) (Scotland) Act 1995 Section 11(5)(a)
Brothel Definition: 'Open and notorious house of lewdness, for the reception of loose and dissolute visitors' (Hume I 468).	*Winter v Woolfe* [1931] 1 KB 549 Place where persons of opposite sexes are permitted to resort for illicit intercourse, whether or not the women are common prostitutes.	
	Milne v McNicol (1965) SCCR Supp 8 M convicted of managing boarding house as a brothel, after typhoid outbreak in Aberdeen caused scarcity of tourist business. No evidence that M had sought business from prostitutes but ample evidence that boarding house acquired notoriety as place where prostitutes could obtain room.	
More than one woman using premises.	*Singleton v Ellison* [1895] 1 QB 607 House occupied by one woman only for purpose of prostitution (with no other women being allowed to use the premises for a similar purpose). *Held* not a brothel.	
Individual rooms in a house let out to individual prostitutes may constitute a brothel.	*Donovan v Gavin* [1965] 2 QB 648 Landlord let out separate rooms to separate tenants. Three rooms on ground floor let to prostitutes, who used them to ply their trade. Per Lord Parker CJ: 'It seems to me that ... whether they were independent and separate lettings is an immaterial matter.'	
	R v Tan [1983] 3 WLR 361	
	Donovan v Gavin [1965] 2 QB 648 at 661, per Lord Parker CJ	
Knowingly permitting	*Mattison v Johnson* (1916) 26 Cox CC 373	
Habitual prostitution Includes habitual prostitution in premises by an *individual* prostitute.	*Girgawy v Strathern* 1925 JC 31 Over a period of time, a large number of prostitutes resorted to a furnished flat of which two men were the tenants and occupiers. Several of the prostitutes went repeatedly. Occupiers were convicted of knowingly permitting premises to be used for habitual prostitution. Observed, that (1) if prostitution had been with the occupiers of the flat only, no offence would have been committed, in respect that the occupiers could not 'permit' their own acts; (2) immaterial that accused made no profit.	Section 11(5)(b)

'Keeping open and notorious house of lewdness.'	*Herron v Macdonald* (1973, unreported) Occupier of house in which pornographic films shown, and live sexual display performed, prosecuted in sheriff court for 'keeping an open and notorious house of lewdness for the reception of loose and dissolute visitors' (Hume I, 468). But quaere: now would he be prosecuted under 'shameless indecency'?	
Other statutory offences.		Theatres Act 1968
		Indecent Displays (Control) Act 1981
		Post Office Act 1953
		Indecent matters not to be sent by post.
		Unsolicited Goods and Services Act 1971, s 4(1), prohibits sending of unsolicited sex manuals.
Living on immoral earnings.	*Soni v HMA* 1970 SLT 275 Landlord convicted of living on immoral earnings. *Held*, on appeal, that it did not have to be proved that rents charged were exorbitant, if it could be proved otherwise that the accused was participating or assisting in activities of the prostitute.	Criminal Law (Consolidation) (Scotland) Act 1995 Section 11(1)(a). It is an offence knowingly to live on earnings of prostitution.
		Section 11(3). Where a male person is proved to live with or to be habitually in the company of a prostitute or is proved to have exercised control over her movements, he shall, unless he can satisfy the court to the contrary, be deemed to be knowingly living on the earnings of prostitution.
Solicitation.		Section 11(1)(b). It is an offence in any public place persistently to solicit or importune for immoral purposes.
Homosexual brothels.		Section 13(9)–(11).
Allowing a child to be in a brothel.		Section 12(1). Any person with parental responsibilities or having charge of care of child between 4 and 16 who allows that child to reside in or frequent a brothel is guilty of an offence.

References: Hume I, 468-469; Gordon, 909.

INDECENT OR OBSCENE PUBLICATIONS

Indecent or obscene publications are those which have a **tendency to deprave and corrupt** the minds of those into whose hands the publication may fall and the **sale, publication or display** of which may be held to be **shamelessly indecent conduct.**

COMMENTARY	CASE LAW	STATUTE LAW
		Provisions of Burgh Police (Scotland) Act 1892 and local statutory provisions repealed by s 137 of Civic Government (Scotland) Act 1982 subject to provisions for postponement of repeal contained in s 134 of same Act.
Indecent or obscene Terms once generally held to be synonymous must now be viewed independently subject to distinctions implied by separate provisions of Indecent Displays (Control) Act 1981, s 1(1), and Civic Government (Scotland) Act 1982, s 51, although see:	*Watt v Annan* 1978 JC 84 Complaint of shameless indecency alleged that the accused had exhibited 'a film of an obscene or indecent nature'.	
	Ingram v Macari 1981 SCCR 184; 1982 SCCR 372 Words 'indecent or obscene convey a single idea'. 1981 report relates to relevancy; 1982 report relates to final disposal.	Indecent Displays (Control) Act 1981. Offence of making, causing or permitting the display of indecent matter in, or so as to be visible from, any public place. Section 1(3) makes provisions for the exclusion in certain limited circumstances from the provisions of s 1, where specific requirements as to warning notices, etc, are complied with, although such a warning may be viewed as incriminating evidence in a charge of shameless indecency.
Indecent What constitutes indecency remains a question of fact.	*Galletly v Laird* 1953 JC 16 G convicted of exhibiting for sale 'indecent or obscene books'. Per LJ-G Cooper: 'Inevitable that the character of the offending books or pictures should be ascertained . . . by reading the books or looking at the pictures. The book or picture itself provides the best evidence of its own indecency or obscenity or the absence of such qualities.'	
Exposing for sale.	*Robertson v Smith* 1979 SLT (Notes) 51 *McGowan v Langmuir* 1931 JC 10 Per LJ-G Clyde: 'Everything depends on the mode and circumstances of each act of sale, loan or exhibition and on the character and circumstances of the persons who are parties to these acts.'	
Obscene Again, question of obscenity remains one of fact to be considered in all the circumstances.	*Galletly v Laird* 1953 SC 16 *McGowan v Langmuir* 1931 JC 10	Civic Government (Scotland) Act 1982. Section 51 creates offences relating to publication, sale, distribution or display of obscene material. Section 51(5) allows court to convict a person found not guilty under s 51(1) on the basis that the material was indecent and not obscene, of the offence under s 1(1) of the Indecent Displays (Control) Act 1981 of displaying indecent material. (Provisions of this section indicate, therefore, that the terms 'indecent' and 'obscene' can no longer be treated as synonymous.)

Obscenity may be of a non-sexual nature.

John Calder (Publications) Ltd v Powell [1965] 1 All ER 159
Book dealing with drug-taking and addiction.
Held obscene.

DPP v A & BC Chewing Gum Ltd [1968] 1 QB 159
Bubble gum cards depicting battles.
Held that magistrates were wrong in excluding evidence of child psychiatrists.

Publications
Applies particularly to books, pictures, drawings, films and articles of such nature which are capable of exhibition, display or sale.

Section 51 of Civic Government (Scotland) Act 1982 and s 1(1) of Indecent Displays (Control) Act 1981 do not apply to broadcasts by the BBC or IBA, nor do they apply to performances of a play which are regulated under s 2(2) of Theatres Act 1968.

May take form of electronic pulses or similar.

Smith v Downie 1982 SLT (Sh Ct) 23
Video-cassette.

Civic Government (Scotland) Act 1982, s 51(8), gives definition of 'material'.

Ross v HMA 1998 SCCR 359
Convicted under s 51(2) of operating computer bulletin board system which contained visual images and text files of an obscene nature.
Held, text files included under description of recording of visual images but in any event the statutory definition was merely inclusive and not delimiting and text files were material.

Essence is 'publication' to general public or part thereof by exhibition or sale.

Annan v Nolan 1980 Crown Office Circular
Record by the Sex Pistols.

Galletly v Laird 1953 JC 16
Per LJ-G Cooper, two elements in offence: (1) 'book or picture is of such a nature as to be calculated to produce a pernicious effect in depraving and corrupting those who are open to such influences; and (2) such book or picture is being indiscriminately exhibited or circulated or offered for sale in such circumstances as to justify the inference that it is likely to fall (and perhaps intended to fall) into the hands of persons liable to be so corrupted'.

Publication to private groups or individuals also criminal.

Watt v Annan 1978 JC 84
Indecent films shown behind locked doors of public house.
Held to constitute shamelessly indecent conduct at common law.
Per Lord Cameron: 'Neither publicity nor privacy of locus of conduct necessarily affects . . . criminal quality of conduct.'

Generally the circumstances of the publication must be taken into account.

McGowan v Langmuir 1931 JC 10
Per Lord Sands: 'There is always an element of relativity. Charts and realistic coloured illustrations which might be exhibited in a medical classroom, might be grossly indecent as adornments of a place of public worship or even of a private sitting-room.'

Tendency to deprave and corrupt
Criteria satisfying this qualification follow those necessary for indecent or obscene.

Ingram v Macari 1981 SCCR 184; 1982 SCCR 372
Attempted to introduce expert evidence on question of whether or not magazines were liable to deprave and corrupt the morals of the lieges.
Held, on appeal, that such evidence could not be admitted. 'It was the duty of the sheriff to make up his own mind from examination of the magazines whether they were indecent or obscene in the sense of being likely to deprave and corrupt the morals of their readers.'

Sale, publication or display
Provisions of Civic Government (Scotland) Act 1982 supplement those of the common law and extend liability to situations not previously covered.

Tudhope v Barlow 1981 SLT (Sh Ct) 94
Held, inter alia, that shameless indecent conduct was a crime of intent and could not be committed recklessly or negligently and accordingly in view of the accused's ignorance of the contents of the magazines in question the necessary criminal intent had not been established and accused found not guilty. This was a common law charge.

Rees v Lees 1996 SCCR 601
Convicted, inter alia, under s 51(2). Sheriff found obscene and explicit covers visible through wrappers and that it was a feature that no warning signs outside. Argued since magazines in clear wrappers they were not liable to deprave and corrupt. *Held*, in circumstances sheriff was entitled to hold magazines were obscene.

Indecent Displays (Control) Act 1981, s 1

Civic Government (Scotland) Act 1982
Section 51(2): publishes, sells, distributes, or with a view to eventual sale or distribution, makes, prints, has or keeps obscene material.
Section 51(4): due diligence to avoid committing the offence is a defence to the charge.

Shamelessly indecent conduct
This common law offence has now been applied to indecent or obscene publications.

Robertson v Smith 1979 SLT (Notes) 51
Shopkeeper charged with shamelessly indecent conduct by selling, exposing for sale and having for sale indecent and obscene magazines. Conviction by sheriff confirmed on appeal.

Ingram v Macari 1981 SCCR 184; 1982 SCCR 372

'All shamelessly indecent conduct is criminal' (Macdonald, 150).

McLaughlan v Boyd 1934 JC 19
Publican convicted of lewd and libidinous practices towards a number of persons. Lord Clyde approving statement by Macdonald to cover such conduct.

Intention or knowledge for this common law crime must be proved.

Watt v Annan 1978 JC 84
W showed an obscene film to a number of persons in a hotel. Convicted of shameless indecency.
Lord Cameron: 'Conduct to be criminal must be directed to some person or persons with an intention or knowledge that it should corrupt or deprave those towards whom the indecent or obscene conduct was directed.'

Dean v Menzies 1981 JC 23
Held a company could not be deemed to possess the necessary mens rea for the offence at common law.

Civic Government (Scotland) Act 1982, s 51, and Indecent Displays (Control) Act 1981, s 1, now obviate this gap in the common law since the statutory offence does not require mens rea.

Exposing for sale.

Scott v Smith 1981 SLT (Notes) 22
Police constable purchased obscene magazine produced from a drawer.
Held that stock held in readiness for sale was being 'exposed for sale'.

Tudhope v Sommerville 1981 SLT 117
Obscene publications—possession for circulation and distribution to retailers.
Held that mere possession without any exposure to the public does not constitute a crime at common law.

References: Gordon, 991; Gane and Stoddart, 680; Macdonald, 152-153.

PUBLIC ORDER OFFENCES

BREACH OF THE PEACE

Disorderly conduct causing or likely to cause public disturbance.

COMMENTARY	CASE LAW	STATUTE LAW
Disorderly conduct Conduct is disorderly when it is in breach of public order,	*Mackie v MacLeod* (1961, unreported) High Court (see Gordon, p 988) M, infatuated with a young woman, habitually waited for her outside her workplace and followed her and her fiancé about. Convicted.	
or public decorum.	*Docherty v Thaw* (1962, unreported) High Court (see Gordon, p 985) D, a participant in a sit-down demonstration, obstructing street traffic. Convicted.	
	Colquoun v Friel 1996 SCCR 497 Conviction of breach of the peace upheld on appeal. Road protestor sat on a felled tree with his back to a workman who was cutting it with a power saw. He refused to move despite being asked. *Held*, this was conduct which might reasonably cause a person to be alarmed as to what might ensue.	
	Palazzo v Copeland 1976 JC 52 P, a shopkeeper, discharging shotgun into the air to scare off 'a number of unsavoury and drunken youths' engaged in a fracas outside his premises. Argued that that which was calculated to stop a breach of the peace was not itself a breach. 'A man may not take the law into his own hands . . . a man may not commit an offence to stop another.' Convicted.	
	Craig v Normand 1996 SCCR 823 Accused shouting and swearing at police after being removed from bus by police when apparently drunk. Conviction of breach of the peace and assaulting a police officer upheld on appeal.	
	Jas Ainslie (1842) 1 Broun 25 A took off his clothes in public and uttered threats. Convicted.	
	Raffaelli v Heatly 1949 JC 101 R, a 'peeping tom', staring at women through chink of curtains at lighted window of dwellinghouse late at night. Convicted.	
	Bryce v Normand 1997 SLT 1351 Accused charged with breach of the peace for taking secret video of neighbour's 15-year-old daughter getting undressed and showing it to another neighbour who was shocked. She informed complainer's friend who told complainer who was disgusted. Conviction upheld on appeal, on ground that if accused had been discovered while filming, the reaction would have shown the conduct had necessary quality to amount to breach of the peace.	

MacDougall v Dochtree 1992 SCCR 531
'Peeping tom', accused looking into solarium from locked toilet cubicle, discovered when suspicious attendant looked under·door. On appeal *held* that a member of the public could have discovered conduct and become alarmed.
Observed: okay to look into cubicle when suspicious. If no one could see into the cubicle, might not be a breach of the peace. Per Lord McCluskey: even if unlikely to be discovered might be shamelessly indecent conduct.

Young v Heatly 1959 JC 66
Y, a depute headmaster of technical school, at four separate interviews with adolescent pupils made 'grossly improper remarks and suggestions' to them. Convicted.

Lauder v Heatly (1962, unreported)
L, a 'kerb-crawling' motorist, stopped his car opposite two women, opening nearside door; no evidence that he spoke to them. Convicted.

McAvoy v Jessop 1989 SCCR 301
M in charge of Orange procession accompanied by band. Police officer asked band to stop playing as procession neared Catholic church outside which worshippers were being greeted by the priest. M ordered band to resume playing and convicted of breach of the peace.

Fisher v Keane 1981 SLT (Notes) 28
Glue-sniffing in absence of evidence of alarm or annoyance.
Held not to be a breach of the peace.

Hughes v Crowe 1993 SCCR 320
Playing music and making banging sounds in flat between 7.15 and 8.15 am 'all exceedingly loudly'. Convicted. Upheld on appeal: facts show a gross lack of consideration for others present.

See also Civic Government (Scotland) Act 1982, s 54, as amended by s 24 of the Crime and Disorder Act 1998.

Taylor v Hamilton 1984 SCCR 393
Breach of the peace. T and another seen sniffing glue from plastic bags in public; woman saw them swaying, staggering and walking round in circles; she phoned police. T convicted.
Per Sheriff Forbes (quoting LJ-G in *Montgomery v McLeod* 1977 SLT (Notes) 77; (1977) SCCR Supp 164): 'There is no limit to the kind of conduct which may give rise to a charge of breach of the peace. All that is required is . . . some conduct such as to excite the reasonable apprehension . . . or . . . create disturbance and alarm to the lieges. . . .'
On appeal, the sheriff's verdict upheld: there was sufficient evidence that a breach of the peace had taken place.
Fisher v Keane 1981 SLT (Notes) 28, distinguished.

Thompson v MacPhail 1989 SCCR 266
T charged with breach of the peace in that he injected himself with an unknown substance in the locked toilet cubicle of a restaurant. When manager became suspicious he alerted police who unlocked door and found T removing syringe from arm. There was blood on the walls and floor. Convicted. On appeal *held* that while there might be circumstances where similar conduct would constitute breach of the peace, in the present case there was insufficient evidence: no evidence of what was in syringe; activities had taken place behind locked door; no evidence as to length of time T was in cubicle or what the demand for cubicles was.

Donaldson v Vannet 1998 SCCR 422
Appellant convicted of breach of the peace for begging. Magistrate found he was not abusive, but that
all the females seemed to be in a state of alarm.
Held, on appeal, objective test that conduct likely
to cause fear and alarm and subjective reactions of
victims may be strong evidence but cannot be conclusive, and conviction quashed.
Per Lord Johnston: 'Since beginning itself cannot
be classified as breach of the peace, each case of
this type must depend upon the way the begging
operation is being conducted . . . In this respect we
think *Wyness v Lockhart* 1992 SCCR 808 is distinguishable because there was physical contact with
the victims.'

Causing or likely to cause
Where actual disturbance does not
occur disorderly conduct constitutes breach of the peace if,
viewed objectively, it is likely to
provoke such disturbance or cause
alarm or annoyance to others.

Turner v Kennedy (1972) SCCR Supp 30
T distributed to schoolgirls aged 12 to 14 pamphlets
referring inter alia to adolescent sex. Convicted.

Sinclair v Annan 1980 SLT (Notes) 55
S made indecent remarks to a woman in the hear-
ing of a girl of 18 who was embarrassed.
Convicted.

Wilson v Brown 1982 SCCR 49
Gesturing and swearing at opposing team supporters at football match. Acquitted by sheriff, but convicted on appeal by Crown.
Per Lord Dunpark: 'test . . . is whether the proved
conduct may reasonably be expected to cause any
person to be alarmed, upset or annoyed.'

See also:

Raffaelli v Healy 1949 JC 101
Evidence that one of the women stared at was
afraid to inform her husband in case he was
tempted into a breach of the peace.
Per LJ-C Thomson: 'Where something is done in
breach of public order or decorum which might reasonably be expected to lead to the lieges being
alarmed or upset or tempted to make reprisals at
their own hand the circumstances are such as to
amount to breach of the peace.'

Butcher v Jessop 1989 SCCR 119
B and W, both professional footballers, convicted
of breach of peace in the course of a football
match between Rangers and Celtic. As result of
incident on pitch, there was a disturbance among
spectators, which led police to fear invasion of
pitch.
Held (diss Lord Murray) that sheriff had taken
proper account of context of 'physical contact'
sport, that test of breach of peace was objective,
that actions of appellants were deliberate and
likely to cause alarm. Appeals refused.

Young v Heatly 1959 JC 66
No finding of alarm being created to spectators or
the public, none of whom either saw or heard what
took place, nor was there any finding of alarm to
the boys themselves.
Per LJ-C Clyde: '. . . it is not essential . . . that witnesses should be produced who speak of being
alarmed or annoyed . . . if the nature of the conduct giving rise to the offence [is] so flagrant as to
entitle the court to draw the necessary inference
from the conduct itself.'

Stewart v Lockhart 1990 SCCR 390
Man dressed as a woman in an area frequented by female prostitutes. Conviction upheld on appeal. Red light area, real possibility of public disturbance.

HMA v Forbes 1994 SCCR 163
Housebreaking with intent to rape. F entering house, removing clothes, prowling around and making a hood.
Held on appeal, could be a breach of the peace but motive irrelevant.

See also:

McKenzie v HMA 1992 SCCR 14
Wyness v Lockhart 1992 SCCR 808
Cameron v Lockhart 1992 SCCR 866

Swearing at the police.

Logan v Jessop 1987 SCCR 604
Appellants convicted of causing breach of the peace by shouting and swearing at two police officers and then running off.
Held that in the absence of any finding that the words complained of were uttered in the presence of others who might have been expected to react to them, there was insufficient evidence to justify conviction.

Cavanagh v Wilson 1995 SCCR 693
Appellant charged with breach of the peace for swearing at two police officers who had called at her home after she made a complaint of assault. No one was present and there was no finding the police were alarmed, upset or annoyed, nor was it found that there was reasonable cause to apprehend the police would be so upset, alarmed or annoyed.
Held, on appeal, in absence of such findings there was insufficient evidence, and conviction quashed. *Logan v Jessop* 1987 SCCR 604 applied.

Compare:
Norris v McLeod 1988 SCCR 572
Accused verbally abused police officers who were themselves annoyed and upset, although no members of the public present.
Held to amount to breach of peace.

Mackay v Heywood 1998 SCCR 210
Appellant convicted of breach of peace for swearing at police officers from her car. They had asked her to roll her window down after noticing her road tax had expired. One constable said he was upset; the woman constable said she was not. Upheld on appeal and fined £100.
Note: LJ-C Cullen points out that in *Logan v Jessop* 1987 SCCR 604 there was no finding that either of the two police officers was upset and the incident happened within the house.

Cardle v Murray 1993 SCCR 170
M 'breakdancing' in street. Police officer holding his arm attempting to warn him after he bumped into shopper. M resisted, shouted and swore. Acquitted.
Held that as the original breakdancing could not be regarded as a breach of the peace, the officer's action was unjustified. M entitled to refuse to accept detention as the officer was not acting under a warrant or exercising a statutory right on suspicion of M having committed some offence.

But see:

Woods v Normand 1992 SCCR 805

Saltman v Allan 1988 SCCR 640
Held that it was not the law that if the only persons present at the scene were police officers there can be no breach of the peace nor that a police officer is not to be regarded as liable to be affected by disorderly conduct.

Mens rea or motive is irrelevant.

Ralston v HMA 1988 SCCR 590
R charged with breach of the peace by mounting protest on prison roof. R stated that his actions were a peaceful protest against prison conditions. Sheriff directed jury that they were entitled to convict even if R's motives were blameless.
Held on appeal that R's behaviour deliberate and sheriff's direction adequate. Appeal refused.

Public disturbance
Can result from disorderly conduct taking place in private.

Ferguson v Carnochan (1889) 2 White 278
The holding of a noisy party in a private dwelling-house caused disturbance of the peace to those in neighbouring dwellinghouses, and in the street outside, and conviction followed.

Can result if the disorderly conduct taking place in private is likely, viewed objectively, to provoke public alarm and annoyance and thereby public disturbance.

Young v Heatly 1949 JC 101
Per LJ-G Clyde: 'It is well settled that [breach of the peace] can take place in a private house.'

Part of a disorderly crowd.

MacNeill v Robertson and Others 1982 SCCR 468
Charge libelling that accused did form part of a disorderly crowd, members of which did shout, swear and commit a breach of the peace.
Held on appeal by Crown, charge irrelevant.

Tudhope v Morrison 1983 SCCR 262 (Sh Ct)
Disorderly crowd.

Montgomery v Herron (1976) SCCR Supp 131
M was member of crowd preventing access to public meeting.
Held that findings showed that appellant formed part of crowd and in absence of any explanation by him the only reasonable inference was that he participated in breach of the peace.

Tudhope v O'Neill 1983 SCCR 443
A breach of the peace can be constituted by forming part of an 'amorphous group' of people; even where there is no evidence as to how each accused behaved.

Threats of violence by police officer; whether breach of the peace.

Carey v Tudhope 1984 SCCR 157
Police officer convicted of breach of the peace committed in course of his duty. Appeal against conviction dismissed.
Per LJ-C Wheatley: 'In many cases it becomes a matter of judgment for the judge to decide whether in the context and atmosphere of what occurred the facts did constitute the offence of breach of the peace in the law of Scotland.'

Provocation cannot operate in exculpation.

MacNeill v McTaggart (1976) SCCR Supp 150
McT charged with breach of peace by fighting with R in public place. McT argued he was responding to R's provocation.
Held that provocation cannot be pled in charge of breach of the peace.

References: Hume I, 439; Macdonald, 137-138; Gordon, 985; Gane and Stoddart, 693.

SENTENCING POLICY

Tait v Allan 1984 SCCR 385—Sheriff accepted that allowances should be made in sentencing otherwise respectable citizens for offences committed in the course of an industrial dispute. However, different considerations applied in this case and 60 days' imprisonment imposed.
Per LJ-G Emslie, upholding sentence. '. . . he was not in any sense an official picket engaged on what could fairly be regarded as a picketing activity. . . .'

Donaghy v Tudhope 1985 SCCR 118—D convicted of breach of the peace in that in pursuit of CND objectives he climbed up onto and remained on crane at Ministry of Defence premises. Sentence of 60 days' imprisonment upheld on appeal.
Per LJ-G Emslie: '. . . this was a very bad example of the offence of breach of the peace. . . . We are not concerned with the motive which led to the commission of this offence.'

McGivern v Jessop 1988 SCCR 511—M convicted of breach of peace by taunting rival football supporters and shouting and swearing.
Held that three months' detention not excessive as conduct could lead to serious consequences and must be severely discouraged.

Worsfold v Walkingshaw 1987 SCCR 17—Appellant pleaded guilty to swearing at police officer and police cadet who had warned him that he was parking illegally. Sheriff fined him £100.
Held that £100 excessive, fine reduced to £25.

Linton v Ingram 1989 SCCR 487—L pleaded guilty and admitted three analogous previous convictions. Sentence deferred for one year for him to attend alcohol education course. He did so and was of good behaviour. When he reappeared for sentence he was fined and appealed against sentence on ground that having complied with conditions of deferment he should only have been admonished.
Held court still has discretion as to appropriate sentence, and justice entitled to impose fine.

Smillie v Wilson 1990 SCCR 133—S pleaded guilty to breach of the peace by driving car in a way which placed occupants of another car in state of fear and alarm. Sheriff made compensation orders of £100 in favour of each of four occupants of other car.
Held that as no personal injury, loss, or damage, there was no justification for compensation order. Fine of £200 substituted.

Cameron v Lockhart 1992 SCCR 866—Kicking ball in street causing hindrance to vehicles and pedestrians. On appeal £60 fine reduced to £25.

Hepburn v Howdle 1998 SCCR 363—Appellant, who had a long record for dishonesty, sentenced to three months each for theft and breach of the peace to run consecutively. *Held*, (1) no consequence what combination of sentences followed so long as overall total of six months not exceeded; (2) where Parliament has provided a higher maximum sentence there is no principle which would justify placing a limit on it other than that derived from the maximum on any single charge. Concession by Crown wrongly made in *Fleming v Munro* 1997 SCCR 327, and *Hamilton v Heywood* 1997 SCCR 783 not followed. Appeal refused.
Note: Gordon's commentary: 'This case removes the confusion created by the Crown's concession in the two 1997 cases and makes it clear that the law is as it has always been thought to be.'

McAlpine v Friel 1997 SCCR 453—Appellant, 29-year-old first offender, convicted of breach of peace committed over period of more than two years by sending letters and packages to 32-year-old woman, following her and causing her fear and alarm. Three-month sentence upheld on appeal as not excessive.

PUBLIC DISORDERS

Meetings, street processions and **offences occasioned by procession or assembly** are covered in various statutes.

COMMENTARY	CASE LAW	STATUTE LAW
Meetings Permission must be sought to hold a meeting. Holding a meeting on or in private premises without consent of owner or occupier is an offence.		Public Order Act 1936 Civic Government (Scotland) Act 1982 *Note:* Provisions of Civic Government (Scotland) Act 1982 are intended to be complementary to Public Order Act.
Public parks, open spaces, etc, are invariably governed by local bye-laws or local legislation.	*Aldred v Miller* 1925 JC 21 Accused challenged bye-law requiring that permission be sought from local authority before holding meeting. Conviction upheld.	
Streets and roads, too, are subject to local regulations.	*Aldred v Miller* 1924 JC 117 A began lecturing in a street, causing a large number of people to assemble, and thereby occasioning obstruction. A convicted under Glasgow Police Act 1866. Per LJ-G Clyde: 'If anybody causes an obstruction in a public street or hinders other members of the public in exercising the public right of free passage upon it—he selfishly engrosses the public right to himself, and his action is justly condemned.'	
Street processions No such prior sanction is required for a procession although powers exist to prohibit or regulate proposed march or to prevent march actually taking place. Notice of intention to hold a procession is required.	*Loyal Orange Lodge v Roxburgh District Council* 1981 SLT 33 Power of district council to issue orders prohibiting or regulating processions is a wide one.	Public Order Act 1936, s 3 Civic Government (Scotland) Act 1982: s 62, requirement to give notice to regional council of a public procession; s 63, power of chief constable to prohibit and impose conditions; s 64, appeals against power granted by s 63.
Offences occasioned by procession or assembly		Civic Government (Scotland) Act 1982, s 65 sets out penalties relating to offences committed by disregard of conditions laid down in ss 62 and 63 of the same Act.
	Deakin and Others v Milne (1882) 10 R (J) 22 Salvation Army parade. Officers convicted of committing a breach of the peace.	
	Marr v McArthur (1878) 5 R (J) 38 M and another convicted of statutory breach of the peace in that they played flutes in a public place. Tune played was of political nature. *Held,* on appeal, that the mere playing of such a tune, without further proven detail of actual breach of the peace, was insufficient and conviction quashed.	

References: Gordon, 971; J.L. Murdoch, 144.

The **wearing of certain forms of uniform, provoking a breach of the peace, stirring up racial hatred** or **disrupting a lawful public meeting** may each in themselves be statutory offences.

COMMENTARY	CASE LAW	STATUTE LAW
Wearing of certain forms of uniform	*O'Moran v DPP; Whelan v DPP* [1975] 1 All ER 473 O'M and others arrested at funeral of Irish Republican hunger-striker, wearing dark berets, dark glasses and black pullovers. Similar items worn on separate occasion during Sinn Fein rally by W and others. Conviction upheld, per Widgery CJ.	Public Order Act 1936. Section 1 prohibits wearing of uniforms which signify association with a political organisation or object, in a public place or at any public meeting.
Provoking a breach of the peace	*Jordan v Burgoyne* [1963] 2 QB 744 A speaker must take his audience as he finds them; test *not* of a hypothetical audience of reasonable citizens. Section has also been used against disorderly football fans, 'streakers' and persons disrupting an Armistice Day silence.	Section 5, as substituted by Race Relations Act 1965, s 7 prohibits in any public place or at a public meeting use of threatening, abusive or insulting words or behaviour or distributing or displaying any such form of writing or sign with intent to provoke a breach of the peace or whereby a breach of the peace is likely to be occasioned.
Stirring up racial hatred	*R v Britton* [1967] 1 All ER 486 B smashed windows of M.P.'s flat and left racialist poster on door. *Held* no distribution to public; conviction fell. *R v Malik* [1968] 1 WLR 353 Black Power leader jailed for using words at a public meeting of a threatening, abusive and insulting nature. Both cases prosecuted under Race Relations Act 1965, s 6(1).	Section 5A, as inserted by Race Relations Act 1976, s 70, makes it an offence to publish or distribute written matter which is threatening, abusive or insulting, or to use in a public place or at a public meeting words of like character, where hatred is likely to be stirred up against any racial group.
Meaning of 'public place'.	*Cawley v Frost* [1976] 3 All ER 743 Track between spectators' area and football pitch at stadium held 'public place' even though public not ordinarily permitted access thereto.	Section 9: includes any highway or any other premises or place to which at the material time the public have or are permitted to have access whether on payment or otherwise.
Disrupting a lawful public meeting	*Burden v Rigler* [1911] 1 KB 337 Meaning of 'lawful public meeting' considered. *Held*, on appeal, that the fact that a public meeting is held on a highway does not necessarily make it unlawful; whether or not an obstruction is caused will depend on the circumstances in which it is held.	Public Meeting Act 1908, Representation of the People Act 1983, s 97. Any person at a lawful meeting acting in a disorderly manner to prevent transaction of business commits an offence and any person who incites others to commit such offence.

Reference: Gordon, 971.

MOBBING

A mob is a **gathering,** intent on a **common purpose** to be effected illegally and to the alarm of the public, in which **mere presence** may be sufficient for guilt.

COMMENTARY	CASE LAW	STATUTE LAW
Gathering The number needed to constitute a mob is determined by their conduct and is not fixed.	*Sloan v Macmillan* 1922 JC 1 Per LJ-C Scott Dickson: 'The law is that the number of people required to constitute a mob depends on what these people do, the violence they show, the threats they use.'	
There need be no actual violence.	*Sloan v Macmillan* 1922 JC 1 Per LJ-C Scott Dickson: '. . . lied persistently . . . in order to produce terror . . . by saying that there were hundreds of desperate men outside. That seems to me to be enough to make the appellant constitute part of a riotous mob.'	
Common purpose Unless there is a common purpose there is no mob.	*Daniel Blair and Ors* (1868) 1 Couper 168 Crowd assembled to pull down all gates. Per Lord Deas: 'The mere number of people, there may be thousands and thousands, does not constitute a mob. In order to constitute a mob there must be not merely a great number of people but a *common purpose*—and that common purpose must be illegal.' *Francis Docherty and Ors* (1841) 2 Swin 635 Per Lord Hope: 'Mobbing is not simply a breach of the peace by a number of persons; to constitute that crime it is absolutely necessary that there should be a common object.'	
But the purpose need not be antecedent to the formation of the mob,	*Alex Orr and Ors* (1856) 2 Irv 502 Accused attacked and burned a chapel. Also charged with mobbing and rioting. Per Lord Hope: 'If a mob take up a purpose, although it may not have been concerted beforehand, or may not at first have been known to the individuals at the bar; if the persons at the bar accompany that mob . . . they are guilty of the outrages committed by that mob.'	
and need have no motive other than to engage in disruptive behaviour.	*Michael Hart and Ors* (1854) 1 Irv 574 H was charged with forming part of a mob whose purpose was to attack Orangemen. There was insufficient evidence to support latter part of the libel but the jury were directed that they could nevertheless convict of mobbing and rioting.	
Evidence necessary to prove common purpose,	*Hancock and Ors v HMA* 1981 SCCR 32 Convictions of mobbing quashed on appeal. Crown failed to prove accused intent on a common purpose, but only 'a series of unconnected and fortuitous events . . . without any evidence of preknowledge or support or encouragement or countenance'.	
but when proved, **mere presence** in a mob may be sufficient for guilt,	*HMA v Cairns and Ors* (1837) 1 Swin 597 Person can be guilty of mobbing by mere presence alone. But he may also be the very soul of the mob without doing much—a word, a nod may excite the mob and be the cause of all the mischief that follows.	
and where a mob arises there is a duty to quell or at least withdraw from it (Alison I, p 520).		

Macdonald (5th edn), p 135; also Hume I, 421. It is not necessary to infer guilt that the accused should have been present at the moment when a particular act was committed, or that he should have been personally present at all. The rule that the instigator be as guilty as the perpetrator applies with special force to the case of mobbing.

'It is no defence that the mob's purpose was to prevent something being done by others which the mob thinks to be contrary to what the law allows' (Macdonald, p 132).

References: Hume I, 416; Alison I, 509; Macdonald, 131; Gane and Stoddart, 691.

SENTENCING POLICY

Millsopp v HMA 1997 GWD 9-381—M (aged 21) and T (aged 25) were sentenced to three years' imprisonment for mobbing and rioting. They were part of a mob of 15 to 20 people which attacked two police officers. M's record included six offences of breach of the peace. T's record included seven offences of breach of the peace and one police assault.

High Court on appeal *held*, sentence was excessive, mainly on grounds of comparative justice where co-accused X (aged 21) had similar sentence reduced to two years. Two years and two years respectively substituted.

HARASSMENT

A non-harassment order requires a person to refrain from such conduct towards the victim of the offence as may be specified in the order, for which period as specified. It can be made in addition to any other disposal which may be made. Such an order is a sentence for the purpose of an appeal. Harassment is defined as a course of conduct including causing alarm or distress on at least two occasions.

COMMENTARY	CASE LAW	STATUTE LAW
		Criminal Procedure (Scotland) Act 1995
Non-harassment order		
On application of prosecutor.	*McGlennan v McKinnon* 1998 SCCR 285 Respondent convicted of breach of the peace for shouting at ex-girlfriend. Prosecutor sought a non-harassment order but was refused on grounds that there were no averments of conduct on two occasions. Prosecutor appealed arguing, inter alia, account could be taken of previous convictions for assaulting lady. *Held*, (1) harassment involves a course of conduct on at least two occasions; (2) the offence for which the accused has been convicted of when the order is sought which must itself involve a course of conduct, and it was not legitimate to look back over previous convictions to construct a course of conduct, and appeal refused. Observed, the exact scope of the dictum regarding not considering the details of previous convictions might require to be determined some day.	Section 234A. Where a person is convicted of an offence involving harassment, the prosecutor may apply for a non-harassment order against him. This will require him to refrain from such conduct to the victim of the offence as may be specified in the order, for such period (includes indeterminate period) as specified, in addition to any other disposal which may be made. Such an order is a sentence for the purposes of an appeal. For this section 'harassment' is defined, in s 8 of the Protection from Harassment Act 1997, as a course of conduct which amounts to harassment, including causing alarm or distress. A course of conduct must involve conduct on at least two occasions.
Order to specify conduct to be refrained from and period.		
Definition of harassment.		
On the balance of probabilities.		Section 234A(2). The court may make a non-harassment order if satisfied on the balance of probabilities that it is appropriate to protect the victim from further harassment.
Penalties.		Section 234A(4). Breach of non-harassment order is an offence and penalties are: (a) on indictment, to imprisonment for a term not exceeding five years or fine, or both; (b) on summary, to imprisonment not exceeding six months or fine not exceeding statutory maximum, or both.

Revocation/variation of order.	*Robertson v Vannet* 1998 SCCR 668 Appellant subject to interim interdict by woman, C. Sheriff made non-harassment order for appellant not to approach or attempt to contact C or her father for five years.	Section 234A(6). Both parties can apply to court to vary or revoke the order which it can do if appropriate on the balance of probabilities, but not so as to increase the period for which the order is to run.
Appeal.	*Held*, refusing appeal, that s 8(5) of the Protection from Harassment Act 1997, which states court may not grant interim interdict and harassment order for same prohibition, applied only to civil proceedings and did not prevent criminal courts from making a non-harassment order. *Note*: father was a victim, because he knew of threats and was frightened. *Note*: Complainers can raise civil proceedings under the Protection from Harassment Act 1997.	Section 175(4) (as substituted by the Crime and Punishment (Scotland) Act 1997) entitles the prosecutor to appeal to the High Court against, inter alia, a decision not to make a non-harassment order. (For the procedure, see s 186.)
		Racially aggravated harassment Criminal Law (Consolidation) Scotland Act 1995
New offence of racially aggravated harassment.		
As from 30 September 1998.	*McGlennan v McKinnon* 1998 SCCR 285	Section 50A. Person guilty of racially aggravated harassment if he: (a) pursues a racially aggravated course of conduct which amounts to harassment of that person, and (i) it is intended to amount to harassment; or (ii) it occurs in circumstances where it appears to a reasonable person that it would amount to harassment of that person; or (b) acts In a manner which is racially aggravated and which causes, or is intended to cause, a person alarm or distress.
Definition of racially aggravated course of conduct.		Section 50A(2). A course of conduct is racially aggravated if: (a) immediately before, during or immediately after the course of conduct or action the offender evinces towards the person malice and ill-will based on that person's membership (or presumed membership) of a racial group; or (b) the course of conduct or action is motivated (wholly or partly) by malice or ill-will towards members of a racial group based on their membership of that group. Crime and Disorder Act 1998, s 96. Where an existing crime is proven to be racially aggravated the court shall take this into account in sentencing. See Sentencing below.

OFFENCES AGAINST THE COURT

CONTEMPT OF COURT

Contempt of court is conduct offending against the **dignity** or **authority** of a court, **within or outwith its precincts.**

COMMENTARY	CASE LAW	STATUTE LAW
The **dignity** of a court is offended by disorderly conduct.	*John Allan* 1826 Shaw 172 A, a witness, attended court so drunk as to be unable to give evidence.	Criminal Procedure (Scotland) Act 1995.
	Robert Clark or Williamson 1829 Shaw 215 'Rudely, indecently and contemptuously addressed the court . . . to be a gross contempt.'	
	Blair-Wilson, Petr 1997 SLT 621 Sheriff refused to allow defence lawyer to play tape, postponing decision until after cross-examination. Solicitor asked for clarification and found in contempt. Fine of £750 suspended on appeal: solicitor entitled to clarification and not wilfully defying court.	
	McKinnon v Douglas 1982 SCCR 80 Solicitor, due to misunderstanding, arrived late at district court. Opinion of the court: '. . . to arrive late in the circumstances . . . was not contempt . . . no neglect of the obligation to support the dignity of the court. There was no wilful or reckless interference with the administration of justice. All there was, was a late arrival [which was] wholly excusable.'	Section 92(2) makes provisions for an accused to be removed and for trial to proceed in his absence, where he misconducts himself to the extent of making a proper trial impossible. Legal representation is essential during such absence.
	Young v Lees 1998 SCCR 558 Complainer opened court door and shouted 'You guffy' at sheriff. Arrested and found in contempt. Later, when he had legal representation present, sentenced to 60 days. *Held*, on appeal, no need to grant legal representation before making finding of contempt.	

The **authority** of the court is challenged, when a witness prevaricates, refuses to answer questions or to take an oath or affirmation when required to do so,

Caldwell v Normand 1993 SCCR 624
Accused half an hour late, slept in.
Held on appeal that mere lateness not contempt unless wilful defiance of the order of the court.

Aitken v Carmichael 1993 SCCR 889
Spectator found in contempt for putting on headphones when leaving court at an adjournment.
Held on appeal that sheriff had grossly overreacted.

McMillan v Carmichael 1993 SCCR 943
Accused awaiting trial, yawned 'openly and unrestrainedly', found in contempt.
Held on appeal that there was no intention to affront the authority of the court. A warning would have been enough.

Riaviz to Howdle 1996 SCCR 20
Section 155(2). Sheriff sent complainer to prison for three months for failing to answer questions (memory lapse meant he could not remember details of or if motorbike stolen). Record did not specify the acts or statements.
Held, upholding conviction, appeal court could look at report to achieve justice.

Mowbray v Valentine 1991 SCCR 494
Party defender found in contempt for time wasting, asking obscure, rambling questions and ignoring directions.
Held on appeal that some latitude is required with party litigants. Behaviour not designed to insult the court.

Omond v Lees 1994 SCCR 389
Complainer, a Crown witness, could not remember statement as put to her on basis of police notes and detained overnight. Sheriff held hearing next day and complainer convicted.
Held, on appeal, finding suspended as sheriff had embarked on procedure beyond powers.
Observed, sheriff failed to follow LJ-G memorandum: he should have ascertained if Crown intended to bring criminal proceedings against complainer before deciding to deal with matter as contempt.

Bacon, Petr 1986 SCCR 265
B, a defence witness, prevaricated in answer to question which he believed would incriminate him. Judge held him to be in contempt of court. On petition, held that in these circumstances it could not be affirmed that his conduct amounted to contempt.

Dawes v Cardle 1987 SCCR 135
Complainer refused to leave cell to appear before sheriff. Sheriff and other court officials visited cells to warn that she might be in contempt if she failed to appear. She then appeared in court but refused to tender a plea.
Held that sheriff was entitled to find complainer in contempt.

Summary procedure
Section 155(1). A witness who fails to attend after due citation, unlawfully refuses to be sworn; or after the oath has been administered to him refuses to answer any question which the court may allow; or prevaricates may be punished forthwith for contempt or prosecuted by way of formal complaint.

Note: Section 291 contains similar penalties to s 155(1) for precognition on oath of defence witnesses who fail to attend, answer questions within knowledge, produce evidence in possession or prevaricate.

Section 155(2). The clerk of the court shall enter in the record of the proceedings the acts constituting the contempt or the statements forming the prevarication.

Section 155(4). Any witness who, after being duly cited in accordance with section 140 of this Act—
(a) fails without reasonable excuse, after receiving at least 48 hours' notice, to attend for precognition by a prosecutor; or
(b) refuses when cited to give information within his knowledge regarding any matter relative to the commission of the offence, shall be liable to punishment.

or where an order of the court is not implemented.

HMA v Airs 1975 SLT 177

A, a journalist, a prosecution witness at a trial, refused to say whether he had met one of the accused.

Opinion of the court: 'Subject only to the single qualification [ie, s 344 Criminal Procedure (Scotland) Act 1975] contempt of court is not a crime within the meaning of our criminal law. It is the name given to conduct which challenges or affronts the authority of the court or the supremacy of the law itself whether it takes place in or in connection with civil or criminal proceedings. The offence of contempt of court is an offence sui generis ... any witness ... who declines to answer a competent and relevant question in court must realise that he will be in contempt.'

Contrast:

Macara v MacFarlane 1980 SLT (Notes) 26

M, a solicitor at one court unable to get to another court on time, had anticipated this and arranged for a replacement solicitor to take his place if necessary. When case called M did not appear and replacement took the case. Sheriff convicted M of contempt.

Conviction quashed on appeal on basis that M having taken the proper steps to ensure that the business of the court would be able to proceed, the sheriff had no material before him at all which justified a finding of contempt of court.

See also Contempt of Court Act 1981, s 15, re penalties for contempt in all Scottish courts. Section 10: No court may require a person to disclose, nor is any person guilty of contempt of court for refusing to disclose, the source of information contained in a publication for which he is responsible, unless it is established to the satisfaction of the court that disclosure is necessary in the interests of justice or national security or for the prevention of disorder or crime.

or where, for example, a witness ignores citation to appear.

HMA v Bell 1936 JC 89

Witness failed to attend. Guilty of contempt and sentenced to one month's imprisonment.

Urquhart v Hamilton 1996 SCCR 217

Accused failed to attend social work interview for SER (said he did not have bus fare). Found in contempt of court and ordered to perform 40 hours' community service.

McGlinchy or Petrie v Angus (1889) 2 White 358

P cited to appear as witness in trial of her brother for assault. She failed to heed adequate citation and did not turn up at court. Convicted of contempt and conviction upheld on appeal.

Per LJ-C Macdonald: 'In all such cases it is in the power, and, indeed, it is the duty of the court, in order to protect the dignity, quietness, and regularity of its proceedings, and to prevent defiance of its orders, to deal with such acts of contempt . . .'

Chappell v Friel 1997 SLT 1325

Witness tried but failed to arrange childcare. She phoned PF's office two hours after due to appear and told warrant issued for arrest. Found guilty of contempt. Upheld on appeal since no explanation and failure wilful.

Anderson v Douglas 1997 SCCR 632

Complainer failed to pay fine and attend means enquiry court because of failure to ensure receipt of citation.

Held, on appeal, failure to pay fine not contempt of court and although neglect in collecting mail, no proof of wilfully defying court and finding and fine suspended.

The conduct may be **within the precincts of the court** either wilfully

Pirie v Hawthorn 1962 JC 69; 1962 SLT 291
Accused failed to appear in sheriff court to answer summary complaint, the explanation being that his father omitted to inform him of the date. On appeal his conviction quashed.
Per LJ-G Clyde: 'There was no wilful defiance of the court. The essential element of contempt of court is thus absent.'

Leys v Leys (1886) 13 R 1223
Non-delivery of child to be handed over held to be contemptuous.
See also:

McKinnon v Douglas 1982 SCCR 80

Cameron v Orr 1995 SCCR 365.
Complainer late for diet trying to find suitable jacket. Sheriff found him in contempt and fined him £50. Sentence suspended as on face value he was endeavouring to show respect to the court.

or carelessly,

Muirhead v Douglas 1979 SLT (Notes) 17
M, a solicitor, due to defend an accused in a trial second on a list of three, absented himself from court after the first trial started anticipating that it would last two hours. Court business was delayed for half an hour when the first trial finished earlier than expected. He appealed unsuccessfully against conviction for contempt of court.
Per Lord Cameron: 'The variety and quality of the acts or omissions which in particular cases may fall within "contempt of court" are not capable of precise delimitation or formulation. On the other hand, it may be said that where there has been a failure to obey or obtemper an order or requirement of a court, such a failure demands satisfactory explanation and excuse, and in the absence of such may be held to constitute a contempt of court of varying degrees of gravity. I can see no reason in principle, and there is certainly none in authority, for an assertion that failure due to carelessness alone may, in no circumstances, constitute contempt of court.'

Ferguson v Normand 1994 SCCR 812
Solicitor late for trial because appearing in other court and expected business to finish early. Fined £250, suspended on appeal: error of judgment but not acting in wilful fashion against court.

or the conduct may be **outwith the precincts of the court,** for example, where the administration of justice is prejudiced by publishing material calculated to cause prejudice.

Stirling v Associated Newspapers Ltd 1960 SLT 5
Newspaper printed a photograph of accused a day after his initial detention along with an article about him and the crime.
Held to be contempt. Test was: Is the course adopted by the newspaper such as to prejudice the impartiality of the trial?

Hall v Associated Newspapers Ltd 1978 SLT 241
Accused in police custody in connection with a murder inquiry. While in custody newspaper published extensive reports about the inquiry and the accused.
Held that from the moment of arrest, or the moment the warrant to arrest is granted, the person concerned is under the care and protection of the court. At either of these points relevant proceedings have commenced so as to bring into play the contempt jurisdiction of the court where prejudicial publication is concerned.

In summary matters, jurisdiction starts from the time of arrest or service of the complaint, whichever is the earlier.

See also:

Kemp, Petr 1982 SCCR 1
Press reports during a conspiracy trial indicated that witnesses who had given evidence were at a secret address under police custody. Trial judge's finding of contempt quashed by appeal court, as the reports were narratives of fact not likely to prejudice the minds of the jury.

Robb v Caledonian Newspapers Ltd 1994 SCCR 659
Petitioner released on bail on charge of lewd practices and petition brought ten months after article and paper gave undertaking not to publish further articles, which made prohibition unnecessary.
Held, if claim of breach of strict liability rule it should be as soon as practicable, and if long delay and repetition unlikely court disinclined to make order.

HMA v Stuurman 1980 SLT 182
Prejudicial pre-trial publicity, even if it constitutes contempt, does not necessarily bar the subsequent trial taking place. Plea in bar of trial rejected.

HMA v Caledonian Newspapers Ltd 1995 SCCR 330
'Evening Times' published article and photograph of escaped prisoner it correctly said was on remand.
Held, (1) the question of prejudice is assessed at stage of publication, there must be a substantial risk and the proceedings must be active at time of publication; (2) the article created only a remote risk of prejudice but the photo created risk of affecting witnesses and strict liability rule applied against publishers and editor; (3) mitigating circumstances of concern for public safety and fined £2,500 and £250 respectively. Observed, in practice decision by LA to authorise publication will remove risk of finding contempt.

HMA v Daily Record 1995 SCCR 330
Paper published article and photo of escaped prisoner but made no reference to robbery charge he was on remand for but erroneously said he had been earlier convicted of culpable homicide (it had in fact been set aside).
Held, only relevant prejudice is to active proceedings and the strict liability rule was not breached.
Note: Boyle pleaded guilty to robbery in High Court in Glasgow on 27 March 1995.

Muir v BBC 1996 SCCR 584
Prison officers facing trial for assaulting prisoners petitioned court to prohibit broadcast of programme containing allegations of assault on prisoners by unnamed officers. Allegations made by prison doctor.
Held, order granted as distinct risk doctor's interview could be held by juror as of great importance. (Accused were acquitted on a submission of no case to answer. The Crown did not call the prison doctor as a witness.)

Contempt of Court Act 1981, ss 1 and 2, strict liability provisions in relation to publications which create a substantial risk that course of justice in particular proceedings will be seriously impeded or prejudiced; s 4, postponement of reporting of proceedings.
For discussion of provisions, see *New Law Journal*, 1981, pages 923, 1167 and 1191.

Cox and Griffiths, Petr 1998 SCCR 561
Section 2(2) of the Contempt of Court Act 1981;
Article 10 ECHR: Freedom of expression.
Petitioners found in contempt for article about
transfer of high security prisoners for trial.
Held, no reason to suppose article would create
risk of serious impediment or prejudice. Observed
by Lord Prosser: 'Even when articles in press do
contain germs of prejudice it will rarely be appropriate to bring these to the attention of the court,
. . . far less for the issue to be treated as even
potentially one of contempt.'

HMA v Express Newspapers plc 1998 SCCR 471
Article published when proceedings were deserted
pro loco et tempore. PF indicated to writer that proceedings still active and she should contact publisher's lawyers who in fact gave go ahead.
Conceded article in contempt as risk of prejudice
to live prosecution and publishers fined £50,000
and editor £2,500.

*HMA v News Group Newspapers; HMA v Scottish
Express Newspapers Ltd* 1989 SCCR 156
Man arrested and charged with attempted murder.
Article in *Sun* and *Scottish Daily Express* next day
reported arrest and described the attempted
murder as the attempted political assassination of
a Yugoslav political exile. Impression given by article that the arrested person was guilty.
Held that publisher must not only try to avoid committing contempt of court but must succeed in
doing so. Having regard to the spectacular nature
of the crime and the 110-day rule, time lag
between publication and trial not long enough to
avoid prejudice. Found guilty.

Moot point whether contempt of court extends to public inquiries, etc, as not strictly courts of law.

But see:
HMA v Airs 1975 SLT 177
Contempt: 'Conduct which challenges or affronts
the authority of the court or the supremacy of the
law itself whether it takes place in or in connection
with civil or criminal proceedings.'

Restriction on press and TV in proceedings involving person under sixteen.

Caledonian Newspapers, Petr 1995 SCCR 576
A on trial for attempted murder of wife and child.
Trial judge dispensed with statutory restrictions on
condition, inter alia, of no photographs of wife and
child. Petitioners sought to publish photo of wife.
Held, trial judge's order incompetent, since statute
does not absolutely prohibit publications of photographs of persons other than child and order
recalled.
Observed, per LJ-G: even though photographs of
persons other than child not absolutely prohibited,
not allowed to publish in manner calculated to lead
to identification of child.

Criminal Procedure (Scotland) Act 1995, s 47, makes it an offence to publish a picture or reveal the name, address or school, or include any particulars calculated to lead to the identification of a person under 16 years in any newspaper where that person is involved in any proceedings in a Scottish court. (This includes radio and television reporting.) The court or the Secretary of State may lift such reporting restrictions. *Note:* This protection extends to a witness who is under 16 years where the accused is also under 16. It does not apply where the accused is over 16 and the witness is under 16, unless the court so directs.

Facts which constitute contempt may also constitute crime, eg perjury.

Manson, Petr (1977) SCCR Supp 177.

References: Gordon, 1088-1096; Hume I, 405-406; Gane and Stoddart, 718.

SENTENCING POLICY

Ellen Hislop, Petr 1986 SCCR 268—H was defence witness in drugs trial. Refused to name those who had supplied her with drugs other than one man whom she did name. Sentenced to nine months' imprisonment for contempt.
Held not to be excessive.
Contempt of Court Act 1981, s 15(2) provides that maximum imprisonment for contempt of court in Scottish proceedings shall be two years.

McInally, Petr 1993 SCCR 212—Witness prevarication. Seventeen-year-old, first offender. Eighteen months' detention on appeal reduced to nine months. Contempt as bad as it could be, custody inevitable but some appreciation now of the gravity of her conduct.

Forrest v Wilson 1993 SCCR 631—Witness prevaricating given 42 days' summary imprisonment. On appeal *held* that the restrictions on first imprisonment did not apply as court not sentencing but summarily punishing. Period should have been 21 days under s 334 of CP(S)A 1975.

Gallagher, Petr 1996 SCCR 833—Menacing stares at jurors by petitioner after conviction of brothers. Sentenced to six months.
Held, on appeal, not so extreme as to justify exemplary sentence, and three months substituted.

PERJURY

Perjury is the **deliberate falsification** of **material, relevant and competent** evidence given on oath or affirmation in **judicial proceedings.**

COMMENTARY	CASE LAW	STATUTE LAW
Deliberate falsification Express denial of a fact under oath,	*HMA v Cairns* 1967 JC 37 C gave evidence at his own trial under oath that he did not stab the deceased. Found not proven. Later tried for perjury on basis of this denial. *Held* to be nothing contrary to natural justice in prosecuting a false denial of guilt in a trial.	Criminal Law (Consolidation) (Scotland) Act 1995, ss 44–46. Section 44(1). Person commits crime if he wilfully makes a statement on oath which he knows to be false or does not believe to be true.
or express assertion of a fact under oath.	*Elizabeth Muir* 1830 Alison I 469–470 M gave false evidence that the police officer arresting the accused in the trial where M was a witness had been drunk. *Held* to be perjury. *Simpson v Tudhope* 1987 SCCR 348 S, police officer, charged with perjury in that he deponed he was accompanied by a female officer JD, when he knew that he did not know whether he had been accompanied by her. *Hold* to be guilty of perjury, Sheriff Gordon comments: 'It is perjury to state that one cannot recollect something when one can . . .' conversely it is perjury to claim one does recollect something of which one had no recollection.'	Section 44(2). False statement in certain material (eg a statutory declaration) not on oath made knowingly and wilfully is a crime. Section 45. Any person who aids, abets etc another person to commit offence against s 44 shall be proceeded against as if principal offender. Section 46. Summary criminal proceedings for offences against s 44 may be commenced at any time within one year from the date of commission of offence, or within three months from the date when evidence sufficient in the opinion of the Lord Advocate comes to his knowledge, whichever period last expires (certificate signed as to that date conclusive thereof).
It is not constituted by omitting to volunteer evidence in one's possession. **Material, relevant and competent**	*Hall v HMA* 1968 SLT 275 H, in evidence, falsely denied making a particular statement to the police, a matter relevant only to credibility. *Held* that this evidence was both material and relevant to the perjury charge. *Aitchison v Simon* 1976 SLT (Sh Ct) 73 S deponed that he had not made a certain statement to a police constable. The evidence contained in the statement was material evidence in the trial, and the question of whether statement was made was material to S's credibility as a witness. Argued as evidence given by S in the original trial related to a conversation by S outwith the presence of the accused, it therefore could not have been competent evidence against accused and no perjury could attach. *Held* that evidence was relevant for testing S's credibility, therefore competent to support charge of perjury.	

Lord Advocate's Reference (No 1 of 1985) 1986 SCCR 329

Per LJ-G Emslie: 'Whether a false statement is material and relevant to the issue in the proceedings in which it is made is a question of law. . . . It would be well if the word "material" ceased to be employed in describing the crime. All that is required is that it should be clearly understood that a charge of perjury will not lie unless the evidence alleged to be false was both competent and relevant at an earlier trial, either in proof of the libel or in relation to the credibility of the witness.'

Normally an opinion cannot constitute perjury. However, the corrupt origin of a pretended opinion may infer perjury or a professional person may take a bribe to give false evidence on opinion (Macdonald, p 164; Alison I, p 468).

Judicial proceedings
Occurs not only in law courts but before tribunals where an oath can be administered.

Section 46(1)(a). Form of an oath immaterial if accepted as binding.

Section 46(1)(b). Affirmation equivalent in effect to oath.

References: Hume I, 366; Alison I, 465; Gordon, 1063; Gane and Stoddart, 701.

SENTENCING POLICY

Hagen v HMA 1983 SCCR 245—Perjury in course of trial. Sentence of four years' detention imposed. Appealed. In view of H's age, and background of threats, sentence was excessive, and one of three years' detention substituted.

Gordon v Hamilton 1987 SCCR 146—G was 17 years of age and unemployed. At trial refused to inculpate accused in assault case. Sentenced to three months' detention. By time of appeal had obtained employment and sentence of £500 fine substituted.

HMA v McKinlay 1998 SCCR 201—Attempted subordination of perjury. Respondent convicted of attempting to pervert the course of justice by attempting to suborn a witness with the intent of procuring false evidence for the appeals of certain persons convicted of terrorist offences. Respondent attempted to get person to swear affidavit that evidence he gave at trial untrue. On appeal sentence of two years' imprisonment substituted for original sentence of three years' probation and 240 hours' community service work.

MISCELLANEOUS

ROAD TRAFFIC

Definitions

Road Traffic Act 1988, ss 185–192, provides a series of definitions of important terms.

COMMENTARY	CASE LAW	STATUTE LAW
Driver Includes separate person engaged in steering the vehicle as well as another person engaged in controlling the vehicle.		Road Traffic Act 1988 Section 192(1)
More than one person may drive the car at the same time,	*Tyler v Whatmore* [1976] RTR 83 One person controlling the steering of the car from passenger seat, while person in driver's seat controlled propulsion. Both held to be driving. *Langman v Valentine* [1952] 2 All ER 803 Learner driver and instructor in dual-control car Both held to be drivers.	
but each must be exercising some degree of control,	*Evans v Walkden* [1956] 3 All ER 64 Qualified driver simply sat beside learner driver. Although able to reach brake and steering wheel did not do so. *Held* not to be in control, thus not driving.	
although the **degree** may be minimal.	*Ames v MacLeod* 1969 JC 1 A car ran out of petrol. Pushed car down straight incline while walking alongside it with one hand on the wheel to steer. *Held* to be driving, because 'in a substantial sense controlling the movement and direction'. But see: *R v MacDonagh* [1974] RTR 372 States differing English approach. In *McArthur v Valentine* 1989 SCCR 704 a five-judge appeal court held that the test applied in *Ames v MacLeod* is to be preferred to the English test in *R v MacDonagh*. M had been drinking and arranged for S to drive him home. In course of helping S to start car by jump starting, M pushed car with one hand on steering wheel. *Held* to be driving.	
Mechanically propelled vehicle Test of mechanical propulsion—will be regarded as mechanically propelled, even if broken down, unless there is no reasonable prospect of the vehicle ever being made mobile again.	*Newberry v Simmonds* [1961] 2 QB 345; [1961] 2 All ER 318 Engine removed from car. Evidence showed that it might be replaced shortly and power restored. *Held* still to be a mechanically propelled vehicle. *Smart v Allan* [1962] 3 All ER 893; [1963] 1 QB 291 Vehicle had no gearbox and engine in such bad repair that future mobility was not possible. *Held* not to be mechanically propelled.	Section 185(1)

Tudhope v Every 1977 SLT 2
Car had clutch slipping. Gear box stuck in second gear.
Held that this car was a motor vehicle and ought only to be released from that classification when it reached such a state of structural or mechanical decrepitude that it would offend common sense to call it a 'mechanically propelled vehicle'. It was also held that the vehicle required to be insured although only parked.

Intended or adapted for use on roads

Carstairs v Hamilton 1997 SCCR 311
Appellant was convicted of driving a go-kart dangerously. Upheld, inter alia, it did not matter whether state arose recently or was built into vehicle in first place.

Nichol v Heath [1972] RTR 476   Section 185(1)
Car rebuilt solely for auto-cross racing.
Held still to be for use on road, although owner did not intend to use it for such.

Test is objective.

Woodward v Young 1958 SLT 289
Agricultural tractor may be a vehicle intended or adapted for use on roads.

Childs v Coghlan (1968) 112 SJ 175
Held that a machine whose primary use was not on roads, which regularly went on roads from one site to another, was intended for use on roads.

Holliday v Henry [1974] RTR 101
Roller skates placed under each wheel of a vehicle so that it was not actually 'on' the road.
Held still to be on the road for purposes of s 8, Vehicles (Excise) Act 1971.

Roads
Any highway and any other road to which the public has access.

Roads (Scotland) Act 1984, s 151(1); Road Traffic Act 1988, s 192(2)

Public access may be a matter of fact or circumstance.

Harrison v Hill 1932 JC 13; 1931 SLT 598
Any road may be regarded as a road to which the public have access where members of the public are to be found who have not obtained access either by overcoming a physical obstruction or in defiance of prohibition express or implied.

'Private' notes are not conclusive proof that the road is not public.

Hogg v Nicholson 1968 SLT 265
Road marked 'Private'. However, used by police cars and delivery vans, and also for access to post office.
Held to be a road.

Public access to, eg, car parks and forecourts does not render them roads per se, unless they could be naturally and ordinarily described as such.

See:
Purves v Muir 1948 JC 122; 1948 SLT 529
Henderson v Bernard 1955 SLT (Sh Ct) 27

Griffin v Squires [1958] 3 All ER 468
Car park held not to be a road simply because public had access. 'Nobody . . . would think of a car park as a road.'

But see:

Paterson v Ogilvy 1957 JC 42
Held that a private field being temporarily used as a car park was a 'public place'.

Vannet v Burns 1998 SCCR 414
Held, car park was no less a public place because frequented by a special section of public (patrons), and case of driving with excess alcohol remitted to sheriff to proceed as accords.

Brown v Braid 1984 SCCR 286
Held that garage forecourt is a public place if there is a high probability of the presence of pedestrians on it.

Beattie v Scott 1992 SCCR 435
Young v Carmichael 1992 SCCR 332

Dick v Walkingshaw 1995 SCCR 307
Appellant convicted of driving without insurance on the car deck of a ferry at a time when the deck was connected to a ramp on the deck and the cars were disembarking. Upheld on appeal: since public had access, albeit restricted, car deck was road at time ramp in place.

Rodger v Normand 1994 SCCR 861
Conviction of careless driving. Upheld on appeal: playground was a public place, since used outside school hours by public as leisure park, and persons not trespassers as this use tolerated by owners.

Dangerous and careless driving

Road Traffic Act 1988, as amended by Road Traffic Act 1991:
Section 1: 'A person who **causes** the death of **another** person by driving a mechanically propelled vehicle **dangerously** on a road or other public place is guilty of an offence.'
Section 2: 'A person who drives a mechanically propelled vehicle **dangerously** on a road or other public place is guilty of an offence.'
Section 3: 'If a person drives a mechanically propelled vehicle on a road or other public place **without due care and attention,** or **without reasonable consideration for other persons using the road** or place, he is guilty of an offence.'

COMMENTARY	CASE LAW	STATUTE LAW
Causes Accused's driving need not be a substantial cause of the accident, only a material cause.	*R v Hennigan* [1971] 3 All ER 133 H drove dangerously fast but other motorist he killed was also blameworthy. Per Lord Parker CJ: 'so long as the dangerous driving is a cause and more than de minimis the statute operates.' *Watson v HMA* [1978] SCCR Supp 192 Jury directed by trial judge that W could only be acquitted if other party 'wholly to blame'. *Held* that this was a misdirection and conviction quashed.	
Another Can be a passenger in same car.	*R v Klein* (1960) Times, 3 April K's passenger died as a consequence of K's reckless driving. *Davidson v HMA* 1996 SCCR 736 D convicted of causing death by dangerous driving. He was taking friend to work and took bend too fast. *McCluskey v HMA* 1989 SLT 175 Driver who caused injuries to unborn child which died as a result, convicted under this section.	
Dangerous	*Abbas v Houston* 1993 SCCR 136 A driving at 108 mph on motorway in good road conditions. Conviction upheld on appeal. Such a conviction possible under RTA 1988, s 2A when accused driving at a grossly excessive speed. See also: *McQueen v Buchanan* 1996 SCCR 826. *Mitchell v Lockhart* 1993 SCCR 1070 Dangerously driving. M driving 61 mph on 15 mph esplanade. Esplanade empty at the time. Convicted. Upheld on appeal. Under RTA 1988, s 2A a driver must have regard to potential dangers, in this case of pedestrians walking onto the esplanade. Observed that RTA 1988, s 2A based on the language in *Allan v Patterson* 1980 JC 37.	Road Traffic Act 1988, s 2A(1). Person driving dangerously if (a) driving far below that expected of a competent and careful driver and (b) it would be obvious to such a driver that such driving would be dangerous.

Trippick v Orr 1995 SCCR 736
Conviction of dangerous driving upheld on appeal, where driver doing 114 mph in 70-mph limit. Only car on road and good road conditions.
Held, potential risks combined with grossly excessive speed created danger. *Brown v Orr* 1994 SCCR 668 distinguished.

Brown v Orr 1994 SCCR 668
Conviction of dangerous driving for doing 104 mph on A9 where limit 60 mph quashed and conviction for speeding substituted as road conditions good.

Note:
Alternative verdicts

Road Traffic Act 1991, s 24. Various alternative verdicts open eg conviction for careless driving competent in a charge of dangerous driving.

If accused charged with RTA 1988, s 1 and the evidence showed he did not cause the death, he can still be convicted under RTA 1988, s 2.

It can be a defence to a charge of dangerous driving that the driver without fault of his own was deprived of control of the vehicle by a mechanical defect which he did not know about or could not with reasonable diligence have discovered.

R v Spurge [1961] 2 All ER 688
Driver convicted—knew of defect but continued to drive.

It is unclear whether there can be a defence of necessity.

McNab v Guild 1989 SCCR 138
Held that if defence of necessity is available, it could only be made out if immediate danger to life or of serious injury at the material time, which was not the case here.

Court cannot assume without evidence that vehicle must have developed defects.

Habjohns v Burgar [1972] Crim LR 46
B's car hit bridge wall on dry road on a clear day. Two skid marks behind car. B gave no explanation for collision. Prosecution did not have to prove that there was no steering defect.

Without due care and attention
Standard of due care and attention is an objective one, inferred from the circumstances and is therefore a question of fact.

Jarvis v Williams [1979] RTR 497
Solitary car damaged in accident. Unexplained accident not attributable to road surface, weather or defect in vehicle.
Held, on appeal, that the inference was that the defendant was not driving with due care and attention.

RTA 1988, s 3

Careless driving.

Sigournay v Douglas 1981 SCCR 302
Careless driving. Driver hit pedestrian who ran in front of her on dual carriageway. Convicted. Appealed.
Held that the appellant had reasonable grounds for believing that the risk of pedestrian crossing road had passed and had no reason to anticipate pedestrian's actions; there was no evidence to support the suggestion that a swerve could have avoided the accident. Conviction quashed.

RTA 1988, s 3

MacPhail v Haddow 1990 SCCR 339
H using a hand-held telephone while driving. No evidence of lack of control or danger to others. Convicted. On appeal *held* that although such driving is contrary to the Highway Code, unless there is actual or potential danger demonstrated it is not an offence in itself.

See also:
Rae v Friel 1992 SCCR 688
Stock v Carmichael 1993 SCCR 136

Inexperience or error of judgment is not an excuse to this offence.	*McCrone v Riding* [1938] 1 All ER 157 Learner driver found guilty of offence under s 3. *Held* irrelevant that carelessness was due to inexperience. *Simpson v Peat* [1952] 1 All ER 447 If a driver does not exercise that degree of care and attention which a reasonable and prudent man would exercise in the circumstances, he is guilty, whether or not committing an error of judgment.
Knowledge of the carelessness not an essential element of careless driving.	*Hampson v Powell* [1970] 1 All ER 929 Lorry driver who was not aware he had hit a stationary vehicle was held to be rightly convicted of careless driving. *Farquar v McKinnon* 1986 SCCR 524 Driver of large articulated vehicle reversed slowly along road without assistance, using only mirrors, in area where he was aware children were playing. Ran over child and found guilty of careless driving because he had reversed without clear vision to rear, notwithstanding that lorry showing hazard light. *Brunton v Lees* 1993 SCCR 98 Speeding, 60 mph in 40 mph zone. Speed held to be excessive but not grossly so. Conviction upheld on appeal. Speed in itself sufficient for careless driving.
No exemption from prosecution exists for emergency services.	*Wood v Richards* [1977] Crim LR 295 Police officer convicted of careless driving. *Held* that there is no special exception or standard to be applied to emergency services. *Husband v Russell* 1997 SCCR 592 Appellant pleaded guilty to dangerous driving. He was driving fire engine on emergency and struck vehicle trying to overtake. Fined £100 and endorsed three points. *Held*, on appeal, minor degree of want of care and absolute discharge appropriate.
Without reasonable consideration	*Dilks v Bowman-Shaw* [1981] RTR 4 DC Motorway with two-lane carriageway. Accused moved into left-hand lane and overtook. No inconvenience caused to other driver. *Held* that although the manæuvre was in contravention of the Highway Code, no one was actually endangered or inconvenienced. No conviction and appeal court upheld decision of lower court and rejected Crown appeal. But see Wheatley, p 36. This authority might not be followed in Scotland.
Other persons using the road Includes passengers in the vehicle being driven by the accused.	*Pawley v Wharldall* [1966] 1 QB 373 Driver of double-decker bus. Five passengers gave evidence that accused's driving caused panic and alarm to them. No evidence that anyone else outside the bus was treated without reasonable consideration. Convicted.
Proof by road marks.	*Ryrie v Campbell* 1964 JC 33 Tyre impression on wrong side of road and matching paint on lamp-post and at collision were enough to convict despite no eye-witnesses.

No offence of 'causing death by careless driving'.

McCallum v Hamilton 1985 SCCR 368
Careless driving. McC drove car in such manner that it collided with another car causing the latter to mount pavement thereby injuring two pedestrians and killing another. Details of these consequences in complaint objected to as irrelevant. Sheriff repelled objection.
Held, on appeal, that the consequential injuries were relevantly detailed in complaint. However, the word 'fatal' was irrelevant and must be deleted. To do otherwise would effectively create by the back door offence of causing death by careless driving- a crime unknown to statute.
Per LJ-C Ross: '. . . the complaint reads as though it were libelling an offence of causing death by careless driving. There is no such offence under the Road Traffic Acts. . . .'

Sharp v HMA 1987 SCCR 179
Held that it was wrong for sheriff to take into account the fatal consequences of a piece of careless driving in considering sentence.

Drink-related offences

Road Traffic Act 1988, s 4.
Section 4(1). **Driving** or **attempting to drive** a motor vehicle while **unfit to drive** through **drink or drugs**.
Section 4(2). **Being in charge of** a motor vehicle while **unfit to drive** through **drink or drugs**.
Section 4(3). It is a defence to a charge under s 4(2) that there is **no likelihood of driving** while unfit through drink or drugs.
Road Traffic Offenders Act 1988.
Section 15(3) provides a defence of **post-incident drinking** if the prosecution relies on analysis of breath, blood or urine specimen.

COMMENTARY	CASE LAW	STATUTE LAW
Driving When motor vehicle moving subject to one's control and direction.	*R v Kitson* (1955) 39 Cr App R 66 K was a passenger in car and awoke to find car moving with no one in driving seat and no key in ignition. K steered car onto grass verge. *Held* that K was driving.	Road Traffic Act 1988 Section 4(1)
	Ames v MacLeod 1969 JC 1 A walking beside car. Car engine not running. Guided car downhill by use of steering wheel. *Held* driving.	
Attempting to drive Intention may be inferred from the circumstances.	*R v Cook* [1964] Crim LR 56 C found in front seat of car fiddling with dashboard which was lit up. Later admitted would have driven away if not caught. *Held* attempting to drive.	
	Guthrie v Friel 1992 SCCR 932 G found in car asleep with engine and lights on. Convicted. *Held* on appeal that the facts showed that G may have been preparing to drive but not actually attempting ie would need handbrake to be off.	
but there must be de facto control.	*Harman v Wardrop* [1971] RTR 127 Motorist effectively prevented from driving at time of breath test as his keys had been taken by another person. *Held* not driving.	
Driving as result of coercion or necessity may prove a valid defence.	*Tudhope v Grubb* 1983 SCCR 350 (Sh Ct) G locked himself in car to avoid violent attack by several persons. Drove off to escape further injury to car and self. *Held* attempted to drive to avoid further injury following unprovoked assault. Acquitted.	
	But see *MacLeod v MacDougall* 1988 SCCR 519 Driving must cease as soon as necessity is over.	
	Moss v Howdle 1997 SCCR 215 (see Coercion). *Roxton v Lang* 1998 SCCR 1 (Sh Ct) (see Coercion).	
Driving in an emergency.	*Watson v Hamilton* 1988 SCCR 13 Court must be satisfied that no other reasonable alternative has been ignored. Pregnant guest in W's house awoke bleeding heavily and fearing miscarriage. W attempted to find phone and get help but at 2 am set off to hospital. It was *held* that it was not reasonable to have expected W to rouse his neighbours at 2 am.	

Unfit to drive

High alcohol content in blood may not indicate unfitness.	*MacNeill v Fletcher* 1966 JC 18 *Held* that although urine sample showed high alcohol content, doctor was entitled not to certify accused as unfit to drive.	Section 4(5)
Normal driving does not raise presumption of fitness.	*Murray v Muir* 1949 JC 127; 1950 SLT 41 *Held* that fact that accused drove 200 yards in proper manner did not create presumption of sobriety which medical evidence could not disprove.	

Drink

	Armstrong v Clark [1957] 2 QB 391 Diabetic took dose of insulin and became incapable of driving properly. Charged under section similar to present RTA 1988, s 4(1). *Observed* that 'drink' probably means alcoholic drink.	

or drugs

	Armstrong v Clark [1957] 2 QB 391 'Drug' means any medicine given to cure, alleviate or assist an ailing body, and includes insulin.	RTA 1988, s 11(2), as amended by Road Traffic Act 1991, Sch 4, para 44, states that drug includes any 'intoxicant other than alcohol', ie wider definition than that given by Lord Goddard CJ in *Armstrong v Clark*.
Solvents having drugging effect.	*Duffy v Tudhope* 1983 SCCR 440; 1984 SLT 107 *Held* that driver whose capacity to drive is impaired because he has been inhaling solvents cannot claim that such solvents are not drugs, if they have a drugging effect.	

Being in charge of motor vehicle.

	Macdonald v Crawford 1952 SLT (Sh Ct) 92 Taxi driver sitting in taxi which had broken down, waiting for tow. *Held* in charge.	RTA 1988, s 4(2)
	Lees v Lowrie 1993 SCCR 1 Accused supervising 'L' driver, not a lesson. Evidence led that he would not have taken over driving. *Held* that the accused was in charge of the vehicle but no likelihood of driving.	
Not in charge.	*Adair v McKenna* 1951 SLT (Sh Ct) 40 *Held* that motor mechanic engaged in repairing fault in vehicle by roadside not in charge.	
	Crichton v Burrell 1951 JC 107; 1951 SLT 365 Car owner waiting for another person with duplicate keys to drive him home. *Held* not in charge of vehicle, as not in de facto control.	
	Dean v Wishart 1952 JC 9; 1952 SLT 86 *Held* that person insensible in back of vehicle which had been immobilised by removal of rotor arm not in charge.	
	Winter v Morrison 1954 JC 7 Car owner in front passenger seat. Wife in driving seat with engine running. Wife's provisional licence expired. *Held* that car owner not in charge.	

No likelihood of driving
Defence to s 4(2) charge.

Neish v Stevenson 1969 SLT 229
Held that burden of proof, on a balance of probabilities, is on accused.

Morton v Confer [1963] 2 All ER 765
Held that court must be satisfied that, on balance of probabilities, there was no likelihood that intention not to drive would be departed from.

Northfield v Pinder [1969] 2 QB 7
Driver found near his car so drunk as to be incapable of driving, finding car, or walking to it.
Held no defence; no evidence that driver would not have driven when worst effects had worn off.

Section 4(3)

Post-incident drinking
Defence to section 4(1) and (2) as well as section 5(1)(a) and (b).

Neish v Stevenson 1969 SLT 229
Standard of proof as in this case.

Hassan v Scott 1989 SCCR 49
Accused may not have to prove exact amount of ale subsequently consumed. If defence evidence demonstrates that there is a reasonable doubt about Crown case, accused entitled to acquittal.

Road Traffic Offenders Act 1988
Section 15(3)

Causing death

RTA 1988, s 3A(1). If a person causes the death of another person by driving a mechanically propelled vehicle on a road or other public place without due care and attention or without reasonable consideration for other persons using the road or place, and
(a) he is, at the time when he is driving, unfit to drive through drink or drugs; or
(b) he has consumed so much alcohol that the proportion of it in his breath, blood or urine at that time exceeds the prescribed limit; or
(c) within 18 hours of that time, he is required to provide a specimen in pursuance of s 7 of this Act, but without reasonable excuse fails to provide it, he is guilty of an offence.

Section 3A(2). For the purposes of this section a person shall be taken to be unfit to drive at any time when his ability to drive properly is impaired.

Section 3A(3). Subsection 1(b) and (c) shall not apply in relation to a person driving a mechanically propelled vehicle other than a motor vehicle.

Alcohol concentration above prescribed limit

Road Traffic Act 1988, s 5.
Section 5(1)(a). Driving or attempting to drive motor vehicle or
(b) in charge of motor vehicle
after consuming so much alcohol that **proportion in breath, blood or urine exceeds prescribed limit**.
Section 5(2). Defence to s 6(1)(b)) that **no likelihood of driving** vehicle while proportion of alcohol in breath, blood or urine remained likely to exceed prescribed limit.
Road Traffic Offenders Act 1988.
Section 15(3). Defence of post-incident drinking.

COMMENTARY	CASE LAW	STATUTE LAW
Proportion in breath, blood or urine	*Jordan v Russell* 1995 SCCR 423 Appellant charged with driving with excess alcohol in his blood. Crown evidence of duplicate test carried out under quality checks gave average of 93 µg from which safety factor of six deducted. Defence test by single analyst gave reading of 80 µg. Conviction upheld: It was all right to reject defence evidence and accept Crown's, which had confirmatory tests and quality checks.	Road Traffic Act 1988 Section 11(2). Prescribed limits are: (a) 35 microgrammes of alcohol in 100 millilitres of breath, or (b) 80 milligrammes of alcohol in 100 millilitres of blood, or (c) 107 milligrammes of alcohol in 100 millilitres of urine, or such other proportion as may be prescribed by the Secretary of State.
Court may discount evidence if, for example, specimen obtained illegally by deception or under duress.	*R v Fox* [1985] RTR 337 Per Lord Fraser: 'If the appellant had been lured to the police station by some trick or deception, or if the police officers had behaved oppressively towards the appellant, the justice's jurisdiction to exclude otherwise admissible evidence . . . might come into play.'	Road Traffic Offenders Act 1988 Section 15(2). All readings, no matter how they were obtained, must be considered. Section 15(4). Specimen of blood will be disregarded unless taken from accused, with consent, by medical practitioner.
Exceeds prescribed limit	*R v Coomaraswamy* [1976] RTR 21 *Held* that if driver's specimen discloses an excess over prescribed limit, it is not necessary to prove a particular degree of excess. *Lockhart v Deighan* 1985 SCCR 204; 1985 SLT 549 It was made clear in this case that because of a letter from the Crown Agent to the Law Society of Scotland, published in the September issue of JLSS, the Crown has effectively barred itself from prosecuting where the breath alcohol level is less than 40 microgrammes. This delimitation was strictly construed in this case and held not to extend to blood alcohol levels. *McConnachie v Scott* 1988 SCCR 176 Motorist provided two specimens of breath of less than 40 milligrammes. *Held* to be incompetent for police officer to require motorist to provide specimen of blood or urine in these circumstances.	
No likelihood of driving Defence to s 5(1)(b) charge.	See: *Neish v Stevenson* 1969 SLT 229 *Morton v Confer* [1963] 2 All ER 765 *Northfield v Pinder* [1969] 2 QB 7	

Preliminary breath test

Road Traffic Act 1988, s 6.

Section 6(1). Constable may require driver to provide specimen of breath for breath test where he has reasonable cause to suspect that:

(a) person driving or attempting to drive, on a road or other public place or in charge of a motor vehicle, has alcohol in body or has committed traffic offence while vehicle in motion, or

(b) person has been driving or attempting to drive or been in charge of a vehicle with alcohol in body and still has alcohol in body, or

(c) person has been driving or attempting to drive or been in charge of vehicle and has committed traffic offence while vehicle in motion.

Section 6(2). After accident constable may require any person who he has **reasonable cause to believe** was driving or attempting to drive or in charge of the vehicle at the time of the accident to provide a specimen of breath for breath test.

Section 6(3). Specimen of breath must be given at or near the place where the requirement is made.

Section 6(4). Failure to provide specimen **without reasonable excuse** constitutes offence.

Section 6(5). Constable may arrest without warrant if

(a) as a result of breath test he has reasonable cause to suspect that proportion of alcohol in person's breath or blood exceeds prescribed limit, or

(b) person has failed to provide specimen of breath and constable has reasonable cause to suspect that person had alcohol in body.

COMMENTARY	CASE LAW	STATUTE LAW
Reasonable cause to suspect	*Copeland v Macpherson* 1970 SLT 87 Suspicion arose out of information given to constable by another officer. *Held* to be reasonable.	Road Traffic Act 1988, s 6(1)
Wide powers to stop vehicles, but these must not be exercised oppressively.	*Chief Constable of Gwent v Dash* [1985] Crim L R 674 Constable may stop a motorist with sole intention of seeing whether or not he has been drinking.	
Public place	*Alston v O'Brien* 1992 SCCR 238 Breath test, 'public place', car on farm drive. *Held* on appeal that the public were not expected to be there so not a public place. See also: *Thomson v MacPhail* 1992 SCCR 513	
Reasonable cause to believe	*Merry v Doherty* 1977 JC 34 Police officers found D alone in car at roadside. Engine was hot, there was damage to front of car, and D had fresh injuries on forehead and nose. No evidence to indicate where accident had happened. D found not guilty of driving with alcohol above prescribed limit as no evidence of reasonable cause to believe that accident had occurred on public highway. *Topping v Scott* 1979 SLT (Notes) 21 Police received anonymous phone call informing them that white van involved in accicent with blue car. Police found white van with traces of blue paint parked outside accused's house. Accused gave positive breath test. *Held* that sheriff entitled to convict. Police had knowledge of accident although they had not witnessed it.	Section 6(2)

MacKenzie v Hingston 1995 SCCR 386

Section 6(1)

Appellant drove to harbour and left vehicle and ran into his boat. Constables followed him on and detected smell of alcohol and required specimen. He refused and was convicted.

Held, prior view of police that road traffic offence committed (as distinct from view he had alcohol on his body) entitled police to require specimen and pursue appellant onto boat as a matter of urgency.

Failure to provide specimen **without reasonable excuse.**

R v Lennard [1973] RTR 252

Per Laxton LJ: '[N]o excuse can be adjudged a reasonable one unless the person from whom the specimen is required is physically or mentally unable to provide it, or the provision of the specimen would entail a substantial risk to his health'.

Once issue of reasonable excuse sufficiently raised, it is for prosecution to rebut it.

Earnshaw v HMA 1982 JC 11.

Reasonable excuse relates to taking of test only.

McNicol v Peters 1969 SLT 261

Not a reasonable excuse for driver to maintain he had not consumed alcohol.

McGrath v Vipas [1984] RTR 58

Not a reasonable excuse that accused not driver at material time.

McLaren v MacLeod 1994 SCCR 478

Constable requiring a specimen under s 7 does not require to ask the person if there are medical reasons why blood should not be taken although the suspect should be told that not giving the specimen without reasonable excuse is an offence.

Provision of specimens for analysis

Road Traffic Act 1988, ss 7, 8.

Section 7(1). Constable may require person suspected of offence under s 3A, s 4 or s 5

(a) to provide two specimens of breath for **analysis by means of a device of type approved by Secretary of State** or

(b) to provide a specimen of blood or urine for a laboratory test.

Section 7(2). Requirement to provide specimens of breath under s 7(1)(a) can only be made at a police station.

Section 7(3). Requirement to provide specimen of **blood or urine** under s 7(1)(b) can only be made at police station or hospital, and cannot be made at police station unless

(a) constable has reasonable cause to believe that for **medical reasons** breath specimen cannot be provided or should not be required, or

(b) **no device or reliable device available**, or

(c) suspected offence is under s 4 and medical advice suggests conditions may be due to drugs.

Section 7(4). If specimen other than breath required, constable decides whether blood or urine is required, unless medical practitioner advises blood cannot or should not be taken.

Section 7(5). Specimen of urine shall be provided within one hour of its requirement, and after provision of previous specimen.

Section 7(6). Failure to provide specimen, without **reasonable excuse**, is an offence.

Section 7(7). Constable must warn that failure to provide specimen may lead to prosecution.

Section 8(1). Where two breath specimens have been provided in pursuance of section 7, the one with the lower proportion of alcohol in the breath shall be used, and the other disregarded.

Section 8(2). If the specimen with the lower proportion of alcohol contains no more than 50 mg of alcohol in 100 ml of breath, the person who provided it may elect to replace it with a specimen of blood or urine, under s 7(4).

COMMENTARY	CASE LAW	STATUTE LAW
Requirement to provide specimen must be corroborated.	*Carmichael v Gillooly* 1982 SCCR 119.	
Analysis by means of a device of type approved by Secretary of State.	*Knox v Lockhart* 1984 SCCR 463 Crown failed to present in evidence at trial that device used was of type approved by Secretary of State. *Held*, on appeal, Crown must prove in evidence that device used is of approved type. See also: *Pickard v Carmichael* 1995 SCCR 76 Proof required that device approved.	
Specimen of blood.		Road Traffic Act 1988, s 11(4). Person must consent to blood being taken by medical practitioner.
Only one breath specimen provided.	*Reid v Tudhope* 1985 SCCR 268 Conviction upheld where R in attempt to frustrate procedure failed to provide second specimen. But compare: *Douglas v Stevenson* 1986 SCCR 519 Accused gave one specimen. After genuine failure to provide second specimen, he was refused opportunity to try again. *Held* that police had not given him fair opportunity for provision of second specimen.	Section 7(1)(a)

Medical reasons.	*Dempsey v Catton* [1986] RTR 194 Decision of constable is subjective, and he is not required to obtain medical advice. Defendant refused to give specimen claiming he suffered from agoraphobia, and phobia of machines. Constable accepted the latter and required blood specimen.	Section 7(3)(a)
No device or reliable device available.	*Gilligan v Tudhope* 1985 SCCR 434 G charged with driving with excess alcohol on basis of blood sample. He had earlier provided two breath specimens. Readings on the visual display showed that it was in working order, but device then produced printout giving nonsensical dates and times. *Held* that analytical function of device working and no justification for requiring blood test. Conviction quashed. See also: *Walker v Walkingshaw* 1991 SCCR 358 *Ramage v Walkingshaw* 1992 SCCR 82 *Carson v Orr* 1992 SCCR 260	
Test is subjective.	*Burnett v Smith* 1989 SCCR 628 B had provided two breath specimens but police concluded device unreliable and required blood specimen. On appeal *held* that proper test is subjective and police entitled to require blood specimen if they concluded on reasonable grounds that device unreliable, even if it was reliable, and appeal refused.	
Blood or urine: constable decides.	*Bain v Tudhope* 1985 SCCR 412 B gave positive breath specimen and elected to exercise right to provide alternative specimen. Required to provide urine, but failed, and convicted on breath specimen. *Held* that decision to require blood or urine was to be left wholly to discretion of constable. See also: *MacLeod v MacFarlane* 1992 SCCR 178 *Simpson v McClory* 1993 SCCR 402	Section 7(4)
Failure to provide specimen without **reasonable excuse.**	See p 81 *McLeod v Murray* 1986 SCCR 369 M, lorry driver, gave evidence that he had been assaulted by police officers who required specimens, and he refused to give specimens because he did not trust officers not to tamper with them. *Held* (1) that accused's evidence, if believed, would constitute reasonable excuse; and (2) onus of proof that there was no reasonable excuse lay on the Crown, and accused had raised reasonable doubt on the matter: accused acquitted. See also: *McIntosh v Lowe* 1991 SCCR 154	Section 7(6)
Accused must raise reasonable excuse at time of requirement if asked why he cannot provide specimen,	*Singh v McLeod* 1986 SCCR 656 At trial S claimed that asthmatic attack prevented him from providing breath specimen. S's doctor gave evidence that any asthmatic attack would have been obvious to anyone. S had not mentioned asthma at time of requirement to provide specimen. *Held* to be sufficient evidence of no reasonable excuse.	

but if not asked no obligation to volunteer information.

Pringle v Annan 1988 SCCR 423
P unable to provide breath specimen as result of injuries suffered.
Held that physical inability constituted reasonable excuse, and there is no general duty on motorist to inform police of the reason for his inability to provide specimen.

McClory v Owen-Thomas 1989 SCCR 402
O-T required to give specimen of blood and refused to do so saying 'There's no way I want to give blood. I tend to get faint . . .'. At trial evidence led of O-T's suffering from phobic fear of needles. Sheriff acquitted. On appeal *held* onus of establishing absence of reasonable excuse lies on Crown; no onus on motorist to disclose anything to police; appeal refused.

But compare:
Milne v Westwater 1990 SCCR 46
M gave evidence that because of earlier amputations he was terrified of doctor putting needles in his arm. Sheriff disbelieved him and convicted. On appeal *held* that onus of proving absence of reasonable excuse was on Crown, but that as sheriff disbelieved him and no rational explanation provided, no merit in appeal.

Manual v Steward 1986 SCCR 121
It is not a reasonable excuse to refuse to give specimen until solicitor arrives.

Accused must **unequivocally** agree to provide specimen,

Beveridge v Allan 1986 SCCR 542
On being required to provide specimen, B replied 'Yes, I refuse'. Officer asked him why and B said 'Oh well, I'll blow the thing'. Officer did not allow him to give specimen, but charged B with failure to provide breath.
Held that sheriff entitled to treat B's initial response as a refusal. Not open to B to change his mind.

and cannot specify part of body from which sample to be taken.

Salesbury v Pugh [1969] 2 All ER 1171
Driver insisted on samples being taken from big toe. Convicted of failure to provide.

Friel v Dickson 1992 SCCR 513
Blood specimen, RTA 1988, s 11(4). Accused under the influence of medication. Sheriff said that the Crown had failed to show consent and exclude the possibility of less than complete consciousness. Appeal.
Held that the Crown must show consent which it had not but need not exclude the possibility of less than complete consciousness. Not convinced here that T knew what was being asked of him.

Police must not exert pressure on driver to provide blood or urine,

Green v Lockhart 1985 SCCR 257

and must inform driver fully of his rights.

Pelosi v Jessop 1990 SCCR 175
Police told P that he could give specimen of blood, without mentioning urine.
Held proper procedure not carried through and conviction quashed.

Police decide whether to require blood or urine.

Bain v Tudhope 1985 SCCR 412.

Timeous objections.

Macaulay v Wilson 1995 SCCR 133
Appellant charged with driving with excess alcohol in urine. Solicitor never objected to Crown evidence, and sheriff never allowed him to lead evidence to contradict the execution of service.
Held, analyst's certificate was sufficient in absence of timeous objection and appeal refused.

See further, Wheatley *Road Traffic Law in Scotland* (2nd edn).

Mitigating circumstances; special reasons

Mitigating circumstances may avoid disqualification which normally results from the 'totting up' of a total of twelve penalty points incurred over a period of three years.
Special reasons for not ordering obligatory endorsement or disqualification.

COMMENTARY	CASE LAW	STATUTE LAW
Mitigating circumstances: all the circumstances both in relation to the offence and the offender, including all previous offences.		Road Traffic Offenders Act 1988 Section 35. Where a driver has incurred twelve points within a three-year period, he must be disqualified for at least six months unless the court is satisfied, having regard to all the circumstances, that there are grounds for mitigation and thinks fit to order a shorter period of disqualification or none at all.
	Smith v Craddock 1979 JC 66 Speeding. Driver by trade and would lose employment if disqualified. Wife and children relied totally on accused for income. Sheriff refrained from disqualification and imposed a fine. *Held*, on appeal by Crown, that sheriff entitled to take such factors into consideration in his exercise of discretion.	RTOA 1988, s 35(4). The court, in considering whether such mitigating circumstances exist, may not take account of (a) triviality of the offence; (b) hardship, other than exceptional hardship; (c) circumstances previously taken into account by any court within the previous three years.
Exceptional hardship—loss of licence involving loss of employment and house.	*Stephens v Gibb* 1984 SCCR 195 S convicted of offence involving discretionary disqualification. S's driving licence contained endorsements showing that the number of penalty points to be taken into account was such as to involve disqualifiation. Appealed. *Held* that '. . . by reason of a combination of factors special and peculiar to this particular appellant, disqualification would result in exceptional hardship. . .'. Appeal allowed; disqualification quashed. But compare: *Holden v McPhail* 1988 SCCR 486 Observed that court should examine very carefully any suggestion of exceptional hardship and hold it established only on clearest possible evidence. *Stephens v Gibb* was a very special case and was not authority for proposition that in every case loss of job and inability to pay mortgage constituted exceptional hardship. *Mowbray v Guild* 1989 SCCR 535 *Held* to be exceptional hardship in that loss of licence would lead to loss of business, affect M and his wife's health, and interfere with child's education. *Howdle v Davidson* 1994 SCCR 751 Exceptional hardship. Accused stood to lose, inter alia, business and income to support family. Crown appealed sheriff's failure to disqualify and relied on *Ewen v Orr* 1993 SCCR 1015 as laying down a rule that exceptional hardship required that persons other than accused's immediate family would suffer. *Held*, no such rule and sheriff entitled to view hardship in case was exceptional and appeal refused. See also cases under Sentencing, Totting Up.	RTOA 1988, s 28 provides for award of penalty points on conviction of contraventions of Road Traffic Act 1988. RTOA 1988, s 35(4): 'No account is to be taken under subsection (1) of . . . (b) hardship, other than exceptional hardship.'

Special reasons

Question of whether a special reason exists is one of law.	*Muir v Sutherland* 1940 JC 66 Speeding charge. *Held* that question whether a special reason existed was one of law and not of discretion.	RTOA 1988, s 34 and Sch 2. Certain offences carry obligatory disqualification. In all these instances disqualification can only be avoided if offending motorist successfully pleads special reasons for not being disqualified.
Special reasons for reducing period of disqualification or ordering not to be disqualified.	*Orttewell v Allan* 1984 SCCR 208 Disqualified driver pushed broken down car off busy main street and then got into driving seat and was pushed into car park where it collided with another vehicle. *Held* to be sufficient grounds to reduce period of disqualification from three years to one year.	
Reason must be special to the facts of the offence and not to the peculiar circumstances of the offender.	*Adair v Munn* 1940 JC 69 Drunk driving charge. *Held* that considerations of hardship and similar mitigating circumstances personal to the convicted person were not 'special reasons' entitling the court to reduce or remit the sentence. *Carnegie v Clark* 1947 JC 74 Charge of driving while disqualified. Fact that sentence might lead to expulsion from university not a special reason. *Muir v M'Pherson* 1953 SLT 307 Charge of drunk in charge of a motor vehicle under Road Traffic Act 1930, s 15(2). Accused was a taxi driver. Fact that disqualification would cause considerable personal hardship held not to constitute a special reason. *Robertson v M'Ginn* 1955 JC 57 Insurance. Submitted as special reasons that offender was a 'man of substance' and required to drive for business as a farmer and for local government affairs. *Held*, no special reason. *Norman v Cameron* 1992 SCCR 390 RTOA 1988, s 5(1)(a) disqualification. Accused said that he had waited until he should have been fit to drive. Accepted by sheriff as a special reason. Overturned on appeal, special reasons must relate to the facts which constitute the offence. See also: *McClelland v Whitelaw* 1993 SCCR 1113	
Medical condition.	*Scott v Hamilton* 1988 SCCR 262 Lady motorist pled guilty to failure to provide specimen but claimed she had been suffering from pre-menstrual tension, and was not amenable to reason. *Held* that this was not special reason for not disqualifying.	
Accused's mistaken belief.	*Robertson v McNaughtan* 1993 SCCR 226 Driving while disqualified, special reasons. R thought his disqualification was suspended pending an appeal but it had revived when his solicitor failed to lodge the appeal timeously. Sheriff imposing penalty points but not disqualifying on the grounds that there were special reasons. Appeal. *Held* that there were special reasons and licence should not even have been endorsed.	

Scott v Ross 1994 SCCR 538
Appellant not disqualified. Sheriff held there were mitigating circumstances, because appellant parked at locus he wrongly thought was not a road. *Held*, by a full bench, allowing appeal: sheriff to consider first whether there are special reasons why the respondent's licence should not be endorsed with penalty points before he decides whether the respondent must be ordered to be disqualified under RTOA 1988, s 35(1).

See also:
Carmichael v Shelvin 1991 SCCR 247

Watson v Adam 1996 SCCR 382
Driver realised that he had drunk alcoholic beer and not non-alcoholic beer as first thought, but decided to drive anyway.
Held, he took risk and one-year disqualification upheld and sheriff wrong to suggest special reasons require corroboration.

Marshall v McLeod 1998 SCCR 317
Appellant convicted of driving another person's vehicle without insurance.
Held, on appeal, overturning sheriff, that special reasons were established where owner told him that he was covered by owner's insurance and no reason to disbelieve owner.

The safety of the public in their use of the roads must be viewed as the vital consideration.

Adair v Munn 1940 JC 69
Considerations tending to show that the safety of the public on the roads would not be prejudiced by a reduction or remission were special reasons.

Fairlie v Hill 1944 JC 53
Insurance contravention under Road Traffic Act 1930, s 35(2).
Held that in considering a remission or reduction in relation to disqualification the protection of the public is the chief criterion. If reasons adduced by offender tend to show public protection will not be prejudiced, the court has a discretion and may have regard to personal hardship.

Lowe v Mulligan 1991 SCCR 551
Driving with excess alcohol. M had moved car a short distance to prevent it being a hazard. The road on which he had originally parked prior to going into the pub was due to become one-way in the morning due to road works.
Held that it was a special reason.

Performance of public duties cannot in itself be a special reason. Exceptions made to this rule during wartime.

Murray v Macmillan 1942 JC 10
Insurance contravention under s 35(2) of Road Traffic Act 1930. Convicted person was a doctor with a number of emergency posts in relation to colliery and aerodrome for which a car was essential.

Compare with:

M'Fadyean v Burton 1954 JC 18
Charge of drunk driving. Officer in Territorial Army used car for related duties.
Held did not constitute special reason.

Triviality of the circumstances of the offence not a special reason.

Tudhope v Birbeck 1979 SLT (Notes) 47
Pedestrian crossing. Fact that circumstances of offence trivial and that no danger caused to anyone did not constitute a special reason.

Circumstances held to have established special reasons include emergencies: accused must prove there was a genuine emergency

Graham v Annan 1980 SLT 28
Driving while disqualified and without insurance. Pregnant woman who was driving car became ill and husband, who was disqualified, took over.
Held, on appeal, that circumstances disclosed a special reason for not ordering further disqualification or endorsement.

and offence must have been committed out of circumstances of real necessity.

Copeland v Sweeney 1977 SLT (Sh Ct) 28
Drunk driving charge. Daughter who suffered from unusual medical condition was stung by wasp. Father drove to his daughter collecting medicine on the way.
Held no special reason. 'Must show not only that the circumstances amounted to a medical emergency but also that the driver had a compelling reason and no alternative in the circumstances but to drive.'

But see:

Norman v Logue 1996 SCCR 797 (Sh Ct)
Special reasons established where disabled woman drove car 10 ft in distraught state to remove it from broken glass from break-in in her street. Car only mode of transport for her and 90-year-old mum. No public interest in disqualifying her.

Lees v Macdonald 1997 SCCR 189 (Sh Ct)
Special reasons where warden of elderly home left flat for fear of assault and drove to friends.
Held, since no record, and concern not to wake residents, it was appropriate not to disqualify her.

Dolan v McLeod 1998 SCCR 653
Held, purpose of driving was to observe ex-boyfriend's gang, not to escape apprehended violence. Convicted and disqualified. Upheld on appeal.

Where driver breaks the law only because he is ordered to do a certain act by a police officer.

Farrell v Moir 1974 SLT (Sh Ct) 89
Refusal to give sample. Convicted. Argued that he should not be disqualified in that he had driven only because police had ordered him to move his car. On appeal, disqualification quashed and admonition substituted.

Onus lies on accused to establish special reasons,

McLeod v Scoular 1974 SLT (Notes) 44
Drugs and driving. Observations made by Lord Justice-Clerk on proper procedure for determining whether special reasons have been established. Onus on accused to satisfy the court that there are special reasons and prosecution should have opportunity to contradict or qualify that evidence.

although such reasons may be established without specific reference to their 'special' quality.

Keane v Perrie 1982 SCCR 377
Careless driving. Plea of guilty by letter. No reference in letter to special reasons as such but referred to certain mitigating factors and his driving record.
Held, on appeal by Crown, that sheriff entitled to refrain from ordering endorsement and not necessary for circumstances to be expressly described as special reasons in the letter.

See also:

Trotter v Burnet 1947 JC 151
Plea of guilty by letter. Where reasons purporting to prejudice the public interest are raised, the court should be slow to pronounce sentence in accused's absence.

Herron v Sharif 1974 SLT (Notes) 63
Small excess of alcohol in blood. Not a special reason.

Keane v Savage, Crown Office Circular A26/82
Accused found guilty after trial of offence of speeding at 44 mph. On conviction fined £15 but sheriff *ex proprio motu* declined to order endorsement. Sheriff was not moved to hold that there were special reasons why he should not endorse. Crown appeal successful.
Held, in absence of special reasons, sheriff should have ordered endorsement.

See also Sentencing Policy, Totting Up, below.

ROAD TRAFFIC

SENTENCING POLICY

Careless Driving

Sharp v HMA 1987 SCCR 179—S charged with causing death by reckless driving and alternately with careless driving. Convicted of careless driving. Sheriff imposed fine of £250 and one year's disqualification, having regard to consequences. S appealed on grounds that sheriff had wrongly taken consequences into account.
Held that grounds of appeal sound. Period of disqualification reduced to six months.

McLean v Annan 1986 SCCR 52—M convicted of careless driving, offence committed ten days after passing driving test. Sheriff disqualified for a month and ordered her to resit test.
Held sentence inappropriate, order to resit test not being penalty, but for case in which driving skills lost through disqualification. Sentence quashed.

McCrone v Normand 1988 SCCR 551—M, driver of mobile shop, reversed in area known by him to be used as children's playground. Collided with and killed 16-month-old child. Fined £400 and licence endorsed. On appeal *held* that fine excessive, fine of £100 substituted.

Malpas v Hamilton 1988 SCCR 546—M, first offender, convicted of careless driving after hitting pedestrian with car. Fined £200 and disqualified for six months. On appeal against disqualification, *held* that disqualification should be imposed for careless driving only in more than usually serious cases. Disqualification quashed and five penalty points imposed.

Buchan v McNaughtan 1990 SCCR 13—B, in receipt of £47 per week invalidity benefit, pleaded guilty to careless driving and driving with excess alcohol in blood. Fined £75 on first charge and £150 on second charge.
Held fine not excessive.

Owens v McNaughtan 1990 SCCR 355—Careless driving conviction, O had a clean licence previously. £500 fine upheld on appeal but nine penalty points reduced to seven.

Neill v Ingram 1990 SCCR 454—Twenty-one-year-old convicted of careless driving, wheelspinning U-turn from parked position.
Held on appeal, six months' disqualification under totting up and a requirement to resit driving test appropriate given that the accused lacked discipline and responsibility.

Ross v Houston 1991 SCCR 102—Lorry driver convicted of careless driving, nine points awarded as he was a professional driver.
Held on appeal, approach incorrect and six points substituted.

Thomas v Lowe 1991 SCCR 943—Careless driving, failing to stop. T alleging pre-menstrual tension. Sentenced to six months disqualification. Appeal.
Held that given PMT, ten penalty points appropriate. PMT 'bad' or 'severe' but mitigation only.

Vannet v Davidson 1995 SCCR 792—*Held*, on appeal, in relation to RTA 1988, s 24(1), that person can be convicted after trial of s 3 (careless driving) as alternative to s 2 (dangerous driving) wherein 'after trial' was constructed as not meaning that the defendant must go to trial.

Excess Alcohol

Weddle v Carmichael 1991 SCCR 64—Family man earning £23,000 a year, 128 µg of alcohol in 100 ml of breath. Sentenced to three months' imprisonment and six years' disqualification. Upheld on appeal, clear that the courts must take a strong and firm view.

Hawthorne v Jessop 1991 SCCR 674—Charge not averring but evidence showing that H very drunk. Disqualified for three years.
Held on appeal that sentence severe but not excessive. Sheriff entitled to take unfitness to drive into account. Court following *Jamsheed v Walkingshaw* 1989 SCCR 75 and disapproving *McParland v Wilson* 1988 SCCR 158.

Cairns v McLeod 1992 SCCR 787—Excess alcohol, third analogous offence, two months' imprisonment. Appeal.
Held that 200 hours' community service appropriate, 'marginal case'.

Brown v McNaughtan 1993 SCCR 399—Excess alcohol, three years' disqualification on the ground that B aware that he had a similar charge outstanding at the time. Upheld on appeal.

Alexander v Hingston 1993 SCCR 431—Excess alcohol, specimen taken six hours after the accident. Sheriff on the basis of a formula to calculate alcohol level at the time of the accident disqualified for 18 months. *Held* on appeal that without specific evidence sheriff not entitled to use the formula. Twelve months' disqualification substituted.

Stirling v Wilson 1988 SCCR 225—S pleaded guilty to driving with breath-alcohol level of 120 µg. Sheriff sentenced S to three months' imprisonment despite favourable social enquiry report. Disqualified for four years.
Held that in all the circumstances, including fact that S would lose job he had held for eight years, fine would meet case. Fine of £750 and three years' disqualification substituted.

McLean v MacDougall 1989 SCCR 625—M pleaded guilty to driving with excess alcohol and admitted recent similar conviction. Unemployed at time and sentenced to 60 days' imprisonment and disqualified for six years. Appealed against sentence of imprisonment. At date of appeal had obtained employment at salary of £10,000 which he would lose if imprisoned. *Held* appropriate to replace imprisonment with fine of £1,000.

Marshall v Carmichael 1990 SCCR 58—M pleaded guilty to driving van with excess alcohol in breath. Two previous analogous convictions. Only drove van short distance as window broken and he was afraid it was vulnerable to theft. Sheriff sentenced M to six months' imprisonment and disqualified for ten years. *Held* sentence excessive, sentence of imprisonment quashed and 150 hours' community service substituted.

Giordano v Carmichael 1990 SCCR 61—G pleaded guilty to driving with blood alcohol level of 220 µg per 100 ml. Two previous convictions in 1981 and 1983. Attending doctor and psychiatrist in connection with alcohol problem and agreed to attend alcohol advice centre. Sentenced to 60 days' imprisonment. Upheld on appeal.

McGrory v Jessop 1990 SCCR 222—M pleaded guilty to driving with excess alcohol and driving while disqualified and to another offence. Sentences to run consecutively. *Held* that as the driving offences had all occurred on same occasion, it was excessive to order sentences to run consecutively. Sentences ordered to be served concurrently.

HMA v Callaghan 1996 SCCR 709—Repeated offences of driving with excess alcohol while disqualified. C had six previous convictions for these offences. Sheriff deferred sentence for alcoholic counselling. *Held*, on appeal, the only appropriate sentence was a custodial one and 18 months imposed.

Middleton v Napier 1997 SCCR 669—Appellant pleaded guilty to driving with 88 µg of alcohol per 100 ml of breath. Had similar previous conviction. Disqualified for four years and ordered to resit test. Appealed against resit. *Held*, resit appropriate after lengthy period of disqualification.

Holland v Howdle 1994 SCCR 772—Conviction of driving with excess alcohol. Record for such offences. *Held*, not appropriate that sheriff disqualified for life and sent appellant to drink-impaired drivers' course. Disqualification for six years substituted.

Craigie v Heywood 1996 SCCR 654—Pleaded guilty to driving recklessly and with excess alcohol after being warned by police not to drive. Disqualified and car forfeited (worth £1,500). Upheld on appeal: appropriate he should not have car to repeat offences.

Carver v Fraser 1997 SCCR 653—Appellant pleaded guilty to driving with excess alcohol in body, and sheriff disqualified for three years on ground that mental condition made him an alcoholic and he needed time to be cured. *Held*, on appeal, sheriff went beyond powers, ie matter for Secretary of State under s 92 of the Road Traffic Act 1988, and one year substituted.

Failure to provide specimen

Aird v Valentine 1986 SCCR 353—A pleaded guilty to failure to provide specimen but evidence led that it had not been proved that A was driving at relevant time. Sheriff took view that obligatory disqualification applied and disqualified him for three years. *Held* that obligatory disqualification arises only when proved that accused driving or attempting to drive; disqualification quashed and case remitted to sheriff.

Tudhope v O'Kane 1986 SCCR 538—O convicted. Sheriff found O was teetotaller and for that reason refrained from imposing obligatory disqualification. On appeal, *held* that present case special and public safety would not be prejudiced by refraining from disqualification.

Goldie v Tudhope 1986 SCCR 414—G had large number of previous convictions, many leading to custodial sentences, but no previous road traffic offences. Sheriff took view that he was committed to life of law breaking and imposed maximum sentence of six months. *Held* that sheriff entitled to look at appellant's record; but that six months was too severe; sentence of three months substituted.

Reynolds v Tudhope 1987 SCCR 340—R pleaded guilty to failing to provide specimens of breath, offence carrying minimum disqualification for one year. Magistrate disqualified her for 18 months on ground that 'this type of quite deliberate action is heard about far too often'. On appeal *held* that magistrate entitled to take the view he did.

McMillan v Scott 1988 SCCR 219—M pleaded guilty to failure to provide roadside test. Fined £100 and disqualified for six months. On appeal against disqualification held to be no reason for sheriff to deviate from normal practice of imposing penalty points. Disqualification quashed, endorsement with four points substituted.

McParland v Wilson 1988 SCCR 158—M first offender, pleaded guilty to failing to provide specimen, careless driving and failure to stay after, or to report an accident. M had had considerable amount to drink. Sheriff sentenced M to three months' imprisonment and referred to public interest in deterring people from driving under influence of drink. On appeal *held* (1) sheriff had wrongly referred to unfitness to drink as no charge under that head and (2) imprisonment inappropriate for first offender, fine of £100 substituted.

Jamsheed v Walkingshaw 1989 SCCR 75—J pleaded guilty to failure to provide specimen, reckless driving and resisting police. Appearance indicated he was heavily intoxicated. Fined £500 and disqualified for three years. On appeal *held* that sheriff entitled to impose substantial period of disqualification, and fine not excessive.

McGuinness v Jessop 1989 SCCR 349—Failure to provide breath a deliberate attempt to avoid providing evidence of how much M had drunk, disqualified for three years.
Held that disqualification not excessive.

Totting Up
McLaughlin v Docherty 1991 SCCR 227—Exceptional hardship. Loss of licence would prevent work being found for three contractors. Disqualification overturned on appeal, hardship made out.

Marshall v MacDougall 1991 SCCR 231—Exceptional hardship, risk of heating business collapsing. Disqualified.
Held on appeal that there was exceptional hardship in the real possibility of the business collapsing.

Edmonds v Buchanan 1993 SCCR 1048
Held on appeal that exceptional hardship made out where there was a possible need to seek urgent medical attention for a newly-born baby, given that there had been one cot death in the family previously.

Bibby v MacDougall 1990 SCCR 121—Not exceptional hardship that B would lose his job as would the employees of the company he managed. Upheld on appeal.

General
Riddick v Normand 1996 SCCR 56—At time of conviction (for driving under influence of drugs) appellant was serving sentence with release date in January 1998, over two years ahead. Sheriff took sentence into account and imposed disqualification for four years. *Held*, not excessive as effective only from release date, therefore disqualification for two years.

See also:
Allan v Crowe 1994 SCCR 596.

Donald, Petr 1996 SCCR 69—Husband convicted of driving while disqualified so transferred car to wife. She gave keys to husband to get friend to drive from work but husband drove. *Held*, failed to take steps to prevent husband driving and forfeiture upheld.

Carron v Russell 1994 SCCR 681—Second conviction for driving with excess alcohol. He was three times over limit and disqualified for four years, ordered to perform community service and ordered to forfeit car. *Held*, given exceptional circumstances and fact no fine, imposed forfeiture not excessive.

Gallacher v Carnegie 1997 SCCR 667—Appellant pleaded guilty to driving car without insurance and without test certificate. Admonished on each charge and disqualified on the insurance charge. *Held*, on appeal, inability to pay fine not good reason for longer disqualification and disqualification quashed and £100 fine and endorsement with three points substituted.

Murray v HMA 1994 SCCR 674—Pleaded guilty to causing death by dangerous driving and sentenced to seven years (maximum is ten years under Criminal Justice Act 1993, s 67). He had excess alcohol in blood and crossed lanes while speeding round bend. He was 25, with previous convictions, and described as a pitiful alcoholic. Sentence upheld on appeal.

Ahmed v McLeod 1998 SCCR 486—Appellant convicted of careless driving and driving without insurance. Both involve obligatory endorsement with penalty points. Disqualified until she passed a driving test for RTA 1988, s 3 offence and on RTA 1988, s 143 charge she was endorsed with eight penalty points. Court took view that Road Traffic Offenders Act 1988 required such endorsement. *Held*, since disqualified on s 3 charge, sheriff not entitled to order that penalty points for RTA 1988, s 143 charge should be endorsed on her licence, and appeal allowed and order for penalty points quashed. *Observed*, for Parliament to consider whether RTA 1988, s 44(1) should be amended so that a court could order disqualification on one offence while ordering endorsement with penalty points in respect of another offence.

Green v O'Donnell 1997 SCCR 315—Complainer convicted of failing to obey traffic signal and driving without insurance. Respectively, given three and six penalty points. The maximum for insurance offence was eight points. *Held*, arose out of same incident and maximum for insurance offence was eight points and this substituted. *Reith v Thomson* 1994 SCCR 577 (Sh Ct) overruled.

McDonald v Howdle 1995 SCCR 216—Appellant convicted of 'causing or permitting' a man to drive her car without insurance. Conviction quashed on appeal, since permission conditional on man being insured as he had falsely claimed. *Newbury v Davis* [1974] RTR 367 followed.

Note:
Forfeiture of vehicles: Road Traffic Offenders Act 1988, s 33A, provides that where person commits culpable homicide by driving motor vehicle, or commits any offence punishable by imprisonment under the Road Traffic Act 1988 by driving, attempting to drive or being in charge of a vehicle, by failing to comply with requirement to provide specimen, or by failing to stop and report an accident, the court (including district court) may on application of prosecutor order forfeiture of vehicle.

MISUSE OF DRUGS

Production, supply and possession of controlled drugs

Misuse of Drugs Act 1971, ss 4, 5.
Section 4(1)(a). It is an offence for a person **to produce** a **controlled drug** unlawfully or to be so concerned.
Section 4(1)(b). It is an offence to **supply** or offer to supply a controlled drug to another unlawfully or to be so concerned, or to be concerned in the making unlawfully of an offer to supply such a drug.
Section 5(1). It is an offence for a person to have a controlled drug in his **possession**.
Section 5(3). It is an offence for a person to have a controlled drug in his **possession**, whether lawfully or not, **with intent to supply** it to another unlawfully.

COMMENTARY	CASE LAW	STATUTE LAW
Produce (or be so concerned)	*R v Farr* [1982] Crim LR 745 CA F allowed C and A to use F's kitchen knowing that C and A were producing pink heroin there. *Held*, allowing F's appeal against conviction of producing a controlled drug contrary to MDA 1971, s 4(2), that there had to be some identifiable participation in the process of producing a controlled drug before a conviction under s 4(2) could be sustained. Appropriate charge should have been under MDA 1971, s 8, allowing premises to be used for production of the drug. F had made no prior arrangements with C and A, and the evidence showed only passive presence. *R v Russell* (1992) 94 Cr App R 351 Court of Appeal upheld that converting cocaine hydrochloride into free base cocaine (crack) amounts to producing class A drug 'by other means', and even though they shared generic term cocaine they had different properties.	Misuse of Drugs Act 1971 Sections 4(2) and 37(1): produce 'by manufacture, cultivation or any other method'.
Controlled drug	*Doherty v Brown* 1996 SCCR 136 Full bench. Conviction under MDA 1971, s 5(3) upheld. Accused mistakenly believed tablets contained ecstasy. *Held*, factual impossibility does not preclude Crown charging an attempt. Where accused knows of impossibility there can be no attempt. *HMA v Anderson* 1928 JC 1 disapproved. See Attempts. *McCallum v McKay* 1997 SCCR 558 Appellant convicted of supplying cannabis. No evidence of analysis of material but those supplied said material was cannabis resin and they had involvement in drugs. Conviction upheld on appeal: evidence was sufficient.	Section 2(1): Any controlled drug, ie, substance or product specified in Sch 2.
Supply	*R v Mills* [1963] 1 QB 522 Per Lord Parker CJ: '. . . "supply" must denote the parting of possession from one person to another . . .'. *R v Harris* (*Janet*) [1968] 1 WLR 769 *Held* that the administration of a controlled drug to another who is already in possession of it does not constitute supplying of the drug by the person administering it.	Section 4(3): '. . . it is an offence for a person—(a) to supply . . . a controlled drug to another. . . .'

Kerr (DA) v HMA 1986 SCCR 81
The offence of being concerned in the supplying of a controlled drug to another, contrary to MDA 1971, s 4(3)(b), may be established even though there has been no actual supply to another person. Per Lord Hunter: 'I consider that section 4(3)(b) was purposely enacted in the widest terms . . . to cover a great variety of activities both at the centre and on the fringes of dealing in controlled drugs. It would include . . . the activities of financiers, couriers and other go-betweens, lookouts, advertisers, agents and many links in the chain of distribution.

Douglas v Boyd 1996 SCCR 44
MDA 1971, s 4(3)(b). Respondent not present when father sold drugs, but she asked for payment a fortnight later. Sheriff held no case to answer.
Held, on appeal, supply not at an end when payment requested, and appeal allowed.

Morrison v Normand 1997 SCCR 469
Appellant convicted of supply and possession with intent to supply. Police officers offered 'hash or jellies' and appellant found in possession of cannabis. Upheld on appeal, since offer was entirely different to fact of possession.

Dickson v HMA 1994 SCCR 478
Observed, bulk buying and separating is covered by MDA 1971, s 5(3) (possession with intent to supply), and involvement before and after date of possession in transactions is covered by MDA 1971, s 4(3)(b) (supply), and jury should be directed to distinctions between sections.

See also:

Kearney v HMA 1998 SCCR 52

Possession
Possession requires more than mere control, ie knowledge.

Lockyer v Gibb [1966] 2 All ER 653; [1967] 2 QB 243
Per Lord Parker CJ: 'It is quite clear that a person cannot be said to be in possession of some article which he or she does not realise is, or may be, in her handbag, or in her room, or in some other place over which she has control. It is necessary to show that the appellant knew that she had the article which turned out to be a drug.'

Warner v Metropolitan Police Commissioner [1969] 2 AC 256
Defendant found with a parcel containing a controlled drug and convicted.
Held, on appeal to the House of Lords, that though there was a very strong inference of fact that a man who possesses a package also possesses its contents, he is entitled to be acquitted if he can show that he genuinely believed the parcel to contain an innocent substance and that he had no reasonable opportunity of examining its contents.

Gill v Lockhart 1987 SCCR 599
Cannabis resin found in accused's golf bag. Accused claimed he had placed it there two years ago and forgotten it. Convicted.
Held on appeal that once a person knowingly has possession of a drug, his possession persists even if he forgets its presence. Appeal refused.

Hughes v Guild 1990 SCCR 527
Possession, drugs found in the living room of flat occupied by two persons.
Held on appeal that drugs lying in the open in room enough for inference of knowledge and control.

Feeney v Jessop 1990 SCCR 565
Possession. Drugs found in F's towel in cell.
Held on appeal that F must have known of them and had control over them.

Davidson v HMA 1990 SCCR 699
Possession. Drugs found in co-accused's room next to scales bought by D.
Held on appeal that given D tried to escape when police raided house there was just sufficient evidence for knowledge and control.

Murray v MacPhail 1991 SCCR 245
Possession. Accused allowing a friend to hide drugs in his room. Convicted.
Upheld on appeal, sufficient knowledge and control.

White v HMA 1991 SCCR 555
Possession. Drugs found in W's flat to which others had access, made statement 'I'm saying nothing about it.' Conviction quashed on appeal, statement not special knowledge.

McTurk v HMA 1997 SCCR 1
Lost purse handed in to nightclub management. Drugs found next to undisturbed credit cards. Conviction under MDA 1971, s 5(3) upheld: no absolute rule that evidence of possession insufficient if more than one party had access.

Bath v HMA 1995 SCCR 323
Drugs found in engine of car in garage rented by appellant and father. Convicted but quashed on appeal: where accused and one other has access, some other evidence is required that accused knew of presence and impossible for jury to say which of them put drugs in engine.

McAllan v HMA 1996 SCCR 899
Drugs found in cigarette packet in compound six days after accident. Conviction under MDA 1971, s 4(3)(b) upheld on appeal: fanciful that drugs planted.
Observed: dictum in *Bath v HMA* 1995 SCCR 323 at 325 not intended as statement of general application, ie each case of possession where access to accused and others must be decided on facts. See Evidence.

See also:

Martin v HMA 1992 SCCR 356
Bain v HMA 1992 SCCR 705

Possession while in the custody of another.

Amato v Walkingshaw 1989 SCCR 564
A a seaman employed on ship plying between Larne and Cairnryan. Posted envelope containing drugs to himself at Larne. Purser kept it for him but became suspicious and handed it to authorities in Cairnryan. Convicted.
Held that A must have known that purser would hold envelope on his behalf, element of knowledge and control present and appeal refused.

See also:

R v Marriott [1971] 1 All ER 595
McKenzie v Skeen 1983 SLT 121

Misuse of Drugs Act 1971, s 37(3): 'For the purpose of this Act the things which a person has in his possession shall be taken to include any thing subject to his control which is in the custody of another.'

Onus.	*R v Cugullere* [1961] 1 WLR 258; [1961] 2 All ER 343 The onus remains throughout on the Crown to prove knowledge. See also:
Inferences.	*Warner v Metropolitan Police Commissioner* [1969] 2 AC 256 *DPP v Brooks* [1974] 2 All ER 840 *Held*, that running away may justify the inference.
Although no provisions as to quantity, important in cases re minute quantities of drugs.	*R v Worsell* [1970] 1 WLR 111; [1969] 2 All ER 1183 W charged with unlawful possession of a tube containing droplets of heroin. *Held* that as the tube was in reality empty (ie the droplets were invisible to the human eye and could only be discerned under a microscope and could not be measured or poured out), it was impossible to hold that there was any evidence that the tube contained a drug. However: *Bocking v Roberts* [1973] 3 All ER 962 Per Lord Widgery CJ: 'When dealing with a charge of possessing a dangerous drug without authority the ordinary maximum of de minimis is not to be applied.'
The quantities of drug found may be small but must be capable of being weighed, measured and identified to sustain prosecution.	*R v Frederick* 53 Cr App R 155 CA; [1970] 1 WLR 107; [1969] 3 All ER 804 Direction that if the jury thought the defendant was in possession of traces they should find him guilty because one must not have any dangerous drug in one's possession, no matter how small the quantity. Upheld. See also:
	R v Graham [1969] 2 All ER 1181 CA; [1970] 1 WLR 113 Scrapings in defendants' pockets sufficient to be measured.
	R v Colyer [1974] Crim LR 243 Traces measurable in the sense that they represented the minimum weight capable of being detected.
	R v Marriott [1971] 1 All ER 595 Traces of drug found on penknife; although it was also necessary to show that the defendant had reason to know there was foreign matter on the knife.
	Hambleton v Callinan [1968] 2 QB 427; [1968] 2 All ER 943 *Held* that when a drug is consumed, it changes its character and it cannot be said that the drug is then in a person's possession, although traces of it are found in his urine.
	Keane v Gallacher 1980 JC 77; 1980 SLT 144 Police discovered on top of sideboard a small quantity of resinous material which was visible and could be measured. Argued by defence that the quantity was not 'useable'. Sheriff acquitted. G convicted on appeal. 'It is possession of the drug which is an offence, not its potential use.'

Murdo McKay v Hogg (1973) SCCR Supp 40; 1973, Crown Office Circular 1224
Appellant asleep naked on couch. Search of his clothes on the chair disclosed nothing. After he had dressed, 16 tablets of LSD were found on seat cover. No one had anything to do with the chair except the appellant. He must have had the tablets for a second or two.
Held that such fleeting contact was not enough to justify possession in terms of MDA 1971.

Defence to 'possession' offence		MDA 1971, s 5(4)(a): It is a defence to prove that the accused 'took possession [of the drug] for the purpose of preventing another from committing . . . an offence . . . and that as soon as possible . . . he took all such steps as were reasonably open to him to destroy the drug or to deliver it into the custody of a person lawfully entitled to take custody of it; or (b) that . . . he took possession of it for the purpose of delivering it into the custody of a person lawfully entitled to take custody of it . . . '
Possession for valid medical reason must be proved by defendant.	*Wood v Allan* 1988 SCCR 115.	Regulation 10(2) of Misuse of Drugs Regulations 1985, SI 1985/2066.

Possession with intent to supply

	Morrison v Smith 1983 SCCR 171 M admitted unlawful possession of a controlled drug, but denied knowledge of a large amount of other drugs found in house. Convicted. *Held*, in absence of an explanation for possession, that the sheriff was entitled to infer intention to supply from the value, quantity and diversity of the drugs.	MDA 1971, s 5(3): '. . . it is an offence for a person to have a controlled drug in his possession, whether lawfully or not, with intent to supply it to another in contravention of section 4(1) . . . '

Haq v HMA 1987 SCCR 433
H convicted of possessing cannabis resin with intent to supply. H in possession of large block of the drug weighing 91 g. No evidence of intent to supply other than size of block and evidence from one police officer that block too large for personal use. Appeal against conviction refused.
Held to be sufficient evidence to infer intent.

See also:

Bauros v HMA 1991 SCCR 768

Donnelly (Mary) v HMA 1984 SCCR 419
Heroin. Possession with intent to supply. D occupier of house where 'considerable quantity' of diamorphine found in separate envelopes with street value of £10 or £20 each. Appeal against conviction refused.
Per Lord Dunpark: '. . .where a large quantity of controlled drugs, separately packaged in quantities normally sold in the streets, are found in the possession of a person, it is open to a jury to infer that that person intended to supply them to another. If the appellant . . . did no more than allow [S] to uplift drugs in her physical possession, she was thereby supplying them to another, namely, [S].'

See also:

Sim v HMA 1996 SCCR 77
Appellant convicted of possession with intent to supply. Search of house found opaque grocery bag containing 16 bags with 100 temazepam capsules. Trial judge directed Crown required to prove bag and contents in accused's physical control and he knew general character of contents but not that they were particular drugs.
Held, direction correct and conviction upheld. *McKenzie v Skeen* 1983 SLT 121 followed.

References: Gordon, 1000; Bovey, 6, 7; 20-39; 55-85.

Cultivation of cannabis

Misuse of Drugs Act 1971, s 6. It is an offence to **cultivate** any **plant of the genus** *Cannabis* unlawfully.

COMMENTARY	CASE LAW	STATUTE LAW
Not lawful to **cultivate** any **plant of the genus** *Cannabis.*		MDA 1971, s 6.
	Tudhope v Robertson 1980 JC 62; 1980 SLT 60 *Held* that the position of plants to secure the light (ie at a window) necessary to the growth, the condition of the plants, the presence of the seeds and the accused's objective in having the plants in the house, all pointed to the conclusion that the plants were being 'cultivated' and the offence was thus being committed.	
Produce	*Henderson v HMA* 1996 SCCR 71 Production of cannabis for own use. Eighteen months' imprisonment upheld on appeal. Observed, Parliament intended cultivation of cannabis to be entirely different offence from simple possession.	MDA 1971, s 4(2)(a)
	Wilson v HMA 1998 SCCR 437 Appellant, first offender pleaded guilty to producing cannabis for own use and sentenced to 12 months' imprisonment. *Held*, on appeal, normally court would sentence to community service but since ruled out by accused's mental health she would be placed on probation with additional condition she undergo medical treatment. *Note*: this may suggest *Henderson v HMA* 1996 SCCR 71 is no longer a generally applicable guide to sentencing.	
	Robertson v Derry 1998 SCCR 599 Appellant had three previous convictions for possession and was convicted under MDA 1971, s 4(2)(a) and sentenced to four months' imprisonment. He used a sophisticated growing system and had 16 plants with street value of £270. *Held*, cultivation more serious than possession, even if for personal use, and appeal refused.	

Reference: Bovey, 27-29.

Offences committed by occupiers etc of premises by permitting certain activities to take place there

Misuse of Drugs Act 1971, s 8. A person commits an offence if, being the **occupier** or concerned in the **management of** any **premises**, he **knowingly permits** or **suffers** any of the following activities to take place on those premises, ie
(a) producing or attempting to produce a controlled drug contrary to s 4(1);
(b) supplying or attempting to supply a controlled drug to another or offering to supply a controlled drug to another contrary to s 4(1);
(c) preparing opium for smoking;
(d) smoking cannabis, cannabis resin or prepared opium.

COMMENTARY	CASE LAW	STATUTE LAW
Occupier	*Christison v Hogg* 1974, Crown Office Circular 1281 *Held* that the word occupier must be given its ordinary meaning: 'It is a person who has possession of the premises in question—in possession in a substantial sense involving some degree of permanency and who as a matter of fact exercises control of the premises and dictates their use.' Every case will depend on its own facts.	Misuse of Drugs Act 1971, s 8
	Bruce v McManus [1915] 3 KB 1 Per Lusk J: '. . . the person indicated by those words ["occupier of premises"] is the person who is in legal occupation and in control of the premises'.	
	R v Bradbury [1996] Crim LR 808 *Held*, acquiescence was not enough to amount to control: there had to be assistance or encouragement as indicated by the court in *R v Conway and Burkes* [1994] Crim LR 826 (referred to in Shiels at p 365).	
	R v Mogford [1970] 1 WLR 988 Two sisters, aged 20 and 15, were charged with permitting premises to be used for the purpose of smoking cannabis at their parents' home when they were away on holiday. *Held* that the defendants' control did not amount to the nature and measure of control envisaged by MDA 1971.	
	Bamber v MacKinnon 1996 SLT 1180 This concerned an occupier of premises under Fire Precautions Act 1971. *Held*, on appeal, that somebody away temporarily on holiday remained the occupier if occupier before he left and intended remaining the occupier when he returned.	
Management of premises	*Sweet v Parsley* [1969] 1 All ER 347; [1970] AC 132 The defendant, the tenant of a farm, sublet rooms there, while living elsewhere. She used her own room occasionally when collecting rent, letters, etc, and rarely stayed overnight. Unknown to her, a sub-tenant used cannabis and the defendant was convicted under the Dangerous Drugs Act 1965, s 5 (equivalent of MDA 1971, s 8). *Held* that her appeal be allowed since: (1) the offence was not absolute and (2) she had no mens rea.	

Knowingly permits

Sweet v Parsley [1969] 1 All ER 347; [1970] AC 132
Per Lord Diplock: '. . . where the prohibited conduct consists in permitting a particular thing to be
done, the word "permit" connotes at least knowledge or reasonable grounds for suspicion on the
part of the permittor that the thing will be done and
an unwillingness to use means available to him to
prevent it . . .'.

Suffers

Rochford RDC v Port of London Authority [1914]
83 LJKB 1066; [1914] 2 KB 916
If a person is in a position to prevent a thing without committing a legal wrong and does not do so,
then in the common use of language, that person
suffers that thing. Of course, one cannot be said to
suffer a thing which one cannot prevent, or, which
by law one ought not to prevent.

Yeandel v Fisher [1966] 1 QB 440
Per Lord Parker CJ: 'It seems to me that the
legislation had in mind making those . . . who were
on the spot and concerned with the management
of premises absolutely liable if those premises
were used for those purposes, whereas they had
in mind that in the case of the occupier who might
be an absent occupier . . . he would only be guilty
if he wilfully and knowingly permitted.'

Sweet v Parsley [1969] 1 All ER 347; [1970] AC 132
Lord Parker CJ: 'If somebody is a mere occupier
he can only be guilty of an offence if it is proved
that he permitted, which as we all know involves
some knowledge or constructive knowledge.'

Reference: Bovey, 86-92.

Drug enforcement: statutory powers

COMMENTARY

Corporate liability
Drugs offence committed by a body corporate either with the consent or due to the neglect of a director, manager, secretary or similar officer.

Police powers
The police have powers to search and arrest those suspected of committing drugs offences.

Reasonable grounds of suspicion required.

Obstruction.

Confiscation orders
Prosecution authorities may seek to confiscate the proceeds of drug dealing from an offender.

CASE LAW

Weir v Jessop 1991 SCCR 242
MDA 1971, s 23(2): reasonable grounds for search. Police given anonymous evidence that a person at a certain locus in possession of drugs. W found, admitted being involved with drugs in the past, searched and drugs found. Appeal.
Held that constable had reasonable grounds.

See also:

Campbell v HMA 1992 SCCR 35

Wither v Reid 1980 JC 7
Held, clear distinction between power under MDA 1971, ss 23(2) and 24(1). A purported arrest under MDA 1971, s 23(2)(a) was unlawful as the section only contains power to detain.

Stuart v Crowe 1992 SCCR 181
Accused coming to house the police were searching, under MDA 1971, s 23(3) warrants, for drugs. S searched then separate warrants obtained to search his house and garage where drugs were found. Warrants upheld on appeal. S at house of known drug dealer without valid reason, police entitled to suspect that he was involved with drugs.

Vannet v Taylor 1998 SCCR 30
Accused charged with obstruction under MDA 1971, s 23(4)(a). Acquitted because sheriff held no evidence that accused had put something in mouth. Upheld on appeal: sheriff not bound to make such finding and as a result the charge must fail.

Normand v McCutcheon 1993 SCCR 709
MDA 1971, s 23(4): obstructing a search. M swallowing drug when approached by the police. Only one constable gave evidence that M told why he was being detained. Acquitted.
Held on appeal, accused knew why they were being detained, conviction substituted.

See also:

Annan v McIntosh 1993 SCCR 938

HMA v McLean 1993 SCCR 917
Supply of drugs valued at £270,000. Confiscation order sought. Deemed proceeds well in advance of the realisable property so order made for the value of the property. No fine imposed.

STATUTE LAW

Misuse of Drugs Act 1971, s 21
The officer involved, as well as the body corporate, shall be guilty of the offence committed.

Section 23(1): gives power to enter the premises of drugs producers to inspect drugs and stock.

Section 23(2): 'where a constable has reasonable grounds to suspect a person is in possession of controlled drugs, he may—
(a) search the person and detain him for that purpose
(b) search any vehicle or vessel in which he believes drugs may be found
(c) seize and detain anything which he believes to be evidence.'

Section 23(3). Justice of the Peace may grant warrant for search of premises if he is satisfied by information on oath of reasonableness of grounds.

Section 23(4). It is an offence, inter alia, intentionally to obstruct or conceal from person acting under this section.

Section 24(1): 'Constable may arrest without warrant a person he reasonably suspects to have committed an offence under the 1971 Act if:
(a) he believes the person will abscond; or
(b) name and address of the person are unknown to him and cannot be ascertained; or
(c) he is not satisfied the name and address given are true.'

Confiscation is now dealt with by the Proceeds of Crime (Scotland) Act 1995 (see Sentencing).

Evidence as to controlled drugs and medicinal products.

Criminal Procedure (Scotland) Act 1995, s 282, deals with evidence as to controlled drugs and medicinal products (see Evidence).

SENTENCING POLICY

Meighan v Jessop 1989 SCCR 208—M pleaded guilty to possessing heroin and disubstituted barbituric acid contrary to s 5(2) of Misuse of Drugs Act 1971. Placed on deferred sentence to be of good behaviour for a year. By time of deferred diet he had obtained employment as a drugs counsellor. Sheriff imposed fines of £150 and £50, and M appealed against these as excessive.
Held that had M not been of good behaviour he could have expected custodial sentence. Fines relatively small, and appeal refused.

Bates v HMA 1989 SCCR 338—Possessing heroin with intent to supply. B and C each sentenced to ten years' imprisonment. B appealed on ground that C nine years older than B and had been sentenced to six years' imprisonment for assault and robbery in 1976. B had number of minor convictions, one previous sentence of three months' detention and fined for drugs offences in 1985.
Held that distinction should have been made between B and C, and B's sentence reduced to seven years.

Hemphill v HMA 1989 SCCR 433—H sentenced to three years' imprisonment for possessing cannabis resin with intent to supply. No previous convictions.
Held that sentence not excessive.

Hudson v HMA 1990 SCCR 200—H pleaded guilty to possessing cannabis with intent to supply. Non-commercial supply to friends. Sentenced to four years' imprisonment. On appeal *held* sentence not excessive.

Smith v HMA 1990 SCCR 251—Supplying drugs. Whether account has to be taken of the fact that one accused older and had supplied the purchasing funds.
Held on appeal that there was not need to differentiate.

Kennedy v HMA 1990 SCCR 417—Possession of £15 worth of lysergide and cannabis. Sentenced to 18 months' imprisonment. Appeal.
Held that the sentence was excessive, nine months substituted. Possession of 0.1 grammes of cocaine. First such charge in the area, sheriff imposing six months' imprisonment as a deterrent. Upheld on appeal.

Isdale v Scott 1991 SCCR 491—Possession of cannabis. 60 days' imprisonment after failing to tell court who was his supplier. Appeal.
Held that providing such information could have mitigating effect but failure didn't provide justification for imprisonment. One year deferred sentence substituted.

Kerr v HMA 1991 SCCR 774—Supplying small amounts of cannabis and buprenorphine to a prisoner. Sentenced to two years' and 18 months' consecutively. Appeal.
Held that this was a serious known evil that required to be dealt with severely. Sentence upheld.

McQueen v Hingston 1992 SCCR 92—Possession of 9.5 grammes of cannabis, previous convictions. Sentenced to 60 days' imprisonment. Appeal.
Held that as M had a family, was unemployed and last offence was three years ago, the sentence was excessive and £1,500 fine substituted.

Howarth v HMA (No 2) 1992 SCCR 525—Three accused convicted of importing 0.5 million tonnes (£100 million worth) of cocaine. Accused sentenced to 25, 15 and 15 years' imprisonment respectively. Upheld on appeal, sentence reflecting the fact that it was Class A drugs, their amount and value.

Gibson v HMA 1992 SCCR 855—First offender supplying cannabis to friends only. £35 worth found. Sentenced to nine months' imprisonment. Appeal.
Held that sentence should be severe but not excessive. 180 hours' community service substituted.

Ravenall v Annan 1993 SCCR 658—First offender, 35-year-old, employed, family. Possession of £20 of Class A Ecstasy. Sentenced to six months' imprisonment. Appeal.
Held that the sheriff had not treated the case on its merits, £250 fine substituted.

Stephen v HMA 1993 SCCR 660—Supplying Class B drug, packaged and ready for sale at folk festival. Valued at £370. Sentenced to 12 months' imprisonment. Increased on appeal to two years.

McCleary v Walkingshaw; Calderwood v Walkingshaw 1996 SCCR 13—Appellants in each case convicted of possessing small quantities of cannabis. Sheriff fined them £250 and £300 respectively as a deterrent to prevent district being flooded with drug abuse. Upheld on appeal, since particular areas may require deterrent sentences for local reasons.

Reid v HMA 1997 SCCR 532—First offender pleaded guilty to supply of cannabis over two-month period. 110g of cannabis and 385g of resin with street value £2,000 and he had £3,600 cash. Sentenced to five years.
Held, on appeal, since first offender and class B drug, four years' imprisonment substituted.

Miscellaneous – Misuse of drugs

O'Mara v Heywood 1997 SCCR 371—Medical student convicted of supplying cannabis over seven weeks, initially to friends then to others.
Held, on appeal, three months' detention not excessive given persistence.
Observed, hoped professional bodies would not allow court sentence to have a doubled effect on the career of anyone.

Baxter v Munro 1997 SCCR 368—Appellant convicted of supplying cannabis to friends on one occasion worth £120. Six months' imprisonment upheld on appeal.

Clark v HMA 1995 SCCR 521—Appellant pleaded guilty to possession of cannabis resin but said holding it for someone else he refused to name. Four-year sentence upheld: no mitigatory aspects in absence of name. *Isdale v Scott* 1991 SCCR 491 distinguished.

Paterson v McGlennan 1995 SCCR 42—Seventeen-year-old pleaded guilty to supplying and possessing cannabis with intent to supply and given four months' imprisonment concurrent on each.
Held, on appeal, custodial sentence normally appropriate but 18-month delay between commission and sentence exceptional and 240 hours' community service substituted.

Carlin v HMA 1994 SCCR 763—Appellant pleaded guilty to MDA 1971, s 4(1), s 4(3) and s 5(3) offences and agreed C and four friends had combined to buy amphetamine for own use. Sheriff imposed one-year imprisonment. Upheld: not excessive and common excuse but court takes serious view whether friends or strangers.

Munro v HMA 1994 SCCR 220—Woman pleaded guilty to possession of 36 deals of heroin (value £720). Said it was put into her jacket by boyfriend, ie she intended to return it. Sentence of two years upheld as appropriate for drug 'of this nature'.

O'Neill v HMA 1994 SCCR 223—Convicted of possession of 2.699 grammes of cannabis resin, contrary to MDA 1971, s 5(2). One similar previous conviction. Given six months' imprisonment.
Held, on appeal, fine with no time to pay or 30 days' imprisonment more appropriate and the latter substituted.

HMA v McPhee 1994 SCCR 830—M (19) pleaded guilty to supply of single tablet of LSD to two girls (aged 13 and 14). Sheriff sentenced to one-year probation with special conditions that he perform 200 hours' unpaid work and attend drug rehabilitation project.
Held, on appeal, sentence unduly lenient given age of girls and class A drug and custodial sentence unless strong mitigation, and three years substituted.

Harkins v HMA 1998 SCCR 603—Appellants (16 and 17) pleaded guilty to being concerned in supply of amphetamine and attempting to be in possession with intent to supply ecstasy (in fact aspirin) at under 18s disco. 16-year-old co-operated and said drugs from 17-year-old. He refused to say where drugs from. Consecutive sentences of 15 and 12 months' detention quashed on appeal. Made consecutive for 17-year-old, and due to mitigation deferred for 12 months on 16-year-old who was pregnant (noted likely community service order would be made at end of that time).

References: Shiels, 365.

OFFENSIVE WEAPONS

The **carrying** of an **offensive** weapon, or a weapon **intended for use** as such, in a **public place** without lawful authority or **reasonable excuse.** It is now also an offence to carry a knife in a public place.
The law is now to be found in the Criminal Law (Consolidation) (Scotland) Act 1995, ss 47–50.

COMMENTARY	CASE LAW	STATUTE LAW
Carrying The offence is the carrying, not the use, of a weapon.	*Bates v Bulman* [1979] 3 All ER 170 Nature of offence under Prevention of Crime Act 1953, s 1(1) is the carrying and not the use of a weapon. Person who borrowed a clasp knife, not offensive per se, with the immediate intention of using it as an offensive weapon is not guilty of an offence under this Act (in England at least). See also: *R v Jura* [1954] 1 QB 503 Airgun held not to be offensive weapon.	Criminal Law (Consolidation) (Scotland) Act 1995. Section 47(1). Any person who without lawful authority or reasonable excuse, the proof whereof shall lie on him, has with him in any public place any offensive weapon shall be guilty of an offence.
'has with him'	*Smith v Vannet* 1998 SCCR 410 Appellant had with him offensive weapon and knife. Weapons six feet away in car and he had keys in pocket. Conviction upheld on appeal: 'with him' purposively interpreted as meaning readily available to him, albeit not on his person. *McVey v Friel* 1996 SCCR 768 distinguished because that case was under the Firearms Act 1968, and accused was in bedroom and separated from car containing the weapon by greater distance.	Section 47(2). Where person convicted of offence under subsection (1) the court may order forfeiture or disposal of weapon. Section 47(3). A constable may arrest without warrant any person whom he has reasonable cause to believe is committing an offence under subsection (1), if not satisfied as to person's identity or address or to prevent further offence in course of which offensive weapon might be used.
Offensive (1) Offensive per se, eg swords, daggers, coshes, knuckledusters	*Tudhope v O'Neill* 1982 SCCR 45 *Held*, a flick knife is an offensive weapon intended for use for causing injury and was therefore an offensive weapon per se. *Woods v Heywood* 1988 SCCR 434 W charged with possessing machete. Sheriff held that machete offensive weapon per se. *Held* on appeal that machete had twofold purpose, ie as a weapon and as a tool, and could not be described as an offensive weapon per se, and conviction quashed. *McGlennan v Clark* 1993 SCCR 334 Shuriken Chinese throwing star is an offensive weapon per se. Only purpose was for causing personal injury. *McKee v MacDonald* 1995 SCCR 513 Prevention of Crime Act 1953, s 1(4). Souvenir in shape of police truncheon. Accused convicted on basis article made for causing personal injury. *Held*, on appeal, article made from light wood and could not be compared to truncheon. Sentence quashed.	Section 47(4): ' "offensive weapon" means any article made or adapted for use for causing injury to the person or intended by the person having it with him for such use by him.' or by some other person.
(2) Adapted for use for causing injury, eg bicycle chain with razor-blade attached, or broken bottle.		

(3) Not offensive per se but intended for use for causing personal injury.

R v Petrie [1961] 1 WLR 358
Held that an ordinary razor was not an offensive weapon per se but would be offensive under Prevention of Crime Act 1953, s 1(4) if intention proved.

Glendinning v Guild 1987 SCCR 304
Flail not per se offensive. Waving it in the air does not render it offensive.

Coull v Guild 1985 SCCR 421
Sheath knife not per se an offensive weapon.

Houston v Snape 1993 SCCR 995
Seven-inch dagger did not stop being an offensive weapon per se just because it was in a sheath.

Intended for use

R v Petrie [1961] 1 WLR 358
If not per se an offensive weapon the Crown must prove the intent to use to cause injury.

Statutory question of intention to use is one to be drawn from all the circumstances.

Lopez v MacNab 1978 JC 41
Accused convicted of possession of a kitchen knife in a public place. Argued, Crown failed to prove intention to use it offensively.
Held that intention was to be inferred from the facts and circumstances of the case.

Normand v Matthews 1993 SCCR 856
Accused said he had clasp knife for 'protection' On appeal *held* that this statement corroborated by two witnesses was sufficient evidence of accused's intention.

Ralson v Lockhart 1986 SCCR 400
R charged with having an offensive weapon, ie a modelling knife, with intention to use it for causing personal injury. R was driving stolen car and when stopped by police, ran off. Sheriff inferred from these facts that he intended to use knife as offensive weapon.
Held on appeal that it could not be inferred from his flight from the car that he intended to use knife and sheriff had inverted onus of proof which lay on prosecution to prove R had necessary intention. Conviction quashed. *Lopez v McNab* 1978 JC 41 distinguished.

Intention must be to cause injury.

R v Rapier (1979) 70 Cr App R 17 CA
Rapier convicted of possession of carrying knife, having threatened a doorman with it.
Held, on appeal, that intimidation was not enough unless the person intended to cause injury to the person (in England at least).

Farrell v Rennicks 1959 SLT (Sh Ct) 71
Knife found on accused who pleaded guilty to a housebreaking charge. Accused explained in evidence that knife was to be used as a housebreaking tool.
Held that knife not in accused's possession for the purpose of causing personal injury. Acquitted of offensive weapons charge.

Public place

Philips v Orr 1997 GWD 226
Prevention of Crime Act 1953, s 1(4). Pool cue in a car. Car was in a public place and Parliament had proceeded on the basis that its interior and all its contents were also deemed to be in a public place. Conviction upheld on appeal.

CL(C)(S)A 1995, s 47(4): ' "public place" includes any highway and any other premises or place to which, at the material time, the public have or are permitted to have access whether on payment or otherwise.'

Substantive law

Normand v Donnelly 1993 SCCR 639
Treatment cubicle in a casualty department necessarily private but conviction upheld on the inference that the accused walked through a public place to get there.

R v Theodoulou [1963] Crim LR 573
T convicted of carrying an offensive weapon, namely, an open razor in a public place, namely, a coffee bar. The trial judge assumed this was a public place rather than leaving it to the jury and because of this the conviction reluctantly quashed on appeal.

Owens v Crowe 1994 SCCR 310
Prevention of Crime Act 1953, s 1(1). Possession of lock knife in disco.
Held, sheriff entitled to draw inference of intention to injure.

Wallace v Ruxton 1998 SCCR 701
Held, offensive weapon in 'public place' as not suggested appellant accessed neighbour's garden other than from public path and not suggested he was handed spanner in garden.

See also:
R v Mehmed [1963] Crim LR 780; [1963] CLY 791

Reasonable excuse

Grieve v MacLeod 1967 JC 32
Taxi driver carried a piece of rubber hose tipped with metal. Argued that it was for defensive purposes, taxi drivers often being subject to attack.
Held that he had contravened the Prevention of Crime Act 1953.
Per LJ-C Grant: 'One object of the Act is to ensure that ordinary citizens do not, unless in exceptional and justifiable circumstances, take the law into their own hands.'

See also:

Hemming v Annan 1982 SCCR 432
Nunchaca sticks being carried home very late at night with no reasonable excuse. Convicted.

Concealment. The offence under CL(C)(S)A 1995 is obstruction of, or concealment from, a PC who is exercising his powers of search for an offensive weapon under the Act.

Burke v MacKinnon 1983 SCCR 23
The offence of concealment of an offensive weapon under Criminal Justice (Scotland) Act 1980, s 4(2)(b) can only be established where it is shown that active steps were taken to conceal the weapon; thus failure to reveal possession would not likely lead to a conviction under the section.
Sheriff Gordon in his commentary at p 25 states that whether or not a carrier will be prosecuted under this section, as well as, or instead of, under the Prevention of Crime Act 1953 will depend on the policy of the prosecutor.

Criminal Law (Consolidation) (Scotland) Act 1995, s 48. It is an offence to obstruct a PC or conceal an offensive weapon from him in the exercise of his powers of search.

Knife or other sharply pointed article

Normand v Walker 1994 SCCR 875
Clerk of Court lent a ruler to two policemen to measure blade and officers gave evidence that blade exceeded three inches. Sheriff upheld no case to answer in absence of evidence as to accuracy of ruler.
Held, on appeal, sufficient evidence and appeal allowed.
Observed, that evidence of use of everyday object like ruler is admissible without further evidence of ruler's accuracy.

Lister v Lees 1994 SCCR 548
L carrying metal spike in railway station, said he had forgotten to throw it away after opening the tin of glue he was sniffing.
Held on appeal that the question was whether at the time of his arrest L had a 'good reason'. Explanation not sufficient here. 'Good reason' different from 'reasonable excuse' under the Prevention of Crime Act 1953 but will still depend on the facts and circumstances of each case.

Brown v Farrell 1997 SCCR 356
Carrying of Knives etc (Scotland) Act 1993, s 1(4).
Held, using a knife to cut cans in preparing heroin for injection was not a 'good reason' for carrying knife.

Donaldson v Vannet 1997 SCCR 689
Appellant charged under s 49 of Criminal Law (Consolidation) (Scotland) Act 1995, and offered to plead guilty as not charged under s 47. Presumably Crown accepted he never threatened anyone with knife. Appellant was re-indicted under s 47. On appeal he argued his reply that knife for self-defence irrelevant to a charge under s 49.
Held, reply would have been admissible to counter any defence of permissible reasons under CL(C)(S)A 1995, s 49(5), and no oppression, and appeal refused.
Observed, Crown will frustrate Criminal Procedure (Scotland) Act 1995, s 258 (agree uncontroversial evidence) if re-indict following discussions with accused.

Stewart v Friel 1995 SCCR 492
Carrying of Knives etc (Scotland) Act 1993, s 1(3). Folding pocketknife was lockable and this additional feature not mentioned in subsection. Conviction upheld on appeal.

CL(C)(S)A 1995

Section 49(1)–(3). Carrying of knife or other sharply pointed article is an offence. This does not apply to a folding pocket-knife with a blade of less than three inches (7.62 cms).

Section 49(4). Defence that the person had 'good reason' or lawful authority for having the article.

Section 49(5). Examples of potential 'good reasons', ie religious reasons, part of national costume, for use at work.

Section 49A. Any person who has article to which s 49 and offensive weapon to which s 47 applies with him on school premises shall be guilty of an offence.

Section 49B. A constable may enter school premises and search for article or offensive weapon if reasonable grounds for suspecting offence under s 49A being committed.

(Section 50 is similar to s 48: it is an offence to obstruct a police constable or conceal an offensive weapon from him in exercise of his powers of search under s 50).

The Knives Act 1997 deals with the marketing of 'combat knives' and is designed to control efforts to advertise and sell knives in a way which portrays them as suitable for violent use.

Reference: Gordon, 861-865.

SENTENCING POLICY

Jacobs v Wilson 1989 SCCR 9—J, first offender, pleaded guilty to having butcher's knife with ten-inch blade in street at 4 am. He stated he had been chased by two youths and had entered his house and come out with the knife, by which time the two youths had gone. Sheriff sentenced J to three months' imprisonment following the sentence in *Smith v Wilson* 1987 SCCR 191.
Held on appeal (1) that sheriff must not be seen to be fettering his discretion, and had come close to suggesting that all offensive weapons should be dealt with by a custodial sentence and (2) that *Smith v Wilson* was distinguishable because weapon not per se offensive. Sentence quashed and order for 120 hours' community service substituted.

Mir v Normand 1993 SCCR 654—Second conviction for possessing a knife. Sentenced to six months' imprisonment and deportation order recommended. Upheld on appeal.

Noble v Lees 1993 SCCR 967—Sixteen-year-old convicted of possessing a knife. Had armed himself to 'settle the score' after an earlier assault. Sentenced to three months' detention. Appeal.
Held that not enough account taken of N's good background. 180 hours' community service substituted.

Prior v Normand 1993 SCCR 118—Possession of lock knife in centre of Glasgow. P telling police he would use it on them. Three months' imprisonment increased to six months' imprisonment on appeal. Carrying knives '. . . always been a problem in Glasgow'.

Reid v Normand 1994 SCCR 475—Breach of the peace, vandalism and offensive weapon charge regarding a baseball bat. Six months' imprisonment on weapon charge upheld on appeal.

Hamilton v Hamilton 1996 SCCR 652—Possession of offensive weapon by 16-year-old who said he was carrying it for protection from creditors looking for payment for drugs.
Held, on appeal, six months' detention not excessive.
Observed, per Lord Sutherland, that custodial sentence not inappropriate for 16-year-old first offender, since it was people of this age who carried and were liable to use knives.

Keaney v Vannet 1997 GWD 19-885—Three months' detention for assault by brandishing knife and six months concurrent for possessing knife.
Held, excessive since K, aged 17, trying to free girlfriend detained in house, K had no previous convictions and recurrence unlikely. 240 hours' community service substituted.

Ross v Reith 1997 GWD 33-1681—R had 12-to-16-inch metal chain with taped handle for protection.
Held, two months' detention for R, a first offender, in employment was appropriate and not excessive.

Miller v Vannet 1997 GWD 16-732—*Held*, three months' detention for first offender for possession of knife (three-to-four-inch sharpened blade) not excessive given dangers of such actions.

McFarlane v Spiers 1997 GWD 20-968—Three months' detention for 16-year-old first offender for carrying knife 'for protection' (M in employment and lived with parents and had stable background).
Held, not excessive.

Reilly v Heywood 1997 GWD 21-1030—Three months' imprisonment for carrying two knives. R in bed and breakfast accommodation and subject to bad influences. Social enquiry report recommended probation to help R move forward.
Held, sentence excessive. One year's probation and 100 hours' community service substituted.

Larkin v Friel 1997 GWD 22-1080—Sixty days' detention for first offender carrying knife in public place 'for protection'.
Held, sentence excessive, since L saving money to go to university, had spent seven days in custody and of good behaviour. Community service substituted.

McIlraith v Vannet 1998 GWD 3-121—Four months for possessing knife in public place. M had analogous conviction in 1991.
Held, sentence excessive, since M had changed lifestyle and was drug-free, in employment and had been given police nomination for helping save a life. Community service substituted.

Arthur v Carnegie 1998 GWD 23-1168—One accused challenged person to a fight and asked other accused to hand him knife with which he threatened to stab person.
Held, 60 days' detention for 16-year-old first offenders excessive and 200 hours' community service and two years' probation substituted.

Boyle v Vannet 1998 GWD 25-1257—Three months for 16-year-old first offender possessing butcher knife with 8-inch blade. He took it to 14-year-old pregnant girlfriend's house because frightened of father. Boy and girl now lived together, and B was in employment.
Held, with hesitation, that sentence excessive, and 240 hours' community service substituted.

PRINCIPLES

ART AND PART GUILT

All persons who **participate** in the commission of a crime **together** are **equally liable for the outcome** of that act irrespective of the particular role played by each individual in its commission.

COMMENTARY	CASE LAW	STATUTE LAW

Participate
Before a person may be held so responsible, he must have actually participated in the crime. Mere presence at, or failure to prevent, the commission of an offence will not, in the absence of any 'special duty', impose guilt for that offence.

HMA v Kerr and Ors (1871) 2 Couper 334
Three accused charged with assault with intent to ravish. One of the accused, Donald, had taken no direct part in the attack but had only stood at the other side of a hedge watching the attack. Had not spoken to his friends or the girl during the attack. *Held* no art and part liability.

Mitchell v HMA 1994 SCCR 440
No averment that accused acted along with another person.
Held, Crown entitled to rely on Criminal Procedure (Scotland) Act 1975, s 45.
Observed, per Lord Clyde, that where the Crown intend to submit accused guilty with others who can be named and identified, the preferable course is for that to be made specific in the indictment.

HMA v Meikleham 1998 SCCR 621.
Held, an averment of art and part guilt still implied in all indictments.

HMA v Hamill 1998 SCCR 164
Two accused charged on indictment with supply of drugs contrary to Misuse of Drugs Act 1971, s 4(3)(a). Question arose as to involvement of third person and objection on ground that there was no averment of art and part against the accused.
Held, breadth of statutory charge meant that there was no room for the common law doctrine of concert, and objection repelled.

Salmon v HMA; Moore v HMA 1998 SCCR 741
Misuse of Drugs Act 1971, s 28. Dictum of LJ-C in *Rodden v HMA* 1994 SCCR 841 on requirement of knowledge in cases of concert disapproved. In *Rodden* LJ-C said where accused charged under MDA 1971, s 4(3)(b), it must be established there was knowledge on the part of each accused that drugs were involved in transaction. LJ-G Rodger said there was no such rule (ie only need prove accused had supplied contents of package and then prove package involved drugs, NOT that accused knew packages contained drugs). LJ-G Rodger and Lord Bonomy also had doubts as per Lord Marnoch in *HMA v Hamill* 1998 SCCR 164 what room if any for concert to apply under MDA 1971, s 4(3)(b).

Criminal Procedure (Scotland) Act 1995, s 293(1) applies the concept of art and part guilt to all statutory offences.

Criminal Procedure (Consequential Provisions) (Scotland) Act 1995, s 6, Sch 6, repeals with savings s 46 of the Criminal Procedure (Scotland) Act 1975. CP(S)A 1975, s 46 provides that it is unnecessary to state in charge that the accused is art and part as every charge now impliedly contains these words.
Note: The effect of the repeal with savings is by no means clear: see Sheriff Gordon's commentary to *HMA v Hamill* 1998 SCCR 164.

Dissociation must be explicit.	*MacNeil v HMA* 1986 SCCR 288 Per L J-G Emslie: 'A person who is an instigator of a contemplated crime or a participator in preparation for it, may successfully dissociate himself from criminal responsibility in the crime, if it is committed by others, if he clearly intimates to them that he is withdrawing and seeks to discourage them from proceeding. . . . In such circumstances he cannot be guilty of the crime if it is nevertheless committed.'
Special duty	*Bonar v McLeod* 1983 SCCR 161 Two police officers. One assaulted prisoner. Senior officer did nothing. *Held* art and part guilty as did not dissociate himself from actions; thus even stronger than position of official standing by and allowing offence; placed in active position as part of escort.
A person may be held to have so participated and thus invoke art and part guilt by several methods: by 'serious, earnest and pointed' instigation or advice whose effect is to induce the commission of a crime (Hume I, 278).	*Spiers v HMA* 1980 JC 36 All accused charged with murder and attempted murder. S was not proven present at attack. Appeal court held S could only be liable art and part if he instigated the attack, this being antecedent concert. Conviction quashed.
'The instigation must be to such an act as was likely to result in the crime charged.' (Macdonald, p 4). 'The connection between the instigation or assistance and the act must continue to the last. If the instigator repent, he is not guilty if he genuinely attempts to dissuade the person whom he instigated. . . .' (Macdonald, pp 5–6).	
Advice of a general nature not directly connected with an imminent crime is not, however, sufficient for guilt.	*HMA v Johnstone and Stewart* 1926 JC 89; 1926 SLT 428 Two accused were charged with procuring an abortion. The accused were unknown to each other and the first accused had only given the name of the second accused to persons seeking an abortion and received no benefit from such a referral. Per Lord Moncrieff: 'It would be straining the law to hold that the mere communication of a name by a party, who was not in actual communication with the party named, was actual participation in the illegal act.' J found not guilty.
By supplying material assistance prior to the commission of the crime, eg supplying a car for a bank robbery where the supplier knows of the imminent plot to commit the crime, or through actual participation in the commission of the crime itself either	*HMA v Semple* 1937 JC 41; 1937 SLT 48 Charge of attempting to procure an abortion through instigation and supply of powders to a pregnant woman held relevant.
by a prior agreement to take part in the crime,	*HMA v Fraser and Rollins* 1920 JC 60; 1920 2 SLT 77 Robbery and murder. Woman lured victim to park where two men were waiting to rob him. Victim died of his injuries. The two male co-accused convicted of murder.

or by a concerted and spontaneous coming together at the time of the offence.

Gallacher v HMA 1951 JC 38; 1951 SLT 158
One of accused started a fight with the deceased and a number of men joined in. All stood round the victim and kicked him to death.
Per Lord Keith: 'If the accused were in a kicking crowd animated by a common purpose, joining in the attack, assisting and encouraging, each and all are responsible for the consequences.' Three of the accused convicted of murder.

But see:

Melvin v HMA 1984 SCCR 113
Held that a jury are entitled, in the absence of intent to kill or any antecedent concerted intention to carry out an assault and robbery, to assess the degree of recklessness displayed by each participant, and to return verdicts of murder or culpable homicide in accordance with that assessment.

Malone v HMA 1988 SCCR 498
Two appellants charged with murdering B after repeated kicks and blows to his face. First appellant found guilty of murder, second appellant who desisted from assault shortly before first appellant found guilty of culpable homicide. Convictions upheld but observed by LJ-G Emslie: 'If a distinction is to be made in a case involving a joint assault causing deaths it could normally only be justified if there were striking differences in the relevant conduct of each of the assailants.'

Hobbins v HMA 1996 SCCR 637
Concert. Misdirection.
Held (Lord Sutherland dissenting), open to trial judge to direct jury that there was sufficient evidence to entitle them to be satisfied that two men were acting in concert, but he was not entitled to tell them that this was something they did not need to decide. Conviction of robbery set aside and authority for new prosecution.

Where accused knew or should have known that a weapon was being used by co-accused,

Walker v HMA 1985 SCCR 150
W and R involved in fight with deceased in discothèque. R's conviction of murdering victim by stabbing him upheld on appeal. W convicted art and part on the basis that he knew or should have known of knife attack but still continued with his own assault. Conviction against W quashed on appeal.
Per LJ-C Wheatley: '. . . it would be reasonable to infer that, if [W] should have known that [R] was using a knife he still persisted in his attack on the victim [then this] would bring into operation the law of art and part and warrant the conviction. But insofar as it has never been established at what point of time the fatal blow was struck it is quite impossible to affirm that the appellant can be involved. . . .'

Mathieson v HMA 1996 SCCR 388
Appellants C and W M took part in attack with other men. S produced knife and stabbed victim while appellants continued to kick victim.
Held, they had witnessed use of knife and were art and part liable of culpable homicide (S convicted of murder).
Per LJ-G Hope: '. . . the knife wounds had already been inflicted during the period when the deceased was still being assaulted by the appellants.'

or if weapon used sufficiently similar to those contemplated.

O'Connell v HMA 1987 SCCR 459
O and three others charged with murder. They had formed common plan to assault deceased with sticks, one of which was three or four feet long. Deceased killed by blow from his own hammer and no evidence as to which accused had wielded it. Trial judge directed jury that where the weapons used were of a broadly similar nature it was for them to decide whether the assailants should have anticipated the use of a broadly similar weapon. Appellant was convicted and his appeal refused.

Art and part guilt applies even where a person could not be convicted as the principal.

Vaughan v HMA 1979 SLT 49
V accused that, acting along with the mother of a small boy, he forced the boy to have intercourse with the mother, contrary to Incest Act 1567. The accused was not related to either the mother or the son and argued that he could not be found guilty since not within the forbidden degrees.
Held, on appeal, that Act did not exclude its application to those art and part in commission of offence. Convicted.

Criminal Procedure (Scotland) Act 1995, s 293(2): '. . . any person who aids, abets, counsels, procures or incites any other person to commit an offence against the provisions of any enactment shall be guilty of an offence . . .'

Together
The essence of art and part guilt is that the accused execute a common plan or, if acting in concert, a spontaneous common purpose.

HMA v Lappen 1956 SLT 109
L charged along with five others with assault and robbery. Convicted.
Per Lord Patrick: 'If a number of men form a common plan whereby some are to commit the actual seizure of the property and some, according to the plan, are to keep watch and some, according to the plan, are to help carry away the loot . . . then, although the actual robbery may only have been committed by one or two of them, every one is guilty of the robbery because they joined together in a common plan to commit the robbery . . . if it has not been proved that there was such a common plan or if it has not been proved that the accused were parties to this previously conceived common plan then in law each is only responsible for what he himself did.'

If the prosecutor cannot prove concert each individual accused is judged only by his own proved actings.

Docherty v HMA 1945 JC 89; 1945 SLT 247
D was charged that, along with another unknown man, he murdered a man in a room of a flat. When blow was struck the other person was in the room and there was no direct evidence to show who in fact struck the blow. Concert was therefore essential to conviction, and D's conviction of murder was quashed because the jury were not explicitly told they must acquit unless concert proved.

Codona v HMA 1996 SCCR 300
Conviction of murder squashed on appeal. Accused had no reason to believe participating in murderous attack which followed her kick, as this was not the nature of two earlier assaults that evening.

Low v HMA 1993 SCCR 493
Trial judge entitled to direct that the first accused did not act in concert but the second accused did act in concert with the first accused, given that each accused treated separately and different evidence admissible for each.

Humphries v HMA 1994 SCCR 205
Misdirection. Conviction of culpable homicide. Judge said could not convict either accused except on art and part.
Held, ample evidence to acquit C alone and acquit appellant, misdirection and conviction quashed.

A party cannot 'dissociate' himself from a crime once it has been perpetrated.

MacNeil v HMA 1986 SCCR 288

Appellant (S) and seven others charged with importing cannabis into UK. S engaged as engineer on vessel which sailed from Oban to West Africa and helped to store cannabis in fuel tank. His defence was that he only became aware that cargo was cannabis after loading it, and thereafter left ship at first opportunity.

Held that there is no defence of dissociation. But compare the case of dissociation *before* perpetration of the offence, above, p 112.

Equally liable for the outcome

Where the common plan or purpose is proved, the accused will be held responsible for any foreseeable consequences of the crime whether or not it was intended.

HMA v Welsh and McLachlan (1897) 5 SLT (Reports) 137

Docherty v HMA 1945 SC 89; 1945 SLT 247

But not for any action of another which goes unforeseeably outwith the common plan or purpose.

HMA v Welsh and McLachlan (1897) 5 SLT (Reports) 137

Two accused charged with murder of old woman having broken into her house and stolen certain articles. Failure by Crown to prove common plan went beyond theft by housebreaking and who in fact murdered the woman. Found not proven.

Boyne v HMA 1980 JC 47; 1980 SLT 56

Three men convicted of murder during assault and robbery. Conviction of murder against two accused quashed since there was no evidence to show that they either knew or had reason to anticipate the use of a knife, or that they continued the attack once the knife was produced.

McLaughlan v HMA 1991 SCCR 733

M joining in serious assault in which one life-threatening blow inflicted. Whether sheriff wrong to direct that M, by joining in, responsible for 'all that has taken place'?

Held on appeal that M only responsible for everything that happened after she joined in, important to know when the life-threatening blow took place

Brown v HMA 1993 SCCR 382

Homicide. Two accused attacking victim with knife and iron bar, both denied inflicting the fatal wound. Culpable homicide withdrawn, convicted of murder. Appeal.

Held that for murder both accused would require the necessary degree of wicked recklessness, if either of their intentions was only to inflict serious injury the culpable homicide open. Culpable homicide convictions substituted.

Elder v HMA 1995 SLT 84

Accused not tried with two co-accused because of insufficient evidence. Co-accused acquitted and precognosced on oath by Crown. Accused incriminated co-accused and argued oppression as prosecuted separately co-accused's statements would be inadmissible as hearsay.

Held, no oppression: Crown had indicted accused on basis of additional information.

References: Hume I, 264; Macdonald, 2; Gordon, 129; Gane and Stoddart, 243.

CONSPIRACY

Conspiracy is complete as soon as two or more persons **have agreed** together to commit a **crime.**

COMMENTARY	CASE LAW	STATUTE LAW
Conspiracy '. . . process is properly brought under this generic name, for any sort of conspiracy or machination, directed against the fame, safety, or state of another, and meant to be accomplished by the aid of subdolous and deceitful contrivances, to the disguise or suppression of the truth . . .' (Hume I, 170).	*Elliot and Nicolson* 1694 Hume I 170, 181 N induced physician to provide poison with which to murder wife. Changed plan to one whereby they conspired to fix on N's wife a false charge of attempting to poison N himself. Conviction for conspiracy and other charges. *Muschet and Campbell* 1721 Hume I 170	
Most recent definition of conspiracy is that made by Viscount Simon in a House of Lords civil appeal case which has subsequently been adopted by the Scottish criminal courts.	*Crofter Hand-Woven Harris Tweed Co v Veitch* 1942 SC (HL) 1 Per Viscount Simon LC: 'Conspiracy . . . is the agreement of two or more persons to effect any unlawful purpose whether as their ultimate aim or only as a means to it, and the crime is complete if there is such agreement even though nothing is done in pursuance of it. *HMA v Wilson, Latta and Rooney* (1968, unreported), High Court—see Gordon, 200 Charge of conspiring to have false evidence led and thus defeat the ends of justice. Viscount Simon's statement adopted by LJ-C Grant. *HMA v Carberry and Ors* (1974, unreported), High Court—see Gordon, 200 LJ-C Wheatley approves Viscount Simon's definition.	
Sheriff Gordon refers to three possible categories of conspiracy:		
(1) Conspiracy where a specific crime has been carried out in pursuance of that conspiracy.	*HMA v Wilson, Latta and Rooney* (1968, unreported), High Court—see Gordon, 200) Charge was a conspiracy to pervert the course of justice and the commission of subornation and attempted subornation in pursuance thereof. LJ-C Grant directed jury that they could acquit in the conspiracy and convict on the subornation. *HMA v Milnes and Ors*, (January 1971, unreported) High Court, Glasgow—see Gordon, 201 Per Lord Avonside: 'If . . . conspiracy has not been proved, your verdict will be not guilty or not proven as regards the conspiracy . . . if you find the heads . . . not proved you will find . . . not guilty . . . but guilty on those which are [proved].'	
However, a conspiracy to do something by criminal means is not a crime unless the criminal means are proved.	*Sayers v HMA* 1982 SLT 220 Charged with conspiring to aid the UVF by criminal means and by contravention of Prevention of Terrorism (Temporary Provisions) Act 1976. Jury found accused guilty of conspiracy but deleted specification of criminal means libelled. Appeal against conviction allowed; charge was irrelevant because of lack of specification and was not a crime known to the law of Scotland.	

(2) Conspiracy where no specified crime is charged in pursuance of the conspiracy, where charge does not set out specified crime by which conspiracy to be effected.

HMA v Walsh and Ors 1922 JC 82—see Gordon, 204
Conspiracy to further the purposes of the IRA by the unlawful use of force and violence by the use of explosive substances to be used to endanger the lives and persons and property of the lieges.

(3) Conspiracy may often be charged as a substitute for attempt. There is an attempt where the person involved goes beyond the stage of preparation for the crime into perpetration. Thus there may be a conspiracy charge where accused person does not move into perpetration but has agreed with another to commit the crime.

See *Elliot and Nicolson* 1964 Hume 1 170, 181

West v HMA 1985 SCCR 248
W and another charged with conspiracy to assault and rob persons employed in named premises. They loitered suspiciously outside these premises and were in possession of blade from pair of scissors and open razor, respectively. Conviction for conspiracy upheld on appeal.
Per LJ-G Emslie: 'Taking all the evidence together . . . we are of the opinion that there was sufficient. . . .'

Have agreed
As soon as two or more persons have agreed to commit a crime they are guilty of a complete crime of conspiracy. The mens rea of the offence is the intention to commit the crime libelled.

Smith and Ors (1975, unreported), High Court—see Gordon, 198
Lord Keith directed the jury that to 'find a conspiracy they would have to be satisfied that matters went beyond the putting forward by one man of his ideas to another with a view to the matter being discussed and possibly agreed upon at another date. There must be actual agreement.'

Crime
Only conspiracies to do what would be criminal if done by one person are criminal conspiracies (Macdonald, p 185).

Smith and Ors (1975, unreported), High Court—see Gordon, 198

Factual impossibility of achievement of the ultimate object of the conspiracy does not act as a defence to the charge.

Maxwell v HMA 1980 JC 40; 1980 SLT 241
Three accused convicted of conspiracy to bribe licensing board to approve transfer of gaming licences. At dates of offence, board did not have legal power to approve transfer since the matter of the issue of the licence was at the time under appeal to sheriff. Conviction sustained on appeal. It is the criminality of purpose and not the result which may or may not follow from the execution of the purpose which makes the crime a criminal conspiracy.

Incitement to murder

Baxter v HMA 1997 SCCR 437
Incitement to murder. Convicted but appealed as no settled plan to kill the victim in a particular way. Appeal refused.
Per LJ-G Rodger: 'A person can incite another to commit a crime without actually instructing him to do so. Depending on the circumstances it may be enough if, for example, he encourages or requests him to do so.'

Conspiracy—sexual offences

Criminal Law (Consolidation) (Scotland) Act 1995, s 16A, inserted by Sexual Offences (Conspiracy and Incitement) Act 1996. Offences involving procuring, organising and promoting unlawful sexual conduct abroad.
Note: It is necessary sexual misconduct is a crime in country where committed and in the UK.

References: Hume I, 170; Alison I, 369; Macdonald, 185; Gordon, 198–204; Gane and Stoddart, 202.

ATTEMPT

A person may be convicted of attempting a crime where he has taken an overt step in pursuance of his criminal intention and has passed from the stage of **preparation** to the stage of **perpetration** but has not completed the crime.

COMMENTARY	CASE LAW	STATUTE LAW
Under statute any person charged with a crime may also be convicted of attempt.		Criminal Procedure (Scotland) Act 1995.
		Section 294(1). Attempt to commit any indictable crime is itself an indictable crime.
		Section 294(2). Attempt to commit any offence punishable on complaint shall itself be an offence punishable on complaint.
The mens rea for an attempted crime is the same as for the completed crime.	*Cawthorne v HMA* 1968 JC 32; 1968 SLT 330 *Held* that attempted murder may be committed either intentionally or recklessly.	
Mere **preparation** shall not suffice. An attempted crime is where the accused failed to complete the crime but had actually taken overt steps in the **perpetration** of it.	*R v John Eagleton* 1855 Dears 376, 515 Parke said: 'The mere intention to commit a misdemeanour is not criminal. Some act is required, and we do not think that all acts towards committing a misdemeanour are indictable. Acts remotely leading towards the commission of the offence are not to be considered as attempts to commit it but acts immediately connected with it are.'	
	HMA v Mackenzie 1913 SC(J) 107; 1913, 2 SLI 48 'The law does not strike at preparation to commit a crime . . . the overt act . . . is essential to a conviction.' Per LJ-C Macdonald: '. . . the preparation of a fraudulent document, or a document intended to be fraudulently used is not in itself a punishable crime . . . it requires an overt act of use to constitute an indictable offence.'	
	HMA v Tannahill and Neilson 1943 JC 150 Per Lord Wark: 'I think you would require some overt act, the consequences of which cannot be recalled by the accused, which goes towards the commission of the crime, before you can convict even of attempt.'	
	(But in certain cases where two or more persons are involved this could be conspiracy—see Conspiracy, p 116.)	
'But the vicious will is not sufficient, unless it is coupled to a wrongful act. And here the question arises, how far must the culprit have proceeded in the prosecution of his wicked purpose, to make him answerable in the tribunals of this world?' (Hume I, 26).	*HMA v Camerons* (1911) 6 Adam 456 Where deciding whether what accused had done amounted to attempted fraud, Lord Dunedin charged the jury that 'the root of the whole matter' was 'to discover where preparation ends and where perpetration begins. In other words, it is a question of degree, it is a jury question'.	
The fact that it was impossible for the accused to complete the crime is no defence against attempt.	*Lamont v Strathern* 1933 JC 33; 1933 SLT 118 Attempted to steal from an empty pocket. Per Lord Sands: 'I am not, I confess, impressed by the metaphysical argument that, whereas one cannot take what is not there, therefore one cannot attempt to take what is not there.' Convicted of attempted theft.	

Doherty v Brown 1996 SCCR 136 (Full Bench)
Appellant charged with and convicted of contravention of Misuse of Drugs Act 1971, s 5(3) and s 19. He possessed tablets he believed contained ecstasy but in fact did not. He thus attempted to have said controlled drug in his possession with intent to supply it to another.
Held, refusing appeal, that fact that impossible to commit complete crime does not preclude Crown from charging an attempt. All court requires to consider is whether the accused had the necessary mens rea and had taken matters further by doing some positive act towards the execution of his purpose AND where the accused knows of the impossibility of what he is doing there can be no attempt.
Observed, per LJ-G Hope: there will be cases where no good purpose in prosecuting a person because actings so wholly misconceived as to cause no risk of harm to anybody.
Observed, per Lord Johnston: in principle the law would recognise that an attempted rape of a transvestite is a relevant charge if it is averred that the accused held the mistaken belief that the accused was a woman.

HMA v Anderson 1928 JC 1 disapproved; *Lamont v Strathern* 1933 JC 33 approved.

However, impossibility may be a defence to certain attempts of abortion.

HMA v Anderson 1928 JC 1; 1928 SLT 651
Court held that it was not attempted abortion to try to abort a woman who was not pregnant.
Per Lord Anderson: 'To attempt to do what is physically impossible can never, in my opinion, be a crime.'

A criminal act may be charged with intent to commit a further crime.

Where murder or culpable homicide is charged and it is not proved that death resulted from the assault, convictions may be assault with intention to murder or kill. Similarly, in assault to danger of life, where it is not proved life was endangered the conviction may be for assault with intent to endanger life.

Strachan v HMA 1994 SCCR 341
Attempted murder. Charge libelled he had brandished knife at officers, threatened them and made to strike them and struggled with them, and repeatedly did strike them. Neither officers could say if actually struck and conviction under deletion of part of charge referring to striking. Conviction upheld on appeal.

References: Hume I, 26; Alison I, 163; Macdonald, 254; Gordon, 163; Gane and Stoddart, 211.

SENTENCING POLICY

Moore v HMA 1984 SCCR 25. Attempted robbery by threats. Attempt to rob a post office by handing employees a note asking for money and adopting a menacing attitude to them. Four years' imprisonment. Appeal dismissed.
Per LJ-G Emslie: '. . . one could hardly have quarrelled with a longer sentence.'

PROCEDURE

BAIL

Admission to bail is competent for all crimes and offences. In cases of **murder** and **treason** and where person charged or convicted of **attempted murder, culpable homicide, rape** or **attempted rape** and **person previously convicted of murder** or **culpable homicide** (and sentenced to imprisonment or hospital order) or one of four crimes above then only the Lord Advocate or the High Court may admit to bail. There are **standard conditions** and there may be **special conditions.** The public interest may require the **refusal of bail.** Bail may be allowed where **reports** are **called for.**

COMMENTARY	CASE LAW	STATUTE LAW
Admission to bail	*Normand v B* 1995 SCCR 128 Misuse of Drugs Act 1971. Crown opposed bail because making further inquiries which would be impeded if bail granted. *Held*, per Lord McCluskey: 'If PF makes a motion to commit ... the court should not seek to go behind that statement.' Sheriff had misdirected himself. *Normand v JL* 1995 SCCR 130 Bail granted. Upheld on appeal. Crown not seeking to detain accused for further inquiries bearing on charge in petition but rather investigating accused's link to offences in England. *Mayo v Neizer* 1994 SLT 931 Bail order continues for so long as accused at liberty. *Lau, Petr* 1986 SCCR 140 Per Lord Justice-Clerk: 'Presentation can only occur when the application has been transmitted to the sheriff.' *Gibbons, Petr* 1988 SCCR 270 Petitioner fully committed for trial on 18.4.88 at 11.30 am and immediately applied for bail. Sheriff adjourned application till 9.45 am the next day. Case not heard till 11.50 am owing to delay in bringing peititioner from prison. Sheriff refused bail and petitioner appealed to High Court. *Held* that requirement of Criminal Procedure (Scotland) Act 1975, s 28(2) was mandatory and petitioner entitled to be liberated.	Criminal Procedure (Scotland) Act 1995, ss 23–33. Bail Applications. Section 23(1). Accused person entitled to apply for bail on any occasion when brought before sheriff prior to his committal until liberated in due course of law. Prosecutor may object. Section 23(2). Discretionary to refuse application until committal stage. Section 23(4). Application, if refused, may be renewed at committal stage. Section 23(5). Grant or refusal of bail within sheriff's discretion. Section 23(7). Application to be dealt with within twenty-four hours of its presentation to the sheriff, failing which liberation forthwith.

Murder and treason

McLaren v HMA 1967 SLT (Notes) 43
Murder. Petition to the High Court to exercise discretionary power refused.
Opinion of the court: 'The fact that there are these discretionary powers in the court is recognised by our standard writers on criminal law (see Hume on Crimes, II, p 90) and they are only exercised when the Court sees reason for such an indulgence in the whole circumstances of the case.'

HMA v Renicks 1998 SCCR 417 (*nobile officium*)
Held, only court which can hear application for bail by person accused or convicted of murder is High Court constituted by quorum of three or more judges. Petition granted and interlocutor of single judge recalled.

Milne v McNicol 1944 JC 151
Theft. M not asked to plead. Bail refused. Appeal to the High Court refused as incompetent because M not committed.
Per LJ-C Cooper: 'It is true that . . . the powers of the High Court of Justiciary to admit to bail any person charged with any crime or offence are preserved, but that section I read as referable to the paramount and overriding authority of the High Court, which has been described as equivalent or similar to the *nobile officium* of the Court of Session; and that is an authority which, as a single judge, I am unable to exercise. . . .'

Bail: circumstances where not available.

Section 26. Where accused charged with or convicted of attempted murder, culpable homicide, rape or attempted rape and already has conviction for murder or manslaughter (and custodial sentence/hospital order) or one of four above crimes then only the Lord Advocate or High Court may admit to bail.

Section 26(3). This section applies whether or not an appeal is pending against conviction or sentence or both.

Standard conditions

MacNeill v Milne 1984 SCCR 427
M pled guilty to some, not guilty to other, charges on summary complaint. Bail allowed on sole condition that M attend all subsequent diets. Appeal by prosecutor against omission of other standard conditions upheld.
Held mandatory to impose standard conditions.
Per LJ-C Wheatley's interlocutor: '. . . finds that the sheriff was wrong in forming the view that the imposition of the standard conditions or any of them was a matter for his discretion.'

Bail and bail conditions.

Section 24(1). All crimes and offences except murder and treason are bailable.

Section 24(2). Nothing in this Act shall affect the right of the Lord Advocate or the High Court to admit to bail any person charged with any crime or offence.

Section 24(4). In granting bail the court shall impose on the accused:
(a) the standard conditions; and
(b) such further conditions as necessary to secure standard conditions observed and that accused available for ID parade or to have print/sample taken from him.

Section 24(5). The standard conditions are that the accused
(a) appears at diets in case;
(b) does not commit offence on bail;
(c) does not interfere with witnesses, nor obstruct course of justice;
(d) makes himself available for inquiries/report to assist court.

Section 24(6). Money bail. Court or Lord Advocate may impose requirement that accused or cautioner deposits sum of money in court where satisfied such condition is appropriate to special circumstances of the case.

Reilly v HMA 1995 SLT 45. Accused admitted to bail. At judicial examination gave different address to that in bail order. Did not appear at diet.
Held, address in order remained domicile of citation. (Under CP(S)A 1995, s 25(2), accused can apply in writing to alter domicile of citation.)

Section 25(1). Court shall specify in order granting bail, copy of which shall be given to accused:
(a) conditions imposed;
(b) domicile of citation.

Section 25(2). Accused may apply in writing to change domicile of citation.

Lockhart v Stokes 1981 SLT (Sh Ct) 71
Assault. S, on petition, granted bail under Bail etc (Scotland) Act 1980. Address given was a fairground site. Attempts to serve indictment unsuccessful because site not in use. Warrant to arrest granted.
Per Sheriff Gow: '. . . a showground which is occupied on a seasonal basis only, and is simply a piece of waste ground at a time when citation is to be effected, is not a "proper domicile of citation" under the Bail Act.'

Special conditions

Note: Bail cannot normally be applied for while a sentence is being served.

Currie v HMA 1980 SLT (News) 187, (1980) SCCR Supp 248.

Breach of bail conditions.

Section 27(1), (2), (7)–(10).

Section 27(1). If accused granted bail fails without reasonable excuse:
(a) to appear at diet of court when given due notice, he commits an offence
(b) to comply with any other condition imposed on bail, he commits an offence.

Refusal of bail

Smith v McC 1982 SCCR 115
Per LJ-C Wheatley: An accused should be granted a bail order unless it can be shown that there are good grounds for not granting it. A complete catalogue of such grounds cannot be compiled. Generally, however, they can fall into two broad categories: (1) the protection of the public and (2) the administration of justice. Previous convictions per se should not be regarded as an automatic reason for refusal of bail, but if there is a significance in the record and the nature of the charge(s) then being preferred against an accused, the consideration of the protection of the public arises. . . . the list which follows is merely illustrative of the more common examples and not exhaustive. . . . (1) . . . already on bail . . .; (2) . . . ordained to appear . . . for trial on another offence; (3) . . . on probation, or undergoing community service order; (4) . . . on licence or parole; (5) . . . on deferred sentence. In such circumstances I take the view that unless there are cogent reasons for deciding otherwise bail should be refused. Other circumstances which warrant refusal of bail are the nature of the offence in very special circumstances, alleged intimidation of witnesses by assaults or threats, absence of a fixed abode, or reasonable grounds for suspecting that the accused will not turn up for his trial.'

G v Speirs 1988 SCCR 517
G charged on petition with assault and robbery and breach of s 3(1)(b) of the Bail etc (Scotland) Act 1980. Prosecutor did not oppose bail and did not give sheriff any information relevant to bail. Sheriff refused bail and accused appealed.
Held that an accused ought to be granted bail unless a sufficient ground produced to justify its refusal; and that as no such grounds were advanced, bail ought to have been allowed. Bail granted.

Maxwell v McGlennan 1989 SCCR 117
Per Lord Brand: 'If the Crown does not oppose bail, grant it'.

Note: These guidelines were reinforced by the Justiciary Office in 1984 SLT (Notes) 271.

Reports called for

Long v HMA 1984 SCCR 161
Fraud. L pled guilty on indictment. Case continued for social enquiry report. Bail refused. Application for review held competent but bail again refused.
Held, on appeal, review procedure incompetent *quoad* Criminal Procedure (Scotland) Act 1975, s 179.
Per LJ-C Wheatley: 'Manifestly, then, the provisions of section 30 [of CP(S)A 1975] have no application to a point in the procedure after the accused has pled guilty and his plea has been accepted.'

Thus review of bail decision under s 30 of CP(S)A 1975 inappropriate at, for example, the stage of remand awaiting best method of disposal or inquiries as to physical or mental condition. At such stage appeal to High Court under CP(S)A 1975, s 179 is the correct procedure.

McGoldrick v Normand 1988 SCCR 83
Appellants, aged 20 and 22 and not previously sentenced to detention, convicted of attempted theft. Sheriff continued case for social enquiry reports and remanded in custody, having refused bail. On appeal *held* that where court has to be satisfied after considering reports that custodial sentence is appropriate, very good reasons are required to justify refusal of bail. Bail granted.

Hill v HMA 1997 SCCR 376
Committing offence on bail. Criminal Procedure (Scotland) Act 1995, s 27(3).
Held, inter alia, incompetent to impose separate period of imprisonment for bail aggravation.
Note: CP(S)A 1995, s 27(3) awaits interpretation in suitable appeal.

Connal v Crowe 1996 SCCR 716.
Held, if appropriate for sentence for substantive offences to run consecutively then same went for sentence for aggravation.
Observed, per Lord Sutherland: 'limit on . . . capacity to impose consecutive sentences . . . is that he [the judge] is limited to a total of six months [for aggravation] . . . which can be imposed over and above the ordinary limits of Sheriff Court.'

Friel v HMA 1998 SCCR 47
Trial judge told jury condition of bail was accused not to commit further offence.
Held, direction not indication accused guilty of main offence.

Section 27. Committing an offence while on bail.

Section 27(3)–(5). Now treated as aggravation of subsequent offence and sentencing court shall have regard to:
(a) fact offence committed on bail, number of bail orders at time of offence;
(b) any previous conviction for breach of bail condition;
(c) the proportion of sentence for previous conviction attributed to aggravation.
Where maximum penalty for subsequent offence specified by enactment this maximum shall be increased to fine up to level 3 in all courts, and up to 60 days' imprisonment in District Court and up to six months in other courts.

Section 27(4A). Bail is a special capacity.

Section 27(6). Court should state extent and reasons where sentence different due to aggravation.

Section 30. Bail Review (Defence).

Section 30(1), (2). Court has power to review decision to grant bail/impose conditions on application of accused. On cause shown may admit to bail or impose different decisions.

Section 30(3). Application shall not be made before fifth day after original decision or before fifteenth day after subsequent decision.

Section 30(4). Review provision shall not affect any right to appeal.

Cochrane v Heywood 1998 SCCR 331
Breach of bail. Sheriff sentenced accused to one month in respect of which one month for breach of bail, intended two-month sentence.
Held, nonsensical, and sentence quashed and concurrent sentence substituted.
Observed, first figure mentioned is total sentence and second figure is amount attributable to aggravation.

Love, Petr 1998 SCCR 161
L, on bail, failed to appear for trial and arrested. Applied for bail and refused and appeal rejected as incompetent by justiciary office. Appealed to *nobile officium* of High Court.
Held (1) appeal should have been accepted; (2) petition incompetent but court would deal with it on merits and petition granted.

Fitzpatrick v Normand 1994 SLT 1263.
Held, recall or modification of a bail order must be subject of express decision by court.

Ogilvie, Petr 1998 SCCR 187
Criminal Procedure (Scotland) Act 1995, ss 30(2), 112. Petitioner lodged note of appeal against conviction and refused bail. Petitioned under CP(S)A 1995, s 30 for review of that refusal.
Held (3 judges): bail granted because (1) petition competent; (2) CP(S)A 1995, s 112 did not require appellant who lodged note of appeal to be granted bail only if there are exceptional circumstances.

Section 31. Prosecution Review On application of prosecutor, where prosecutor puts material information before court which not available to it when granted bail, review its decision. Court may (a) withdraw bail; (b) grant or condone bail either on same or different conditions. Review provision shall not affect any right of appeal.

Section 32. Bail Appeal.

Section 32(1). Where, after full committal or person charged on complaint with an offence, bail is refused or applicant is dissatisfied with the amount of bail fixed he may appeal to the High Court.

Section 32(2). The public prosecutor may appeal the admission of bail if dissatisfied with grant or amount of bail fixed; if admission is appealed the applicant is not liberated.

Section 32(7). Applicant shall be liberated after 72 hours from granting of application, whether the appeal has been disposed of or not, unless the High Court grants order for further detention in custody.

Section 112. High Court may convict person to bail pending appeal, but that it shall not do so where he is the appellant and has not lodged a note of appeal unless in exceptional circumstances.

Section 103(5)(c). Power to admit appellant to bail may be exercised by single judge.

SENTENCING POLICY

Hamilton v Heywood 1997 SCCR 783—Criminal Procedure (Scotland) Act 1995, s 27(5). Subsequent offences committed while accused subject to two bail orders. Maximum penalty available on each charge was three months, but sheriff gave four months to run consecutive on each (one month in each for breach of bail).
Held, in view of Crown's concession (which might need to be reconsidered) concurrent sentences of five months substituted (two months for breach of bail).

Wilson v HMA 1997 SCCR 674—Three subsequent offences while on bail. Sheriff sentenced nine months consecutive on each (three months in each for breach of bail).
Held, excessive as related to same grant of bail, and sentence for nine months on other two quashed and six months substituted.

Nicholson v Lees 1996 SCCR 551—Police assault and driving while disqualified. Charges on two complaints but related to one incident. Sheriff gave six months' consecutive sentence on each.
Held (bench of 5 judges) allowing appeal and ordering sentences to be concurrent: (1) court can impose concurrent or consecutive sentences; (2) where several charges on one complaint (or on more than one complaint for technical reasons) highest custodial sentence is that for charge which carries highest penalty and the same applies where charges on several complaints but fairness requires they be treated as one; (3) no absolute rule that sentence must be concurrent if charges arose out of same course of conduct, and if offences distinctive in nature, time or place the court may consider consecutive sentences appropriate.
Observed, general rule sentences for breach of bail/failing to attend diet should be consecutive.

Young v Friel 1998 GWD 9-443
Held, one-month sentence for breach of bail consecutive to six months for two drugs offences not excessive.

Mackay v McGlennan 1998 GWD 11-541—M received nine months (six months attributable to bail) for threatening witness. *Held*, bail element of sentence was excessive, and three months substituted.

Nicol v Higson 1998 GWD 1-31—Theft/breach of bail.
Held, 24 months excessive since appellant had changed attitude and circumstances, and 18 months substituted by making concurrent the one-month sentences for six failures to appear at diets which had been consecutive.

Compare with:
Nicholson v Lees 1996 SCCR 551
Observed, general rule that sentences for failure to attend to be consecutive.

Ross v Walker 1998 GWD 6-266—Use of weapons. One month each for two offences of failure to appear.
Held, these would be made concurrent as although relating to different complaints they occurred on same day.

Henderson v Munro 1998 GWD 8-372
Held, where four months for theft, and two months consecutive for failure to appear at intermediate diet, sentence not excessive since H knew to inform court, having failed to appear on prior occasions.

JUDICIAL EXAMINATION

When an accused appears on petition he may intimate his wish either to emit or not emit a **declaration.** Whether he does so or not, the prosecutor may then **examine** the accused with a view to eliciting any denial, admission, explanation or justification. The prosecutor may also question the accused on any alleged **confession.**

COMMENTARY	CASE LAW	STATUTE LAW
Declaration Must be entirely the composition of the accused.	*Carmichael v Armitage* 1982 SCCR 475 Accused read a declaration prepared by his solicitor on his instructions. *Held* that declaration was inadmissible, as being more of the nature of a precognition.	Judicial examinations are held in terms of Criminal Procedure (Scotland) Act 1995, ss 35–39 and Chapter 5.5 of the Act of Adjournal (Criminal Procedure Rules) 1996, SI 1996/513. See them for detailed procedures.
Examine The prosecutor may put certain questions to the accused.		Criminal Procedure (Scotland) Act 1995.
		Section 36(5). Questions put by the prosecutor should not be designed to challenge the truth of anything said by the accused; there should be no reiteration of a question which the accused has refused to answer; and there should be no leading questions. The sheriff has the duty to ensure that questions are fairly put to and understood by the accused.
Where the accused declines to answer a question put to him in the examination, his having so declined may be commented on by the prosecutor, judge or any co-accused at subsequent trial even if he declines to answer on the advice of his solicitor.	*McEwan v HMA* 1990 SCCR 401 M giving no response to questions at examination on the advice of his solicitor, gave evidence of an alibi at trial. *Held* on appeal that the judge was allowed to comment on M's silence notwithstanding the legal advice. *Dempsey v HMA* 1995 SCCR 431 *Held*, as appellant not given evidence it was not open to sheriff to pass any comment on silence at judicial examination. *Note*: prosecutor can now comment on accused's failure to give evidence at trial. *McGhee v HMA* 1991 SCCR 510 Murder. At examination M not answering questions regarding an admission he was alleged to have made to the police, on legal advice. Judge commenting that such advice would have been extraordinary if lawyer had known of the proposed alibi defence. *Held* that the judge had gone too far, making comment as to his view of the facts and not relating to the jury M's explanation for not answering. See also: *Moran v HMA* 1990 SCCR 40	Section 36(8). Where the accused declines to answer a question put to him in examination, his having so declined may be commented on by the prosecutor, judge or any co-accused at any subsequent trial, only where accused (or witness called on his behalf) in evidence avers something which could have been stated appropriately in answer to that question. Even if he declines to answer on advice of solicitor. Rule 5.5(4) of Act of Adjournal (Criminal Procedure Rules) 1996, SI 1996/513: 'Trial judge . . . may in determining whether having so declined may be commented on have regard to the terms of the charge to which the questions related.' *Note*: Section 32 of the Criminal Justice (Scotland) Act 1995 repealed s 141(b) of the Criminal Procedure (Scotland) Act 1975. So prosecutor can now comment on accused's failure to lead evidence.

With sheriff's permission, the solicitor for the accused may ask the accused any questions in order to clarify any ambiguity in an answer given by the accused to the prosecutor or to give him an opportunity to answer a question which he has previously refused to answer.

CP(S)A 1995, s 36(7)

Section 36(6). Warning by sheriff: inform accused he has right to consult solicitor before answering any questions; and if answers disclose an ostensible defence the prosecutor shall be under a duty to investigate it to such an extent as reasonably practicable.

Section 36(10), (11). Ostensible defence disclosed: prosecutor under duty to investigate to such extent as reasonably practicable.

Confession

A statement clearly susceptible of being regarded as incriminating.

McKenzie v HMA 1982 SCCR 545
Held that the statement 'Just my luck, I knew I'd be picked out' was clearly a statement susceptible of being regarded as incriminating and thus constituted a 'confession' within the terms of CP(S)A 1975.

Robertson v HMA 1995 SCCR 152; 1996 SCCR 243
Two separate reports dealing with aspects of same case. Failure to comply with provisions for recording declaration.
Held (LJ-C dissenting): this did not render subsequent indictment incompetent, and if accused claimed he suffered grave prejudice he could raise matter by preliminary plea of oppression or during trial.

Reference: Renton and Brown, 5–54.
A useful pamphlet on judicial examination was produced in 1981 by the then Convener of the Criminal Law Committee of the Law Society of Scotland. Copies may be obtained from the Society.

STATUTORY TIME LIMITS

Imposed to prevent undue delay in the commencement of trials.

Solemn procedure: If accused not detained in custody, trial must commence within **12 months** of first appearance on petition. If detained pending liberation in due course of law, indictment must be served within **80 days** of full committal and trial must commence within **110 days** of such full committal.

Summary procedure: If accused detained, trial must commence within **40 days** of bringing of complaint in court. For **statutory offences**, unless otherwise provided, proceedings must commence within **six months** of contravention.

COMMENTARY	CASE LAW	STATUTE LAW
		The question of the time limits for the bringing of a person to trial is essentially regulated by the Criminal Procedure (Scotland) Act 1995, s 65(1) (solemn) and s 136 (summary).
Solemn procedure **Twelve-month** rule. Where accused not detained in custody, trial must commence within 12 months of his first appearance on petition.		**Solemn procedure:** Twelve-month rule regulated by CP(S)A 1995, s 65(1). 'An accused shall not be tried on indictment for any offence unless such trial is commenced within a period of twelve months of the first appearance of that accused on petition in respect of that offence; and, failing such commencement within that period, the accused shall be discharged forthwith and thereafter he shall not at any time be proceeded against on indictment as respects the offence.'
The 12-month period will be extended where the delay is due to the non-appearance of the accused at a diet where a warrant for his arrest has been granted, and the period may also be extended on cause shown.	*McGinty v HMA* 1984 SCCR 176 McG and another first appeared on petition on 20.5.83. Trial arranged for 14.5.84. Last date for service of indictment was 14.4.84. Indictments not served by police. Crown applied for extension of 12-month period. Application granted by sheriff. Appeals dismissed. *Held*, with some hesitation, that sheriff entitled to treat unforeseen illness of policeman responsible for serving indictment as adequate cause for extension. *Observed*, per LJ-G Emslie: '. . . it will not do for the Crown to say that there has not been time to serve an indictment . . . as the result of mere pressure of business.' *Dobbie v HMA* 1986 SCCR 72 An unexpected extra High Court sitting resulted in lack of accommodation for sheriff and jury trial. *Held* that this was not a case of mere pressure of business (see *McGinty v HMA* 1984 SCCR 176) and sheriff entitled to grant extension. See also: *Fleming v HMA* 1992 SCCR 575	For extension of 12-month rule CP(S)A 1995, s 65(1) provides: '(i) Nothing . . . shall bar the trial of an accused for whose arrest a warrant has been granted for failure to appear at a diet in the case; (ii) on application . . . the sheriff or . . . in respect of the High Court, a single judge . . . may on cause shown extend the said period of twelve months.' *Note*: Criminal Procedure and Investigation Act 1996, s 73(3) amends CP(S)A 1995, s 65(1) and specifically provides that the freedom from further process granted in respect of a breach of the 12-month rule is limited to process on indictment, thus overruling *Gardner v Lees* 1996 SCCR 168.

Rudge v HMA 1989 SCCR 105
R appeared on petition on 14.12.87 and indicted for trial on 1.11.88. On 3.11.88 Crown applied for three-month extension on ground of volume of business. Sheriff granted extension.
Held that sheriff entitled to hold that pressure on accommodation could be sufficient reason for extension.
Per LJ-C Ross: '. . . the pressure of business referred to in *McGinty* was pressure of business on the Crown. In the present case the pressure of business is that on accommodation available for holding trials. . . .'

HMA v Swift; Allen v HMA 1984 SCCR 216
S arrested on petition. Indictment prepared. Crown repeatedly failed to serve S with indictment at his domicile of citation. Crown applied for extension of 12-month period. Refused. Crown appealed to High Court. Appeal dismissed.
Held (1)(a) Criminal Procedure (Scotland) Act 1975, s 101 rule is to be departed from only if sufficient reason is shown; (b) nature and degree of fault on Crown's part are relevant; (c) that charges are serious is insufficient reason; (d) sheriff correct to refuse, as only reason offered by Crown was commission of a major error by them.
(2) Shortness of extension requested and little risk of prejudice to the accused are not relevant to consideration of whether sufficient reason shown, but may be relevant to consideration of whether judge should exercise discretion.

Lyle v HMA 1991 SCCR 458
Twelve-month rule. Extension sought and granted. Crown had made a mistake in calculating the date. Overruled on appeal. Rule to be applied except in exceptional circumstances. Mistake in this case inexcusable.

Mejka v HMA 1993 SCCR 978
Twelve-month rule. Crown seeking extension to allow it to try M and his co-accused, who was ill, together.
Held that mere convenience would not justify extension, absence of fault of the Crown not conclusive.

HMA v Davies 1993 SCCR 645
Twelve-month rule. Metropolitan police failed to serve indictment and failed to inform the prosecutor as requested. Extension granted on appeal, prosecutor had no reason to foresee that the police would not comply with his request.

HMA v Brown 1984 SCCR 347
Accused had moved house but had given no notice of this to court. Consequently, they had not received their indictments until shortly before trial, which prejudiced defence preparation. Adjournment granted. Sheriff held that case still to proceed within 12-month period. However, on Crown appeal, extension of three months granted.

Rennie v HMA 1998 SCCR 191
Appellant charged with rape but indicted on a charge of shameless indecency. Plea to relevancy of charge. Sheriff refused leave to amend but granted extension on ground that relevancy raised at last moment and that appellant had opposed Crown motion. Upheld on appeal.

Bennett v HMA 1998 SCCR 23
Held, on appeal, Crown's miscalculation of time-bar period not ground for extension.

HMA v Findlay 1998 SCCR 103
Police 'served' indictment at uncle's address after being told accused no longer lived there. Extension granted since failure to effect service not fault of Crown.

Siddiqi v HMA 1998 SCCR 368
Indictment served at wrong domicile on basis of information from sheriff clerk. Sheriff granted extension. Upheld on appeal.

HMA v Brodie 1996 SCCR 862
Further extension granted, since possibility respondent abroad and extradition proceedings only competent if live proceedings.

Anderson (JJ) v HMA 1996 SCCR 487
Lewd practices. Sheriff clerk's staff gave wrong domicile of citation to prosecutor's staff. Sheriff's decision to grant extension upheld on appeal: reasonable for prosecutor to rely on information.

Ashcroft v HMA 1996 SCCR 608
A and C charged with indecently assaulting 12-year-old girl. Extension granted to allow outcome of C's petition to *nobile officium* (see *X, Petr* 1996 SCCR 436). Further extension granted to enable trial of A and C on same date.
Held, fact that undesirable for complainer to give evidence twice constituted sufficient justification for extension.

Squires v HMA 1996 SCCR 916
On morning of trial Crown told court vital witness ill and unable to travel until next day. Thirty-day extension overturned on appeal.
Held, inquiry should have been made to ascertain likelihood of witness being available later that week or adjourn to next day to ascertain if witness available.

See also
Mair v HMA 1998 SCCR 694
Retrospective extension granted, since essential witness had gone into hiding.

HMA v Sorrie 1996 SCCR 778
Extension granted where productions (bundles of bank notes) stolen from fiscal's office.
Held, not prosecutor's fault and prejudice to defence could be cured by direction of trial judge.

Rodger v Heywood 1996 SCCR 788
As in *HMA v Swift*; *Allen v HMA* 1984 SCCR 216, seriousness of charge not sufficient reason for extension.

But note:

Forrester v HMA 1997 SCCR 9
Extensions granted because of illness of essential Crown witness.
Held, oral evidence was preferable to using hearsay alternative and this was sufficient reason to extend, and whether extension granted or not the seriousness of the offence was a relevant factor.

Compare with:
HMA v Swift; Allen v HMA 1984 SCCR 216
Seriousness is not a sufficient reason to grant
extension, but once sufficient reason exists then
seriousness is issue as to whether or not to use
discretion to grant extension.

HMA v Taylor 1996 SCCR 510
Non-appearance warrant granted, but court officers had directed respondent to wrong court. Re-
indicted after expiry of time limit but sheriff
dismissed.
Held, grant of warrant for failure to appear inter-
rupts 12-month period even if not accused's fault.

HMA v McGill 1997 SCCR 230
Lewd practices alleged to have been committed
between 11 and 21 years earlier. Crown sought
further extension of 12-month period.
Held, extension granted as substantial delay
caused by plea in bar of trial. At trial respondent
acquitted on a submission of no case to answer.

C v Forsyth 1995 SCCR 553
Held, statutory 12-month rule applies only to proceedings on indictment, but even so, not appropriate to authorise private prosecution after lapse of
14 months and reasonable to subject it to similar
constraints, given that private prosecution proceeds in public interest.
Opinion, 110-day rule applies to trials on indictment and to criminal letters.

McKie v HMA 1997 SCCR 30
Lewd conduct. Extension of 12-month period
upheld on appeal where sheriff deserted pro loco
et tempore where he comforted a child witness
who broke down in the course of her evidence and
where prosecutor approached her during adjournment to see if able to continue.

Twelve-month rule does not prevent subsequent summary proceedings on same charge outwith
12-month period.

MacDougall v Russell 1985 SCCR 441
R appeared on petition on 9.5.84, was committed
for trial and liberated on bail. On 13.3.85 a complaint containing the same charges was called
against him in sheriff court. Trial called for 17.6.85
and R tendered plea to competency on ground that
trial not brought within one year of appearance on
petition.
Held that s 101(1) of CP(S)A 1975 should be read
as if the words 'on indictment' were added to it, and
complaint therefore competent.

Twelve-month rule can be retrospectively extended.

HMA v M 1986 SCCR 624
M appeared on petition on 26.9.85. Second indictment served for trial on 22.9.86. On 15.9.86 indictment dismissed as irrelevant. Crown appealed and
appeal upheld on 24.10.86.
Held that it was competent to extend 12-month
period retrospectively and trial diet postponed for
three months. Reasoning in *Farrell v HMA*, 1984
SCCR 301, followed.

McDowall v Lees 1996 SCCR 719

Langan v Normand 1997 SCCR 306

80-day rule.

If an accused is detained in custody being committed for trial until liberated in courts of law, the indictment must be served upon him within 80 days of such committal, otherwise he has to be released, although the Crown can still proceed against him on the charges.

HMA v Walker and Ors 1981 SCCR 154
Accused committed for trial. Indictment which was served within the 80-day period was not called for trial. A second indictment in the same terms as the first was served outwith the 80-day period.
Held, on appeal, that since the original indictment had fallen, there was no valid indictment served within the 80-day period and accused must be liberated.

80-day rule regulated by CP(S)A 1995, s 65(4)(a). An accused who is committed for any offence until liberated in due course of law shall not be detained . . . for a total period of more than (a) eighty days, unless within that period the indictment is served on him, which failing he shall be liberated forthwith. . . .'

The 80-day rule may be extended for any sufficient cause; however, not if the delay is due to some fault by the prosecution.

Farrell v HMA 1984 SCCR 301
Indictments served within 80 days and trial commenced within 110 days. However, due to illness of prosecution witness, trial abandoned. Crown petition for extension of both periods granted by Lord Justice-Clerk and, on appeal, decision upheld by High Court. Notable in that extension of 80-day period granted retrospectively.

McCluskey v HMA 1992 SCCR 920
Eighty-day rule. First indictment within 80 days but not called, second indictment outwith 80 days. Conviction upheld on appeal. Section 101 of CP(S)A 1975 deals only with detention, not with the validity of indictment.

Exception under CP(S)A 1995, s 65(5), (6). 'A single judge of the High Court may . . . for any sufficient cause extend the period. . . . Provided that he shall not extend the said period if he is satisfied that, but for some fault on the part of the prosecution, the indictment could have been served within that period.'

110-day rule.

Where an accused is detained in custody having been fully committed for trial, the trial must actually commence within 110 days of such committal, and if it does not the accused has to be released and the Crown cannot proceed against him any further on these charges.

110-day rule regulated by CP(S)A 1995, s 65(4) '. . . an accused who is committed . . . until liberated in due course of law shall not be detained . . . for a total period of more than . . . (b) 110 days, unless the trial of the case is commenced within that period, which failing he shall be liberated forthwith and thereafter he shall be for ever free from all question or process for that offence.'

The 110-day rule can be extended if the delay is due to the illness or absence of certain vital personnel, or to any other sufficient cause not due to an error of the prosecution.

Gildea v HMA 1983 SCCR 114; 1983 SLT 458
Extension of 110-day period granted because of 'time-tabling, administrative difficulties and pressures'.
Held, on appeal, that extension justified.
Per LJ-G Emslie: 'The Crown undoubtedly took a calculated risk. . . . The question is whether the decision to take that risk was unreasonable. . . .'

See also:
Farrell v HMA 1984 SCCR 301

X, Petr 1996 SCCR 436
Bail condition that child reside in secure unit of List D school. Child transferred to open accommodation at request of Crown after 109 days, but school refused permission to leave.
Held, child detained beyond 110 days, but that detention by attitude of school influenced by considerations unconnected with warrant. Appeal refused.

See also:
Thomson v HMA 1996 SCCR 671

Exception under CP(S)A 1995, s 65(7) 'A single judge of the High Court may . . . extend the period . . . where he is satisfied that delay in the commencement of the trial is due to:
(a) the illness of the accused or of a judge;
(b) the absence or illness of any necessary witness; or
(c) any other sufficient cause which is not attributable to any fault on the part of the prosecutor.'

HMA v Muir 1997 SCCR 677
Accused released on bail after 105 days but failed to appear at diet and warrant issued. He was arrested and Crown applied for extension to 110 days, which judge refused as unnecessary. On appeal, extension granted, since under CP(S)A 1995, s 65(4) the total of the separate periods of detention must not exceed 110 days.

Beattie v HMA 1995 SCCR 606
Trial judge not available to sit in Inverness beyond 19 May and granted extension. Reversed on appeal, because extensions not to be permitted to suit convenience of court administrators and trial judge under responsibility to see if court could make alternative arrangements.
Observed, test to extend 110-day period more exacting than that in regard to 12-month rule.

HMA v Lewis 1992 SCCR 22
L convicted and sentenced in Scotland, transferred to England under s 26(1) of the Criminal Justice Act 1961, escaped and came back to Scotland where after more offences he was caught and committed. Detained beyond 110 days before trial. Crown argued he was being held under the sentence of imprisonment.
Held that the imprisonment to be treated as imposed by the English court, time exceeded and indictment dismissed.

See also:
HMA v Lang 1992 SCCR 642

Appeals for all solemn cases.

Appeal under CP(S)A 1995, s 65(8). 'The grant or refusal of any application to extend the periods mentioned . . . may be appealed against by note of appeal presented to the High Court. . . .'

Commencement of trial.

Commencement of trial under CP(S)A 1995, s 65(9). '. . . a trial shall be taken to commence when the oath is administered to the jury.'

If accused detained successively on full committal warrants, the 110 days run separately and in parallel.

Ross v HMA 1990 SCCR 182
R detained on 20.2.89 in respect of certain charges. Committed for certain other offences on 23.3.89. Indicted on all charges. Trial due to commence 18.6.89 being more than 110 days after 20.2.89. Charges in respect of 20.2.89 committal dismissed but March charges not time barred.

40-day rule.

In the case of summary complaints where an accused is detained in custody his trial must commence within 40 days of the bringing of the complaint in court, otherwise, as with the 110-day rule for solemn procedure, he must be set free and the Crown cannot proceed against him on those charges.

Brawls v Walkingshaw 1994 SCCR 7

Forty-day rule. B released on bail under the condition that he remain within the curtilage of his house. Took plea to the competency of proceedings on the basis that this was in effect detention and 40 days exceeded. Sheriff repelled pleas. Upheld on appeal. Condition did not involve an outside agency and relied on the accused's own willingness to abide by it. Such a condition should be used only exceptionally.

Kerr v Carnegie 1998 SCCR 168

Decision of Crown not to proceed on complaint on which extension granted but to raise fresh complaint.

Held, since not deserted there was throughout warrant for the detention of complainer; the time limit for detention applied to proceedings in respect of the same offence; no question of warrant for detention expiring prior to trial; and no reason for regarding service of second complaint as oppressive.

Summary procedure

Forty-day rule regulated by CP(S)A 1995 s 147(1). 'A person charged with a summary offence shall not be detained in that respect for a total of more than 40 days after the bringing of the complaint in court unless his trial is commenced within that period, failing which he shall be liberated forthwith and thereafter he shall be for ever free from all question or process for that offence.'

Again, as with the 110-day rule, the 40-day rule may be extended where the delay is due to illness or absence of vital personnel, or for any other sufficient cause not due to the fault of the prosecution.

Exception under CP(S)A 1995, s 147(2). 'The sheriff may [on application made to him] extend the period . . . for such period as he thinks fit where he is satisfied that delay in the commencement of the trial is due to

(a) the illness of the accused or of a judge;

(b) the absence or illness of any necessary witness; or

(c) any other sufficient cause which is not attributable to any fault on the part of the prosecutor.'

Appeals.

Appeals under CP(S)A 1995, s 147(3). 'The grant or refusal of any application to extend the period mentioned in subsection (1) may be appealed against by note of appeal presented to the High Court. . . .'

Commencement of trial.

Commencement of trial under CP(S)A 1995, s 147(4). '. . . a trial shall be taken to commence when the first witness is sworn.'

Statutory offences
Six-month rule.
In the case of statutory contraventions, unless the statute otherwise provides, proceedings must be commenced within six months of the contravention. If there is continuous contravention the last contravening point shall be taken for the application of the six-month rule, and the whole continuous contravention shall be chargeable.

Certain additional evidence may be considered.

Commencement of proceedings—requirement that there be no undue delay in execution of warrant.

Tudhope v Lawson 1983 SCCR 435 (Sh Ct)
Offence against Trade Descriptions Act 1968. Summary proceedings 'may be commenced at any time within twelve months from the time when the offence was committed' (s 19(3) Trade Descriptions Act 1968). Date of offence was 28.6.82, proceedings commenced on 28.6.83. L pleaded proceedings incompetent as not having been commenced within prescriptive period.
Held, that in computing period, date of offence not to be taken into account, and complaint competent.

Hamilton v HMA 1996 SCCR 744
Trade Descriptions Act 1968, s 19. Petition warrant obtained within one year, but indictment served outwith one year.
Held, prosecution commenced as soon as warrant granted by court and appeal refused.

See also:

Gray v Normand 1994 SCCR 794

Young v Smith 1981 SCCR 85; 1981 SLT (Notes) 101
Offences against Road Traffic Act 1972. Y appeared voluntarily at court and complaint was served on him there. Convicted. Appeal on ground that proceedings time-barred because warrant not executed, dismissed.
Held, that warrant had not been executed, but requirement for warrant to be executed without undue delay applies only where warrant requires to be and is enforced, and does not apply where, in absence of undue delay on prosecutor's part, the need for execution is elided by the voluntary act of the accused which achieves the entire objective of the warrant.

Chow v Lees 1997 SCCR 253
Offences allegedly committed on 6.12.95. Warrant granted for arrest on 5.6.96 but not executed. Instead, PF wrote and said warrant would not be executed if he appeared at court on 27.6.96. Letter written on 12.6.96 but not posted until 18.6.96. Sheriff held that, since warrant not executed, the question of delay did not arise. Overturned on appeal, and case remitted to sheriff to consider whether undue delay.

Singh v Vannet 1998 SCCR 679
Warrant sent to police HQ on 14.5.98 and received between 15.5.98 and 18.5.98. Sent to local police office on 18.5.98; returned to HQ on 19.5.98 to dispatch to division on 22.5.98. Arrived there on 22.5.98 (holiday weekend). Reached warrants officer on 26.5.98 and executed on 29.5.98. Upheld on appeal: no undue delay, since not fault of PF.

Harvey v Lockhart 1991 SCCR 83
Held on appeal that when considering the question of undue delay, a sheriff should hear evidence from the Crown on its justification for delay.

Six-month rule.

CP(S)A 1995, s 136(1). Proceedings in respect of any offence to which this section applies shall be commenced within six months after the contravention occurred and, in the case of a continuous contravention, within six months after the last date of such contravention, and it shall be competent to include the entire period during which the contravention occurred.

Section 136(2). This section applies to any offence triable only summarily and consisting of the contravention of any enactment, unless the enactment fixes a different time limit.

Section 136(3). Proceedings shall be deemed to be commenced on the date on which a warrant to apprehend or to cite the accused is granted, if the warrant is executed without undue delay.

Melville v Normand 1996 GWD 10-542
A combination of public holidays, the warrant being
sent to the wrong police office and execution being
delayed by police until conclusion of accused's
High Court trial on other charges.
Held, undue delay not established (the last reason
viewed as a sound one).

Alexander v Normand 1997 SLT 370
Delay of 13 days before issuing the warrant to
police where time bar two months away, followed
by three abortive attempts to execute warrant.
Undue delay not established.

MacDonald v HL Friel & Sons Ltd 1995 SCCR 461
(Sh Ct)
Control of Pollution Act 1974, s 16. Prosecution
subject to six-month time limit.
Held, period interrupted by appeal but resumed
once appeal determined and six months had
expired.

*Summary-Smith v Peter Walker and Son
(Edinburgh) Ltd* 1978 JC 44
Per LJ-G Emslie: 'The expression "without undue
delay" implies that there has been no slackness on
his part and that any delay in execution is due to
some circumstance for which he is not responsible, eg the conduct of the accused.'

McGlennan v Singh 1993 SCCR 341
Undue delay. Fourteen days delay, some of which
was due to the sheriff clerk's office. Sheriff said
occasionally extraordinary measures were
required to commence prosecutions.
Held on appeal that no special or unusual measures require to be taken, nothing to show that
delay the fault of the prosecutor.

Tudhope v Mathieson 1981 SCCR 231
Contravention of Road Traffic Act 1972 on 11.1.81.
Warrant for arrest granted on 19.3.81. Prosecutor
did not enforce warrant during period of strike
(23.3–10.8.81) by court clerks and other civil ser-
vants on court staff. M arrested on 24.8.81. Took
plea to competency of complaint on ground that it
was time-barred.
Held, that latitude given to prosecutors by CP(S)A
1975, s 331(3) did not extend to situation where
prosecutor could have executed warrant timeously,
but made conscious decision not to do so in order
to encumber limited court facilities with cases of
type in question. Complaint dismissed as incompetent.

Tudhope v Brown 1984 SCCR 163 (Sh Ct)
Statutory contraventions up to 24.9.83. On 19.3.84
sheriff assigned 30.3.84 as diet. Complaint served
on *first* accused by police on 26.3.84. Accused
pleaded proceedings were time-barred.
Held, that there had been undue delay. It was
irrelevant that citation executed more than 48
hours before assigned diet; complaint dismissed
as incompetent.
Statutory contraventions up to 24.9.83. On 19.3.84
sheriff assigned 30.3.84 as diet. Complaint served
on *second* accused on 21.3.84. Delay was
explained by reference to normal police procedure
for serving citations.
Held, no undue delay. Plea to competency
repelled.

Beattie v Tudhope 1984 SCCR 198; 1984 SLT 423
Contravention of Trade Descriptions Act 1968,
s 1(1)(b). Offence allegedly committed on 18.2.82.
Prosecutor obtained warrant to cite on 17.2.83
(prescriptive period is 12 months for this offence).
Citation served personally, but due to intervention
of weekend, this took six days. Sheriff held no
undue delay. B's appeal dismissed.
Held, that question was one of fact, circumstances
and degree for sheriff, 'that being so, we are
unable to say that in arriving at his decision, he
exercised his discretion in any manner which
would justify us in disturbing his conclusion.'

McCartney v Tudhope 1985 SCCR 373
Road traffic offences allegedly committed on
13.12.84. Prescriptive period ended on 13.6.85.
Warrant to cite obtained by prosecutor on 11.6.85
and handed to police on 13.6.85, but not executed
until 25.6.85. Magistrate decided no undue delay
in execution. On appeal, however, delay held
unreasonable. Excessive workload of policeman
responsible for serving warrant not in itself sufficient to justify delay in absence of any details as to
his work priorities.
Per LJ-C Ross: '. . . I am of opinion that the
stipendiary magistrate did not have material before
him to justify his concluding that the delay was not
undue.'

Buchan v McNaughtan 1990 SCCR 688
Undue delay. B at sea, police not leaving citation
with wife so as to cite personally.
Held on appeal that as it would not have been
quicker to leave citation with wife then there was
no undue delay.

Anderson v Lowe 1991 SCCR 712
Undue delay. Delay in sheriff clerk's office getting
a warrant to the prosecutor.
Held not to be the fault of the prosecutor. No decision on what would have happened had the prosecutor been aware of the warrant.

References: Hume II, 136; Alison II, 96; Macdonald, 211; Renton and Brown, 7–36 and 14–10.

SPECIAL DEFENCES

The special defences of alibi, impeachment or incrimination, insanity, self-defence, automatism and coercion are those which, if established in relation to a relevant charge, are a complete answer to that charge.

GENERAL

COMMENTARY	CASE LAW	STATUTE LAW
Proof of special defences generally.	*Lambie v HMA* 1973 JC 53 Per LJ-G Emslie: 'The only purpose of the special defence is to give fair notice to the Crown ... When a special defence is pleaded ... the jury should be charged in the appropriate language and all that requires to be said of the special defence ... is that if the evidence is believed or creates in the minds of the jury reasonable doubt as to the guilt of, the accused ... they must acquit'. *McDonald v HMA; Valentine v McDonald* 1989 SCCR 165 McD indicted for trial in sheriff court. Purported to lodge a notice under s 82(1) of CP(S)A 1975 of defence to the effect that the indictment was a vindictive and vexatious prosecution brought because of the knowledge of the procurator fiscal and police officers of his wrongful conviction in 1986, and was an attempt to prevent or delay him in exposing their criminal conspiracy. *Held* inter alia that as what was contained in the purported CP(S)A 1975, s 82(1) notice would not necessarily result in acquittal of accused even if established, it did not constitute a special defence in terms of that subsection, and proposed defence was irrelevant. *O'Connell v HMA* 1996 SCCR 614 (see Competent Evidence) *Held*, in terms of s 307(1) of CP(S)A 1995, first diet in s 78 included any continuation thereof, and since substitute special defence in proper form and duly lodged in terms of s 78(3) it ought to have been received, and cause did not require to be shown.	Criminal Procedure (Scotland) Act 1995 Section 78. Plea of special defence to be lodged in a High Court case with the clerk of justiciary and intimated to Crown Agent and to any accused and his solicitor not later than 10 days before the trial diet; in a sheriff court case with sheriff clerk and intimated to the procurator fiscal and to any co-accused or his solicitor at or before the first diet (unless in any case the court, on cause shown, otherwise directs). Section 78 applies to alibi, incrimination, insanity, self-defence, automatism and coercion.

ALIBI

This **special defence** is that at the time of the alleged offence the accused was **not at the locus libelled but at some other specified place**.

COMMENTARY	CASE LAW	STATUTE LAW
A **special defence** intimates that the defence evidence will be of a certain specific nature: the burden of proof is unaltered.	*HMA v Hayes* 1973 SLT 202 Posting packet containing explosives. Special defences of alibi and incrimination. Per Lord Cameron: 'The purpose of a special defence in Scots law is to give to the prosecution proper notice of a particular line which the defence of an accused person may take . . . there is no obligation on an accused person to establish that special defence under a penalty that if he fails to do so then conviction would follow.'	Criminal Procedure (Scotland) Act 1995
	Fraser v HMA 1982 SCCR 458 Assault and robbery. Special defence that F was in public house at time of crimes. Convicted. On appeal conviction sustained. Opinion of the court: '. . . we disagree with the inherent proposition that a judge is bound to give proper and clear direction with regard to the nature, purport and effect of the special defence of alibi. The simple reason is that the special defence has played all the part it has to play in the trial when it has given notice to the Crown of a possible line of evidence which will or may be held on behalf of an accused person.'	**Summary procedure:** Section 149. Notice of intention to lead alibi evidence to be given to prosecutor before first witness is sworn. Notice to be given with particulars as to time and place and of the witnesses by whom it is proposed to prove it. The prosecutor is entitled to an adjournment.
	Gilmour v HMA 1982 SCCR 590 Murder and rape. Special defence that accused was at home alone. Convicted. Per trial judge, Lord Dunpark: 'Now, before I turn to the charge in this case let me just dismiss this so-called special defence of alibi which was read to you at the outset. It is miscalled a special defence because there is no onus on the accused, and I think you should ignore the alibi so-called special defence in this case, because if you believe the evidence of the accused that he was alone in his house between two and four o'clock on 4th November 1981, you would acquit him; and if you were left with a reasonable doubt about that you would also acquit him.' Appeal against conviction dismissed. Per LJ-C Wheatley: 'That direction was in line with current practice, and, rather than constituting prejudice to the appellant, it was to his advantage. We need say no more on that, and in the result we reject both branches of this ground of appeal.'	
	Balsillie v HMA 1993 SCCR 760 Theft by housebreaking. Sheriff not allowing B's explanation as to his whereabouts at the relevant time because no notice of special defence lodged. *Held* on appeal that notice not required where B was saying he was at the locus but did not go into the house. Only where accused saying he was at a specified other place was notice required.	
At the time of the alleged offence the accused was **not at the locus libelled but at some other specified place**. 'The plea is not conclusive unless the alibi . . . makes it not only unlikely but impossible that the [accused] could have done the deed at the time and place libelled' (Alison II, 624).	*William and Alex Fraser* 1720 Hume II, 411 Fire raising. Alibi evidence that accused were in bed at 11 pm on night libelled, and on morning following, disregarded.	

References: Hume II, 410; Alison II, 624; Macdonald,265; Renton and Brown, 7–20 and 7–21.

IMPEACHMENT OR INCRIMINATION

This is a **special defence** that the offence was committed not by the accused but by another person, named if known. It is **competent** to call a **co-accused** as a witness.

COMMENTARY	CASE LAW	STATUTE LAW
A **special defence** intimates that the defence evidence will be of a certain, specific nature; the burden of proof is unaltered.	*Lambie v HMA* 1973 JC 53; 1973 SLT 219 Theft. Others named as responsible for crime. Per LJ-G Emslie: 'The only purpose of the special defence is to give fair notice to the Crown. . . . When a special defence is pleaded . . . the jury should be charged in the appropriate language, and all that requires to be said of the special defence, where . . . evidence in support of it has been given is that if that evidence . . . is believed, or creates in the minds of the jury reasonable doubt as to the guilt of the accused . . . they must acquit.'	
Specific reference to the special defence by the judge is unnecessary if the significance of all the evidence, including the special defence, is brought to the jury's attention.	*Mullen v HMA* 1978 SLT (Notes) 33 Rape. Defence claim that crime committed by principal Crown witness. Convicted. Appeal on misdirection refused. Per LJ-C Wheatley: 'It does not follow that failure by the trial judge to make specific reference in terms to such a special defence necessarily amounts to a misdirection such as to vitiate a conviction.' But contrast: *Donnelly v HMA* 1977 SLT 147 Assault and robbery. Special defence of incrimination. See also: *Mackie v HMA* 1990 SCCR 716 *Collins v HMA* 1991 SCCR 898	
Co-accused's evidence is **competent.**	*HMA v Ferrie* 1983 SCCR 1 Murder and serious assaults. One of the accused, Y, pled guilty to one of the assault charges. Subsequently the prosecution called Y as a witness against his co-accused. Per trial judge, Lord Stewart: '. . . the advocate-depute may call the witness subject only to any representations about delay in such call to enable the taking of defence precognitions . . . the conclusion reached [is] the witness may be called.' *McQuade v HMA* 1996 SCCR 347 *Held,* on appeal, a notice of incrimination not necessary, since evidence could not have secured the appellant's acquittal (see Competent evidence for facts).	Criminal Procedure (Scotland) Act 1995 Co-accused compellable only when giving evidence or pleading guilty: s 266(9), (10). If co-accused gives evidence, an accused may cross-examine and if co-accused pleads guilty (sentenced or not) prosecutor or defence may call him as a witness without notice. Section 266(1), (2). Accused a competent defence witness whether on trial alone or with co-accused but only upon own application.
There is no onus to prove a special defence of impeachment.	*Lambie v HMA* 1973 JC 53; 1973 SLT 219 Per LJ-G Emslie: '. . . we have come to be of opinion that the references in [earlier cases] of *Lennie* and *Owens* to there being an onus upon the defence were unsound. It follows that [this] can now be regarded as an accurate statement of the law only in the case of the plea of insanity at the time.'	

References: Macdonald, 265, 317; Renton and Brown, 7–21 and 18–92.

INSANITY

Insanity at the time of commission of offence

At the time of commission of offence. Where accused is found to have committed the actus reus of the offence but to have been insane at the time he may not be convicted of the offence.

COMMENTARY	CASE LAW	STATUTE LAW
'. . . an absolute alienation of reason . . . such a disease as deprives the patient of the knowledge of the true aspect and position of things . . . hinders him from distinguishing friend or foe,—and gives him up to the impulse of his own distempered fancy' (Hume I, 37).	*HMA v Kidd* 1960 JC 61 K murdered wife and child and pled special defence of insanity at time of offence. *Held* to be insane at time of offence. Per Lord Strachan: 'Must have been some mental defect . . . by which his reason was overpowered and he was thereby rendered incapable of exerting his reason to control his conduct and reactions.'	Criminal Procedure (Scotland) Act 1995 New procedure: see Insanity in bar of trial section for details of examination of facts and disposals. Section 54(6) deals with the special defence of insanity at the time of the offence. Where insanity plea in bar of trial and accused acquitted court shall direct jury to find (and court shall state in summary procedure) whether accused insane at time of offence and whether acquitted on account of his insanity at that time.
At the time of commission of offence Accused may be insane with regard to one area of his life while appearing lucid in all others.	*HMA v Sharp* 1927 JC 66 *HMA v Kidd* 1960 JC 61 Per Lord Strachan: 'If his reason was alienated in relation to the act committed he was not responsible for that act, even although otherwise he may have been apparently quite rational.'	
Self-induced intoxication is not a foundation for a special defence of insanity.	*Brennan v HMA* 1977 SLT 151 B convicted of murdering his father. Defence of insanity on ground of acute intoxication rejected. Opinion of the court: 'There is nothing unethical or unfair or contrary to the general principle of our law that self-induced intoxication is not by itself defence to a criminal charge.' See also: *Smith v M* 1983 SCCR 67 (Sh Ct) Accused was charged in the sheriff court with assault and breach of the peace. Facts of the case not disputed. Defence was that he was insane at the time. He was not suffering from mental disorder at the time of the trial. Sheriff accepted the defence and acquitted the accused. *Held* that CP(S)A 1975, s 376(3) had no application to a person acquitted on grounds of insanity and no hospital order could be made. Only disposal was a simple acquittal. See also: *Ebsworth v HMA* 1992 SCCR 671	

Note: Automatism

Ross v HMA 1991 SCCR 823
Assault. Non-insane automatism, spiked drink—involuntary intoxication.
Held (Five-judge bench), automatism due to an external factor (not disease of the mind), which is not self-induced and which leads to total alienation of reason amounting to a complete absence of self control, is something which the accused is not bound to foresee and is a defence. Crown must always establish mens rea. *HMA v Cunningham* 1963 JC 80; *Clark v HMA* 1968 JC 53 and *Carmichael v Boyle* 1985 SCCR 58 overruled as far as they hold that any mental condition short of insanity relevant only to mitigation.

See also:

Cardle v Mulrainey 1992 SCCR 658

Sorley v HMA 1992 SCCR 396
Automatism, spiked drink. Held that the evidence fell far short of what will be sufficient for this defence. Need expert evidence on state of the accused, total loss of control backed up by eye witnesses.

See also:

MacLeod v Napier 1993 SCCR 303

References: Hume I, 37; Alison I, 664; Macdonald, 265; Gordon, 347; Gane and Stoddart, 291.

Insanity in bar of trial

Insanity in bar of trial. If a person is **insane** at the time of his trial he cannot be tried, whether or not he was insane at the time of the alleged crime. Insanity in this instance is based on accused's **unfitness to plead**. However, a successful plea **cannot be treated as an acquittal.**

COMMENTARY	CASE LAW	STATUTE LAW
Insane Criteria for insanity are based on accused's 'unfitness to plead' and not on those elements regarded in insanity as a special defence.		Criminal Procedure (Scotland) Act 1995, ss 54–56 New procedure. Briefly, when the court finds accused is currently insane in bar of trial (on the evidence of two medical practitioners) the court has to hold an examination of facts pending the completion of which the court remands the accused on bail or commits him under a temporary hospital order. The purpose of the examination of facts is to determine whether the accused carried out the actus reus. Section 55. If it is not proved beyond reasonable doubt that the accused did the act, or there is ground for acquitting him (on the balance of probabilities) then he must be acquitted. If the ground for acquitting is insanity at the time of the offence then this must be stated (s 55(4)). Section 55(2). If proved accused did act and there are no grounds for acquitting the court shall make a finding to this effect (this is not a conviction).
Unfitness to plead A person is unfit to plead if he is incapable of understanding the charge and the proceedings or of properly instructing his defence.	*HMA v Brown* (1907) 5 Adam 312 Charged with murder of woman who had eaten poisoned shortbread intended for someone else. Jury found B to be now insane. Per Lord Dunedin: Accused must be able to 'maintain in sober sanity his plea of innocence and instruct those who defend him as a truly sane man would do'. *HMA v Wilson* 1942 JC 75 Per Lord Wark: 'A man is not fit to be tried if he cannot from mental or physical defect tell his counsel what his defence is and cannot instruct his counsel to defend him, or if he does not understand the proceedings and cannot intelligibly follow what it is all about.'	
An accused may be perfectly lucid in relation to all other matters but insane with regard to the subject-matter of the charge against him.	*HMA v Sharp* 1927 JC 66 S, otherwise intelligent and lucid, had an obsessional disorder in relation to conditions and matters regarding his family. Charged with murder of his two children. Found unfit to plead.	

Exceptionally the judge may call upon the accused to plead, leaving it to the jury to say that he is capable of pleading.

HMA v Wilson 1942 JC 75
Lord Wark's direction to the jury: 'No plea has been taken on behalf of the accused that he is unfit to plead; indeed, . . . it is to be maintained on his behalf that he is fit to do so, but the evidence which you will hear . . . will show that his mental and physical condition is such as to raise a question as to whether any plea can be accepted from him. . . .'

Mere loss of memory by an otherwise sane person is not, however, sufficient for a plea in bar.

Russell v HMA 1946 JC 37
R was charged with a series of frauds. Pleaded in bar of trial that she had suffered from hysterical amnesia covering the period of four years in which the offences took place.
Held that this amnesia was no ground for plea in bar of trial.
Per Lord Sorn: 'It is enough if the accused is sane and normal now, and can rationally tell her advisers all that she knows about her defence and follow the proceedings.'

Mental deficiency alone does not constitute a bar to trial, although the question will depend on the degree of the deficiency and its effect on the accused's ability to understand.

HMA v Breen 1921 JC 30

McLachlan v Brown 1997 SCCR 457
Theft of bottle of vodka by accused alleged to be mentally handicapped, but plea tendered at common law (evidence led by psychologists) and not in terms of CP(S)A 1995, s 54(1).
Held, no place at common law for plea and CP(S)A 1995, s 54(1) applied and court could sustain plea only where satisfied that person insane from the evidence of two medical practitioners.

HMA v Wilson 1942 JC 75
W almost completely deaf and dumb and feeble-minded, making it difficult for him to communicate. High Court accepted that a deaf-mute could be regarded as unfit to plead although in this case accused was allowed to plead.

Barr v Herron 1968 JC 20
Finding of unfitness to plead by reason of mental deficiency accepted by appeal court.

Stewart v HMA (No 1) 1997 SCCR 330
Charged with three charges of rape and seven charges of lewd practices between 1983 and 1993 against four complainers. Evidence that accused was suggestible and had poor concentration but understood what accused of and could tender plea and instruct counsel what defence was. Upheld on appeal that appellant fit to plead.

Stewart v HMA (No 2) 1997 SLT 1056
Held, nothing in CP(S)A 1995 which excluded an accused's right to submit a plea of insanity in bar of trial at a preliminary diet following service of a fresh indictment, despite such a plea being unsuccessful in respect of a previous indictment.

Cannot be treated as an acquittal
Accused cannot be treated as having tholed his assize.

Where a case is remitted from a lower court because there are doubts about fitness to plead by accused.

HMA v Bickerstaff 1926 JC 65
B insane and unfit to plead. Regained sanity, whereupon he was tried.

Herron v McCrimmon 1969 SLT (Sh Ct) 37
Accused pled guilty in the police court to breach of the peace and was remanded in custody for probation and psychiatric reports. Case was deserted pro loco and remitted to the sheriff court.
Held, that a plea of res judicata could not succeed since no sentence had been pronounced.

Disposals
CP(S)A 1995, s 57 applies to insanity as defence (s 54(5)) and insanity in bar of trial (where finding made at examination of facts that he committed act and no grounds for acquitting him).

Note: If accused found insane in bar of trial he will be acquitted simpliciter if finding under CP(S)A 1995, s 55(2) not made at examination of facts.

Section 57(2). In all cases other than murder the court may, as it thinks fit, make:
(a) a hospital order;
(b) a restriction order without limit of time, along with (a) above;
(c) a guardianship order;
(d) a supervision and treatment order (new type of order detailed in CP(S)A 1995, Sch 4);
(e) no order.

Section 57(3). Where the offence is murder the court shall make orders under para (a) and (b) of subsection 2 in respect of that person.

Prosecutor may raise unfitness
If the accused has not stated a plea in bar of trial the prosecutor may bring forward evidence of accused's mental condition.

Jessop v Robertson 1989 SCCR 600 (Sh Ct)
R charged with fraud. Prosecutor submitted report from psychiatrist to effect that she was mentally disordered.
Held, inter alia, that there was an onus on any person alleging unfitness by reason of insanity to satisfy the court by corroborated evidence on the balance of probabilities.

Solemn procedure:
Under CP(S)A 1995, s 67 accused to have intimation of two medical practitioners who may give evidence for Crown of insanity. If the defence wish to raise the issue then they must intimate the details of the two medical practitioners: s 78(4).

Summary procedure:
No duty on the Crown to intimate the issue in advance of the trial.

Section 57(4). The accused is under a duty to give notice of plea of insanity in bar of trial before the first witness is sworn, notice to include details of witnesses and court can adjourn on prosecutor's motion.

Sufficiency of medical evidence
Section 61. A report under s 54 in writing purporting to be signed by a medical practitioner may be received in evidence without proof of the signature or the qualifications of the practitioner, but court may require signatory to give oral evidence.

Appeals
Section 62. Appeal by accused in solemn and summary cases to appeal to High Court against any findings, the refusal to make a finding, that the accused is insane in bar if trial, and orders and findings made at examination of facts. See s 62(2) for time limits of appeals. (These vary with each ground of appeal.)

Section 63 provides the Crown with similar rights of appeal as that given to accused under s 62, but only on point of law. (See s 60 and s 60A for provision detailing appeals against hospital orders.)

References: Hume I, 37; Alison I, 644; Macdonald, 271; Gordon, 376; Gane and Stoddart, 301.

SENTENCING POLICY

Duff v HMA 1983 SCCR 461—Murder charge. D pled guilty to culpable homicide. Suffering from diminished responsibility. Life imprisonment. Sentence appealed.
Held that sentence in the best interests of appellant—as under life sentence, position reviewed from time to time—and in best interest of public. Appeal failed.

SELF-DEFENCE

The use of **reasonable force** against a person is **not criminal** if done in **self-defence** or **defence of others. Provocation** is not such a defence.

COMMENTARY	CASE LAW	STATUTE LAW
Reasonable force Retaliation must not exceed what is necessary in the circumstances although the matter will not be weighed too finely by the law.	*Fraser v Skinner* 1975 SLT (Notes) 84 F, a police officer, 'handed off' an aggressive motorist stopped for speeding believing himself to be under attack. Opinion of the court: 'It is only *cruel excess* which will defeat a plea of self-defence.' *HMA v Doherty* 1954 JC 1 Culpable homicide. C attacked D with a hammer and D responded by striking C in the face with a bayonet supplied to him during the affray by another. Defence of self-defence fell and D convicted of culpable homicide and sentenced to twelve months' imprisonment. Per Lord Keith's charge to the jury: 'Let me remind you ... of the limits of self-defence ... two fundamental things you will keep in mind, that there is imminent danger to life and limb and that the retaliation used is necessary for the safety of the man threatened.' *Whyte v HMA* 1996 SCCR 575 Accused punched victim as thought complainer going to punch mother. He admitted using excessive force and said he did not mean to. Conviction quashed on appeal as should have been left to jury, since excessive blow due to error of judgment in circumstances where hard to judge how strong the blow needed to be. Per LJ-G Hope: 'It is always difficult to judge precisely the force with which a blow may strike a victim.' *Hillan v HMA* 1937 JC 53 Assault. H accused of a minor assault. However, he claimed he was merely acting in self-defence, the case having a sexual connotation. *Held*, on appeal, that H had been acting in self-defence and acquitted. Per Lord Wark, quoting Hume: 'In deciding on pleas of this sort the judge will not insist on an exact proportion of injury and retaliation, but rather be disposed to sustain the defence unless the panel has been transported to acts of cruelty or great excess.' But see: *Crawford v HMA* 1950 JC 67; 1950 SLT 279 *Friel v HMA* 1998 SCCR 47 In direction on self-defence trial judge made no reference to making allowance for heat of the moment. *Held*, no misdirection.	
Cruel excess of violence used.	*Fenning v HMA* 1985 SCCR 219 F killed P on a fishing trip. Alleged that P had become suspicious that there was a relationship between F and deceased's wife. P had thus threatened F with knife and in response F smashed P's head several times with rock. On appeal conviction for murder upheld as there was cruel excess of violence used. Per trial judge Lord Mayfield: '. . . there must be no cruel excess of violence on the accused's part.'	

Where there is a mistaken apprehension of danger, a plea of self-defence is not defeated if there are reasonable grounds for the belief.

Owens v HMA 1946 JC 119
Murder. O killed a man whom he maintained he believed to have had a dangerous object in his hand when he sprang at O. On appeal, conviction quashed.
Per LJ-C Normand: 'Self-defence is made out when it is established . . . that the panel believed he was in imminent danger and that he held that belief on reasonable grounds. Grounds for such a belief may exist though they are founded on a genuine mistake of fact.'

HMA v Kay 1970 SLT (Notes) 66
Murder. K killed her husband with a knife alleging self-defence. Notable in that Lord Wheatley allowed evidence of previous assaults by deceased on K.
Per Lord Wheatley: 'The defence . . . is to the effect that the accused was acting in self-defence, she reasonably believing that there was imminent danger to her life due to an assault intended by the deceased.'

Not criminal
If act is done in **self-defence** it is not of criminal quality.

HMA v Brogan 1964 SLT 204
Assault. B accused of assaulting W by striking him on the head with a chair. B claimed in self-defence that he was first assaulted by W.
Per Lord Cameron's charge to the jury: 'Although a plea of self-defence may be put forward . . . the burden of proof remains with the Crown throughout to prove beyond reasonable doubt . . . the charge.'

M'Cluskey v HMA 1959 JC 39
Culpable homicide. M'C claimed he had killed O when acting in self-defence in that O was forcibly attempting to effect sodomy on him. Convicted of culpable homicide on basis of provocation, self-defence being rejected. Decision upheld on appeal.
Per LJ-G Clyde: 'I can see no justification at all for extending this defence to a case where there is no apprehension of danger to the accused's life . . . but merely a threat . . . of an attack on the appellant's virtue.'

Derrett v Lockhart 1991 SCCR 109
Self-defence open in an assault-type breach of the peace but not where the accused has not looked for an opportunity to retreat before taking pre-emptive strike.

Defence of others
The special defence extends to the use of reasonable force to protect another party from unjustified attack.

HMA v Carson and Anr 1964 SLT 21
M, C's co-accused, alleged that he had struck D with a bottle, only to protect C from a homicidal knife attack by D. M alleged that he was thus acting in self-defence of C.
Per Lord Wheatley: 'If a man sees another man being unlawfully attacked, he is entitled to stop that unlawful attack.'

Pollock v HMA 1998 SLT 880
Accused killed victim by inflicting 70 injuries by jumping on his head. Accused said protecting girlfriend from rape by victim whom he believed had a knife. Trial judge withdrew self-defence but allowed provocation and accused convicted of culpable homicide. Upheld on appeal, savagery of attack went far beyond measures reasonably required to protect girlfriend.

Provocation

Where the accused has acted in unjustifiable self-defence, he may be entitled to plead provocation, but it is not a justification of an attack that there has been provocation.

Crawford v HMA 1950 JC 67; 1950 SLT 279
C killed his father, stabbing him as he was preparing to shave. There had been a family quarrel the previous night and immediately before the stabbing C had been shouted at by his father. Plea of self-defence failed although plea of provocation accepted in mitigation of sentence.
Per LJ-G Cooper: 'Provocation and self-defence are . . . often I fear confused . . . but provocation *is not* a special defence.'

Rutherford v HMA 1997 SCCR 711
Partner told appellant on Friday she had an affair. On Sunday she said affair more serious than previously disclosed. Trial judge withdrew provocation but on appeal High Court said Sunday's account different and should have been left to jury, conviction of culpable homicide substituted.

HMA v Hill 1941 JC 59
H shot his wife and her lover immediately after they had confessed they had committed adultery.
Per Lord Patrick: 'If a man catches his wife and her paramour in the act of adultery and, in the heat of passionate indignation, then and there kills them, his crime is a very serious one, but it is not murder, it is culpable homicide.'

HMA v McKean 1996 SCCR 402
Accused convicted of culpable homicide: responded to information he had been sharing her lesbian partner.
Per Lord MacLean: 'I also see no reason why in the modern context the plea should not also be available to homosexual couples who live together and are regarded in the community as partners bound by close ties of love, affection and faithfulness.'

See also:

McKay v HMA 1991 SCCR 364

Graham v HMA 1987 SCCR 20
G charged with murder. She had quarrel with victim who had knife and threatened to kill her. She successfully disarmed him and killed him. Convicted of murder.
Per LJ-C Ross: 'What is noteworthy is that by the time the killing took place, the appellant had disarmed the victim.'

See also:

M'Cluskey v HMA 1959 JC 39

Test is subjective.

Jones v HMA 1989 SCCR 726
J charged with murder. Victim had threatened J with knife previously and when J later met him in the street, he believed he had knife and stabbed him. Trial judge directed jury that test for self defence and provocation was objective. On appeal *held* to be misdirection. Test to apply is the subjective one, whether accused believed on reasonable grounds that deceased had a knife. Conviction of culpable homicide substituted.

Low v HMA 1993 SCCR 493
Provocation. Deceased inviting L to have sex with him, in following struggle the deceased cut L on the hand, L stabbed deceased 50 times. Provocation withdrawn at trial, upheld on appeal. Gross disproportion between the provocation and the retaliation.
'Gross disproportion' preferred to 'cruel excess' as in *Lennon v HMA*.

See also:

Lennon v HMA 1991 SCCR 611

Robertson v HMA 1994 SCCR 589
Murder, provocation. R had stabbed the deceased 99 times after the deceased had made a homosexual advance to him and had presented a knife at him.
Held on appeal that the trial judge's direction that there must be a reasonable proportionate relationship between the deceased's actions and R's response was the same in effect as saying the retaliation must not be grossly disproportionate.

Withdrawal of special defence.

Williamson v HMA 1980 JC 22
Special defence of self-defence was lodged but later withdrawn prior to empanelling of jury.
Held that Crown entitled to examine the circumstances of the withdrawal of the special defence.

References: Hume I, 217 and 333; Alison I, 132 and 176; Macdonald, 106, 116 and 265; Gordon, 750, Gane and Stoddart, 422, 505.

NECESSITY

Plea of **necessity** may be submitted in **certain limited circumstances** and according to these circumstances may be regarded as a **defence** or merely as a **plea in mitigation.**

COMMENTARY	CASE LAW	STATUTE LAW
Certain limited circumstances Exact circumstances and actions which form foundation of a plea of necessity have been narrowly interpreted.	*HMA v Graham* (1897) 2 Adam 412 Drugs administered to cause an abortion. Convicted. *R v Dudley and Stephens* (1884) 14 QB 273 Two men and a boy cast adrift in open boat. The two men killed the boy, who was ill, after eight days without food and six without water. Fed on flesh of boy. Convicted of murder. Per Lord Coleridge: 'It is not correct to say that there is any absolute or unqualified necessity to preserve one's life.' *Moss v Howdle* 1997 SCCR 215 Accused speeding at over 100 mph on motorway to reach service station as passenger in pain. Pain turned out to be cramp. Accused claimed necessity, but sheriff held he had real choice and was not constrained to commit the offence: he had the alternative of pulling over and finding out what was wrong with passenger. Conviction upheld by High Court, which held that the defence of necessity was available in respect of all offences and the minimum requirement was of immediate danger or great bodily harm to accused or companion and danger may come from a person or natural disaster or illness. *Ruxton v Lang* 1998 SCCR (Sh Ct) 1 Drink driving. Accused returned home after office party with colleague and her boyfriend threw him out and threatened accused with knife so she went off in car intending to drive to brother's house two miles away. She was stopped in street where brother lived. *Held*, defence of necessity available to charge of driving with excess alcohol but not in instance as when stopped by police the danger had already ceased. Accused fined and awarded 11 penalty points, there being special reasons for not disqualifying her. Accused refused leave to appeal.	Abortion Act 1967, s 5(2), excludes defence of necessity by providing that anything done with intent to procure a miscarriage, unless authorised by the Act, is unlawful.
Defence Where, in order to preserve a greater value, there is the commission of a crime, eg stealing a fire extinguisher to save a burning building (Williams, p 737). Where to ensure personal safety there is the commission of a crime.	*Tudhope v Grubb* 1983 SCCR 350 (Sh Ct) Accused charged under s 6(1) of Road Traffic Act 1972. *Held*, that as accused had attempted to drive so as to avoid further injury following an assault, he had established defence of necessity. Acquitted.	

Plea in mitigation

Hume and Alison refer to old law of 'burthensack' as a form of necessity which was regarded as a plea in mitigation, where extreme hunger and want made the theft of a limited amount of food a non-capital offence.

R v Dudley and Stephens (1884) 14 QB 273
Sentence of death for murder commuted to six months' imprisonment.

Graham v Annan 1980 SLT 28
Driving while disqualified and without insurance. Wife, who was pregnant, was driving car. Became ill and husband, who was disqualified from driving and uninsured, took over.
Held, on appeal, that circumstances disclosed special reasons to mitigate penalty by avoiding a further period of disqualification or endorsement.

Road Traffic Offenders Act 1988, s 34, where special reasons established why an otherwise obligatory disqualification or endorsement should not be enforced.

References: Hume I, 55; Alison I, 674; Gordon, 420; Gane and Stoddart, 341; Williams, 722.

COERCION

The plea of **coercion** may operate as a defence to a criminal act or as plea in mitigation. Similarly, where such coercion takes the form of **superior orders** such a plea will have the same effect.

COMMENTARY	CASE LAW	STATUTE LAW
Coercion 'Crime consists in the intentional violation of the rights of others; it follows it cannot be visited with punishment where it has arisen not from intention or voluntary depravity but such coercion as has deprived the party of the free exercise of his will' (Alison I, 668).	*Thomson v HMA* 1983 SCCR 368 Threat must be of immediate harm in circumstances where resort to protection of authorities impossible, and it is impossible to resist or avoid participation. The defence of coercion can extend even to a person playing a principal part, and the question whether the gain, etc, was disclosed to the authorities matters only as regards the credibility of the accused.	
Coercion may take different forms.		
It may be of a public nature,	*James Purdie* 1720 Hume I 52 Charge of mobbing. Acquitted on basis that he was forced and compelled to participate by the mob.	
or be issued by one individual to another, the essence of the plea being the existence of such coercion that the accused 'could not resist without manifest peril to his life or property' (Alison I, 672).	*Docherty and Ors* (1976) SCCR Supp 146 Three men charged with armed robbery. Two of them pleaded that they had been coerced by the third who had threatened them and their mothers. Issue of coercion left to jury to decide. Per Lord Keith: 'In order that coercion may be a defence the position must be that the accused acted in a situation created by a threat to him which he had reason to believe would be carried out.'	
The threat must be imminent.	*HMA v McCallum* (1977) SCCR Supp 169.	
Fear of imminent death or serious injury may operate as a defence even to a serious crime.	*Sayers and Ors v HMA* 1981 SCCR 312 Jury directed that where a person's will is overborne by the will of another so that he is not acting of his own free will, that might be a defence to a criminal charge, but that matter be approached with some caution lest it become an easy answer for those that could not otherwise explain their conduct.	
Gordon, p 429, for position re murder in England.		
	But see:	
	Thomson v HMA 1983 SCCR 368 Cast doubt as to whether coercion could be a defence to murder in Scotland. Per Lord Hunter: '. . . I would, until the question arises for decision, wish distinctly to reserve my opinion as to whether coercion could ever or in any circumstances affect the verdict in a case of murder.'	
	DPP (NI) v Lynch [1975] AC 653 *Abbott v Queen, The* [1977] AC 755	
	However, Sheriff Gordon suggests (1983 SCCR 383 and 384) that there is a difference in the English approach, as stated in *DPP (NI) v Lynch* [1975] AC 653, where the emphasis is concentrated on the overcoming of the accused's will by the force of the threat; whereas in Scotland the concentration is on the requirement that the commission of the crime should be the *only* way to avoid the threatened danger. This is in keeping with Hume's definition and the terms of *Thomson v HMA* 1983 SCCR 368.	

Superior orders

may form the basis of a plea of coercion where a soldier acts under a lawful order or believes that he is so acting.

HMA v Sheppard 1941 JC 67; 1941 SLT 404
Charge of culpable homicide. Private in army part of escort to return a deserter to the regiment. Accused left alone with deserter for a few minutes and deserter attempted to escape. Accused shot and killed him. No clear orders but told by superior officer to 'stand no nonsense and shoot if necessary'. Found not guilty.
Per Lord Robertson: 'It would be altogether wrong to judge his actings so placed too meticulously—to weigh them in fine scales. If that were to be done it seems to me that the actings of soldiers on duty might well be paralysed by fear of consequences with great prejudice to national interests.'

See also:

HMA v Hawton and Parker (1861) 4 Irv 58
Marine firing at boat illegally fishing. Killed fisherman.
Held not guilty of culpable homicide.

References: Hume I, 47–56; Alison I, 668; Macdonald, 11; Gordon 429; Gane and Stoddart, 320.

ERROR

Error of law does not affect criminal responsibility. An **error of fact** may affect responsibility where it is **genuine and reasonable** and where the accused's responsibility would have been affected had the circumstances been as he thought them to be.

Note that **error** is **not a special defence** and s 78 of Criminal Procedure (Scotland) Act 1995 does not apply thereto.

COMMENTARY	CASE LAW	STATUTE LAW
Error of law Every man is presumed to know the law—*ignoratia juris neminem excusat*.	*Clark v Syme* 1957 JC 1; 1957 SLT 32 C, charged with maliciously killing a neighbouring farmer's sheep, pleaded that he thought he had a legal right to do so after giving due warning to his neighbour about sheep damaging his crops. Acquitted by sheriff on ground that he had acted under a misconception of his legal rights; but appeal court rejected this defence. Per LJ-G Clyde: 'The mere fact that his criminal act was performed under a misconception of what legal remedies he might otherwise have had, does not make it any the less criminal.'	
Error of fact Must affect mens rea: a mistake as to identity of the victim is irrelevant unless the mens rea of the particular crime (eg incest) requires knowledge as to the identity of the victim.	*Matthew Hay* 1780 Hume I 22 H put poison in a family's breakfast with the intention of killing his girlfriend. She survived but her parents died. H convicted of murder. *HMA v Brown* (1907) 5 Adam 312 B sent poisoned shortbread through the post, which was eaten by a servant of his intended victim. Murder indictment held relevant, but B found unfit to plead.	
Error must be **genuine and reasonable**.	*Dewar v HMA* 1945 JC 5; 1945 SLT 114 D, the manager of a crematorium, was convicted of theft of over one thousand coffin lids and some coffins. In defence he claimed to believe that it was the general and accepted practice in crematoria for the manager to remove lids at the time of cremation and keep them or use them as he saw fit; in effect to treat them as 'scrap'. Conviction upheld on appeal. Per LJ-C Cooper: '. . . if his beliefs were . . . not founded on rational grounds but founded only on the singular idea of the man himself . . . then . . . you . . . are bound to return a verdict of guilty.' *Crawford v HMA* 1950 JC 67; 1950 SLT 279 C stabbed his father five times after a verbal quarrel in which his father swore at him and made threatening gestures but with no indication of imminent violence. Appeal court upheld the trial judge's withdrawal of self-defence plea. Per LJ-G Cooper: '. . . when self-defence is supported by a mistaken belief rested on reasonable grounds, that mistaken belief must have an objective background and must not be purely subjective or of the nature of a hallucination.' *Jamieson v HMA* 1994 SCCR 181 *Held*, an unreasonable error as to consent will be a defence to rape.	

Error

If the error is found to be genuine and reasonable the accused is judged as if the facts were as he believed them to be.	*Owens v HMA* 1946 JC 119; 1946 SLT 227 O, charged with murder, claimed that after seeing what he thought was a knife in the deceased's hand, he had used his own knife in self-defence in the ensuing struggle. The trial judge told the jury that if O was 'completely wrong' in thinking the other man had a knife, his own use of a knife could not be justified. The appeal court held this to be a misdirection and quashed the conviction. Opinion of the court: '. . . self-defence is made out when it is established . . . that the panel believed that he was in imminent danger and that he held that belief on reasonable grounds. Grounds for such belief may exist though they are founded on a genuine mistake of fact.'	
The defence of error may apply in rape cases.	*Meek and Others v HMA* 1982 SCCR 613 Honest belief that woman consenting is a defence of rape even if not based on reasonable grounds. Quaere whether the decision applies to all common law crime (see commentary by Sheriff Gordon, 1982 SCCR 620).	
There may be a statutory defence of mistake.		Trade Descriptions Act 1968, s 24(1). In any proceedings for an offence under this Act it shall be a defence for the person charged to prove (a) that the commission of the offence was due to a mistake or to reliance on information supplied to him or to the act or default of another person, an accident, or some other cause beyond his control.

References: Hume I, 73; Macdonald, 11; Gordon, 326; Gane and Stoddart, 107.

EVIDENCE

ADMISSIBILITY

BEST EVIDENCE

The best evidence rule requires that primary evidence be given but **secondary evidence is admissible,** *quoad* **credibility in** *de recenti* **statements:** of **taped interview by police**; of statements by an **accused at judicial examination**; of **witness's statements different from those at trial**; but not **statements in precognition**; or if it is **impossible**, or **not reasonably practicable to produce primary evidence.**

COMMENTARY	CASE LAW	STATUTE LAW
Secondary evidence is admissible *quoad* **credibility in** *de recenti* **statements** A *de recenti* statement is of no corroborative value,	*Harrison v Mackenzie* 1923 JC 61 Illegal trawling. Only evidence of identification that of fisherman who read boat mark through telescope and reported to father immediately. *Held* evidence admissible *quoad* credibility. Appeal sustained *quoad* absence of corroboration.	
it bears only on credibility.	*Morton v HMA* 1938 JC 50 Indecent assault. Only identification that of complainer. *De recenti* statement to brother led in evidence. Objection repelled. *Held* that evidence admissible *quoad* credibility. Per LJ-C Aitchison: 'A statement made by an injured party *de recenti* . . . is admissible as bearing upon credibility only, [it is] not evidence of the fact complained of.' (Re: Evidence of distress *de recenti* and corroboration see also Evidence—Sufficiency, p 197.)	
Taped interview by police Better evidence than recollection.	*HMA v McFadden* 1981 *Scolag* 260 Murder. Police interview taped and tape produced as evidence to which defence objected and queried admissibility as to: (1) unfairness, ie accused cross-examined by police; (2) tape contained hearsay statements and matters irrelevant to the indictment. Per Lord Jauncey: 'There is a good deal to be said for the view that where you have a tape recording, that must be the better evidence . . . than a recollection of events some months ago.' *Deb v Normand* 1996 SCCR 766 *Held*, best evidence of what a police officer had witnessed was his own recollection and he could not be compelled to produce his notebook which he had referred to prior to going into the witness box.	
Witness's statements prior to trial.	*Morrison v HMA* 1990 SCCR 235 Where a 'mixed' statement is led in evidence, containing elements of admission as well as exonerating elements, the jury must be allowed to consider the whole statement made by the accused and not just the part on which the Crown relies as constituting an admission.	

Jones v HMA 1991 SCCR 290
Two accused admitted to police involvement in a robbery but denied being party to murder in the course of the robbery, incriminated another man. *Held* on appeal that such a 'mixed' statement could be evidence. *Morrison v HMA* 1990 SCCR 235 followed.

Thomson (UK) v HMA 1998 SCCR 683
Held, evidential character of mixed statement is not altered when accused gives evidence. Judge misdirected that only to test credibility, but no pre-judice and appeal refused and conviction upheld.

Scaife v HMA 1992 SCCR 845
'Mixed' statement. S admitted theft but denied vio-lence.
On appeal (following *Morrison v HMA* 1990 SCCR 235), *held* the jury should have been specifically directed to determine whether they accepted the whole, or part of it, and whether it caused reason-able doubt.

See also:

Smith v HMA 1994 SCCR 72

Geddes v HMA 1997 SLT 392
Convictions upheld despite failure to follow *Morrison v HMA* 1990 SCCR 235 explicitly.

Ridler v HMA 1995 SCCR 655
Opinion reserved whether an accused could dis-charge a burden of proof under the Prevention of Corruption Act 1906 by relying solely on exculpa-tory answers given in a mixed statement at judicial examination.

Earley v HMA 1995 SCCR 267
E charged with assault. Crown relied on a state-ment which appellant denied making.
Held, since no explanation in statements why he could claim self-defence the exculpatory element which is the basis of *Morrison v HMA* 1990 SCCR 235 was absent.

Higgins v HMA 1993 SCCR 542
H said he had stabbed the deceased but only in self-defence.
Held that the judge was entitled to tell the jury that they could isolate parts of the statement that they wished to accept.

Accused at judicial examination

Howarth v HMA (No 1) 1992 SCCR 364
Judge entitled to refer to a statement made by the accused to police even though he denied making the statement at judicial examination.

Criminal Procedure (Scotland) Act 1995, ss 35–39

Sutherland v HMA 1994 SCCR 80
Held on appeal that judge correct to give a direc-tion that jury could not draw an inference from S's failure to give evidence but could draw an infer-ence where the facts were crying out for an expla-nation and none was given. Sufficiently special circumstances.

Robertson v HMA 1995 SCCR 152
LJ-C: 'Although in *Morrison v HMA* the court was not dealing with statements at judicial examination, there is no reason to think that the principles laid down in that case would not cover statements made at judicial examination.'

See also:

Hoy v HMA 1997 SLT 26

Dempsey v HMA 1997 SLT 289
Accused advanced special defence of self-defence for the first time at his trial.
Held, judge's remarks on the accused's silence when he had not given evidence at trial was a breach of statutory provision. Conviction quashed.

Record evidence without witnesses.		**Solemn procedure:** CP(S)A 1995, s 278. Record is evidence without witness. Either party can object to the record or part of it being read; witnesses to it can be called. 'Record', each record, in list of productions. **Summary procedure:** CP(S)A 1995, s 352. Record evidence without witness. Either party can object to the record or part of it being admitted; witness to it can be called. 'Record', each record, sought to be received. Ten days' notice, except on cause shown, to be given of application requesting the court to refuse admission.
Prior statement of witness (other than accused) evidence of contents where witness gives evidence.	*Jamieson v HMA* 1994 SCCR 610 Crown witness said she could not remember what happened or her statement that appellant was kicking the complainer, but said if that's what she told police then true. Evidence led that she told police appellant had been kicking the complainer. *Held*, her evidence that she told police the truth incorporated her statement to police into own evidence. . *Note*: *Jamieson* wider than CP(S)A 1995, s 260 since statement not in document.	CP(S)A 1995, s 260(1), (4). Prior statement in precognition on oath or in other proceedings will be admissible as evidence of any matter stated in it, provided the witness's direct oral evidence on the matter would have been admissible and statement sufficiently authenticated. CP(S)A 1995, s 260(1), (2). Prior statement (other than precognition on oath/made in proceedings) admissible as evidence of any matter stated in it, provided the witness's direct oral evidence admissible AND (a) statement contained in a document; (b) witness adopts it as his evidence; (c) he would have been a competent witness at time statement made.
Witness's statements different from those at trial	*Dunsmore v HMA* 1991 SCCR 849 D giving evidence that at an earlier trial a witness had identified his co-accused not D. On appeal *held* that the jury entitled to have regard to the evidence as a direction otherwise would have meant them ignoring part of D's evidence. *Greenhalghse v HMA* 1992 SCCR 311 Crown putting to witness evidence of a statement made to the police which differed from the evidence she was giving at trial. Judge making no comment about the statement in his charge. *Held* on appeal that the judge should have dealt with the statement because some of it was hearsay.	CP(S)A 1995, s 263(4). Witness may be examined as to whether on specified occasion made different statement; evidence may be led of it.

HMA v Hislop 1994 SLT 333
Witness could not recall what statement she had given police.
Held, non-recollection sufficed to meet the 'different' requirement under CP(S)A 1995, s 263(4).

Young v HMA 1995 SCCR 418
Statement made to police when witness patient in hospital.
Held, wording of section does not exclude possibility that statement unfairly obtained should not be put to the witness, for jury to decide whether fair to take evidence into account.

Paterson v HMA 1997 SCCR 707
Defence agent sought in cross-examination to lead evidence from police witness as to inconsistencies of B's statement.
Court *held* he should have put to B first the specific occasion when statement made and to whom.

McNee v Ruxton 1997 SCCR 291
Witness adopted statement of another witness.
Held, sheriff wrong to prevent defence from using CP(S)A 1995, s 263(4) as no grounds for saying that he sought to put a statement other than the witness's own statement. Conviction quashed.

Hemming v HMA 1998 SLT 213
Court granted order allowing recovery of police witness statements to allow defence to test credibility in terms of CP(S)A 1995, s 263(4). Granted on grounds of the overriding public interest of fair hearing of accused, and given that Crown made similar use of statements.
Observed, need for substantial reasons why recovery necessary in the interests of justice.

See also:

McGhee v HMA 1992 SCCR 324

Statements in precognition
By their nature interviews of defence witnesses are precognitions.

McNeilie v HMA 1929 JC 50; 1929 SLT 145
Attempted theft. Special defence of alibi. Objection to evidence of statements made to police when they interviewed defence witnesses repelled. McN convicted. Conviction quashed on appeal.
Object had been to discover what the witness's evidence was to be, was a precognition, and therefore inadmissible.

KJC v HMA 1994 SCCR 560
Rape trial. Complainer examined on inconsistencies in precognition on oath.
Held, fairness requires that the other party be allowed to put the full statement to show consistency with evidence.

Statements taken when a case is at the stage of active construction are precognitions,.

Kerr v HMA 1958 JC 14; 1958 SLT 82
Theft of goods. Employer gave statement to police in interview which was read as evidence in court. K convicted. Conviction quashed on appeal.
Per LJ-C Thomson: 'There is no dispute that on authority, if this statement was a precognition, it was inadmissible [a precognition] is filtered through the mind of another . . . once the police have begun to build up a case against certain people . . . we have passed beyond the stage of preliminary investigations and have got into the stage of preparation for the leading of evidence.'

Impossible to produce primary evidence

To test whether primary evidence is requisite, the questions to be asked are whether the evidence is necessary and available.

Clements v Macaulay (1866) 4 M 543
Pursuer wanted to produce copy of letter. Pursuer unable to produce original after due diligence. *Held* that copy admissible.
Per Lord Cowan: 'Secondary evidence is admissible only after due exertion is proved to have been made for recovery of the principal document.'

Real evidence not essential.

Maciver v Mackenzie 1942 JC 51; 1942 SLT 144
Accused took possession of wreck without reporting it to receiver. Wreck not produced. Secondary evidence of condition admissible *quoad* marks on timber.
Per LJ-C Normand: 'The question in each case is whether the real evidence is essential for proving the case against the accused.'

Friel v Leonard 1997 SLT 1206
Audiovisual equipment allegedly stolen from house not produced at trial. Sheriff refused to allow evidence. *Held*, sheriff's decision recalled, because production of items not necessary for proof of Crown's case and no prejudice to accused from their absence. LJ-G dictum in *Maciver v Mackenzie* 1942 JC 51; 1942 SLT 144 applied.

Is it reasonably practicable to retain evidence?

Anderson v Laverock 1976 JC 9; 1976 SLT 62
Statutory prosecution for unlawful possession of salmon. Fish destroyed by police before defence allowed to examine them. Condition of fish material. Convicted. Conviction quashed.
Opinion of the court: 'Whether goods are perishable or whether it is reasonably practicable and convenient to retain them as primary evidence . . . will depend on the circumstances and evidence in each particular case.'

Not reasonably practicable to produce primary evidence

Newspapers sold for trading purposes.

Hughes v Skeen 1980 SLT (Notes) 13
Stolen newspapers recovered and returned for distribution, but not produced at trial.
Per Lord Cameron: 'Production of these newspapers . . . neither necessary nor . . . practicable in this particular case.'

No authority to impound whisky bottle and label.

McLeod v Woodmuir Miners' Welfare Society Social Club 1961 JC 5; (1960 SLT 349)
Statutory prosecution for sale of understrength whisky. Objections to oral evidence of details on label on bottle not produced at trial sustained. Crown appeal successful. No authority to impound the bottle, not reasonably practical to produce it.

Photographs of fingerprint 'lifts'.

Hamilton v Grant 1984 SCCR 263
Objection taken to evidence consisting of photographs of fingerprint 'lifts'. Sheriff held photographs inadmissible and said actual 'lifts' required and best evidence rule contravened. Reversed on appeal. No opinion delivered.

Blood samples not produced.

Williamson v Aitchison 1982 SCCR 102; 1982 SLT 399
Drunken driving. Certification lodged re blood samples' results. Objection by defence that blood samples should have been prodced repelled. Appeal rejected. Shown that the blood analysed had been taken from the accused.

Biological material

CP(S)A 1995, s 276. Evidence of characteristics and composition competent notwithstanding neither material nor sample lodged. If party wishes to lead evidence where neither material nor sample lodged he shall make material/sample available for inspection by other party unless material hazard to health or destroyed in process of analysis.

Print-out from breath testing device not available.	*McLeod v Fraser* 1986 SCCR 271 *Held* that best evidence of result of analysis of blood was that of the analyst and it was permissible for him to refer to the register of blood analyses, or the certificate, as an aide-memoire.	
		Documentary evidence CP(S)A 1995, s 279, Sch 8. Provides for certification of documents, in particular business documents (which may contain hearsay) and validates their use as best evidence.
Statutory exceptions to the rule that hearsay evidence is inadmissible. (See Renton and Brown, A 449, for categories of hearsay admissible at common law.)	*Forrester v HMA* 1997 SCCR 9 Hearsay admissible, but oral evidence preferable. Sufficient reason to extend 12-month time limit (see Statutory time limits).	CP(S)A 1995, s 259(1). Evidence of a statement made by a person otherwise than while giving oral evidence shall be admissible where the judge is satisfied that: (a) the person who made the statement will not give evidence because he— (i) is dead or mentally/physically unable to give evidence; (ii) is outwith UK and it is not reasonably practicable to secure attendance or obtain evidence in any other competent manner; (iii) cannot be found and all reasonable steps have been taken to find him; (iv) is authorised by the court to refuse to answer on grounds of self-incrimination; or (v) is called as a witness and refuses to take oath or affirmation or, having sworn, refuses to give evidence; (b) evidence of the matter would be admissible in proceedings if that person gave direct oral evidence of it; (c) person who made statement would have been a competent witness in such proceedings at time statement made; and (d) evidence would entitle judge/jury to find that the statement was made and either it is contained in a document or the person who gave oral evidence of statement has direct personal knowledge of its making. CP(S)A 1995, s 259(3). Evidence of statement above shall not be admissible where judge is satisfied that evidence is unavailable due to actings of person in support of whose case the evidence would be given (or a person acting on that person's behalf).

COMPETENT EVIDENCE

To be admissible, evidence must be competent; **non-compliance with statutory requirements** will make it incompetent. Competent evidence may be **compellable or non-compellable**. In the case of a **witness present during earlier evidence** it is subject to special considerations. By statutory provision evidence in **replication**, and **additional** evidence is competent.

COMMENTARY	CASE LAW	STATUTE LAW
Non-compliance with statutory requirements		Criminal Procedure (Scotland) Act 1995
		Solemn procedure:
Service of (a) copy indictment, (b) list of prosecution witnesses.	*Bennett v HMA* 1995 SCCR 471 Service of copy indictment missing page 2. Nothing on page 2 concerned appellant. *Held*, breach of provisions but in absence of claim appellant misled/prejudiced court required by statutory provision to repel objection and appeal refused.	Section 66(4) (prosecution). Accused to be served full copy of indictment and list of prosecution witnesses.
Declaration or extract conviction.		Section 67(2) (prosecution). Not necessary to list witnesses to declaration of accused or extract conviction.
Witnesses, productions, not in list—notice.	*Torres v HMA* 1997 SCCR 491 Charge of importing cocaine. Short report compiled on lodged sample not shown to defence. *Held*, no breach of statutory provisions as samples lodged and original report made clear what comparisons might be carried out. Per LJ-C Cullen: 'evidence did not introduce any genuinely new material or additional source of evidence.'	Section 67(5) (prosecution). Competent, with leave, to examine witnesses or put in evidence production not included in list, if written notice given not less than two clear days before jury sworn.
Special defence—ten days' notice normally required.	*McQuade v HMA* 1996 SCCR 347 Murder. S admitted shooting deceased in course of robbery and said M present and armed but they never intended to fire. On appeal, convictions for murder upheld. Notice of incrimination not required, since evidence not calculated to exculpate accused. *O'Connell v HMA* 1996 SCCR 614 Special defence tendered at adjourned first diet not accepted as not in proper form. At further diet tendered in proper form but sheriff said special cause required to be shown. On appeal, *held* continued diet was still first diet and since defence duly lodged in proper form cause not required to be shown.	Section 78 (accused). Not competent for accused to state special defence or to lead evidence calculated to exculpate the accused by incriminating a co-accused unless notice lodged ten clear days before trial diet in High Court cases (at or before the first diet in Sheriff Court cases) unless on cause shown.
Notice by accused if witness or production not in prosecutor's list.	*Brown v HMA* 1998 SCCR 461 Before the start of the trial the depute fiscal changed the backing number on production without informing the defence. Sheriff granted extension, but overturned on appeal due to accumulation of errors on the part of the Crown.	Section 78(4) (accused). Not competent to examine witnesses or put in evidence productions not included in prosecutor's list unless ten clear days notice given before jury sworn in High Court cases (at or before the first diet in Sheriff Court cases) unless on cause shown.
Witness or production in other party's list competent.		Section 67(6) (both parties). Competent for prosecutor or accused to examine witness or put in evidence production in other party's list.

Evidence

		Summary procedure:
Alibi—notice in summary cases.		Section 149 (accused). Not competent for accused to found on alibi unless notice of this plea with particulars as to time and place and of witnesses proposed to prove it given to prosecutor prior to the first witness being sworn. Prosecutor, on notice, is entitled to adjournment.
Compellable or non-compellable Accused non-compellable either in his own, or a co-accused's defence although he may elect to give evidence.		Section 266(1), (2). Accused a competent defence witness whether on trial alone or with co-accused but only upon own application.
Co-accused compellable only when giving evidence or pleading guilty.		Section 266(9), (10). If co-accused gives evidence an accused may cross-examine and if co-accused pleads guilty (sentenced or not) prosecutor or accused may call him as witness without notice.
Relatives of accused compellable.		Section 265(3). No objection to admissibility or compellability that witness is father, mother, son, daughter, brother, sister, by consanguinity or affinity, or uncle, aunt, nephew, niece by consanguinity of party adducing witness.
Spouse may be called by accused.	*Hunter v HMA* 1984 SCCR 306 Murder and assault. H father of deceased child. Special defence of incrimination lodged naming wife *quoad* assault. Wife warned that she need not answer any questions. Intimated that she did not wish to do so. H convicted of culpable homicide. Appeal refused. Opinion of the court that one spouse is a compellable witness in the other spouse's defence. *Bates v HMA* 1989 SCCR 338 B and C charged with drugs offences in relation to which spouse is not a compellable witness. B intended to lead evidence incriminating C. Crown called C's wife as witness and she was told by trial judge that she was not obliged to answer questions which might incriminate C. She gave evidence against B but refused to answer any questions put to her in cross-examination. On appeal, *held* that judge's direction was wrong. Ought to have instructed spouse that she could not be compelled to give evidence but that if she did she would have to answer all the questions put to her.	Section 264(1). Spouse of an accused may be called as a witness by accused.
Matrimonial communications—'special category'.	*Harper v Adair* 1945 JC 21; 1945 SLT 133 H charged with stealing property of her husband. Husband competent and compellable witness. Per LJ-G Normand: 'It is admitted that, standing the decision in *Foster v HMA* 1932 SC 75; 1932 SLT 482 the admission of the husband's evidence cannot be impugned.' *Casey v HMA* 1993 SLT 33 'Spouse' does not include a co-habitee.	Section 264(2)(b). Spouse not compellable witness with regard to disclosure of matrimonial communications.

Spouse compellable in personal injury offences and offences against his or her property.

Foster v HMA 1932 JC 75; 1932 SLT 482
Forgery and uttering cheques. Alleged that F forged signature of husband. Husband competent and compellable witness.
Per Lord Anderson: 'If the fundamental considera-tion . . . is necessity—the need for the evidence of the injured spouse to secure conviction, this would seem to operate as strongly in the case of offences against property as in the case of bodily injury.'

Hay v McClory 1993 SCCR 1040
CP(S)A 1975, s 348. Spouse compellable where she would have been at common law. Offence by accused against the house of the spouse did not make her compellable because the offence was not against her, council paid for repairs to the house. Spouse should have been warned that she need not give evidence.

Section 264(2)(a). Spouse of an accused may be called as a witness by co-accused or pros-ecutor without consent of accused, if compellable at common law.

Wife's evidence at previous trial may be admissible even where she is not compellable in present trial.

Lockhart v Massie 1989 SCCR 421.

Socius criminis
No warning need now be given to treat the evidence of a *socius crim-inis* with special care.

Docherty v HMA 1987 SCCR 418
Appellant convicted, by majority, of assault and robbery while acting with three others who had earlier pled guilty on separate indictments, and were called as witnesses for the Crown, giving evi-dence that the appellant had been recruited as dri-ver for a different criminal enterprise (an assault upon a man against whom one of the three sought retaliation for the alleged rape of his step daugh-ter). Appeal that conviction should be quashed because no 'cum nota' warning given. A bench of nine judges was convened to reconsider the soundness of the rule referred to in *Wallace v HMA* 1952 JC 78 in these terms: '(the) evidence [of a *socius criminis*] ought always to be made the sub-ject of a specific and particular warning that . . . it is suspect evidence deserving of close scrutiny'.
Held 'Trial judges need only give to juries in all cases, whether or not any *socius criminis* has been adduced as a witness for the Crown the familiar directions designed to assist them in dealing with the credibility of witnesses and any additional assistance which the circumstances of any parti-cular case may require.'

Witness present during earlier evidence
Reasons to hear evidence required.

Macdonald (Angus) v Mackenzie 1947 JC 169; 1948 SLT 27
Reckless or careless driving. Witness for defence in court during earlier evidence. No objection by procurator fiscal. Evidence disallowed by sheriff.
Per Lord Jamieson: 'It is for the party tendering the witness to satisfy the court that his presence was not due to negligence or, . . . that he had not been or was not likely to have been influenced by what he had already heard.'

Section 267(2). Witness need not be rejected because of presence during earlier evi-dence without permission or consent if presence was not through culpable negligence or criminal intent, if witness not unduly instructed or influenced and injustice will not follow.

Section 267(1). Court may per-mit witness to be in court prior to giving evidence if it appears to the court not to be contrary to the interests of justice.

Note: The statutory requirements do not apply to a defence solicitor as witness.

Campbell v Cochrane 1928 JC 25; 1928 SLT 394
Licensing Act prosecution. Solicitor conducting defence adduced as defence witness. Ruled inad-missible. Appealed.
Held that solicitor competent witness.

Evidence

Witness not present but informed of earlier evidence.	*Keenan v Scott* 1990 SCCR 470 Person in court hearing evidence and then going to witness room to tell the witnesses what had been said. Trial proceeding, appeal. *Held* that the sheriff was correct to allow the trial to proceed as he had repelled the submission of no case to answer holding that evidence was sufficient without the 'suspect' evidence.	
Replication evidence To contradict defence evidence where it could not have been reasonably anticipated.	*Sandlan v HMA* 1983 SCCR 71 Theft. S and K charged. K lodged special defence incriminating S. S lodged special defence incriminating K. In course of cross-examination by Crown, S gave evidence of shopping visit. Crown allowed evidence in replication to show trip took place two days earlier. S gave further evidence and called solicitor as witness. Argued evidence in replication incompetent on grounds that CP(S)A 1975, s 149A only applied to evidence led to contradict evidence of defence witness in examination in chief. Argument rejected by Lord Stewart: evidence in replication competent. On appeal conviction quashed on other matter. Per Lord Hunter: 'I doubt whether the interpretation contended for on behalf of the appellant is well-founded.' *Campbell v Allan* 1988 SCCR 47 *Held*, allowing appeal, evidence in replication cannot be used by Crown to contradict earlier prosecution evidence. *Neizer v Johnston* 1993 SCCR 772 Statutory offence. Sheriff refused to allow replication evidence of witness who had been precognosced by the Crown but not led. Upheld. Per LJ-C Ross: 'Having regard to the notice which the Crown had been given . . . the Crown could reasonably have anticipated the evidence [and] the Crown had in fact precognosced both [witnesses].'	**Solemn procedure:** Section 269. Judge may, after defence case closed and before speeches, permit prosecutor to lead evidence to contradict evidence prosecution could not have reasonably anticipated; or to prove witness made different statement to that at trial although witness or production not listed and witness must be recalled. **Summary procedure:** Section 269. Judge may, before prosecutor's address on evidence, allow him to lead additional evidence to contradict evidence he could not have reasonably anticipated or to prove witness made different statement to that at trial, although witness must be recalled.
Additional evidence	*Cushion v HMA* 1993 SCCR 356 Murder. Before trial began, appellant told advisors of rumours that co-accused, T, had offered two men money to give evidence against him. Appellant unable to provide their names until trial had started. T cross-examined on these allegations, then application made to call the men. Not disputed that evidence material and unavailable when jury sworn, but application refused, since trial judge not satisfied evidence could not reasonably have been made available, and no information given to court of attempts to investigate rumour before trial. Conviction upheld on appeal.	**Solemn procedure:** Section 268. Judge may, before speeches, permit either party to lead additional evidence if he considers that it is prima facie material. Judge must consider that at time when jury sworn the evidence was not reasonably available or its materiality could not reasonably have been foreseen, although witness or production not listed and witness must be recalled.
If material, and not earlier available.	*Wotherspoon v HMA* 1998 SCCR 615 *Held*, since evidence was of a prior consistent statement which was not challenged by the Crown, it would not have been material and if sheriff had applied CP(S)A 1995, s 268 he would have refused the motion.	**Summary procedure:** Section 268. Judge may, before prosecutor's address on the evidence, permit either party to lead additional evidence if he considers that it is prima facie material. Judge must consider that at time when first prosecution witness sworn the evidence was not reasonably available or its materiality could not reasonably have been foreseen, although witness or production not listed and witness must be recalled.

FAIRLY OBTAINED EVIDENCE

To be admissible, evidence must have been fairly obtained. In the case of the **accused**, in determining fairness, it will be considered whether the evidence has been obtained **before suspicion: after suspicion but before charge**; or **after charge**. If **statements to persons other than the police** are made, the particular circumstances will be considered, as will **evidence disclosing previous convictions,** or **evidence of bad character**; and **illegally obtained evidence** can be admissible.

COMMENTARY	CASE LAW	STATUTE LAW
Accused, before suspicion Admissibility will be assessed on fairness and whether evidence was volunteered or elicited. Search uncovering evidence of different crime	*HMA v Hepper* 1958 JC 39; 1958 SLT 160. Theft. H gave police consent to search property in connection with a crime. While searching they found attaché case unconnected with matter under investigation. They took this suspicious article away and it founded charges re the case reported here. Evidence held to be admissible as the police had a duty to inquire further in the circumstances.	
	Brown v Glen 1997 SCCR 636 Police asked if they could search appellant and he agreed. Found drugs concealed in his clothing. Allowing the appeal by the procurator fiscal, Lord Sutherland stated that so long as consent sought of person not suspected of a specific crime, any request need not require a specific warning that the person can withhold consent. *Normand v Cox* 1997 SCCR 24 (Sh Ct) overruled.	
	Graham v Orr 1995 SCCR 30 Appellant's breath test was below statutory limit, but car held until clear test produced. Released from arrest, he became agitated and constable searched car. *Held,* no suspicion of any offence and no power to search; evidence from search inadmissible and conviction quashed.	
	See also: *HMA v Turnbull* 1951 JC 96.	
Confession blurted out at early stage of investigation.	*Bell v HMA* 1945 JC 61; 1946 SLT 204 Rape. B, interviewed during enquiry, blurted out confession. *Held* admissible evidence. Until confession police had no reason to caution or charge B.	
Admission by family member at start of investigation.	*Thompson v HMA* 1968 JC 61; 1968 SLT 339 Murder. Members of victim's family were interviewed, including T who remained at police station while accommodation was being found for him. T blurted out, 'It was either her or me.' *Held* admissible evidence. Per LJ-G Clyde: '[T] had not been cautioned or charged, nor was he being asked questions by the police at the time. Nothing in the nature of bullying or cross-examining had occurred.'	
Accused, after suspicion but before charge Where there is urgency, search without a warrant may be justified.	*Lord Advocate's Reference (No 1 of 1983)* 1984 SCCR 62 Per LJ-G Emslie: 'A suspect's self-incriminating answers to police questioning will indeed be admissible in evidence unless it can be affirmed that they have been extracted from him by unfair means . . . In each case . . . it will be necessary to consider the whole relevant circumstances in order to discover whether or not there has been fairness.'	

HMA v McGuigan 1936 JC 16; 1936 SLT 161
Murder, rape. Evidence obtained during search without warrant led to charges of murder, rape and theft being brought. Evidence held admissible on ground of urgency.

Search without consent or warrant justified if evidence could have been lost.

Walsh v MacPhail 1978 SLT (Notes) 29
Possession of drugs. Servicemen on an air base were suspected of possessing drugs. Search made without consent and on an invalid warrant. Evidence held admissible on ground that drugs could have been disposed of or lost.

Evidence obtained improperly but in good faith admitted.

Fairley v Fishmongers of London 1951 JC 14; 1951 SLT 54
Salmon poaching. Evidence against F was discovered by a private inspector and a government official.
Held that although the evidence was improperly obtained it was admissible, as they had acted in good faith.

See also:

Hepburn v Vannet 1997 SCCR 698

Genuine but mistaken belief that search authorised.

Lawrie v Muir 1950 JC 19; 1950 SLT 37
Illegal use of milk bottles. Two inspectors of the Scottish Milk Bottle Exchange searched L's premises believing mistakenly although in good faith that they had authority to do so; incriminating evidence found held inadmissible.
Opinion of the court: 'Persons in the special position of these inspectors ought to know the precise limits of their authority and should be held to exceed these limits at their peril.'

Reasonable belief that obtaining of warrant is necessary.

HMA v Rae 1992 SCCR 1
Held that a police officer swearing that he has reasonable grounds is sufficient to allow a justice to grant a warrant under s 23(3) of the Misuse of Drugs Act 1971.

Scope of warrant exceeded.

Leckie v Miln 1981 SCCR 261; 1982 SLT 177
Theft. Police told householder of L's arrest on warrant and said they wished to search house. She consented. Incriminating evidence found.
Held inadmissible. Officers unaware of scope of warrant, consent not given for active unlimited search.

Innes v Jessop 1989 SCCR 441
I charged with reset of driving licence and tax exemption certificate found by police while searching for firearms and ammunition. Justice repelled objection to evidence having been irregularly obtained and convicted.
On appeal *held* that removal of other articles carried implication that search was random one and it would be unsafe to sustain conviction.

Tierney v Allan 1989 SCCR 334
T charged with reset of gas cylinders and a typewriter. Police officers had searched T's house on a warrant referring only to gas cylinders. In course of search typewriter found under cot, similar to some typewriters known to have been stolen.
Held that the evidence was admissible.
Per LJ-G Emslie: 'This was not a case of random search as in *Leckie v Miln* [1981 SCCR 261; 1982 SLT 177]. It was the unexpected discovery of an article which aroused suspicion during the course of a lawful search for material listed in warrant.'

HMA v Turnbull 1951 JC 96
Fraud. Police obtained warrant and searched T. Removed property in relation to another alleged crime and kept it for six months. Inadmissible because police had acted outwith the scope of warrant.

Davidson v Brown 1990 SCCR 304
Illegal search. Police stopping car of known shoplifters asking to see contents of a bin.
Held, not an illegal search as the request had been voluntarily complied with.

See also:

HMA v Hepper 1958 SC 39; 1958 SLT 160

Burke v Wilson 1988 SCCR 361
Police obtained warrant for search of premises for video recordings for which no classification certificate had been obtained. In course of search they removed unlabelled videos which they subsequently found to be obscene. B charged, objected that evidence irregularly obtained.
Held that the police had come upon videos by accident in course of authorised search and had not acted improperly.

Dental impressions taken under warrant.

Hay v HMA 1968 JC 40
Murder. H inmate of List D school suspected. Police took dental impressions for comparison with bite marks on body. Applied for warrant to take further impressions, granted. Upheld by High Court. '. . . obtaining of the warrant prior to the examination in question rendered the examination quite legal . . . evidence which resulted from it was therefore competent.'

Note: Police powers with regard to persons in detention under the Criminal Procedure (Scotland) Act 1995.
Invasive searches.

Grant v HMA 1989 SCCR 618
G questioned by police during six-hour period, but detention not terminated until arrest after the expiry of six hours.
Held that fact that detention exceeded six hours did not invalidate things done lawfully within period.

Walker v Lees 1995 SLT 757
Theft.
Held, on appeal, that warrant to take blood samples involved some degree of loss of liberty, but allowed because crime serious and samples necessary, provided warrant modified to exclude detention of suspect.

See also:

Brodie v Normand 1994 SCCR 924

Williamson v Fraser 1995 SCCR 67
Same test applied in summary as in solemn proceedings. It is competent to grant such a warrant until the case comes to trial. Bail refused.

Criminal Procedure (Scotland) Act 1995.

Section 14. Police may question suspect detained under s 14. Detention must not exceed six hours.

Section 18(1). This section applies where a person has been arrested and is in custody or is detained under CP(S)A 1995, s 14(1).

Section 18(2). Constable may take fingerprints, palmprints or other external prints.

Section 18(6). With the authority of an officer not below the rank of inspector, may take sample of hair, nail cuttings or blood, body fluid, tissue or other material, or saliva, by means of swabbing or rubbing.

Section 19. Briefly, gives police power within one month of (a) conviction; (b) written intimation that sample was unsuitable or insufficient, to obtain prints, samples.

The juncture at which questioning should be discontinued unless a caution is given is determined by the extent to which suspicion has been focused and having regard to fairness.

Manuel v HMA 1958 JC 41
Murder. M confessed. Gave location of corpse and commented on its condition. Convicted. Appealed. Alleged his condition motivated by inducements. Appeal rejected, no evidence of inducement.

Statement containing discrepancies, further questioning allowed.

HMA v McPhee 1966 SLT (Notes) 83
Assault and culpable homicide. McP gave statement containing discrepancies. Came under suspicion of having committed offence. No caution given. McP blurted out admissions when questioning was resumed. Evidence held admissible, mere suspicion does not mean that caution is required.

Person arrested but not yet charged.

Johnston v HMA 1993 SCCR 693
Questioning need not cease when person arrested but not yet charged.

See also:

Hay v HMA 1998 SCCR 634

HMA v Penders 1996 SCCR 404
Break in interview of robbery suspect to formulate charge. On resumption caution administered, accused admitted guilt and then questioned on details and cautioned and charged.
Held, only when formal charges levelled are further questions precluded, and whether it was fair for police to renew interview should be left to the jury. Jury by majority found charges not proven. *Codona v HMA* 1996 SCCR 300 distinguished.

Miller v HMA 1997 SCCR 748
Police informing accused that they were going to charge him and asking him twice if he had anything to say. Appellant confessed and made further admissions. Conviction upheld on appeal.
Held, it is only when a charge is made, as opposed to an intention to charge, that further questions with regard to that charge are precluded.

Compare with:

Johnston v HMA 1993 SCCR 693
Gives police right to question arrestee who has not been charged.

When does a person become 'a suspect'?

Miln v Cullen 1967 JC 21; 1967 SLT 35
Drunken driving. C pointed out as one of the drivers involved in a collision. Police officer asked C whether he had been the driver. Response held admissible.
Per Lord Wheatley: 'The point at which a person becomes a "suspect" in the eyes of a police officer may be difficult to define with exactitude. The test is basically a subjective one, but the police officer may have to justify his attitude by reference to the facts in his possession or the knowledge which he had at the given point of time. . . . In each case the issue is—was the question in the circumstances a fair one? . . . The question asked . . . was merely to discover whether the respondent was the driver of the car, not whether he had caused the accident or was drunk. If a question had been asked without a caution being administered, and the question had been directed to elicit an admission of culpability for the accident or an admission that he was drunk in charge of his car, then the question might have been properly objected to.'

Tonge v HMA 1982 SCCR 313
Held (1) that it is a requirement of law that a charge must be preceded by a full common law caution; (2) that where a statement is made in reply to an accusation, whether or not in the words of a formal charge, any reply induced by that accusation will be inadmissible unless preceded by a common law caution, or at least that such a caution was given as soon as it became clear that accused might be about to incriminate himself.

HMA v Middler 1994 SCCR 838
Murder. First accused not cautioned before being interviewed, despite suspicions by police of inconsistencies between witness's statements and accused's earlier statement, and despite search warrant obtained for accused's house to search for clothing worn by accused at locus. On appeal conviction upheld.
Per Lord Marnoch: '... the question of ... at what stage a caution should be given falls to be determined as part of the more general test of fairness.'

Questioning of a suspect.

Chalmers v HMA 1954 JC 66; 1954 SLT 177
Murder. C brought under suspicion to police, cautioned, then interrogated. Replied to caution and charge: 'I did it. He struck me.' Evidence held inadmissible. Conviction quashed.
Held, that if suspicion is such that the person is viewed as the likely perpetrator of the crime then any further interrogation amounting to cross-examination may render any confession extracted inadmissible.

McClory v MacInnes 1992 SCCR 319
MacI found asleep in vehicle at side of road, woken up by police, no caution given and asked what had happened. MacI said that he had crashed.
Held, statement unfairly obtained, police were obviously suspicious but gave no caution.

Young v Friel 1992 SCCR 567
F interviewed by police. F seeking incentive from police to give a statement.
Held that sheriff correct to allow interview where the police officer had said that he was not sure whether any such offer could be made. One caution sufficient to cover statements made in relation to two different offences.

Threats and inducements

Black v Annan 1995 SCCR 273
Person detained on a Saturday on charge of reset. Told if he did not co-operate he would be kept in until Monday.
Held, on appeal, no need for pressure to be the cause of the statement, which was not shown to be fairly obtained, and conviction quashed.

Harley v HMA 1995 SCCR 595
Theft by housebreaking. Appellant accused of obtaining information about house from married woman. Told if he spoke up they would phone her: otherwise they would visit the house, which might lead to her husband finding out.
Held, unfairly obtained: the matter should not have been left to the jury, and conviction quashed.

Stewart v Hingston 1996 SCCR 234
Suspect declined to give statement at home and constable said he would have to detain her and take her to a police station and he would arrange for social worker to look after children.
Held, policeman just being practical and statement fairly obtained.

Requirement for caution depends on nature of police questioning.	*Custerson v Westwater* 1987 SCCR 389 C accused with having offensive weapon. Evidence consisted of evidence by complainer that C waved knife at him, and statement by C that he had knife with him for protection. C made statement voluntarily in response to question. C appealed on ground that he had not been cautioned (see *Tonge v HMA* 1982 SCCR 313). *Held* that this case distinguishable from *Tonge* in that statement made in response to unobjectionable question rather than an allegation.
Youthful suspect—is the evidence spontaneous and voluntary?	*HMA v Rigg* 1946 JC 1; 1946 SLT 49 Murder. R reported discovery of body to police and gave a statement. Later his condition being described as excited. R collapsed trembling and shuddering and gave another statement, which was held inadmissible. Statement was not spontaneous and voluntary, more like a detailed precognition. Ultimate test is fairness to the accused.
	Codona v HMA 1996 SCCR 300 Murder trial. On appeal, statement by 14-year-old girl held inadmissible because it was unfairly obtained due to: the length of interview (over three hours); her distress; her age; and the form of questioning which pressurised her into changing her answers.
	Blogojevic v HMA 1995 SCCR 570 Appellant denied being at locus. During a break in the interview, told not doing himself any favours with denial. On resumption he admitted being at locus and stabbing man who punched him. At trial appellant never gave evidence but defence produced psychological report that appellant vulnerable to changing story if pressurised. Conviction upheld on appeal, since in absence of evidence from police or appellant on the matter there was no factual basis for the claim.
Statement by person not only possible suspect.	*Brown v HMA* 1966 SLT 105 Murder. B cautioned. Statement contained discrepancies. B warned of these and cautioned further at which he broke down saying 'I killed her.' B cautioned again and charged. Subsequently, items were recovered from where B had indicated. Evidence held admissible. Police were not cross-examining the accused or treating him as the only possible suspect.
Admission volunteered.	*Costello v Macpherson* 1922 JC 9; 1922 SLT 35 Theft. C asked by railway police to open parcel he was carrying, which contained coal. C said he obtained it from a bunker. Regular police became involved and C volunteered that he had stolen the coal. Evidence held admissible, not improper to lead evidence of a statement made voluntarily without questioning being required.
Search without warrant where crime seen to have been committed.	*Jackson v Stevenson* (1897) 2 Adam 255; 24 R(J) 38; 4 SLT 277 Assault. Water bailiffs stopped and searched J, who resisted arrest and was charged with assault. Conviction quashed. Per LJ-G Robertson: 'The right of the bailiffs is to exercise the powers . . . of constables. . . . A constable is entitled to arrest, without a warrant, any person seen by him committing a breach of the peace and [having done so] . . . search him. But it is a totally different matter to search a man in order to find evidence to determine whether you will apprehend him or not.'

Statutory power to search after 'reasonable suspicion'.	*Ireland v Russell* 1995 SCCR 685 Misuse of Drugs Act 1971, s 23(2). Appellant searched by constable acting on information received two months earlier. On appeal conviction quashed, since no reasonable grounds existed at time of search. See also: *Gavin v Normand* 1995 SCCR 209 *Stark v Brown* 1997 SCCR 382 *Barr v Normand* 1997 SCCR 511 *Vannet v Taylor* 1998 SCCR 30 *Chassar v Macdonald* 1996 SCCR 730 Civic Government (Scotland) Act 1982, s 60(1). Appellant's friend arrested on theft charges. On way to station officer told appellant he was going to search turn ups in trousers and appellant co-operated and cannabis resin found. Conviction upheld on appeal: statutory powers of search without warrant negated need for consent far less intimation that consent can be withheld. *Cooper v Buchanan* 1996 SCCR 448 Police had information B in possession of drugs in car. Passenger found to have them in search. Upheld on appeal: power to search vehicle covered passengers with suspects when stopped.	Misuse of Drugs Act 1971, s 23(2), (3)
Unless there is urgency, physical evidence from the person of an accused should be obtained under warrant or after charge.	*McGovern v HMA* 1950 JC 33; 1950 SLT 133 Safe blowing. McG suspected of safe blowing. Nail scrapings taken. McG subsequently charged. Evidence held inadmissible as the charge should have come before the scrapings. *Bell v Hogg* 1967 JC 49; 1967 SLT 290 Theft of telephone wires. Verdigris on B's hands. Before any charge had been preferred, police took palm rubbings without warrant but with consent. Evidence held admissible on basis of urgency.	
Conversation taped without the accused's knowledge.	*HMA v Graham* 1990 SCCR 56 Police secretly taped a meeting between G and a civilian witness with the help of the civilian; flagrant transgression of the rules of fairness. G had previously been interviewed by the police. Should have had the right not to self-incriminate. Situation distinguished from that where police eavesdropping on the commission of a crime.	
There is no defence of entrapment in Scots law.	*HMA v Harper* 1989 SCCR 472 Police officer who suspected drugs being sold approached van, asked for and was sold drugs. Objection taken to evidence as unfairly obtained through entrapment. *Held* no defence of entrapment, and in the absence of any evidence of deception, pressure or encouragement to commit crime, evidence admissible.	
Evidence from accused after charge Questioning at trial re change of plea.	*Williamson v HMA* 1980 JC 22 Assault. W pled self-defence initially but later withdrew that plea. Change of plea questioned by Crown in cross-examination. W convicted. Appeal refused. Per LJ-C Wheatley: 'This question was a legitimate and competent one. . . . The objection taken by the appellant's counsel was in anticipation of what the answer might be, and not the question itself.'	

175

Comment by the judge on accused's failure to give evidence.	*Brown v Macpherson* 1918 JC 3 Reset. Evidence led that B had identified one of the thieves. Judge took into account fact that B did not give evidence on his own behalf. B convicted. Appeal refused. Per LJ-G Strathclyde: 'The judge may, and in my opinion ought to . . . comment on the fact [that] the only man in full possession of the facts refrains from going into the witness box for the purpose of establishing his own innocence.'
Subject to the test of fairness, evidence of the accused's actings or statements after charge is admissible.	*Forrester v HMA* 1952 JC 28 Safeblowing. F arrested, cautioned and charged. Thereafter his hand was examined for cut. Search made without F's consent. F convicted. Appeal refused.
Grant of warrants depending on the circumstances, including public interest.	*HMA v Milford* 1973 SLT 12 Rape. M charged with rape, refused to give blood sample voluntarily. Prosecutor petitioned for warrant to take sample. Granted as reasonable in these exceptionally grave circumstances. *Morris v MacNeill* 1991 SCCR 722 Sheriff granting warrant to take blood sample from accused, balancing public interest and the minimal invasion involved. Upheld on appeal. *G v Lees* 1992 SCCR 252 Warrant granted to take blood sample but limited to finger pricks as the accused had a phobia of needles. *Smith v Cardle* 1993 SCCR 609 Murder investigation, one of a set of twins suspected. Warrant sought and obtained to measure S and compare this with evidence from a video to eliminate twin brother. Warrant granted, non-invasive procedure, reasonable in the public interest.
Accused's answer to question not directed to him inadmissible.	*HMA v Leiser* 1926 JC 88 Murder. After being charged, L answered a question which was not addressed to him. Reply held inadmissible. Judge not satisfied accused had not made a mistake.
Reply to caution and charge re lesser offence.	*McAdam v HMA* 1960 JC 1 McA charged with assault to severe injury and subsequently attempted murder. Objection taken at trial to admissibility of reply to McA to caution and charge quoad lesser crime. Reply admitted. Admissibility confirmed on appeal. As both charges contained the element of assault they could be seen as within the same category. *Carmichael v Kinnie* 1993 SCCR 751 Objection to statements made to police about the offence charged and a number of similar offences. *Held* that the police could not ask about the offence already charged but could ask about unrelated matters. Interview only inadmissible as far as matters not already charged.
Entitlement to communicate with solicitor.	*HMA v Cunningham* 1939 JC 61; 1939 SLT 401 Murder. C cautioned and charged. En route to the cells his attention was drawn by police officer to a notice stating that a prisoner was entitled to communicate with a law agent. Made statement after being reminded of earlier caution. Statement held admissible, police observed every requirement of fairness.

Admission by one accused put to co-accused in presence of first accused.

Stark and Smith v HMA 1938 JC 170; 1938 SLT 516
Theft. Two co-accused. Admission by one accused in reply to police interrogation repeated to other accused in presence of first. Both convicted. On appeal, statement held inadmissible against either accused.

Presence of accused when co-accused cautioned and charged.

HMA v Davidson 1968 SLT 17
Attempted murder. D cautioned and charged, brought to bar of police station where co-accused was about to be cautioned and charged. D not advised that his presence would make any incriminating reply by co-accused admissible in evidence against him.
Held that in effect the accused was providing evidence against himself contrary to the fundamental rule that he need not do so once charged, reply inadmissible.

See also:

McNicol v HMA 1993 SCCR 242
Buchan v HMA 1993 SCCR 1076

Fingerprint taken after arrest.

Adair v McGarry 1933 JC 72; 1933 SLT 482
Theft. McG arrested. Fingerprints taken from him held admissible.
Per L.J-G Clyde: '. . . provided a person has been legally arrested by the police, they may search him for stolen goods, or weapons, or other real evidence connecting him with the crime, and . . . neither his consent nor a magistrate's warrant is required for that purpose.'

Namyslak v HMA 1994 SCCR 140
Theft. Fingerprints taken without consent while not under arrest or detention in respect of theft charge led in evidence to prove theft charge. Conviction upheld on appeal.
Held, irregularity excused: no unfairness, since the police had recently obtained fingerprints lawfully for a different charge and could ask for a further set prior to accused being fully committed on this original charge.

HMA v Shepherd 1997 SCCR 246
Accused released on bail without fingerprints taken. Then arrested for further offence and fingerprinted.
Held, fingerprints admissible to prove earlier offence and nothing in CP(S)A 1995, s 18(2) prevents the use to which records of prints lawfully taken may be put in evidence.

Begley v Normand 1992 SCCR 230
Warrant granted to take palmprints after B fully committed as the original prints taken turned out to be defective.

White v Ruxton 1998 SLT 105
Theft. Officer destroyed finger and palm prints in belief accused not to be prosecuted. After trial diet fixed, sheriff allowed warrant for fresh prints.
Held, administrative error: no basis for saying that sheriff wrong in using discretion, and appeal refused.

No further questioning after arrest.	*Wade v Robertson* 1948 JC 117; 1948 SLT 491 Theft. W arrested for theft of whisky. Police showed him bottle recovered from his lodgings and told him he would be questioned about the offence charged. Without any questions W made a self-incriminating statement. *Held*, statement inadmissible. Police not entitled to question further with regard to that particular charge.
	Fraser v HMA 1989 SCCR 82 Appellants charged with assault. In separate cells in police station. Visited by police officer, W, with whom they were friendly and made statements to him. At trial evidence of these statements left to the jury by the sheriff. Appellants appealed on ground that statements induced by W and unfairly obtained. It was conceded in the appeal that issue properly left to jury under proper directions. *Held* that in view of the concession it was not possible to say that the jury were not entitled to have regard to the statements, and that they were entitled to hold that they were not procured by inducement. Appeal refused.
Statements to persons other than the police Questioning by employer.	*Waddell v Kinnaird* 1922 JC 40; 1922 SLT 344 Theft. Quantity of oil in possession of W, a railwayman. Arrested by railway police and cautioned. Later questioned by stationmaster in presence of civilian police. W convicted. Appeal rejected, allowed to seek an explanation so long as there is nothing to suggest improper motive.
Interview by employers' investigators.	*Morrison v Burrell* 1947 JC 43; 1947 SLT 190 Fraud, attempted fraud. Horseracing bets placed by M, a sub-postmaster, who falsified date-stamping of envelopes. M interviewed under caution as suspect by Post Office investigators. Statement admitted and M convicted. Appeal rejected. *Held*, domestic investigation into public service department. Can be no objection to replies voluntarily given.
Confidentiality restricted to spouse and solicitor.	*HMA v Parker* 1944 JC 49; 1944 SLT 195 Murder. P, Canadian serviceman, visited in prison by brother to whom he made statement about how death occurred. Objection to admissibility repelled at trial. *Held*, only spouses and solicitors protected by the doctrine of confidentiality.
Incriminating remark accidentally overheard.	*HMA v O'Donnell* 1975 SLT (Sh Ct) 22 Assault. O'D in custody shouted incriminating remark to a co-accused which was overheard by police officers. Objection to admissibility repelled. Per Sheriff Macphail: 'It is clear that the incriminating statement was voluntarily emitted by the fourth accused, that no inducement was offered to him, that the witness who overheard the statement had not been ordered to do so but spontaneously stopped and listened when the accused shouted, and that the witness neither knew that the fourth accused was in custody, nor had any reason to suspect him of having been implicated in the assault.'

Prolonged questioning by Customs investigators.

HMA v Friel 1978 SLT (Notes) 21
Tax frauds. F, with others, interviewed by Customs and Excise investigators, first for three and a half hours, then, after caution, for another twelve and a half hours. At trial, objection to admissibility of answers in second interview sustained.
Held that questioning unfair, in the nature of cross-examination and pressure placed on the accused.

Immigration officers.

Williams v Friel 1998 SCCR 649
Immigration officer never accused appellant of offence, but asked to interview him because he believed passport was a forgery.
Held, statement on way to interview not unfair and therefore admissible.

Statement made by suspected shoplifter to shop manager.

McCuaig v Annan 1986 SCCR 535
Manager saw McC put articles in pocket and leave without paying. Followed her and removed articles. She agreed to return to the office and made statements without having been cautioned.
Held that evidence admissible as the test was whether what had happened was fair to the appellant.

Evidence disclosing previous convictions
Unless evidence of previous conviction(s) is necessary to prove the offence(s) charged, it is inadmissible to elicit it.

Cannot be invoked where accused leads evidence of his own good character from his own witnesses (CP(S)A 1995, s 270 is available).

Murphy v HMA 1978 JC 1
M pled guilty to charges of theft, assault and breach of the peace and admitted previous convictions. M induced his solicitor to make false representations which mitigated the penalty and was subsequently charged with perverting the course of justice.
Held relevant to incorporate reference to admission of previous convictions as evidence in causa of substantive charge and to show the mitigating effect of the false information.

Nelson v HMA 1994 SCCR 192
Crown leading evidence of N swallowing a substance on being approached by the police, an offence in itself, to prove a charge of supplying drugs. Allowed on appeal.
Per LJ-G Hope: 'The Crown can lead any evidence relevant to the proof of a crime charged, even though it may show or tend to show the commission of another crime not charged, unless fair notice requires that that other crime should be charged or otherwise expressly referred to in the complaint or indictment.'

Criminal Procedure (Scotland) Act 1995

Accused cross-examined as to character and previous convictions
Section 266(4). Accused not to be asked questions tending to show commission of an offence other than those charged, or bad character, unless—
(a) proof of offence admissible *quoad* offence charged; or
(b) evidence of accused's good character led or character of complainer impugned or nature of defence is such as to involve imputations of character of prosecution or prosecution witness or complainer; or
(c) accused has given evidence against any co-accused.

Section 266(5), (6). If prosecutor wishes to invoke s 266(4)(b) he must apply to the trial judge for permission in the absence of the jury.

Section 270. Evidence not to be led that the accused has committed an offence other than those charged or is of bad character unless—
(a) evidence of accused's good character led or character of prosecution or prosecution witness impugned; or
(b) nature or conduct of the defence to tend to establish the accused's good character or involve imputations on character of prosecution or prosecution witness.

CP(S)A 1995, s 270 mirrors CP(S)A 1995, s 266(4)(b), and closes the loophole where accused does not give evidence.
Note: In CP(S)A 1995, s 270(1)(b), the definition of nature of defence is wider to also include 'such as tend to establish the accused's good character'.

In case of prison breaking disclosure of previous convictions is inevitable.

Varey v HMA 1985 SCCR 425
V and others charged with prison breaking. Indictment specified length of sentences and crimes for which imposed.
Held that to prove appellants were lawfully confined at date of charge, Crown required to prove date and length of sentences, and appeals dismissed.

Previous convictions

Solemn procedure:
Section 101(1), (2). Previous convictions not to be laid before jury or reference made to them before verdict unless as evidence in support of a substantive charge or where crown permitted to lead evidence in terms of CP(S)A 1995, s 266 or s 270.

Milne v HMA 1995 SCCR 751
Charge of driving while disqualified and without insurance. In cross-examination appellant changed plea to guilty and was then charged with perjury. At perjury trial Crown led evidence that earlier trial concluded with plea of guilty.
Held, competent to lead evidence in support of perjury charge and appellant convicted.

Section 101(3). Previous convictions must not be laid before judge until prosecutor moves for sentence.

Road traffic disqualification listing of previous convictions where not competently supporting substantive charge not allowed.

Mitchell v Dean 1979 JC 62; 1979 SLT (Notes) 12
Driving while disqualified and without insurance. Trial evidence included extract conviction *quoad* disqualification which referred to admission of six previous convictions. M convicted.
Held, on appeal, that evidence in relation to six previous convictions not competent to support substantive charge and conviction quashed.

Summary procedure:
Section 166(1), (3)–(8). Previous convictions not to be laid before judge until charge proved unless as evidence in support of a substantive charge or under CP(S)A 1995, s 266 or s 270 of this Act.

Boustead v M'Leod 1979 JC 70; 1979 SLT (Notes) 48
Driving while disqualified and without insurance. Trial evidence included extract conviction referring to public mischief offence. B convicted.
Held, on appeal, evidence inadmissible and conviction quashed. Prejudice to be confined within the narrowest limits.

But see:

Criminal Law (Consolidation) (Scotland) Act 1995, s 5(5). Defence that being a man under the age of 24 years who had not previously been charged with like offence had reasonable cause to believe that the girl was of or over the age of 16 years.

Strictly construed.

Robertson v Aitchison 1981 SCCR 149; 1981 SLT (Notes) 127
Driving while disqualified. At trial evidence incorporated extract conviction which referred to an offence additional to that which had led to R's disqualification. R convicted.
Held, on appeal, that reference to previous conviction was a fatal flaw and conviction quashed.
Opinion of the court: 'The words of the statute are clear, the risk of prejudice is guarded against by the strictness of its prohibition which operates "in any proceedings".'

Breach of statutory prohibition not necessarily sufficient to constitute miscarriage of justice.

McAvoy and Jackson v HMA 1982 SCCR 263; 1983 SLT 16
Theft by housebreaking. J, in a voluntary statement to police, made reference to 'two guys who I know from the jail'. Statement given in evidence. No direction in charge to jury to disregard implied reference to previous convictions. Jury, on sheriff's suggestion, took voluntary statement to jury room while deliberating. J convicted.
Held, on appeal, that the reference to previous conviction had been a breach of CP(S)A 1975, s 160(1), but no miscarriage of justice and appeal refused. No objection raised by the defence at the time.

Disclosure of previous convictions creating no risk of prejudice.

Moffat v Smith 1983 SCCR 392
Driving while disqualified. M convicted. Trial evidence incorporated extract conviction referring to two offences (for driving without licence and without insurance) in respect of which M disqualifed. Submission, that reference to one would have been sufficient, repelled and appeal dismissed. No risk of prejudice.

Robertson v HMA 1995 SCCR 497
Witness referred to helping appellant in SACRO (Scottish Association for Care and Resettlement of Offenders). Judge in charge told jury to ignore extraneous matters. Conviction upheld on appeal, since (1) unlikely jurors knew what SACRO stood for; and (2) if they did, they were covered by the judge's charge.

Harkin v HMA 1996 SCCR 5
Appellant charged on indictment of driving while disqualified. Procurator fiscal depute in speech to jury said they must ignore fact that disqualification result of previous conviction. Conviction upheld on appeal: no miscarriage of justice, although comment unnecessary and sheriff entitled to take view that less harm to appellant by not referring to it.

Maclean v Buchanan 1997 SLT 91
Police witness asked by fiscal to read out part of form recording why accused refused Camic breathalyser procedure. Revealed accused had answered he had been convicted earlier of an offence.
Held, no miscarriage of justice, since witness not pressed unreasonably and sheriff could put it out of his mind.

Where credibility in issue.

Graham v HMA 1983 SCCR 315; 1984 SLT 67
G tried on four charges. Offer of plea of guilty to charges 2, 3 and 4 rejected. On first charge, wife assault, credibility at issue. Evidence elicited of reply to caution and charge *quoad* charge 2 (breach of the peace) which was: 'That cow's got me the jail again.' Jury directed to disregard reply.
Held deliberate eliciting of evidence irredeemably prejudicial, and conviction on charge 1 quashed.
Per LJ-G Emslie: 'So grave was the breach, and so important was the issue of credibility, that we are satisfied that the effect of the breach of the peremptory direction in [CP(S)A 1975,] section 160(1) upon the minds of the jurors could not reasonably be expected to have been obliterated by anything the sheriff tried to do. . . .'

Previous convictions elicited by questioning.

Slane v HMA 1984 SCCR 77
S tried for conspiracy to rob with two others. During Crown evidence, counsel for one of the co-accused elicited in cross-examination of a Crown witness that S had previous convictions. 'Ample evidence' of S's guilt. Judge gave direction to jury to disregard evidence of previous convictions.
Held that questions should not have been asked, action of counsel inexcusable, but no miscarriage of justice.

McLean v Tudhope 1982 SCCR 555
McL charged with breach of the peace. On cross-examination by prosecutor, McL was asked whether he regarded himself as honest with a previous conviction. No reply. On re-examination by defence solicitor McL stated one previous conviction. Because of revelation of earlier conviction, McL liberated on appeal. Violation of CP(S)A 1975, s 346(1)(f) (replaced by CP(S)A 1995, s 266(4)).

Kepple v HMA 1936 JC 76
Assault on wife. Libel evincing previous violence and malice. At trial wife made reference to 'previous convictions'. K convicted. Appeal refused, it being *held* that the information had been volunteered not elicited.

Haslam v HMA 1936 JC 82

Fraud. H charged with fraud offences had at police station at first given false name. At trial evidence by police witness that H had been asked if name was Haslam and that witness, for identification purposes, had then examined hand wound. H convicted. Appeal refused but in the course of his judgment LJ-C Aitchison observed obiter. 'When a reference is made to a previous conviction by an officer of the police, who ought to know better, it is obviously prejudicial to a fair trial . . . an accused is not fairly tried if an inspector of police, when he gets an opening in a question inadvertently addressed to him, makes a reference, direct or indirect, to the record of the man who is standing his trial.'

See also:

Armstrong v HMA 1993 SCCR 311

Special rules re reset.

Deighan v Macleod 1959 JC 25

Theft. Two accused. Police witness speaking of accused being 'known thieves'. Conviction upheld, not act of prosecutor.

Watson v HMA (1894) Adam 355

Reset. W charged with reset. During trial evidence of previous conviction for reset tendered. W convicted. Appeal dismissed.

Per Lord Rutherford Clark: 'Under the statute the previous conviction may be given in evidence in order to prove guilty knowledge . . . at any stage in the proceedings provided only that evidence has been given that the stolen property has been found in the possession of the accused. . . .'

Prevention of Crimes Act 1871, s 19. In prosecution for reset competent to lead evidence that accused in possession of other stolen property within previous twelve months. Previous offence of fraud or dishonesty within the preceding five years may be taken into consideration.

Disclosure of manner of accused's identification no reference to previous conviction.

Corcoran v HMA 1932 JC 40

Housebreaking. C convicted. Fact that C's arrest based upon identification from a police photograph album disclosed in court.

Held, on appeal, that disclosure fell short of reference to previous conviction.

HMA v McIlwain 1965 JC 40

Assault and robbery. Special defence of alibi. Objection to leading of evidence *quoad* identification by police officers repelled. Not always incompetent to lead evidence just because it may incidentally reveal previous convictions.

Exception to general prohibition: reference rebutting defence of innocence.

Carberry v HMA 1975 JC 40; 1976 SLT 38

C and two others charged with conspiracy to rob. Evidence led at trial that co-accused of C had made voluntary statement, before arrest, that he had obtained car, allegedly used in furtherance of conspiracy, from man 'met in Barlinnie'. C convicted. Appeal refused.

Opinion of the court: 'The jurisdiction is a delicate one and in its exercise it is necessary to keep firmly in view that the statutory prohibition is designed in the interests and for the protection of accused persons and, therefore, that there is a heavy onus on a prosecutor who seeks to support the competence of evidence which directly or indirectly brings to the knowledge of judge or jury or leads to the drawing of the inference, that the accused has been previously convicted. One of the categories of possible exception from the consequences of breach of the statutory prohibition is where the reference tends to rebut a defence of innocence which might otherwise be open to the accused . . . each case must depend on its own facts and circumstances. . .'

Police referring to accused as a housebreaker.	*Smith v HMA* 1975 SLT (Notes) 89 S, charged with theft, identified by police witness who referred to him twice as, 'known to me as Smith, a housebreaker'. No warning to jury to disregard evidence. S convicted, quashed on appeal. *Held* that the trial judge should have directed the jury to ignore such evidence.
Relevant evidence of collateral matters will be admitted if fairness requires it.	*HMA v Kay* 1970 JC 68; 1970 SLT (Notes) 66 Murder of K's husband. Indictment libelled previous evincing of malice and ill-will. At trial K's counsel allowed to lodge hospital records relating to treatment after alleged assaults by deceased. *Held* admissible to lead evidence of these to show the accused had reason to apprehend danger. Departure from general rule justified.
Accused forced to admit he was in prison at specified time.	*Cordiner v HMA* 1978 JC 64; 1978 SLT 118 Extortion. C, with another, indicted inter alia on a charge of extortion. Special defence of alibi that he was in prison at the time. At trial, evidence of date of conversations grounding charge imprecise and charge withdrawn. C convicted on other charges. *Held*, on appeal, that C had been compelled to disclose record, and conviction quashed. Opinion of the court: 'We cannot say that the jury would have convicted if the Crown had not erred at the outset in forcing the appellant to admit that he was in prison in June 1976.'
Evidence revealing previous assaults bearing on conclusions in medical reports.	*Gemmill v HMA* 1980 JC 16; 1979 SLT 217 Murder. G's mental condition at issue *quoad* diminished responsibility. Medical evidence disclosed previous assaults on females. G convicted by jury. *Held*, on appeal, that evidence introduced for purposes connected with G's medical history not admissible *quoad* guilt and that the judge should thus have directed the jury to disregard this evidence. However, not misdirection sufficient to require quashing of conviction. *Note:* G was convicted of culpable homicide, not murder.
Caution and charge referring to previous convictions—insufficient miscarriage of justice.	*McCuaig v HMA* 1982 SCCR 125; 1982 SLT 383 McC convicted on a number of charges. Police witness speaking to caution and charge disclosed to jury that charge referred to previous convictions. *Held*, on appeal, that there had been a breach of the statutory provisions, but miscarriage of justice not sufficient to set aside conviction.
Disclosure accidental.	*Johnston v Allan* 1983 SCCR 500 Driving without licence. J tried on a number of road traffic contraventions including driving without a licence. During trial a computer printout was production to establish J did not hold a licence. Sheriff asked for and was handed printout he saw on 'production table', which was, however, a different printout disclosing previous convictions. J convicted. Appeal refused, previous convictions not 'laid before the court' by the prosecutor, just an unfortunate accident. *Grugen v HMA* 1991 SCCR 526 Witness spontaneously implicating G in a crime with which he was not charged. Prosecutor commenting on this matter in his charge to the jury. Conviction upheld on appeal. Prosecutor entitled to make such comment as evidence spontaneous.

Cross-examination on character.	*Leggate v HMA* 1988 SCCR 391 L charged with assault and robbery. Evidence came from two police officers who spoke to an admission by L and two other officers who said that L took them to where weapon hidden. L alleged that police had 'fitted him up' and were lying. Trial judge, relying on *Templeton v HMA* 1985 SCCR 357, allowed Crown to cross-examine L as to character, and he admitted various analogous convictions. *Held* by bench of seven judges (1) where nature or conduct of defence is such as to involve imputations on the character of Crown witnesses, accused is liable to cross-examination on his character in terms of CP(S)A 1975, s 141(1)(f)(ii), and whether or not it was necessary for an accused to conduct his defence in this way in order to establish his defence fairly is irrelevant, but that s 141(1)(f)(ii) does not apply where the accused merely asserts that a Crown witness is lying; (2) that a trial judge has a wide discretion to refuse to allow an accused to be cross-examined on his character, that the fundamental test is one of fairness, having regard both to the position of the accused and the public interest in bringing wrongdoers to justice, and that a significant factor in the exercise of the discretion is whether the questions asked of the Crown witnesses were integral and necessary to the defence or were a deliberate attack on the character of the witness; (3) that while s 161(1) of Criminal Procedure (Scotland) Act 1975 prohibits the prosecutor from laying a list of the accused's previous convictions before a judge, it does not prevent him making reference to them by giving judge relevant information; and (4) trial judge had erred in not exercising his discretion and there had been miscarriage of justice. Appeal allowed and conviction quashed.
Penalty notice applicable to second offence.	*Bryce v Gardiner* 1951 JC 134; 1952 SLT 90 Licensing Act offences. B, a licence holder, charged with breach of conditions of certificate and contravention of statute. Penalty liability referred to in complaint disclosed implicitly that it was a second offence which was alleged. Conviction quashed on appeal. *Held* that an alert judge would have seen the penalty and known there was a previous conviction.
Separate libelling of charges.	*McGregor v Macdonald* 1952 JC 4; 1952 SLT 94 Theft. McG and others charged with theft and, being 'known thieves' loitering with intent to steal. List of previous convictions annexed to indictment. Conviction on theft charge quashed. *Held* that charges should have been separately libelled. Statutory provision designed to exclude prejudice but effect here was to nullify that purpose since one charge within general rule and other not.
Inadvertent disclosure of endorsement on licence.	*Clark v Connell* 1952 JC 119; 1952 SLT 421 Comparison drawn between Connell's handwriting and signature on licence. Examination of licence by sheriff inadvertently disclosed endorsement, although not offence for which imposed. Connell's objection to evidence upheld by sheriff and Connell acquitted. On appeal by Crown court held sheriff to have been mistaken in sustaining objection to competency as information not 'laid before' the sheriff, but appeal dismissed on other grounds.

Evidence of bad character
(i) of the accused
Cross-examination of wife—who was accused—on fidelity.

HMA v Grudins 1976 SLT (Notes) 10
Murder of husband. G asked by Crown whether she had remained faithful to husband during separation. Defence objection on basis that question attempted to impugn G's character sustained.
Per Lord Stewart (quoting LJ-C Thomson in *O'Hara v HMA* 1948 JC 90; 1948 SLT 372): '"The fundamental consideration is a fair trial and there may be cases where the price which the accused may be called upon to pay if cross-examined will be out of all proportion to the extent and nature of the imputations cast on the witnesses who testify against him." I would have no hesitation here in using my discretion in favour of disallowing the line of cross-examination. . . . There must be a limit to what can be explored.'

Accused giving evidence against co-accused is open to question on record.

McCourtney v HMA 1977 JC 68; 1978 SLT 10
Manufacture of controlled drug. McC convicted along with four co-accused. Appealed on basis that judge had allowed a co-accused's counsel to ask questions of McC which elicited his previous convictions, McC having given evidence already against co-accused. Conviction upheld.
Opinion of the court: 'Once an accused has given evidence against a co-accused there is no discretion in the trial judge to refuse to the co-accused the right to cross-examine him as to his criminal record.

Burton v HMA 1979 SLT (Notes) 59
B and co-accused J tried on charge of attempted extortion. J acquitted, B convicted. B appealed on basis that J's counsel had been allowed to cross-examine B on issue of character, B having given evidence already against J. Appeal dismissed.
Held, B's evidence against J was damaging, J entitled to cross-examine.

Reluctant witness—evidence relevant to explain reluctance.

Manson v HMA 1951 JC 49; 1951 SLT 181
Assault. M charged with assault (razor slashing). At trial hesitant witness claimed she had been threatened by, allegedly, M's wife about giving evidence. M convicted. On appeal submitted that jury should have been directed to disregard evidence of intimidation, presumably as suggesting bad character of M. Appeal refused.
Held, not evidence against M but evidence to explain the reluctance of the witness.

(ii) of the witness
Witness's conversation with complainer relevant *quoad* credibility.

Donald McFarlane (1834) 6 SJ 321
Assault with intent to ravish.
Held competent to ask witness about his conversation with victim with a view to testing her credibility, but not competent to ask another witness what first witness had repeated to him in an attempt to prove 'latent acts of individual unchastity'.
Per Lord Neaves: 'Such a course would be contrary to the principles of justice, and of judicial inquiry.'

Sinclair v MacDonald 1996 SCCR 466
CP(S)A 1975, s 346(1)(f)(ii). Dangerous driving. Witnesses accused of lying. Stated that Mrs P, activated by malice, accelerated to prevent appellant returning to his own side of the road. Sheriff took view that this went beyond suggestions of perjury and involved serious imputations on their characters and granted leave to cross-examine appellant as to character. Upheld on appeal: sheriff used discretion correctly.

185

One witness not to be asked about character of another.	*Thomas Wight* (1836) 1 Swin 47 Theft and horsestealing. *Held* incompetent for prosecutor to ask prosecution witness about general character of one of defence witnesses. Per Lord Meadowbank: 'Even in cases of rape, where the character of the woman is so material a point, such questions are not allowed, unless a special defence impugning her character has been given in.'
Evidence of general disposition but not specific acts of violence.	*James Irving* (1838) 2 Swin 109 Cutting and stabbing. I attempted to prove that his alleged victim had perpetrated specific acts of violence on other occasions, and led evidence to show 'passionate disposition' of victim in support of claim that offence committed in self-defence. *Held* competent to lead evidence of victim's 'passionate disposition' having given notice in his defences of intention to do so, but not to prove specific acts of violence committed by victim. *Brady v HMA* 1986 SCCR 191 B convicted of attempted murder and pleaded self-defence. Sought to lead evidence of assaults by complainer on third parties. Appealed on ground that trial judge was wrong to reject this evidence. *Held*, following *James Irving* (1838) 2 Swin 109 that evidence of specific acts of violence by complainer against third parties was inadmissible except in exceptional circumstances, as in *HMA v Kay* 1970 JC 68; 1970 SLT (Notes) 66. *Robert Porteous* (1841) Bell's Notes 293 Murder. *Held* competent for Crown to ask whether deceased was quarrelsome or inoffensive, although his character had not been impugned by P, but incompetent to ask whether another individual involved, who was not an injured party, was quarrelsome or inoffensive.
General character, but not specific acts of unchastity.	*David Allan* (1842) 1 Broun 500 Rape or assault with intent to ravish. A pled not guilty. Gave in special defences that alleged victim was of unchaste character and had previously had sexual intercourse with other men. *Held* (1) principal witness in such a charge not bound to answer questions whether on particular previous occasions she had intercourse with other men; (2) incompetent for panel to prove this by evidence of witnesses although notice had been given in special defences that the proof was proposed; (3) proof of general reputation of witness in respect of chastity allowed. *Walter Blair* (1844) 2 Broun 167 Rape, murder, assault with intent to ravish. B submitted special defences setting forth that attack on character of victim would be made. *Held* (1) incompetent to prove by examination of mother of injured party in rape charge that her daughter, since deceased, and from whom a dying declaration had been taken, had been convicted of theft; (2) proof tending to show in terms of special defences lodged that victim had shortly before had voluntary intercourse with B admissible. Opinion of the court: On special notice being given, competent for party accused of rape to prove that alleged victim had previously had criminal intercourse with other men.

John McMillan (1846) Ark 209

Rape.

Held competent for prosecutor to lead evidence of alleged victim's good character, even although McM had not lodged special defences impugning her character, but this evidence should not be brought forward at commencement of trial.

Held, character relevant as making it likely the woman did or did not consent.

James Reid and Others (1861) 4 Irv 124

Rape or assault with intent to ravish. Special defence of alibi, and statement that victim of unchaste character and unfaithful to her husband with other men.

Held (1) in a charge of rape, although the unchaste character of the woman said to have been ravished is not matter of defence, due notice must be given to prosecutor if panel intends to lead evidence of a woman's unchastity; (2) incompetent to lead evidence in respect of character other than that at or about time of alleged offence; (3) incompetent to lead evidence of character on points collateral to the issue, not forming part of *res gestae*.

Per Lord Ardmillan: 'It would be most unfair to the woman to admit evidence of what is said to have taken place, it may be 12, 15, or 18 years ago. . . . The rule [as applicable to charges of rape] applies to proof of unchastity at, and immediately before, the time when the rape is said to have been committed.'

Bremner v HMA 1992 SCCR 476

Rape. Character of the complainer, CP(S)A 1975, s 141B. B wished to lead evidence of a previous sexual relationship with the complainer. Leave refused, appeal.

Held that it was a matter for the trial judge to decide in the interests of justice. No interference here. Time gap of eight months between the relationship ending and the alleged offence.

Sexual character

Criminal Procedure (Scotland) Act 1995

Section 274(1). Briefly, in a trial on sexual offence the court shall not allow questioning by defence designed to show the complainer:

(a) is not of good sexual character;

(b) is a prostitute; or

(c) has at any time engaged with any person in sexual behaviour not forming part of subject matter of charge.

Section 275(1). There are exceptions to the above rule where—

(a) question designed to rebut or explain evidence otherwise than by accused;

(b) question under s 274(1)(c) above is relevant to defence of incrimination or relates to sexual behaviour which took place on same occasion as that forming subject matter of charge; or

(c) contrary to interests of justice to exclude question.

Section 275(2). Where questioning allowed, court may limit the extent at any time as it thinks fit.

Section 275(3). Application to be made in course of trial but in absence of jury, complainer, witnesses and public.

Illegally obtained evidence may
be admissible.
Urgency.

Bell v Hogg 1967 JC 49; 1967 SLT 290
Theft of copper wire. Police intercepted van carrying B and others and cautioned but did not charge
them. Palm rubbings taken but B not told expressly
that he was entitled to refuse. B convicted. Appeal
refused. Per LJ-G Clyde: 'The urgency of the matter is its justification.'

Edgely v Barbour 1994 SCCR 789
Radar device retrieved from car without search
warrant. Conviction upheld on appeal: irregularity
excusable on grounds of urgency, since impracticable to obtain search warrant by leaving locus for
several hours. Unlikely the appellant could have
been detained in car for this period, and would
have ample time to dispose of the device.

Welbey v Ritchie 1997 SCCR 472
Charge of theft of three squash racquets. While
accused in detention for four hours, police traced
car and searched it and found racquets. Police
said the reasons for the search were the risk of
removal; inexperienced officer available to guard
vehicle; and fear that warrant could not be
obtained before detention ended.
Held, urgency excused search and appeal
refused.

HMA v McGuigan 1936 JC 16; 1936 SLT 161

Walsh v MacPhail 1978 SLT (Notes) 29

Fairley v Fishmongers of London 1951 JC 14;
1951 SLT 54

Lawrie v Muir 1950 JC 19; 1950 SLT 37

Leckie v Miln 1981 SCCR 261; 1982 SLT 177

Hay v HMA 1968 JC 40

Non-urgency.

McGovern v HMA 1950 JC 33; 1950 SLT 133
Theft by opening lockfast place. McG not charged
or apprehended in connection with safe blowing,
but kept in police station for six hours during which
police obtained scrapings from fingernails of McG
for chemical analysis. McG later charged.
Held evidence inadmissible, as no question of
urgency, and no knowledge by police as to
whether scrapings would yield any evidence of
McG's connection with offence.

Forrester v HMA 1952 JC 28.

Wilson v Brown 1996 SCCR 470
Appellant attended rave and was searched by
stewards without consent and found with controlled drugs.
Held, no authority for search. It could not be
excused on grounds of urgency, since stewards
could have detained appellant until police arrived.
Appeal allowed and conviction quashed.
Observed, search for offensive weapon might
have been justified in circumstances.

SUFFICIENCY

As evidence requires to be sufficient, there must be corroboration of the essential facts of **the identification of the accused** and **the commission of the crime**, except when there is a **statutory non-requirement for corroboration**. There need not be corroboration of **procedural matters** or **incidental matters**. Special considerations apply in the case of **the *Moorov* doctrine** (named after *Moorov v HMA* 1930 JC 68; 1930 SLT 596) and **the circumstantial confession**. There may be **inferential corroboration from *de recenti*** possession.

COMMENTARY	CASE LAW	STATUTE LAW
The identification of the accused It is essential that identification of the accused be explicit.	*Bruce v HMA* 1936 JC 39 Wilful fire raising. B convicted on evidence of witnesses not asked expressly to identify B, but certain of whom referred 'to the accused James Bruce'. On appeal conviction quashed because B not directly identified in court.	
	Wilson v Brown 1947 JC 81 Sale of adulterated whisky. W convicted on evidence of witnesses not asked expressly to identify her. One witness said he knew the owner of the hotel to be Mrs Wilson, another that he knew licence holder to be Mrs J W S Wilson. On appeal conviction quashed because no express identification of accused by witnesses.	
During trial, accused under no duty to facilitate ID.	*Beattie v Scott* 1990 SCCR 296 *Held* on appeal that the sheriff erred in requiring the accused to stand up to assist the Crown with the ID. Accused had no duty to do so, so long as not taking positive steps to conceal his identity.	
Evidence of earlier identification is admissible.	*Muldoon v Herron* 1970 JC 30; 1970 SLT 228 Breach of the peace. Witnesses could not identify M in court and one denied having identified M to police previously. Police evidence of previous identification by witnesses held to corroborate evidence by witnesses that identification made to police at the time of the offence. Per LJ-C Grant: 'The evidence of the police as to who was identified is primary and direct evidence of that matter and no question arises of hearsay evidence in the sense of evidence designed to establish the truth of a statement by proving that the statement was made.'	
	Bennett v HMA 1976 JC 1; 1976 SLT (Notes) 90 Assault to severe injury. D identified on day of assault by victim and two other witnesses none of whom able to identify him at the trial. Police officer gave evidence of previous identification of B by witnesses and victim. B convicted. Appeal refused. *Held*, identification need not be visual. Concurrences of independent fact even if each spoken to by only one witness may be enough when taken together.	
	McGaharon v HMA 1968 SLT (Notes) 99 Breach of the peace and assault. Two witnesses unable to identify McG at trial. Police evidence of identification by these witnesses to police at time of the incident held to be sufficient identification. McG convicted. Per Sheriff Middleton: '. . . evidence by policeman that a particular witness identified a particular person at the time may be very much better than identification by a witness himself six months later in the witness box.'	

Neeson v HMA 1984 SCCR 72
Murder. Two police witnesses gave evidence that N identified at identification parade by witness. This witness unable to identify N in court. N convicted and appeal dismissed.
Held, corroborative material from what happened at the identification parade.

See also:

Maxwell v HMA 1990 SCCR 363
Hawkins v Carmichael 1992 SCCR 348
McEwan v HMA 1990 SCCR 401

Corroboration of identification normally required unless there is statutory provision to the contrary.

Morton v HMA 1938 JC 50; 1938 SLT 27
Indecent assault. M identified by complainer at identification parade and at trial. The only other witness failed to identify M. M convicted. On appeal conviction quashed.
Held, insufficient evidence.
Opinion of the court: '. . . by the law of Scotland no person can be convicted of a crime or a statutory offence except where the legislature otherwise directs unless there is evidence of at least two witnesses implicating the person accused with the commission of the crime or offence with which he is charged.'

Robson v HMA 1996 SCCR 340
Appellant's conviction of using lewd practices towards brother and sister upheld on appeal despite one complainer not asked to point out appellant in court.
Held, sufficient that man described by children was complainer along with parent's identification and circumstantial detail.
Observed, Crown should have complied with rule for identifying accused in court.

Harrison v Mackenzie 1923 JC 61; 1923 SLT 565
Illegal trawling. Name of vessel read through telescope by only one witness. H convicted. Quashed on appeal.
Per Lord Hunter: '. . . it is always essential that vital testimony given by a single witness against the person accused should be corroborated, either by the testimony of other witnesses, or by facts and circumstances.'

Dudley v HMA 1995 SCCR 52
Appellant convicted of rape. Complainer did not attend identification parade and court was cleared when she pointed out appellant. Conviction upheld on appeal: issue for jury to determine and in any event other evidence overwhelming.

Bainbridge v Scott 1968 SLT 871
Criminal damage. B admitted to police that he had damaged car and van with paint stripper. B had also freely admitted to owners of two vehicles that he was responsible for the damage.
Held that the accused's special knowledge sufficient to corroborate admission to the police but observed that evidence of confession to the owners did not corroborate evidence of confession made to the police.

Sinclair v MacLeod 1962 JC 19
Careless driving. Driver of the car owned by S not identified at locus. Later, police arrived at S's house to find wife locking the car door. S in bed admitted to police he was the driver. S convicted. Quashed on appeal, insufficient corroboration.

Reilly v HMA 1981 SCCR 201
Assault and robbery. Corroboration relied on by Crown consisted of weak sometimes contradictory pieces of circumstantial evidence. Conviction quashed on appeal.
Opinion of the court: 'The question . . . is whether that evidence, in character, quality and strength, is apt to entitle the jury to treat it as corroborative of the evidence of [the witness]. We have come to be of the opinion that it was not.'

Mair v HMA 1997 SCCR 44
Robbery conviction upheld on appeal.
Held, where positive identification by one witness all that was needed was other evidence consistent in all respects with positive identification.

Ralston v HMA 1987 SCCR 467
R convicted of assaulting a security guard and attempting to rob him. Evidence consisted of positive identification at identification parade and in court by victim and weak evidence from two other guards that R's face resembled that of the assailant.
Held that where one starts with a positive emphatic identification by one witness, very little else is required provided that it is consistent with the positive evidence. Appeal refused.

Winter v Heywood 1995 SCCR 276
Conviction of driving while disqualified upheld on appeal. Appellant registered keeper of car gave false information as to identification of driver.
Held, reply not simply false denial and giving false information sufficient with fact appellant registered keeper to corroborate eyewitness.

Souter v Lees 1995 SCCR 33
Accused convicted of careless driving had denied car at locus since he had key. Upheld on appeal since no explanation of theft, and sheriff had not treated reply as admission but held on basis of other evidence that his car involved and he was driver.

Nelson v HMA 1988 SCCR 536
One positive identification sufficiently corroborated by identification by build.

MacDonald v HMA 1997 SCCR 116
Convicted of murder, assault and robbery.
Held, on appeal, complainer's evidence that appellant 'doesn't look unlike' and 'same build, also facially' fell short of amounting to a positive identification (even if treated as equivalent that appellant looked like driver of car). Conviction quashed.

Murphy v HMA 1995 SCCR 55
Murder. Question of identity. Witness described appellant as 'just the height and the dark hair colour'. Conviction upheld on appeal.
Held, evidence of resemblance capable of corroborating positive identification (also there was other evidence strengthening witness who spoke to resemblance).

Fisher v Guild 1991 SCCR 308
Road traffic. Passenger identifying accused as the driver. Only two in the car and as passenger held to be credible there was sufficient identification.

See also:

Webb v HMA 1996 SCCR 530
Judge should warn jury of care needed with eye-witness identification.

Cuthbert v Hingston 1993 SCCR 87

Kelly v HMA 1998 SCCR 660
One positive identification. At identification parade, complainer said 'either number three or four'. Appellant was number four.
Held, it was not fatal that more than one person was picked out as resembling individual in question. Conviction upheld.

Contradictory evidence of identifying witnesses.

Robertson v HMA 1990 SCCR 142
R identified by two witnesses who differed as to his clothing. Convicted.
Held on appeal, up to jury to assess reliability, one reliable witness alone would have been sufficient to corroborate the special knowledge admission R had made.

See also:

McDonald v Scott 1993 SCCR 78
Gilmour v HMA 1994 SCCR 133
McGeoch v HMA 1991 SCCR 487

Evidence of identification can be corroborated by the accused's actings at the time of the offence.

O'Donnell v HMA 1979 SLT (Notes) 64
Assault. Evidence of principal eyewitness held by sheriff as corroborated only by circumstantial evidence of O'D being seen at the locus at least ten minutes after crime. O'D convicted. Conviction quashed on appeal.
Per LJ-C Wheatley: 'No reasonable jury could have accepted that evidence as corroboration. . . .'

Gracie v Allan 1987 SCCR 364
G convicted of theft by housebreaking. Principal evidence that of Mrs F who identified him as being in the back garden of the house in question. Mrs F said accused very like the person she saw. For corroboration Crown relied on evidence that G found acting suspiciously a quarter of a mile away twenty minutes after the housebreaking.
Held that it was not necessary that identification witness be 100 per cent certain and there was sufficient other evidence to corroborate that identification.

MacNeill v Wilson 1981 SCCR 80
Use of lorry carrying insecure load. W identified by one of his passengers as driver of the lorry, also seen by another witness examining the lorry after accident. W made no admissions to the police but produced damaged strop and said this was being used at the time the load fell from the lorry. W acquitted. On Crown's appeal conviction ordered, evidence that the respondent was the driver.

Maclennan v Macdonald 1988 SCCR 133
Road traffic offences. Question of whether M had been driving his car when it collided with parked car. Witness gave evidence of seeing M walking from his car to the parked car. No other traffic present. Damage to parked car consistent with M's car having reversed into it. M's explanation that someone else had been driving his car was not believed by sheriff and witnesses had not heard anyone running off.

Held that the evidence showed that car involved in collision was the appellant's, seen walking towards the car and no-one else present.

Proctor v Tudhope 1985 SCCR 403
P convicted of housebreaking with intent to steal. Clear identification by householder some hours after offence. In addition to this R ran off when pointed out while walking along the street by householder to policeman.
Held, witness credible and P's reaction sufficiently eloquent of guilt to be corroboration.

Stillie v HMA 1990 SCCR 719
Robbery. Complainer identified S. Corroboration in that police officers identified two persons running as or similar to the two accused. Conviction upheld on appeal. Complainer was a debt collector on his rounds, reasonable inference that the purpose of the attack was robbery.

Henderson v HMA 1993 SCCR 1005
Mobbing and rioting. Complainer identified H as did a witness who spoke to H telling him of the proposed riot and inviting him to join in.
Held, sufficient corroboration of H's identification.

Identification by voice.

McGiveran v Auld (1894) 1 Adam 448; 21 R (J) 69
Causing street obstruction. McG alleged to have made statements earlier to witnesses through telephone. Only means of identification of speaker was similarity of voice. McG convicted. Upheld on appeal.
Per LJ-C Macdonald: 'The evidence is practically the same as that given by a person outside a house who identifies his voice, and such evidence has never been held incompetent.'

See also:

Lees v Roy 1990 SCCR 310

Identification by video recording.

Bowie v Tudhope 1986 SCCR 205
Assault and robbery incident recorded on video tape. Video viewed by two police officers who identified B as one of the men seen committing the offence on film.
Held that evidence of constables sufficient to identify appellant.

Fingerprint identification.

HMA v Hamilton 1934 JC 1
Opening lockfast place, theft. H convicted on evidence of two fingerprint identification experts who found prints on bottle in shop. No other evidence. Appeal dismissed.
Per LJ-G Clyde: '. . . no chain is stronger than its weakest link. . . . Accordingly the strength of the link provided by the finger-mark depends on the degree of reliability which—on the evidence presented to them—the jury thought should be attributed to the finger-mark method as applied by the police and the experts in the present case.'

Langan v HMA 1989 SCCR 379
L charged with murder. Only evidence consisted of bloodstained fingerprint on tap in sink of house where crime committed. Fingerprint identified as L's. L claimed to have never been in the house but offered no explanation for presence of the print.
Held that in the absence of any explanation the jury were entitled to hold that it was made by the murderer.

Handwriting identification.	*Richardson v Clark* 1957 JC 7

Forgery and uttering. R and his wife convicted on the evidence of handwriting analysis experts in relation to wife's handwriting. Appeal refused.
Per LJ-C Thomson: '. . . it was for the sheriff, as a jury question, to decide whether and to what extent, the handwriting evidence led before him was careful, reliable and scientific, having in view . . . the skill and experience of the investigators and the amount and nature of the materials available to them for comparison.'

Campbell v Mackenzie 1974 SLT (Notes) 46
Fraud. C convicted of writing letters to chief constable making unfounded allegations about other persons and subscribed by false signature. Appeal rejected, competent and sufficient expert evidence not contradicted.

Palm print identification.

HMA v Rolley 1945 JC 155
Theft by housebreaking. Palm print found in house identified with palm print of R. Police evidence that no case of identity between prints of two different person's palms had ever been found. R convicted.
Per LJ-C Cooper: ' . . the evidence in its quality and substance [must be] of a character to carry conviction to the jury, whose duty it is to determine upon its value.'

DNA identification.

Welsh v HMA 1992 SCCR 108
Murder. Blood found at the scene matched to that of W by use of DNA profiling.
Held on appeal that DNA could be used. While DNA is not unique as with fingerprinting there was only a chance of 1 and between 88 and 99 million that the blood not that of W. No set statistical mark must be reached, up to jury whether to accept an identification using this process.

Identification by blind person.

Hill v Copeland (1976) SCCR Supp 103
H convicted of assaulting a blind person. Complainer said he had been assaulted by person who had brought him home. Threads found in complainer's house similar to those used to repair H's jacket. H had admitted taking complainer home but stated that he had left him in the close and not entered the house. Sheriff believed the complainer and determined that the threads constituted sufficient corroboration.

Identification by admissions of guilt—unequivocal

Keane v Horne (1978) SCCR Supp 225
Theft by opening lockfast car. Accused seen near locus but ran off. Described by owner of car. Two sets of car keys found on the accused's person, who said on apprehension, 'Honest we didn't take anything', and replied to caution and charge, 'I'm sorry, I didn't mean to take anything'.
Held, sufficient corroboration.
Opinion of the court: 'It has been said time and time again that when you are dealing with an unequivocal and clear admission of responsibility, only a very little evidence in corroboration of such an admission is required in law.'

McNab v Culligan (1978) SCCR Supp 222
Careless driving. Collision. Two occupants of car ran off. Later, respondent seen with facial injuries. Car belonged to respondent's father. Registered driver not driving, had handed car over to respondent who said, 'I might as well tell you the truth, it was me', to the police.
Held sufficient corroboration, even a clear admission requires some element of independent evidence.

	Meredith v Lees 1992 SCCR 459 Lewd practices. Sheriff holding that the evidence of the four-year-old complainer provided the 'very little' required to corroborate the confession of M. *Held*, appeal sustained, even a clear and unequivocal confession required corroboration.	
—equivocal.	*Sinclair v Clark* 1962 JC 57 Careless driving. S admitted to two witnesses that he was the driver. Other evidence showed S one of those in car and that he reported to the police station. S convicted. On appeal *held* sufficient corroboration. Per LJ-C Thomson: '. . . short of a solemn plea of guilt, an admission of guilt by an accused is not conclusive against him unless it is corroborated by something beyond the actual admission.'	
	Greenshields v HMA 1989 SCCR 637 G charged with murder and attempting to pervert the course of justice. Replied 'You don't think I did it myself do you; but I'm telling you nothing about it until I see my lawyer.' Appealed on the ground of insufficiency of evidence. *Held*, even when confession is not clear and unequivocal it is of evidential value and in present case constituted critical ingredient of case based on circumstantial evidence. Appeal refused. See also: *King v Normand* 1993 SCCR 896 *McDonald v Normand* 1994 SCCR 121	
Inconsistent account by the accused.	*Wright v Tudhope* 1983 SCCR 403 Careless driving. Collision with parked car. W identified by driver of parked car did not deny then that he was driver. Later W said that he was passenger and actual driver could not be traced. W convicted. Appeal dismissed.	
Identification established by answering summary complaint.	*Smith v Paterson* 1982 SCCR 295 Breach of the peace. Witnessed by two policemen who arrested P but were not asked to identify him in court. Defence submitted 'No case to answer'. Fiscal founded on statutory presumption that person who answers summary complaint is person charged by police unless the contrary is alleged and argued that there was sufficient evidence to convict. P acquitted. Crown appeal by stated case allowed. Per LJ-G Emslie: 'In most cases the presumption of limited scope provided by [the statute] will have no part to play at all in proof of the essential facts in a prosecution, viz (i) that the offence libelled was committed and, (ii) that the person who committed it was the accused.' See also: *Hamilton v Ross* 1991 SCCR 409	Criminal Procedure (Scotland) Act 1995 Section 280(9). Identification answered by answering summary complaint. Presumed person who appears in answer to the complaint is the person charged by the police unless the contrary is alleged.
Extract conviction and police evidence as proof of disqualification.	*Andrews v McLeod* 1982 SCCR 254 Driving while disqualified. Extract conviction showed disqualification, police evidence identified A as driver. *Held*, sufficient evidence.	
The commission of the crime	*Hay v HMA* 1968 JC 40 Murder. Suspicion fell on H because impression of bite marks on deceased's body corresponded with impression of H's teeth. H convicted.	

Cause of death—postmortem evidence desirable.	*Brown v HMA* 1964 JC 10 Causing death by dangerous driving. Evidence of only one doctor that death caused by multiple injuries and shock. Evidence from other witnesses of prior good health provided corroboration of this. Per LJ-C Grant: 'It is unfortunate that the Crown did not follow the normal and proper practice of proving the cause of . . . death by medical evidence based on a postmortem dissection. Such evidence, where the cause of death is in issue, is not a sine qua non, but it is highly desirable that it should be led, and grave difficulties may arise if it is not.'
Police evidence may corroborate evidence of *socius criminis*.	*O'Hara v Tudhope* 1986 SCCR 283 Car theft. O convicted on evidence of I who pled guilty but incriminated O. Car was stopped after a chase and O was sitting in the back seat. *Held* that I's evidence was sufficiently corroborated by police evidence that O was a passenger in the car.
It is necessary that there be evidence that the crime was carried out in the manner described.	*McDonald v Herron* 1986 SLT 61 Theft. Witness said McD had been on premises acting suspiciously. No evidence that stolen property found in McD's possession. McD convicted. *Held* on appeal, not enough corroboration to establish that the theft took place and conviction quashed. But see: *Mackay v HMA* 1997 SCCR 743 Robbery. Witness saw complainer and appellant go into lane, heard shouting, and on emerging saw complainer distressed, pleading 'give me it back'. *Held*, corroborated evidence that ring taken by violence or intimidation, and therefore sufficient evidence of robbery. *Campbell v Vannet* 1998 SCCR 207 Assault. Only part of complainer's account corroborated. Conviction of entire charge upheld on appeal.
	Miller (J) v HMA 1994 SCCR 377 Murder. Evidence of one witness that appellant stabbed deceased in toilet. Evidence of another witness that accused punched deceased in hall. On appeal conviction quashed: two inconsistent accounts did not provide corroboration. *Young v HMA* 1997 SCCR 405 Corroboration. Complainer said appellant put hand inside clothing and touched breast. Witness said thought rubbing complainer's tummy. Conviction of lewd practices upheld on appeal: both witnesses' evidence that complainer touched sufficient for conviction. *Cassidy v Normand* 1994 SCCR 325 Assault. Conviction upheld on appeal. *Held*, evidence of suspicious behaviour (walking along roof at relevant time and jumping down near spot) sufficient to corroborate complainer's evidence.' *McGrory v HMA* 1995 SCCR 237 Assault. Appellant told witness she would be sorry if she gave evidence. Conviction upheld on appeal. Observed, threat to witness is not corroboration, but court can look at remark in light of other evidence.

McLeod v Mason 1981 SCCR 75

Forcing open lockfast cars with intent to steal and attempting to steal. Sheriff acquitted, holding complaint should have indicated intent to steal either the contents of the car or the car itself and insufficient evidence to show attempt to steal the car not just drive it away unlawfully. Crown appealed successfully.

Opinion of the court: 'There was no need for the Crown in order to establish the commission of a completed crime to show that it was the intention of the respondents to steal the car or its contents or both. It is quite sufficient to libel the opening of a lockfast motor car with the criminal intent of theft and in many cases it will be impossible to prove more.'

Distress cannot corroborate complainer's evidence of what occurred, but can corroborate withholding consent.

Fox v HMA 1998 SCCR 115

Clandestine injury.

Held (full bench): (1) complainer's distress could corroborate her evidence that she did not consent; (2) corroborative evidence must support or confirm the direct evidence of a witness; (3) it is not the law that circumstantial evidence is corroborative only if it is more consistent with direct evidence of Crown than the account given by the accused; (4) circumstantial evidence can provide corroboration even where the accused puts forward an innocent explanation where the jury rejects this explanation. Conviction upheld on appeal. *Mackle v HMA* 1994 SCCR 277 overruled.

See Sheldon, 'Corroborational Relevance' 1998 SLT (News) 115; Brown, 'Two Cases on Corroboration' 1998 SLT (News) 71.

Gracey v HMA 1987 SCCR 260

Rape. G charged with rape and his defence was that the complainer had consented to intercourse. *Held* that where evidence is led of the distressed state of the complainer it is for the jury to assess that evidence, and if accepted as genuine, it is capable of corroborating the complainer.

Geddes v HMA 1996 SCCR 687

Corroboration. Conviction of assault charge quashed on appeal.

Held, distress at medical examination of anus five days after incident relied on for corroboration was too remote and could be attributed to intrusive examination.

See also:

Cannon v HMA 1992 SCCR 505
Martin v HMA 1993 SCCR 803

McLellan v HMA 1992 SCCR 171

Lewd practices. Crown leading evidence of child complainer's distress. Judge not directing the jury on a possible alternative source of distress that the complainer was not supposed to be visiting M's house. Conviction quashed on appeal.

Smith v Lees 1997 SCCR 139

Accused convicted of using lewd practices towards a young girl, causing her to handle his penis. Distress relied on for corroboration.

Held, on appeal (bench of five judges): distress cannot corroborate complainer's evidence of what occurred (but can corroborate withholding consent). *Stobo v HMA* 1993 SCCR 1105 overruled.

Observed, per Lord McCluskey: mere consistency not enough for corroboration: need evidence pointing positively towards truth of essential facts.

197

Vetters v HMA 1994 SCCR 305
Indecent assault. Crown alleged distress as corroboration. Sheriff did not specifically direct the jury on the distress evidence. Conviction quashed on appeal.
Held that judges must give the jury directions where there is distress evidence.

Distress in non-rape cases.

Horne v HMA 1991 SCCR 174
Abduction.
Held that distress evidence also relevant in cases other than rape. (Following *Mongan v HMA* 1989 SCCR 25 and *Bennett v HMA* 1989 SCCR 608.)

Thomson v HMA 1998 SCCR 56
Conviction of assault upheld on appeal despite misdirection of availability of distress as corroboration to fact of assault.
Held, no miscarriage, since evidence of physical injury at time of distress available for jury to consider.

Insufficient evidence that an individual committed a specific crime.

Shannon v HMA 1985 SCCR 14
Reset. S's conviction of possessing illegal sawn-off shotgun upheld on appeal.
Held, however, that although S's actings inferred knowledge of possessing the shotgun there was insufficient evidence to infer that he knew gun had been stolen.

See also:

West v HMA 1985 SCCR 248 (Conspiracy, p 117)

Statutory non-requirement for corroboration

Criminal Procedure (Scotland) Act 1995

Solemn and summary procedure:

Autopsy report.

O'Brien v HMA 1996 SCCR 238
F gave evidence that actual analysis carried out by C; objection to evidence as hearsay repelled. Conviction upheld on appeal.
Note: opinion reserved if neither of the two signatories had carried out the work.

Section 281(1). Autopsy report presumed to relate to deceased identified therein unless contrary is alleged by defence by notice not less than six days before trial or later in special circumstances.

Signatories to autopsy or forensic science report.

Donnelly v Schrikel 1994 SCCR 640
No statement in certificate that drugs analysed by signatories of certificate.
Held, on appeal, that parties' joint minute that report was joint report relieved need to rely on statutory provision, and sheriff to proceed accordingly.

O'Brien v McCreadie 1994 SCCR 516
No statement in report that drugs analysed by signatory of report. Sheriff acquitted respondent. Conviction overturned on appeal, since document was a report and not a certificate, which had different requirements. Sheriff to proceed accordingly.

Section 281(2). Evidence of one of two signatories to autopsy or forensic science report sufficient on contents and signatories' qualifications if intimation to accused of intention to call only one specified signatory given when report lodged as production unless notice given by accused requiring other signatory, not less than six days before trial, or later in special circumstances.

Sufficiency

Summary procedure:

Act of Adjournal (Criminal Procedure Rules) 1996, SI 1996/513, rule 27.2. The autopsy report must be lodged no later than 14 days before the trial if the Crown are to rely on CP(S)A 1995, s 281.

SI 1996/513, rule 27.3. Prosecutor must serve notice on accused or his solicitor, along with copy of report, no later than 14 days before trial.

Forensic science reports.

Criminal Procedure (Scotland) Act 1995

Section 280(4)–(6). A report purporting to be signed by two authorised forensic scientists shall be sufficient evidence of any fact or conclusion contained in the report and of the authority of the signatories only where notice served and no counter notice issued in terms of s 280(6)(a), (b) above.

Solemn and summary procedure:

Certificates.

Law Mining v Carmichael 1996 SCCR 627
Control of Pollution Act 1974. Test carried out by F using standard laboratory procedures agreed with superior, D. D was not present during analysis, but independently checked results. Conviction upheld on appeal.

McCrindle v Walkingshaw 1994 SCCR 299
Conviction under s 5(2) of the Misuse of Drugs Act 1971 (possessing cannabis). Sufficient corroboration of principal analyst that second analyst checked the lab reference number against the plate, the slide and lab records, despite the second analyst not present when cannabis removed from bag and put on plate and slide.

Pickard v Carmichael 1995 SCCR 76
Speeding.
Held, necessary in circumstances to prove Gatso radar device an approved device. Conviction quashed.

Section 280(1)–(6), Sch 9. Speedometer, odometer, radar meter, measuring apparatus—signatories: two police testers. Substance allegedly controlled drug—signatories: two qualified / authorised analysts. Benefits payments, eg social security, child and supplementary benefits—signatory: authorised officer.

Certificate signed by person in column 2 certifying matter in column 3 in relation to offence in column 1, shall be sufficient evidence of that matter and of authority/qualification of that person where:
(a) copy served on other party at least 14 days before trial; and
(b) other party does not challenge matter, qualification or authority, by serving a counter notice within 7 days after service of copy (or as court in special circumstances allows).

Forgery and Counterfeiting Act 1981
Section 26. Arrival, entry particulars—signatory: authorised officer.

		Solemn and summary procedure:
Conviction or extract sufficient to show disqualification.		Criminal Procedure (Scotland) Act 1995
		Section 286. Conviction or extract sufficient evidence if copy served on accused at least 14 days before trial diet, purportedly signed by clerk of court having custody of record containing the conviction, unless notice denying conviction given by accused within 7 days of service of notice.
		Road Traffic Offenders Act 1988, s 19 (as amended), has identical provisions to CP(S)A 1995, s 286 in relation to proof of disqualification from driving, and remains in force.
		Criminal Procedure (Scotland) Act 1995 Section 285(6)–(8). Briefly, extract conviction issued by officer sufficient without being sworn to by witnesses, unless challenged by notice (in solemn procedure five days before first day of sitting of trial) and if challenged Crown may prove previous convictions from witnesses not in list.
		Criminal Procedure (Scotland) Act 1995 Section 285(1)–(5). Provides for proof of previous convictions by fingerprints.
Bail—extract of minutes.		Criminal Procedure (Scotland) Act 1995 Section 28(6). Extract of minutes bearing to be signed by clerk of court sufficient evidence.
Road traffic—blood specimen; analyst's report.		Road Traffic Offenders Act 1988 Section 16(3) and (4). Certificate of medical practitioner taking blood specimen and analyst's report thereon sufficient evidence only if copy served on accused not less than seven days before trial, and accused does not serve notice that certificate's signatory required to attend trial. This notice to be served not less than three days before trial, or later in special circumstances.

There is provision by statute that one witness is sufficient to prove certain offences.	*Lees v Macdonald* (1893) 20 R(J) 55 Trespass in pursuit of game. Appeal by prosecutor from decision of sheriff that title to shooting rights required corroboration sustained. *Held*, day poaching, one credible witness sufficient.	Game (Scotland) Act 1832 Sections 1, 2 and 6. Contraventions may be proved by the evidence of one credible witness.
Poaching.		
Game offences.	*Anderson v Macdonald* 1910 SC(J) 65 Unlawful pursuit of game. Sheriff dismissed complaint against M found in possession of rabbits on grounds that evidence of only one witness was led. Crown appeal sustained. Per Lord Ardwall: 'Section 3 of the Act of 1862 imports into that Act the whole provisions regarding procedure in the Act of 1832.'	Poaching Prevention Act 1862 Section 3. Conviction of offences on evidence of single credible witness, by way of adopting the terms of the Game (Scotland) Act 1832.
Salmon poaching.	*Jopp v Pirie* (1869) 7 M 755 Taking salmon during closed time. Appeal from decision of sheriff that proof by one witness only applied where there was a 'paucity of evidence' sustained. Per Lord Neaves: 'By the common law of Scotland, the evidence of one witness, however credible, is not sufficient for a conviction, but this Act has said it shall be sufficient. The sheriff seems to have thought this was only where there was a *penuria testium*; but there is nothing to that effect in the Act.'	Salmon Fisheries (Scotland) Act 1868 Section 30. 'All offences' under the Act (found in ss 15, 17 to 24) can be proved by one credible witness. Salmon and Freshwater Fisheries (Protection) (Scotland) Act 1951 Section 7(3). Conviction is lawful on evidence of one witness (for illegal possession of salmon or trout or means for taking them).
Road traffic.	*Inwar v Normand* 1997 SCCR 6 Careless driving. Crown failed to lead evidence that traffic lights in working order. Appeal allowed and conviction quashed. *Donaldson v Valentine* 1996 SCCR 374 Charge of speeding on a motorway. Only evidence that locus was motorway was from two constables. *Held*, sufficient. *Donnelly v Carmichael* 1995 SCCR 737 Conviction of drinking in prohibited place. Lodging of bylaws without accompanying plans. *Held*, this was insufficient evidence, which could not be made good by evidence from police officers or private knowledge of justice. Conviction quashed.	Road Traffic Regulation Act 1984 Section 120(1). In respect of any of the offences described in s 120(2) conviction is lawful on the evidence of one witness. Road Traffic Offenders Act 1988 Section 21(3). Conviction is lawful on the evidence of one witness for contravention of the Road Traffic Act 1988, s 35(1) (failure to obey traffic direction by police constable or traffic sign).
Routine evidence: controlled drugs and medicinal products.		Criminal Procedure (Scotland) Act 1995 Section 282. Evidence by a forensic scientist that a substance is a controlled drug or medicinal product, by reference either to the label on a sealed container or the characteristic appearance of the substance, shall be sufficient evidence of identity of substance, notwithstanding that no analysis of the substance has been carried out. Notice to be served not less than 14 days before trial diet and counter notice of non-acceptance within 7 days, in which case these provisions will not apply.

Note: There are similar provisions as regards sufficiency and notification procedure for: CP(S)A 1995, s 283 (evidence as to time and place of video surveillance recordings); s 284 (evidence in relation to fingerprints); and s 277 (transcripts of police interviews—accused has 6 days before trial to challenge accuracy of transcripts by counter notice).

Procedural matters

Rights re medical examination.

Farrell v Concannon 1957 JC 12; 1957 SLT 60
Drunken driving. Sheriff returned 'not proven' verdict. Appeal by Crown allowed.
Held, on appeal, that the fact that an accused was told he need not consent to medical examination should be proven, but could be done by only one witness.

Breath test procedure.

MacLeod v Nicol; Torrance v Thaw 1970 JC 58; 1970 SLT 304
Drunken driving. At trial of N one police witness spoke to circumstances of breath test. At trial of To one policeman spoke to fact he was in uniform and device used was of approved style. Sheriff found charge against N not proven. To convicted. In N's case, Crown appealed and in To's case accused appealed.
Held, that procedural steps in issue could be spoken to by one credible witness.
Per LJ-C Grant: '. . . in any case any fact can be proved by one witness although the whole case cannot be so proved. . . . All that the law demands is that there should be two witnesses to prove a case; and provided that is so, any fact in the case may be provided by the testimony of one credible witness.'

Incidental matters

Security of premises.

Cameron (1839) 2 Swin 447
Theft by housebreaking. Only one witness to washhouse being locked up before offence took place. Aggravation proved. Conviction upheld on appeal.

Davidson (1841) 2 Swin 630
Theft by opening lockfast place. Locking spoken to by only one witness.
Held only one witness necessary, now fixed law.

Evidence of real facts.

Ryrie v Campbell 1964 JC 33
Driving without due care and attention. No eye witness but tyre marks on the wrong side of the road observed by the police. Paint marks on lamp standard matched car. Appeal refused.
Held evidence of eyewitness not essential, real facts eloquent of what happened.

The *Moorov* doctrine

The interlinking of evidence on separate charges, if sufficiently idiosyncratic, will furnish corroboration even if there is only one witness speaking to matters.

HMA v Moorov 1930 JC 68; 1930 SLT 596
Indecent assault. M convicted of series of indecent assault over a period of years. On appeal, *held* evidence in support of any one charge was competent corroboration of evidence in support of other charges.
Per LJ-G Clyde: 'Before the evidence of a single credible witness to separate acts can be used as providing material for mutual corroboration, the connection between the separate acts indicated by the external relation in time, character or circumstance must be such as to exhibit them as subordinates in some particular and ascertained unity of project, campaign, or adventure, which lies beyond or behind, but is related to, the separate acts.'

See also:

Ainsworth v HMA 1996 SCCR 631

Pettigrew v Lees 1991 SCCR 304
Two charges of indecent exposure. In both incidents only one witness could identify the accused. The presence of others at one incident did not make the doctrine inapplicable as there was only one identification on each occasion.

Quinn v Lowe 1991 SCCR 881
Held on appeal that *Moorov v HMA* 1930 JC 68; 1930 SLT 596 could apply to two incidents arising out of the same matter in each of which the same complainer was the only witness.

See also:

Lindsay v HMA 1993 SCCR 868
Carpenter v Hamilton 1994 SCCR 108

Offences connected in time.

Ogg v HMA 1938 JC 152
Sexual offences. Ten charges over seven years. In first three, complainer the only witness.
Held that *Moorov v HMA* 1930 JC 68; 1930 SLT 596 not applicable in view of the time between offences and lack of corroboration.
Per LJ-C Aitchison: '*Moorov* . . . laid down the general proposition in relation to sexual crimes, although not entirely limited to such crimes, that similar sexual crimes each deponed to by a single credible witness may afford mutual corroboration, provided always that they are so inter-related by character, circumstances and time—the presence of all these features is not essential—as to justify an inference that they are instances of a course of criminal conduct systematically pursued by the accused person.'

Russell v HMA 1990 SCCR 18
Interval of two years between two incidents held to be fatal to the application of the doctrine.

Turner v Scott 1995 SCCR 516
Held, charges of indecent assault separated by three years borderline case, but sufficient coherence in character and circumstance to apply Moorov doctrine (*Moorov v HMA* 1930 JC 68; 1930 SLT 596). Conviction upheld on appeal.

See also:

Coffey v Houston 1992 SCCR 265

Bargon v HMA 1997 SLT 1232

Offences must be of the same genus.	*HMA v WB* 1969 JC 72 Incest and lewd, indecent and libidinous practices. Five offences over some years. Two incidents separated by interval of fifteen months. *Moorov* doctrine applied despite time interval. *Held*, evidence of incest included indecency and could corroborate evidence of lewd practices but not vice versa as incest much more serious than lewd practices.
	Smith v HMA 1995 SLT 583 *Moorov* doctrine successfully applied to two charges of lewd conduct and one of sodomy. *Held*, essential element was indecent assault, and similarities meant there was not too great a gap.
	Compare with:
	HMA v Cox 1962 JC 27 'Incest and sodomy are different in nature and cannot corroborate each other.'
	Mackintosh v HMA 1991 SCCR 776 *Held* on appeal that *Moorov* doctrine could not apply to a charge of theft by housebreaking and assault with intent to rob because one incident involved violence and the other did not.
	P v HMA 1991 SCCR 993 Trial judge holding that *Moorov* doctrine could be applied to two charges of sexual offences against a young boy and girl. Course of criminal penetrative abuse.
	Carpenter v Hamilton 1994 SCCR 108 *Moorov* doctrine: offences must be of the same genus. Indecent exposure and jumping out at women making a suggestive noise (Hannibal Lector 'slither'). *Held*, to have underlying similarity of character and conviction of breach of peace upheld.
	O'Neill v HMA 1995 SCCR 816 Armed robberies. Moorov doctrine not used by Crown but introduced in judge's charge despite robberies lacking necessary unity of purpose. *Held*, conviction set aside and authority granted for new prosecution.
	Thomson (L McK) v HMA 1998 SCCR 657 Armed robbery, judge made no reference to need for underlying unity of purpose. *Held*, conviction set aside and authority for new prosecution: jury had to consider whether single course of criminal conduct by appellant.
	See also:
	Russell v HMA 1992 SCCR 257 *Farrell v Normand* 1992 SCCR 859
	See also:
	W v HMA 1996 SLT 51
An attempted crime may corroborate a completed one.	*PM v Jessop* 1989 SCCR 324 PM charged with sodomy and attempted sodomy in relation to two boys. Convicted using *Moorov* doctrine. *Held* that the sodomy and attempted sodomy so closely related that evidence of attempted act may corroborate evidence of completed act.

Moorov doctrine also applied to non-sexual crimes.

McDudden v HMA 1952 JC 86—bribery
HMA v McQuade 1951 JC 143—razor attacks
Harris v Clark 1958 JC 3—reset
McIntosh v HMA 1986 SCCR 496—supply of drugs

Hutchison v HMA 1997 SCCR 726
Held, on appeal, although assault charge could provide corroboration of breach of the peace the converse was not the case. Since *HMA v Moorov* 1930 JC 68; 1930 SLT 596 was put to the jury, there was a miscarriage of justice. Authority given for new prosecution.

Austin v Fraser 1997 SCCR 775
Charge of breach of the peace involved two incidents, 80 days apart on same stretch of road, of obstructing motor car behind by forcing driver to proceed at slow speed and come to a halt respectively. Conviction upheld on appeal: *Moorov* doctrine applicable.

Reynolds v HMA 1995 SCCR 504
Two assaults and robberies. Both similarities and dissimilarities. *Moorov* doctrine left to the jury. Conviction upheld on appeal.

The *Howden* rule
If proved both crimes committed by same person and proved one of them committed by appellant, then there is sufficient proof second crime committed by him.

Howden v HMA 1994 SCCR 19
Appellant charged with robbery of bank and building society in different parts of Edinburgh 14 days apart. Positive identification in building society, tentative identification in bank. Conviction upheld on appeal: if proved both crimes committed by same person and proved one of them committed by the appellant, then sufficient proof second committed by him.

The *Townsley* approach
Where there are three charges, but only one positive identification on one charge and tentative identification on other two charges, *Moorov* doctrine may be applied to first two charges, and *Howdon* rule applied to convict accused of all three charges.

Townsley v Lees 1996 SCCR 620
Appellant charged with three offences of theft. Three tentative identifications on first charge; positive identification on second charge; complainer in third charge could only say appellant similar in build and age. Conviction upheld on appeal.
Held, that the *Moorov* doctrine applied to the first two charges, and since evidence that all three offences committed by same person sheriff entitled to hold appellant involved in all three. *Howden v HMA* 1994 SCCR 19 approved.

The circumstantial confession
Where a confession by an accused or a suspect details information which would have been in the possession of the perpetrator of the crime, the terms of the confession supply corroboration of it.

Manuel v HMA 1958 JC 41
Murder. Statement by M as to whereabouts of victim's body which was subsequently discovered by police held sufficient corroboration and conviction upheld on appeal.

Beattie v HMA 1995 SCCR 93
Conviction of murder upheld on appeal. Appellant's statement not a special confession: it displayed special knowledge, and this required corroboration from other evidence in addition to that required to demonstrate accuracy of detailed knowledge of circumstances.

Connolly v HMA 1958 SLT 79
Theft. Particularised and detailed confession with extraneous evidence of its accuracy. Independent evidence of the accused acting suspiciously in car near locus held sufficient corroboration.
Held, confession shows crime committed and accused must have been the perpetator or privy to its perpetration.

Mitchell v HMA 1996 SCCR 97
Corroboration. Attempted murder. Two witnesses in house spoke to chap at window and shot but unable to identify gunman. C said appellant admitted chap and shot; L said appellant admitted shot to him. Conviction upheld on appeal.
Held, not necessary for each element of confession said to constitute special knowledge to be spoken to by two witnesses.

Woodland v Hamilton 1990 SCCR 166
Held not to be special knowledge admission where the alleged special knowledge could have been given to W by his co-accused.

Robertson v HMA 1990 SCCR 345
Art and part assault. Statement by R to police, 'You've got this wrong, I've never stabbed anyone' consistent with R knowing of the incident in question but not sufficient to infer she knew or ought to have known that a knife was to be used.

Smith v HMA (1978) SCCR Supp 203
Theft by housebreaking. Confession amounting to account of offence and some of the items stolen held sufficient corroboration.
Per LJ-G Emslie: 'A confession can receive corroboration if there is not only proof of the commission of the crime to which it related but proof *aliunde* of the truth of the confession.'

Wilson v McAughey 1982 SCCR 398
Vandalism. Details in confession as to how mechanical digger had been started and what thereafter occurred held sufficient corroboration.
Per LJ-C Wheatley: 'The law in the situation here could be summarised in the phrase that the respondent could not have been able to make the statement which he did if he had not been present at the time when the offence libelled had been committed.'

Campbell (T) v HMA 1998 SCCR 214
Held, evidence of appellant expressing thanks in circumstances related to crime should be regarded as incriminating remarks rather than an admission and could corroborate the appellant's admission to police, and appeal on this ground refused.

Admissions partly consistent with facts.

Gilmour v HMA 1982 SCCR 590
Rape and murder. Two admissions of guilt by G incorporating information, some consistent, some inconsistent with the proved facts. On appeal held sufficient corroboration of investigating officers' existing information.
Held on appeal, corroboration found in that the statement contained material facts, established independently, which accused could have known if he had been present when the offence occurred.

See also:

Hutchison v Valentine 1990 SCCR 569

Reilly v Fraser 1996 SCCR 26
Assault. Only corroboration was witness in pub with complainer, who said appellant left ten minutes after complainer and returned and said 'You'd better make sure your mate is OK'. Conviction quashed on appeal, since not entitled to infer that remarks were admission, and insufficient evidence.

Confession must be corroborated by findings in fact.

Allan v Hamilton 1972 SLT (Notes) 2
Theft. A told police where stolen savings stamps were cashed and admitted theft. A convicted. Appeal dismissed.
LJ-C Wheatley observed that there had been a very full confession by the accused admitting the theft, and that was corroborated by findings in fact.

McDonald v Normand 1994 SCCR 121
Conviction of assault upheld on appeal. Appellant admitted kneeling on arm; complainer identified accused as man who twisted her arm.
Held, description sufficient to corroborate general allegation of assault.

Admission by one accused may be corroborated by another accused.

Annan v Bain 1986 SCCR 60
Theft. B and H charged with theft of car. Respondents seen in car and subsequently chased by police. B admitted that he 'stole white car' before police had indicated that this was the reason for apprehension. H also admitted 'We stole it'.
Held that confessions contained special knowledge and were sufficiently corroborated by presence in car; and that statement of each respondent corroborated that of the other.

See also:

Low v HMA 1993 SCCR 493

Inferential corroboration from *de recenti* possession
In the absence of an explanation, an inference of guilt can be drawn from the possession in criminative circumstances of recently stolen property.

Christie v HMA 1939 JC 72; 1939 SLT 558
Theft by housebreaking. C found in possession of part of stolen property and evidence of *de recenti* pawning of stolen article. On arrest C gave detailed statement that goods were obtained from named person, who denied it. No evidence given by C at trial. Appeal against conviction refused.
Per Lord Fleming: 'According to the authorities, which extend over a long period of time, it has in practice been recognised that where there is no reasonable explanation of such possession, the jury are entitled not merely to infer that the accused is guilty of reset, but to go further and hold that he was actor or art and part in the actual theft charged.'

L v Wilson 1995 SCCR 71
Appellant in possession of pension book one week after taken from complainer in robbery.
Held, on appeal, possession not sufficient evidence he was robber and conviction quashed and conviction for reset substituted.

Hamilton v Friel 1994 SCCR 748
Theft of boat and trailer. Appellant had receipt for articles.
Held, on appeal, that appellant's inability to give details about seller did not amount to incriminative circumstances and conviction quashed.

Corroboration not necessary to establish that items stolen (Alison p 324).

Findlay v HMA (1953) SCCR Supp 1
Theft by housebreaking. Crown relied on evidence of recent possession of stolen articles, the only evidence that the articles were stolen being that of the householder.
Held that the finding of articles in accused's possession in suspicious circumstances sufficient to corroborate evidence of owner as to their having been stolen.

But compare:

Bennet v HMA 1989 SCCR 608
Appellants charged inter alia with robbing taxi driver of a watch and £35. No corroboration of complainer's evidence that he had a watch. There was evidence that complainer had money at outset of journey but no evidence that he had no money when he reported the incident.
Held to be no corroboration of robbery.

Other criminative circumstances in addition to possession necessary.

Fox v Patterson 1948 JC 104; 1948 SLT 547
Reset. P, scrap merchant, sold stolen metal. P had receipt for his purchase of the metal.
Held that there was no presumption of guilt to be rebutted. Eventual conviction for reset quashed on appeal.
Per LJ-C Cooper: '[For the doctrine of recent possession to apply] three conditions must concur: (a) that the stolen goods should be found in the possession of the accused; (b) that the interval between the theft of the goods and their discovery in the accused's possession should be short . . .; and (c) that there should be "other criminative circumstances" over and above the bare fact of possession.'

Watt v Annan 1990 SCCR 55
Six months is too great an interval for application of doctrine of recent possession, but may be sufficient to convict of reset.

De recenti possession must not merely be transporting of items on another's behalf.

HMA v Simpson 1952 JC 1; 1952 SLT 85
Theft by opening lockfast place. Stolen goods found in possession of dealer to whom S had taken them as another's servant. Conviction quashed on appeal because no presumption of guilt to be rebutted as S not in 'possession' of the goods.

Gilchrist v HMA 1992 SCCR 98
Theft. G spotted by police driving car similar to one seen at the scene of a crime, pursued by police. Car slowed to allow a person to jump from the car. G stopped and jewellery found in the back seat.
Held on appeal that given the discovery of the jewellery and the manner in which G drove the car there was sufficient evidence to infer that G was aware of the stolen goods.

Present possession not required—past possession sufficient.

Brannan v HMA 1954 JC 87; 1954 SLT 255
Theft by housebreaking and opening lockfast place. Evidence that B had possession of stolen goods initially although recovered elsewhere. B convicted. Appeal refused because held that presumption of guilt arising from recent possession had not in this case been rebutted.
Per LJ-G Cooper: 'Possession may be constructive, and it does not necessarily follow that possession which has been parted with need not be explained.'

Stolen goods not 'in person's possession' as premises open to other people.

Cryans v Nixon 1955 JC 1; 1954 SLT 311
Theft. C occupier of two sheds kept unlocked, with customers having access. Part of stolen property found concealed in C's premises. C denied all knowledge. C convicted. Conviction quashed on appeal. *Held* no presumption of guilt to be rebutted, other people had access to premises, goods not in accused's possession.

Silence, when charged, not a criminative circumstance.	*Wightman and Anr v HMA* 1959 JC 44; 1959 SLT (Notes) 27 (*sub nom* Collins) Theft. Scrap metal found in W's possession. When cautioned and charged W replied: 'I am saying nothing, not one iota.' Other appellant did not reply, neither did he give evidence. Both convicted. On appeal, held that neither the failure to reply nor the failure to give evidence could constitute a criminative circumstance and no presumption of guilt to be rebutted. Per LJ-G Clyde: (quoting LJ-G Cooper in *Robertson v Maxwell* 1951 JC 11): '. . . no legitimate inference in favour of a prosecutor can be drawn from the fact that a person, when charged with crime, either says nothing or says that he has nothing to say. He is entitled to reserve his defence, and is usually wise if he does so.'	But note: Criminal Justice (Scotland) Act 1995, s 32, repealed Criminal Procedure (Scotland) Act 1975, s 141(b): ie prosecutor can now comment on accused's failure to lead evidence. See also Criminal Procedure (Scotland) Act 1995, s 36(8), and page 127 above: declining to answer a question at judicial examination can be commented on. Criminal Procedure (Scotland) Act 1995 Section 14(9). Detained person under no obligation to answer any question other than to give name and address.
Fingerprints and attempt to dispose of items—*de recenti* possession.	*Cameron v HMA* 1959 JC 59 Theft by opening lockfast place. Box of stolen goods thrown out of window when police arrived at C's house. C's fingerprints found on stolen articles in box. C convicted. Appeal refused. *Held*, evidence of the box confirming evidence as regards possession. *Slater v Vannet* 1997 SCCR 578 Fingerprints. Palm prints on plastic bag found in lockfast unit. Appellant claimed to be customer in another shop in market. Conviction of theft quashed on appeal: evidence inconclusive, since the public had access and possibility prints came on to bag some time other than crime. *Crowe v Dealsey* 1996 SCCR 1 (Sh Ct) Location of accused's fingerprints on cheques shortly after being stolen sufficient for conviction of reset and uttering. Compare with: *Burke v Macphail* 1984 SCCR 380	
Fingerprint evidence alone—not *de recenti* possession.	*Reilly v HMA* 1959 JC 59 Theft. R co-appellant with Cameron (see *Cameron v HMA* 1959 JC 59). Only evidence of possession fingerprints on sheets of stamps. Conviction quashed on appeal because no presumption of guilt to be rebutted. Per LJ-G Clyde: '. . . the presence of fingerprints alone is not sufficient to establish possession . . . of the articles alleged to have been stolen . . . one of the three necessary conditions for applying the doctrine of recent possession has not been satisfied.'	

Uncontroversial evidence.

Criminal Procedure (Scotland) Act 1995

Section 258. Where party considers facts unlikely to be disputed by other party he can prepare and sign a statement specifying facts. Not less than 14 days before trial diet he can serve copy on other party. Other party has 7 days (or longer if court allows in special circumstances) to serve counter notice challenging statement. Otherwise, facts deemed conclusively proved. Court may, on application of either party, if special circumstances, and shall on joint application, direct that presumption shall not apply. Applications to be made after commencement of trial and before prosecutor's address on the evidence. If direction then court shall adjourn unless parties agree otherwise and will permit leading of evidence notwithstanding not in list nor notice as required by CP(S)A 1995, s 67(5) and s 78(4).

Note: see CP(S)A 1995, s 257 for general duty of each party to take reasonable steps to secure agreement of evidence which they consider unlikely to be disputed.

SENTENCING

ABSOLUTE DISCHARGE

An absolute discharge may be granted for offences where the sentence is not fixed by law, if the circumstances of the offence and/or the offender make it appropriate. A right of appeal is not affected. Although not a conviction, it can be laid before a court in subsequent proceedings.

COMMENTARY	CASE LAW	STATUTE LAW
In solemn procedure, absolute discharge follows upon conviction. In summary procedure, it comes after the court is satisfied the offender committed the offence.		Criminal Procedure (Scotland) Act 1995
		Solemn procedure:
Not available where sentence is fixed by law.		Section 246(2). Where a person is convicted on indictment of an offence (other than one for which sentence is fixed by law), if it appears to the court, having regard to the circumstances including the nature of the offence and the character of the offender, that it is inexpedient to inflict punishment and that a probation order is not appropriate it may instead of sentencing him make an order discharging him absolutely.
Nature of offence to be considered.		
Nature of offender to be considered.		
Inexpedient to inflict punishment.		
Probation order not appropriate.		
		Summary procedure:
	Kheda v Lees 1995 SCCR 63 Nurse convicted of breach of the peace and fined. On appeal High Court said sheriff never attached sufficient weight to appellant's good character and repercussions conviction would have on career, and absolute discharge substituted.	Section 246(3). Where summary offence (other than one for which sentence is fixed by law) and the court is satisfied he committed offence, the court having regard to the circumstances including the nature of the offence and the character of the offender, is of opinion that it is inexpedient to inflict punishment and that a probation order is not appropriate may, without proceeding to conviction, discharge him absolutely.
	Galloway v Mackenzie 1991 SCCR 548 Careers officer convicted of minor assault and admonished. He appealed, since occupation exempt from provisions on convictions becoming spent, which meant he would have to disclose conviction. High Court substituted absolute discharge.	
While not a conviction, an absolute discharge can be referred to in subsequent proceedings.		Section 247(1). Absolute discharge or probation order shall be deemed not to be a conviction, but can be laid before court as previous conviction in subsequent proceedings.
		Section 247(2). Absolute discharge (and also probation order) disregarded for the purposes of any enactment which imposes any disqualification or disability upon convicted persons (unless the relevant Act specifically extends to persons granted an absolute discharge).

Section 247(4). Right of appeal not affected.

Section 247(6). *Note:* if offender (not less than 16 at time of conviction) is placed on probation as in CP(S)A 1995, s 247(1) and is subsequently sentenced for the offence, provisions for treating it as previous conviction shall cease to apply.

ADMONITION

A court may, if it appears to meet the justice of the case, dismiss with an admonition any person convicted by the court of any offence.

COMMENTARY	CASE LAW	STATUTE LAW
No statutory limit to the use of admonition. Can be used with other order, eg disqualification.		Criminal Procedure (Scotland) Act 1995 Section 246(1). A court may, if it appears to meet the justice of the case, dismiss with an admonition any person convicted by the court of any offence.

ANTI–SOCIAL BEHAVIOUR ORDER

The Crime and Disorder Act 1998 provides for anti-social behaviour orders (s 19) and sex offender orders (s 20) which prohibit the subject from doing anything described in the order. The applicants are the local authority and the chief constable respectively. Both orders proceed by way of summary application (civil procedure). See the Crime and Disorder Act 1998 for detail of orders. It is an offence if without reasonable excuse a person breaches these orders by doing anything prohibited by the order.

COMMENTARY	CASE LAW	STATUTE LAW
		Crime and Disorder Act 1998
It is an offence to breach an anti-social behaviour order or a sex offender order.		Section 22(1). If without reasonable excuse a person breaches an anti-social behaviour order / sex offender order by doing anything which he is prohibited from doing by the order, he shall be guilty of an offence.
Where accused is charged with a separate offence, the court, when sentencing, shall take into account the fact that offender subject to order.		Section 22(2). Subsection (3) applies where the breach of the order consists in the accused having acted in a manner prohibited by the order which constitutes a separate offence and the accused has been charged with that separate offence.
		Section 22(3). The accused shall not be liable to be proceeded against for breach of order but the court which sentences him for that separate offence shall have regard to the following in determining the appropriate sentence or disposal: (a) the fact offence was committed by him while subject to order; (b) number of orders he was subject to at time of offence; (c) any previous conviction under s 22(1); (d) the extent to which any previous conviction differed by virtue of this subsection from what would otherwise have been imposed.
		Section 22(4). The court shall not regard fact offence committed by accused subject to order unless so specified in indictment/complaint.
		Section 22(5). The fact a separate offence was committed by the accused while subject to an order shall unless challenged be held as admitted (**solemn procedure:** by notice of preliminary objection under the Criminal Procedure (Scotland) Act 1995, s 72(1)(b); **summary procedure:** by preliminary objection before plea is recorded).

CAUTION

Caution consists of a specified amount of money as security for good behaviour over a specified period of time. Failure to find caution within specified period then alternative of imprisonment may be imposed. Caution can be consigned or there can be a bond of caution; if further offence then caution is forfeited; otherwise at end of period caution refunded.

COMMENTARY	CASE LAW	STATUTE LAW
		Criminal Procedure (Scotland) Act 1995
		Solemn procedure:
Conviction.		Section 227. Where a person is convicted on indictment of an offence (other than an offence the sentence for which is fixed by law) the court may, instead of or in addition to imposing a fine or a period of imprisonment, ordain the accused to find caution for good behaviour for a period not exceeding 12 months and to such amount as the court considers appropriate.
Caution consists of a specified amount of money as security for good behaviour over a specified period of time.		
		Summary procedure:
		Section 7(7). In district court period not exceeding six months and maximum not exceeding level 4 on the standard scale.
		Section 5(2). In sheriff court maximum amount is the prescribed sum and maximum period for which caution may be required is 12 months.
Caution is consigned.		Section 168(2). Caution may be found by consignation of the amount with clerk of the court, or by bond of caution signed by the cautioner.
If further offence committed, caution is forfeited.		Section 168(3). Where caution becomes liable to forfeiture, forfeiture may be granted by the court on the motion of the prosecutor, and, where necessary, warrant granted for the recovery of the caution.
Failure to find caution.		Section 168(4). If cautioner fails to pay amount under his bond within six days after he has received charge to that effect, court may: (a) order him to be imprisoned for maximum applicable under CP(S)A 1995, s 219 or until payment made; (b) if it considers it expedient, on application of cautioner grant time for payment; or (c) order recovery by civil diligence in accordance with CP(S)A 1995, s 221.

General

There is no caution by instalments.

Provisions relating to payment of fines and default— CP(S)A 1995, ss 214, 216, 219(2)–(6)— apply equally to caution.

Note: there is no provision for caution by instalments.

COMMUNITY SERVICE ORDER

A Community Service Order (CSO) is available where offence punishable by imprisonment (excluding murder); does not apply where sentence fixed by law; accused must be person over 16; order to be explained to offender and offender's consent required; suitability to be considered by court; requires unpaid work for a certain number of hours.

COMMENTARY	CASE LAW	STATUTE LAW
		Criminal Procedure (Scotland) Act 1995, ss 238–245
CSO is a direct alternative to custody.	*Guisti v Walkingshaw* 1996 SCCR 61 Appellant convicted of obstructing police. Sheriff discounted fines because appellant could pay them without difficulty, said imprisonment was excessive and imposed CSO. *Held*, wrong approach: (i) a large fine can cause difficulty; (ii) if sheriff discounted imprisonment then it followed that CSO must also be discounted. CSO quashed and fine of £800 at £20 per week substituted.	Section 238(1). Where person over 16 convicted of offence punishable by imprisonment (other than where sentence fixed by law) the court may, instead of imposing a sentence of imprisonment, make a CSO requiring him to perform unpaid work for number of hours specified in order.
Offence must be punishable by imprisonment.		
Does not apply where sentence fixed by law.		
Accused must be 16 or over.		
Not less than 80 hours.	*Kidd v Russell* 1993 SLT 1028 Accused pled guilty to inter alia a contravention of s 5(1)(a) of the Road Traffic Act 1988. Sheriff fined accused and made CSO for 120 hours. *Held*, on appeal, incompetent to make CSO along with fine for same offence, and fine quashed.	*Note:* the minimum length of an order in all cases is 80 hours; the maximum for summary cases is 240 hours; the maximum for solemn cases is 300 hours: CP(S)A 1995, s 238(1) (as amended by the Community Service by Offenders (Hours of Work) (Scotland) Order 1996, SI 1996/1938).
Other considerations to be observed by court before making order.	*McQueen v Lockhart* 1986 SCCR 20 Appellant pleaded guilty to theft of car and on same day pleaded guilty to second complaint of theft by housebreaking. Sheriff ordered 120 hours' CSO on first offence and 60 days' detention on second. Upheld since no basis two complaints should be treated as one.	Section 238(2)(a). Offender must consent to CSO.
		Section 238(2)(b). CSO can be made only if necessary arrangements available where offender lives.
		Section 238(2)(c). Offender must be suitable person to perform work under CSO (court must consider local authority report on offender and his circumstances).
		Section 238(3). Copy of report by local authority officer to be supplied to offender or his solicitor.
		Section 238(2)(d). Court must be satisfied that provision can be made through the social work department for the offender to perform work under the order.

Explanation of CSO and its effect to offender before making order.		Section 238(4). Court shall explain to offender in ordinary language: (a) the purpose and effect of the order and the obligations of the offender; (b) the consequences which may follow if he fails to comply; and (c) that the court has the power to review the order either on the application of the offender or the supervising officer.
Court makes order.		Section 238(8). CSO shall: (a) specify locality of residence; (b) require local authority to appoint a supervising officer; (c) state number of hours offender required to perform. Section 238(10). Copy order must go to offender, local authority and 'appropriate court'. Section 239(2). The work shall be performed during the period of 12 months beginning with the date of the order; but, unless revoked, order will remain in force until full number of hours worked.
Can be imposed concurrently with or consecutive to other CSO or probation order containing 'unpaid work' requirement.		Section 238(9). An order may be consecutive or concurrent (to both CSO and probation order with unpaid work requirement) but at no time shall the offender have an outstanding number of hours to perform in excess of maximum under CSO.
		Section 249(1)(2). An offender may pay compensation and perform CSO in respect of same charge. Section 238(7). In addition to CSO court can impose (a) disqualification (b) forfeiture order (c) caution. **Requirements:**
Obligations on person subject to order.		Section 239(1)(a). Must advise supervising local authority officer without delay of any change of address or of any changes in times of work.
Obligations on local authority supervising officer.		Section 239(1)(b). Must perform specified hours on such work and at such times as instructed by local authority officer.

Failure to comply with order.

Section 239(3). Instructions, so far as practicable, must avoid conflict with offender's religious beliefs and normal working hours or attendance at educational establishments.

Section 239(4). Breach of community service order. When CSO in force, where it appears to court on information from local authority office that offender failed to comply with s 239(1)–(3) (including failure to perform work satisfactorily) court may issue warrant for arrest or citation to appear.

Evidence of failure required.

If evidence of failure proved satisfactorily, court can impose a fine, vary number of hours or revoke order.

Gilbert v Buchanan 1997 SCCR 642
Criminal Procedure (Scotland) Act 1995, s 239(5): breach of order. Appellant breached CSO and sentenced to three months for original offence and two months consecutive for breach.
Held, on appeal, no such crime as breaching CSO. If CSO revoked then only sanction is to deal with original offence and two months' sentence quashed.

Section 239(5). If such breach proved (evidence of one witness sufficient) court can:
(a) impose a fine;
(b) revoke order (order ends) and deal with offender in any manner in which he could have been dealt with if order had never been made; or
(c) vary number of hours (subject to statutory limits).
Right of appeal not affected by making of order.

Appeal.

HMA v Hood 1987 SCCR 63
Question as to relevancy of complaint of breach of CSO since related to period later than 12 months after making order.
Held, complaint against offender irrelevant since in absence of court extension he could not lawfully be required to carry out work and complaint dismissed.
Opinion, competent to apply for extension even after expiry of 12 months.

Court may extend, vary, revoke order or deal with offender.

Amendment and revocation:

Section 240(1). On application of offender or local authority office, if it appears to court that it is in the interests of justice to do so having regard to circumstances which have arisen since order was made, court may:
(a) extend 12-month period;
(b) vary number of hours specified (subject to statutory limits); or
(c) revoke order (order ends), and deal with offender in any manner in which he could have been dealt with if order never made.

Commission of offence while CSO in force:

Commission of offence while order in force.

Section 241. If offence committed by individual performing CSO (or within three months of expiry of that order) and in place where unpaid work carried out or previously performed, the court which sentences for that offence shall in determining the appropriate sentence have regard to the fact that offence was committed in those circumstances.

Section 241(3). Section 241 applies only if aggravation libelled in indictment or specified in complaint. Fact offence committed in aggravating circumstances in CP(S)A 1995, s 241 shall be held as admitted unless challenged (a) in solemn proceedings, by giving notice of objection under CP(S)A 1995, s 72(1); or (b) in summary proceedings, by preliminary objection before the plea is recorded.

When order completed in satisfactory manner, the order ends.

References: Nicholson, 1–145 to 1–172 and 10–43 to 10–49; Renton and Brown, 23–33.

COMPENSATION ORDER

A Compensation Order (CO) may be made instead of, or in addition to, other disposal. Cannot be made on (a) absolute discharge; (b) probation order; or (c) deferred sentence. Compensation order requires offender to pay compensation for personal injury, loss or damage caused (other than loss because of death of a person or arising due to a motor vehicle accident). Order is sentence for purpose of appeal or review. Court has power to enforce order generally as if it were a fine.

COMMENTARY	CASE LAW	STATUTE LAW
		Criminal Procedure (Scotland) Act 1995, ss 249–253.
Conviction.	*Carmichael v Siddique* 1985 SCCR 145 (Sh Ct) Compensation order for £1,000 upheld against shopkeeper selling firework to underage boy who injured eye. *Held*, statute designed to prevent injuries suffered, and no such restrictions as argued by defence (ie defence argued CO competent only where legal position clear and damage capable of precise valuation).	Section 249(1). Where person convicted of an offence the court, may instead of or in addition to other disposal make a CO requiring him to pay compensation for any personal injury, loss or damage caused, whether directly or indirectly by the act which constituted the offence.
	Bruce v McLeod 1998 SLT 173 Accused person charged with assault but convicted under deletion of words 'repeatedly striking her to her injury' and justice imposed compensation order. On appeal quashed. Per Lord Sutherland: 'the Court requires that the Crown present some information ... which could provide a factual basis for the making of a compensation order.'	Section 249(2). A CO cannot be made on (a) absolute discharge; (b) probation order; or (c) deferred sentence.
	HMA v Nelson 1996 SLT 1073 Accused pleaded guilty on indictment to aggravated assault. Sheriff made CO requiring accused pay £250 to complainer and £1,000 to victim support. *Held*, only competent to make CO in favour of person who had suffered loss, and order quashed.	
	Wilson v Transorganics 1996 SLT 1014 Incompetent to suggest to an accused that if donation made to a local trust fund he will be admonished.	
Covers personal injury, loss or damage caused by acts constituting offence.	*Nazir v Normand* 1994 SCCR 265 Criminal Procedure (Scotland) Act 1995, s 249(4). Road accidents excluded except damage, not loss, of vehicle. CO to owner of other car damaged by appellant's brother driving without insurance. *Held*, order not excessive and appeal refused.	Section 249(3), (4). COs do not cover loss because of death of a person; or arising due to motor vehicle accident, except where damage caused in case of offence under Road Traffic Act 1988, s 178(1) (taking motor vehicle without authority and property recovered but damaged).
Court to consider means of offender.	*McEvoy v McGlennan* 1997 SCCR 385 Theft by housebreaking. CO of £2,200 at £7.50 a week. He had disposable income of £20 a fortnight. High Court *held* the financial circumstances of the appellant should not be wholly ignored and order excessive and CO for £1,000 substituted.	Section 249(5). If going to make compensation order, court to consider means of offender.
	Storie v Scott 1990 SCCR 284 Appellant pleaded guilty to theft from employers and CSO made and also CO imposed for £1,137: £100 to be paid in four weeks, and the rest at £5 per week. *Held*, four years' repayment period excessive and CO for £350 substituted. *Note:* repayment period not usually more than two years.	Section 249(6). No account shall be taken of earnings contingent upon offender obtaining employment after release.

Amount.

Section 249(7). Solemn proceedings: no limit to amount.

Section 249(8)(a). Summary proceedings before sheriff or stipendiary magistrate: amount not exceeding prescribed sum (£5,000).

Section 249(8)(b). District court before lay magistrate: amount not exceeding level 4 on the standard scale (presently £2,500).

Section 249(9). Payment to clerk of court who shall account for amount to person entitled thereto.

Court has power to enforce order generally as if it were a fine.

Section 249(10). Only the court can enforce CO.

Where order and fine are concurrent, order takes precedence over fine.

Section 252(2). Court has power to enforce order generally as if it were a fine.

Section 250(1). Where in respect of offence a court considers a fine AND a CO appropriate but offender has insufficient means to pay appropriate levels of both, a CO should be preferred.

Section 250(2). Where there is both a fine and a CO, payment shall first be applied in satisfaction of CO.

Appeal.

Brown v Normand 1988 SCCR 229
No CO where more than minimal provocation by complainer. Appellant chased by gang including complainer whom he hit with brick. £650 CO quashed on appeal: since not entitled to compensation from Criminal Injuries Compensation Board there was no reason he should get it in a court order.

Section 250(3). Order is sentence for purposes of appeal or review.

Section 250(4). Payment to court retained until determination of appeal.

Review of CO:

Review of compensation order.

Reduction of amount possible.

Section 251. At any time before CO complied with or fully complied with, on application of person against whom order made, court may discharge the CO or reduce the amount if it appears to the court that:
(a) injury, loss or damage has been held in civil proceedings to be less than it was taken to be for the purposes of the CO; or
(b) property, the loss of which is reflected in the CO, has been recovered.

Section 252. All the provisions of CP(S)A 1995 relative to the payment, remission, transfer and enforcement of fines apply to CO, as appropriate.

Alternative disposal.

Ely v Donnelly 1996 SCCR 537
Appellant on income support given CO of £540 at £7 a week for breach of peace and vandalism. Appealed on grounds that sentence excessive, and asked for case to be continued to find out if complainer were recovering money from insurers. Motion for continuation refused.
Held, (1) fact victim insured irrelevant; (2) CO not same as fine and guidelines on time to pay fine did not apply.

Landsborough v McGlennan 1997 SCCR 464
Housebreaking. CO of £1,360 at £10 a week.
Held, LJ-G Rodger dismissing appeal against CO, CO unlike fine, and fact repayment period longer than appropriate in case of fine not in itself reason to say order is inappropriate. (Repayment period here of two years.)

But *note:* guidelines which apply to length of time within which a fine should be paid do not apply to CO (see eg *Ely v Donnelly* 1996 SCCR 537; *Landsborough v McGlennan* 1997 SCCR 464).

Section 252(3)(a). A court may impose imprisonment in respect of a fine and decline to impose imprisonment in respect of a CO, but not vice versa.

Section 252(3)(b). Where a court imposes imprisonment both in respect of a fine and a CO, the amounts are to be aggregated for the purposes of calculating the maximum period imposed.

References: Renton and Brown, 23–65 to 23–71.

DEFERRED SENTENCE

Court can defer sentence after conviction on such conditions as the court may order. No limit on length of period of deferment. If conviction of another offence during period of deferment the court may sentence offender—deferment ends prematurely. At date of deferment court may further defer sentence eg to allow longer period to show good behaviour, otherwise court sentences offender.

COMMENTARY	CASE LAW	STATUTE LAW
		Criminal Procedure (Scotland) Act 1995
On such conditions as the court may order. No limit on length of period of deferment.	*Cameron v Webster* 1997 SCCR 228 Theft. Sheriff deferred sentence for a year and asked appellant to bring £300 to court as compensation at that time. He brought £180 but case continued and he spent it and imprisoned. *Held*, sentence quashed and CO and fine imposed: not appropriate to defer sentence to enable accused to save up for CO ie that is what instalments are for.	Section 202(1). Competent for a court to defer sentence after conviction for a period and on such conditions as the court may determine.
	Lennon v Copeland 1972 SLT (Notes) 68 Sheriff sentenced accused to three months on second charge (possessing LSD) but deferred sentence on first charge (possessing cannabis). *Held*, question of sentence not in bill of suspension so court cannot dispose of it. Observed approach contrary to practice ie should have sentenced on both or admonished on cannabis charge.	
	McElwaine v Cardle 1993 SCCR 619 Complainer convicted of breach of the peace and committing offence on bail. Sentence deferred on breach of the peace and fined on bail charge. *Held*, approach inappropriate as might fetter judge's discretion as to appropriate penalty on each charge taken as a whole and fine set aside and sentence also deferred. *Note:* offence on bail is now an aggravation.	
Conviction for another offence during period of deferment: court may sentence offender—deferment ends prematurely.	*Borland v HMA* 1976 SLT (Notes) 2 *Held*, competent for one sheriff to remit accused to High Court despite fact another sheriff presiding when accused found guilty.	Section 202(2), (3). Conviction for another offence during period of deferment: (a) by court making original order: court may sentence for new offence and original offence; (b) by different court (anywhere in Great Britain): court which originally deferred sentence may compel appearance of accused before it by warrant or citation and may sentence.
Lord Advocate's appeal.		Lord Advocate may appeal against deferment of sentence (on indictment, under CP(S)A 1995, s 108(1)(g)); in summary procedure, under CP(S)A 1995, s 175(4A)(v) on a point of law only).
Competent to make probation order after period of deferment.		Competent to make a probation order after period of deferment (see Renton and Brown, 23–155).

Deferred sentence

Date of deferment: court may further defer sentence. Otherwise, court sentences offender.

Laing v Heywood 1998 SCCR 458
Complainer placed on deferred sentence in district court and told if of good behaviour then absolute discharge. At end of period in which he was of good behaviour another justice admonished him.
Held, justice not bound by earlier occasion and no flaw.
Observed, if any indication they should be given in ways which do not suggest there will be a definite outcome.

References: Nicholson, 10–03 to 10–21; Renton and Brown, 23–155.

DRUG TREATMENT AND TESTING ORDER

A Drug Treatment and Testing Order (DTTO) can be made in relation to an offender (other than where offence for which sentence fixed by law) aged 16 or over who is dependent on or has a propensity to misuse drugs and the court considers a DTTO expedient rather than sentencing. The offender's consent is required. Order must be between six months to three years and contain a treatment requirement that the offender submit to a treatment provider with a view to reduction or elimination of drug dependency/misuse.

The testing requirement requires offender to provide samples to the treatment provider. The offender shall also be under the supervision of a supervising officer who shall receive result from samples and report offender's failure/progress to appropriate court. The order may be amended or revoked on application of offender or supervising officer.

The DTTO shall provide for a periodic review at intervals of not less than one month. There shall be a review hearing in court where offender need attend and the order may be amended with the offender's consent. If progress satisfactory future reviews may be made in chambers in absence of parties. If breach of order without reasonable excuse court may fine or vary or revoke order. If court revokes order it may dispose of offender in any way competent at time order made. DTTO may be combined with probation order.

COMMENTARY	CASE LAW	STATUTE LAW
		Criminal Procedure (Scotland) Act 1995, ss 234B–234J, as inserted by ss 89–95 of the Crime and Disorder Act 1998.
		Criminal Procedure (Scotland) Act 1995
Offender 16 years or over.		Section 234B(1). 16 years or over convicted of offence other than fixed by law.
Court may make DTTO if expedient.		Section 234B(2). Court may make DTTO if expedient. (a) Effective for period of six months to three years.
Arrangements must be available in local authority area.		Section 234B(3). A court shall not make DTTO unless– (a) notified that arrangements available in area;
Offender must have drug dependency/misuse susceptible to treatment.		(b) obtained a report from local authority office about offender and his circumstances; and (c) is satisfied offender is a suitable person for such order and that he has a dependency or propensity to misuse drugs which is susceptible to treatment.
Treatment requirement.		Section 234C(1). DTTO shall include a treatment requirement that offender shall be treated by a treatment provider with a view to reducing or eliminating dependency on drugs.
		Section 234C(2). Nature of treatment need not be specified, only need specify institution, time period and resident / non-resident status.

Testing requirement.		Section 234C(4). DTTO shall include a testing requirement. Offender shall provide samples as required by treatment provider.
		Section 234C(5). Testing requirement shall specify the minimum number of samples required each month.
Appointment of supervising officer.		Section 234C(6). DTTO shall specify area where offender to reside and local authority to appoint supervising officer.
		Section 234C(7). Offender to keep in touch with supervising officer and notify change of address, officer to be given details of test samples.
Reports to court on offender's progress.		Section 234C(8). Supervising officer shall report offender's progress/failure to comply to court.
Explanation to offender about order.		Section 234D(1). Court must explain to offender in ordinary language the effect of order, its requirements, the consequences of failure, that order may be varied or revoked, that order will be periodically reviewed at times specified in order
Copy of order.		Section 234D(2). Copy of order shall be given to offender, treatment provider, chief social work officer.
		Amendment and revocation:
Amendment and revocation of order.		Section 234E(1). Offender or supervising officer may apply to the appropriate court for variation or revocation of order (court may do so if it appears in interest of justice and offender consents).
		Periodic Review:
Periodic review of order (intervals not less than one month).		Section 234F(1)–(4). DTTO shall provide for order to be reviewed periodically at intervals of not less than one month at a review hearing, which the offender shall attend. Supervising officer to give court progress report before each hearing (includes test results). Court can amend order with offender's consent. If no consent court to revoke order.
		Section 234F(5), (6). If progress satisfactory court may provide for each subsequent review without a hearing (in chambers without the parties present).

		Breach:
Breach: court may fine or vary or revoke order.		Section 234G(1). If it appears to court failure to comply it may issue a citation to appear or warrant to arrest.
		Section 234G(2). If proved (evidence of one witness sufficient) that the offender has failed without reasonable excuse to comply with any requirement of order, the court may vary or revoke the order or impose a fine.
		Disposal:
DIsposal		Section 234H(1). If court revokes order it may dispose of offender in any way which would have been competent at time order made.
		Section 234H(2). Court shall regard time order in operation.
		Section 234H(3). Where court revokes DTTO and offender subject to probation order or restriction of liberty order court shall discharge / revoke those other orders before disposing of DTTO.
Combination of orders.		Section 234J. Combination of orders.
		Section 234J(1). Court can make both DTTO and probation order concurrent if expedient to do so.
		Section 234J(2). In so deciding court shall regard circumstances including the nature of offence and character of offender and report.
		Section 234J(3). Copy of each order to be sent to treatment provider, local authority officer, probation officer.
		Section 234J(4). Where offender breaches either DTTO or probation order and either one varied, the court may also vary the other order.
		Section 234J(5). If both breached court may opt to vary either or but not both.

FINES

Court may impose fine following conviction. Maximum fine depends on jurisdiction of the court. Means of the offender must be considered by court in fixing the amount of the fine. Deductions may be made from income support. Court may allow time to pay or payment by instalments or refuse time to pay if there are reasons for doing so. Offender may be under the supervision of a Fine Supervision Order (FSO) while paying. Court may impose the alternative of imprisonment in default of payment (period depends on amount of fine: see below). Court may instead of imposing alternative of imprisonment make a Supervised Attendance Order (SAO).

COMMENTARY	CASE LAW	STATUTE
		Criminal Procedure (Scotland) Act 1995, ss 211–226.
		Maximum fines:
Maximum fine depends on jurisdiction of court.		Section 211(1). For conviction of common law offence on indictment there is no maximum.
		Section 211(2). For conviction of a statutory offence on indictment there is no maximum.
		Section 225(1). For conviction of common law offence triable only summarily, the current prescribed sum (£5,000). For conviction of statutory offence the maximum fine is one which does not exceed the level on the standard scale prescribed by statute.
Standard scale.		Section 225. There shall be a standard scale for offences triable only summarily:

Level	Amount
1	£200
2	£500
3	£1,000
4	£2,500
5	£5,000

COMMENTARY	CASE LAW	STATUTE
Means of offender must be considered by court in fixing the amount of the fine.	*Milligan v Jessop* 1988 SCCR 137 Appellant on social security pleaded guilty to breach of the peace and police assault. Magistrate said appellant unable to meet level of fine required and imprisoned him. *Held*, approach flawed, as possibility of fine rejected because of appellant's means and fines of £100 on each charge at £5 per week imposed. *Forsyth v Cardle* 1994 SCCR 769 Theft of bird eggs, income of £80 a fortnight. Fined total of £16,000 with three months to pay. *Held*, excessive, and fine of £2,000 at £5 per week imposed. Not proper to impose fines completely beyond capacity of offender, even over very long period (normally, fines payable in not much more than a year). *Picto Ltd v Lees* 1994 SCCR 775 Company breached trading standards over safety claims regarding Christmas tree lights. *Held*, on appeal, £2,500 fine not excessive given means of offender regardless of fact company a first offender.	Section 221(7). Means of offender shall be taken into consideration in determining the amount of the fine.

Reynolds v Hamilton 1994 SCCR 760
Breach of trade descriptions for falsely claiming engines rebuilt. Appellant, on income support, fined £1,200.
Held, failure to regard means of offender and not reasonable or proper fines would take six years to pay. Fine of £300 at £5 per week substituted.

Buchan v McNaughtan 1990 SCCR 13
Appellant pleaded guilty to breach of ss 3 and 5 of the Road Traffic Act 1988. In receipt of £47 per week invalidity benefit. Fined total of £225.
Held, if appellant could not pay fines he must have recourse to means enquiry court.

Hamilton v Scott 1987 SCCR 188
Appellants plead guilty to assault and fined £600 at £10 per week.
Held, that as a result of fines, appellants would almost certainly end up in prison for non-payment, and fines excessive and reduced to £300 at £5 per week.

Time to pay:

Court may allow time to pay.

Section 214(1). At least seven days must be allowed to pay fine or first instalment.

Court may refuse time to pay if there are reasons to do so.

Elder v Crowe 1996 SCCR 38
Appellant convicted of offering to supply counterfeit perfume with street value of £3,000. More than £2,000 in cash at house seized at time. Sheriff fined appellant £2,000 and allowed no time to pay. Decision upheld on appeal, since appellant had sufficient means.
Note: court can refuse time to pay if it appears there are sufficient means.

Section 214(2). Court may refuse time to pay the fine if:
(a) offender appears to have means to pay immediately; or
(b) offender does not wish time to pay; or
(c) offender has no fixed abode; or
(d) court is satisfied that there is any other special reason to refuse time to pay.
If court refuses time to pay and offender fails to pay it may impose imprisonment, stating the special reasons for its decision.

Alternative prison sentence may be imposed.

Barbour v Robertson 1943 JC 46
Brothel keeping. Fined £100 and refused time to pay in view of nature of offence.
LJ-C Cooper held: 'nature of offence rarely a relevant consideration' as to whether time to pay should be granted.
Note: special reason does not include the nature of the offence.

Section 214(4). On the occasion of the imposition of a fine when allowing time to pay or payment by instalments, the court may only impose the alternative of imprisonment in the event of future default if:
(a) the offender is personally present; and
(b) the court determines, having regard to the offender's character and nature of offence, or other special reason, that it is expedient to do so. Where a court so determines it shall state the special reason.

Robertson v Jessop 1989 SLT 843
Held, on appeal, magistrate's reason for refusing time to pay ie 'unrealistic since accused in custody' was itself unrealistic and appeal allowed and time to pay allowed for payment of fine.

Court may allow further time to pay.

Section 214(7). Where time to pay, court may on application by offender, and after giving prosecutor an opportunity of being heard, allow further time to pay.

Section 215(4). Such application may be oral or in writing.

Court may allow payment by instalments.

Note: generally, if instalments, fine payable in a year or so.

Tonner v Hamilton 1995 SCCR 469
Road Traffic Act 1988 offence. £350 fine at £5 a fortnight.
Upheld on appeal, since appellant had requested this repayment.

Brown v McGlennan 1995 SCCR 627
Appellant offered to pay £5 per week and ordered to do so on fine for £800.
Held, £5 per week reasonable but repayment time (over 160 weeks) unreasonable and appealed allowed and fine reduced to £400 at £5 per week.

Paterson v McGlennan 1991 SLT 832
Criminal Procedure (Scotland) Act 1995, s 214. Accused fined £450 at £5 per week with alternative of 60 days' imprisonment if default on grounds of record (16 previous convictions).
Held, (bench of five judges)· (1) 90 weeks' repayment period excessive; (2) alternative of imprisonment on grounds of accused character not justified since he had paid fines in the past. Fines reduced and default order quashed.

Section 215(3). Court may only refuse such application if satisfied:
(a) that failure to pay is wilful; or
(b) that there is no reasonable prospect of securing payment if further time allowed.

Section 215(8). Where court has imposed fine, court may of its own accord or on application of offender order payment by instalments of such amounts and at such time as it thinks fit.

Section 215(9). Where court has ordered payment by instalments it may allow further time to pay or order payment of lesser amounts or at longer intervals than those originally fixed.

Restriction on imprisonment for default.

Buchanan v Hamilton 1988 SCCR 379
Drink-driving offence. Fined £250 with default order because of nature of offence.
Held, nature of offence not a relevant reason for imposing the alternative and appeal allowed and alternative of imprisonment quashed.

Finnie v McLeod 1983 SCCR 387
First offender fined £100 for shoplifting and imprisonment in default due to 'nature of offence' which sheriff described as 'barefaced shoplifting'.
Held, very case where appropriate for the sheriff to impose the alternative.

Compare with:

Buchanan v Hamilton 1988 SCCR 379
Difference is that in Finnie the sheriff referred to gravity of offence rather than just merely the nature.

Restriction on imprisonment for default:

Most sheriff courts issue warning letters on default before issuing citation to a means enquiry court.

Section 216(1). Where court has imposed a fine, without imposing imprisonment in default of payment it shall not impose imprisonment for failing to make payment unless on an occasion subsequent to that sentence the court has enquired into the reason why the fine has not been paid, in his presence.

Section 216(2). Subsection (1) shall not apply if offender is in prison.

Fine defaulter may be cited to attend a means enquiry court.

Dunlop v Allan 1984 SCCR 329
Careless driving, motor cyclist killed. Sheriff fined appellant and imposed alternative of imprisonment.
Held, not competent to impose alternative of imprisonment on ground of gravity of offence (careless driving) which was not punishable with imprisonment in the first instance.

Section 216(3). A fine defaulter may be cited to attend a means enquiry court, or a warrant may be issued for his arrest.

Section 216(7). Where a child would, if adult, be liable to imprisonment in default of payment of any fine, the court may order the child to be detained for period not exceeding one month. Only where court considers no other disposal suitable.

As an alternative disposal, court may make a Fine Supervision Order (FSO).

Supervision pending payment:

Section 217(1). When given time to pay the offender may be under the supervision of local social work department while paying.

Section 217(4). Detention of an offender under 21 as an alternative disposal when a fine is unpaid is not competent unless a Fine Supervision Order (FSO) has been made.

Section 217(5). Subsection (4) does not apply unless court is satisfied that it is impracticable to place offender under FSO and states the grounds on which it is so satisfied.

Section 217(6). Where an FSO has been made, the court must obtain a report from the supervising authority before imposing the alternative.

Periods of imprisonment for non-payment.

Periods of imprisonment for non-payment:

Section 219(1). When imposing a fine a court may impose a period of imprisonment in default of payment. If no such order made and person fails to pay fine or instalment in time the court may impose imprisonment for such failure.

Section 219(2), (4), (5). Maximum period of imprisonment is determined by amount of fine still unpaid:

Amount of fine				Period of imprisonment
Below £	200			7 days
Over £	200	below £	500	14 days
,, £	500	,, £	1,000	28 days
,, £	1,000	,, £	2,500	45 days
,, £	2,500	,, £	5,000	3 months
,, £	5,000	,, £	10,000	6 months
,, £	10,000	,, £	20,000	12 months
,, £	20,000	,, £	50,000	18 months
,, £	50,000	,, £100,000		2 years
,, £100,000		,, £250,000		3 years
,, £250,000		,, £1 million		5 years
,, £1 million				10 years.

Section 219(3). If fines were imposed by same court on same day, the period of imprisonment will be determined by the total of the fines imposed.

Section 220. In the event of imprisonment being imposed as an alternative, the offender may secure his release or reduce the period spent in prison by making payment in whole or in part while in prison (in proportion to amount of fine outstanding).

Section 224. All warrants for imprisonment in default of payment of a fine shall specify a period at the expiry of which the sentence shall be discharged, notwithstanding that the fine has not been paid.

Section 213. Fine may be remitted in whole or part by any court which is at that time responsible for its enforcement (High Court fines enforced by sheriff court). Attendance of accused unnecessary.

Criminal Justice Act 1991, s 24: court may apply to the Secretary of State to have sums deducted from income support to secure payment.

Sum may be deducted from income support to secure payment.

Court may make a Supervised Attendance Order (SAO)

Alternative to imprisonment for non-payment of fine.

Offender must attend a place of supervision and carry out instructions of supervising officer.

Consent of offender **not** required.

Supervised Attendance Orders (SAOs):

Criminal Procedure (Scotland) Act 1995, ss 235–237, Sch 7 Court may make a supervised attendance order. Offender aged 16 years or over convicted, fine imposed, offender has failed to pay, the court instead of ordering the alternative of imprisonment may make a supervised attendance order. Offender must attend a place of supervision for not less than 10 hours and not more than 50 hours where the unpaid fine is less than level 1 (£200); in all other cases not more than 100 hours and carry out the instructions of a supervising officer. Offender's consent is not required.

A supervised attendance order may be made in the following situations:

Discretionary SAO.		**Discretionary orders:**
		(a) CP(S)A 1995, s 235(3). SAO available if offender 18 or over, imprisonment in default would have been imposed but the court considers SAO more appropriate than prison.
		(b) CP(S)A 1995, s 237. SAO available when further time to pay is given in case of future default if a request for further time to pay under s 215(1) has been granted.
Mandatory SAO.		**Mandatory orders:**
		Section 235(4). Court shall make SAO where offender over 18 and not serving sentence of imprisonment, imprisonment in default would have been imposed, the unpaid fine does not exceed level 2 (£500) and court is prescribed for purposes of subsection.
Orders in place of fines for 16- and 17-year-olds		**Orders in place of fines for 16- and 17-year-olds:**
		Section 236. Applies where 16- or 17-year-old convicted of offence by court of summary jurisdiction and court considers fine appropriate. The court shall determine the amount of the fine and whether offender likely to pay it within 28 days. If offender not likely to pay SAO must be made immediately.

References: Nicholson, 1–64 ff; Renton and Brown, 23–29 ff.

IMPRISONMENT AND DETENTION

Imprisonment is competent only for adult offenders (21 years or over). Detention is competent for young offender (not less than 16 but under 21 years of age). Court may not pass prison sentence on adult offender not previously sentenced unless no other disposal appropriate and must first consider background reports. Court may not sentence young offender to detention unless no other disposal appropriate and must first consider background reports. No court may sentence to imprisonment or detention if offender is not legally represented and not previously sentenced to imprisonment or detention unless refused legal representation or failed to apply.

Note: full bench dealt with question of consecutive or concurrent sentences in *Nicholson v Lees* 1996 SCCR 551 (dealt with under Bail above).

COMMENTARY	CASE LAW	STATUTE LAW
		Criminal Procedure (Scotland) Act 1995, ss 204–210
		Imprisonment:
Imprisonment.	*Nicholson v Lees* 1996 SCCR 551 Full-bench decision on concurrent/consecutive sentences: see Bail above.	Only competent for adult offenders: 21 years or over.
Adult offender not previously sentenced to imprisonment or detention.		Section 204(2). Court may not pass prison sentence on adult offender not previously sentenced to imprisonment or detention by UK court, unless it considers that no other method of dealing with him is appropriate. For this purpose court shall from an officer of local authority or otherwise obtain such information as it can about offender's circumstances (eg Social Enquiry Report). Court must also take account of any information before it relating to offender's character and his physical and mental condition. It has power to make a hospital order in addition to imposing a sentence of imprisonment. (Summary court must state reason for sentence of imprisonment and enter reason in record of proceedings).
Alternative?		
Custodial sentence being considered.		
Court must first consider background reports.		
Court must, when taking account of previous sentences, disregard suspended sentences not brought into effect.		Section 204(4). Court must, when taking account of previous sentences: (i) disregard suspended sentence (English/Irish) which has not been brought into effect; (ii) interpret detention as meaning a young offenders' institution or detention centre, but not borstal training (except in England and Wales).

If first sentence, offender should be allowed legal representation, irrespective of offender's age.

Section 204(1). No court may pass sentence of imprisonment or detention (or impose such sentence as immediate alternative to fine under CP(S)A 1995, s 214(2)) if the offender is not legally represented and has not previously been sentenced to imprisonment or detention by a UK court. But legal representation not a prerequisite if offender either:
(a) has been refused legal aid on financial grounds; or
(b) has failed to apply for legal aid after having been informed of his right and having had the opportunity to do so.

Section 204(5). These provisions apply to all courts and all sentences of imprisonment or detention, except those fixed by law.

Detention:

Detention.

Young offender.

Young offenders' institution.

Is there any other method of dealing with offender appropriately?

Section 207(1), (5). Young offender: not less than 16, but under 21 years of age. All young offenders serve sentence in young offenders' institution. Maximum and minimum sentences are same as for imprisonment.

Section 207(3). A young offender not to be sentenced to detention unless no other way of dealing with that person is appropriate. Reason for imposing detention to be given and, except in High Court, entered in the record of proceedings.

Bain v Wilson 1998 SCCR 454
On 18 February 1998 sheriff proceeded to sentence appellant to detention without obtaining any further report (as CP(S)A 1995, s 207 requires), since he had dealt with appellant on other matters and appellant was known to sheriff from reports provided in January 1998.
Held, to allow sheriff to proceed from recollection would ride roughshod over CP(S)A 1995, s 207(4). Observed, per LJ-G Rodger, court can obtain information from up-to-date reports from other proceedings.
Note: case shows LJ-G Rodger's observations are not to be given wide interpretation.

Section 207(4). For purposes of CP(S)A 1995, s 207(3), court shall obtain information from office of local authority or otherwise (SER) and court must also take into account any information before it relating to offender's character, and his physical and mental condition.

Additional points:

Supervised Release Orders

Fyfe v HMA 1997 SCCR 755
Breach of SROs. 'Date of first proven failure' is the date on which failure occurred.

(i) Supervised Release Orders (SROs): CP(S)A 1995, s 209. Only on indictment cases where period of custody 12 months to four years where court considers it necessary to protect public. Again, court must first consider report from local authority officer about offender and his circumstances. Applies to adult and young offenders and prisoner's consent not required. Breach of SRO (proved by one witness) means that court can vary order or order that offender be returned for whole or part of period beginning with date of order for return and equal to period between first proven failure referred to in statement on oath and date on which supervision under SRO would have ceased (see s 209 for details).

Guilty pleas.

(ii) Guilty pleas: CP(S)A 1995, s 196(1). In determining what sentence to pass on, or what disposal or order to make in relation to, an offender who has pled guilty to an offence, a court may take into account:
(a) the stage in the proceedings for the offence at which the offender indicated his intention to plead guilty; and
(b) the circumstances in which the indication was given.

Note: CP(S)A 1995, s 196 offectively overrules *Strawthorn v McLeod* 1987 SCCR 413. May be applied where children saved from giving evidence. CP(S)A 1995, s 196 may also allow increased sentence where circumstances merit it, eg very late plea causing great inconvenience.

References: Nicholson, chapter 2; Renton and Brown, 23–01 to 23–22.

OFFENCES RACIALLY AGGRAVATED

Where it is libelled in an indictment or specified in a complaint and proved that an offence has been racially aggravated the court shall take that aggravation into account in determining the appropriate sentence. An offence is racially aggravated if offence is motivated by ill-will or malice towards members of a racial group based on their membership thereof OR if offender evinces towards victim malice and ill-will based on membership (or presumed membership) of that group. Evidence from a single source is sufficient to establish that an offence is racially aggravated.

COMMENTARY	CASE LAW	STATUTE LAW
Court shall take racial aggravation into account when sentencing.		Crime and Disorder Act 1998, s 96 Section 96(1), (5). Where it is libelled in an indictment or specified in a complaint and proved that an offence has been racially aggravated, the court shall take the aggravation into account in determining the appropriate sentence.
Racially aggravated Malice or ill-will based upon victims membership of a racial group.		Section 96(2). An offence is racially aggravated if: (a) at time of offence or immediately before or after the offender evinces towards the victim (if any) malice or ill-will based upon the victim's membership (or presumed membership) of a racial group; or (b) the offence is motivated (wholly or partly) by malice and ill-will towards members of a racial group based on their membership of that group. Evidence from a single source sufficient to establish that offence is racially aggravated.
'membership'		Section 96(3). In CDA 1998, s 96(2)(a) 'membership' includes association with members of that racial group; 'presumed' means presumed by the offender. Section 96(4). It is immaterial for purposes of CDA 1998, s 96(2)(a), (b) whether or not the offender's malice or ill-will is also based on— a) the fact or presumption that person belongs to any religious group; or (b) any other factor not mentioned in that paragraph.
'racial group'		Section 96(6). 'Racial group' means a group of persons defined by reference to race, colour, nationality (including citizenship) or ethnic or national origins.

PROBATION ORDER

A Probation Order (PO) may be made where offence is one for which sentence not fixed by law. Consideration by court of various factors before making probation order (see below). Explanation to, and agreement of, the offender required before order made. Right of appeal not affected. Supervision for specified period by officer of local authority. Court has discretion re additional requirements. Residential requirement may be added. Unpaid work requirement may be included. Treatment for mental condition may be included. Compensation requirement may be included. In event of failure to comply with requirements of order court may impose fine or vary requirements or make a Community Service Order (CSO). If further offence committed, court may sentence for offence for which order made, as well as for offence committed during period of probation.

COMMENTARY	CASE LAW	STATUTE LAW
		Criminal Procedure (Scotland) Act 1995, ss 228–234
Offence must be one for which sentence not fixed by law.	*HMA v Heron* 1998 SCCR 449 Pensioner stabbed estranged partner. *Held*, on appeal, probation not unduly lenient. (See Assault notes above.)	Section 228(1). Where accused convicted of offence (where sentence not fixed by law) and court is of opinion it is expedient to do so, having regard to circumstances includ ing the nature and character of offender (having obtained report on this), court may make a probation order (PO) requir ing the offender to be under supervision for a period of not less than six months and not more than three years.
Court must consider various factors before making a probation order: nature of offence; character of offender; reports on character of offender; home surroundings of offender; whether suitable arrangements can be made by appropriate local authority.		
		Section 228(2). Court shall not make PO unless the appropri ate local authority can make suitable arrangements for supervision.
Order to be as nearly as may be in form prescribed.		Section 228(3). PO shall be as nearly as may be in the form prescribed and: (a) name the local authority area in which offender is to reside or resides; and (b) make provision for the offender to be under the super vision of a local authority offi cer in that area.
Explanation to, and agreement of, offender required before order made.		Section 228(5). Before making a PO, a court must explain, in ordinary language, to the offender the effect of the order, including any additional requirement, and result of fail ure to comply. Agreement of offender required before order can be made. Requirements to be included to be stated.
Copy of probation order given to relevant parties.		Section 228(6). Copy of proba tion order to be given by clerk of the court to supervising offi cer, probationer, and person supervising place of residence (if necessary).

Additional requirements:

Court has discretion re additional requirements.

Section 229(1). Court has discretion re additional requirements and such requirements as may be made to secure good conduct or prevent repetition by offender of offence or the commission of other offences.

Residential requirement may be added.

Section 229(2), (3). Residential requirement may be added. Before making such order, court must consider home surroundings of offender. If such order made, it must specify name of residence and may involve change of surroundings. Period of residence to be for not more than 12 months from date requirement order made or beyond expiry date of order.

Unpaid work requirement may be added.

Section 229(4). Unpaid work may be included: not less than 40 and not more than 240 hours.

Compensation requirement may be included.

Section 229(6). Compensation requirement may be included: lump sum or instalments for any personal injury, loss or damage caused. Compensation provisions of CP(S)A 1995 applied.

Section 229(7). Where such compensation requirement then:
(a) payment must be not more than 18 months after making of order and not later than two months before end of probation, whichever first occurs;
(b) court may vary terms on application of offender or local authority officer;
(c) in proceedings for breach where only failure is failure to comply with compensation requirement, document purporting to be certificate signed by clerk of court shall be sufficient evidence of such breach.

Requirement of treatment for mental condition:

Treatment for mental condition requirement may be added.

Section 230(1). Treatment for mental condition may be included. Evidence re mental condition of offender to be given by registered medical practitioner. Period of treatment not to extend beyond 12 months from date of requirement specified.

Section 230(2). Treatment will be one of the following:
(a) as a residential patient in a hospital (not a state hospital);
(b) as a non-resident patient;
(c) by or under the direction of specified registered medical practitioner or chartered psychologist.

Section 230(3). A court shall not make PO unless satisfied that arrangements made for treatment specified in order, and, if offender to be resident patient, for his reception.

Section 230(4)–(7). Treatment or place of treatment may be changed with consent of probationer and supervising officer. Officer must notify the court of the new arrangements. Treatment must still be by registered medical practitioner and, if patient to be resident, must have arrangements for him to be received as such.

Section 232(5). Refusal of probationer to undergo any surgical, electrical or other treatment will not be failure to comply with order if court considers refusal reasonable.

Section 232(6). Without prejudice to CP(S)A 1995, s 233, failure to comply will not include probationer being convicted of offence during probation period.

Section 231(1). CP(S)A 1995, Sch 6 applies in relation to amendment and discharge of POs.

Section 231(2). Where, under CP(S)A 1995, s 232, a probationer is sentenced for an offence for which he was on probation, the PO shall cease to have effect.

Failure to comply with requirement:

Failure to comply with requirements of order.

Warrant for arrest or citation to appear.

Valentine v Kennedy 1987 SCCR 47
If breach denied, failure to comply has to be proved beyond reasonable doubt.
Note: under CP(S)A 1995, s 232(3) proof by one witness is enough.

Section 232(1). If it appears to court on information from local authority officer that probationer has failed to comply with order, it may issue warrant for his arrest or cite him to appear.

Proof of failure.

Court may impose fine, vary requirements or make a CSO.

Section 232(2), (3). If breach proved (one witness shall be sufficient) the court may:
(a) impose a fine (except in a case of failure to comply with compensation requirement) which may be levied without prejudice to continuation of PO and not exceeding level 3 on the standard scale; or
(b) sentence offender for offence for which order was made; or
(c) vary requirements of PO - any extension of probation period must terminate not later than three years from date of PO; or
(d) make a CSO to run with PO.

Commission of further offence:

Commission of further offence.

Warrant for arrest or citation to appear.

Section 233(1). If it appears to a court that the probationer has been convicted by a court in Great Britain of an offence committed while on probation and he has been dealt with for that offence, the court may issue a warrant for his arrest or cite him to appear. The court may, if it thinks fit, sentence the offender for the offence for which the order was made.

Conviction for offence by court which made order.

Section 233(2). Where probationer convicted by the court of an offence committed while on probation, it may, if it thinks fit, sentence him for the offence for which the order was made as well as for the offence committed during the period of probation.

If offence committed as part of unpaid work requirement, this is an aggravation.

Section 233(3)–(5). As with CSO, if unpaid work requirement to PO and offence committed in that work place during or within three months of PO, then court which sentences him for that offence shall have regard to fact that the offence was committed in those circumstances (in effect an aggravation). Circumstances which satisfy aggravation must be libelled.

Section 233(6). As with CSO, unless challenged circumstances of aggravation shall be held as admitted (in effect a kind of special capacity).

Order may be amended at request of probationer or supervising officer.

Section 231, Sch 6, paras 2 and 3.

Order may be discharged at request of probationer or supervising officer, or when time period expires.

Section 231, Sch 6, para 1.

References: Renton and Brown, 23–123 ff.

PROCEEDS OF CRIME

Forfeiture

The Proceeds of Crime (Scotland) Act 1995 provides for the forfeiture of property used to facilitate crime and the confiscation of the proceeds of crime. Court may make a suspended forfeiture order in respect of property used to facilitate the commission of any offence. The order is made on application of the prosecutor. In general, property is not forfeited right away. Moveable property is forfeited 60 days after making order unless perishable etc whereby it is forfeited immediately. Heritable property is forfeited six months later.

COMMENTARY	CASE LAW	STATUTE LAW
		Proceeds of Crime (Scotland) Act 1995
		Suspended Forfeiture Orders: s 21.
Court may make SFO in respect of property used to facilitate the commission of **any** offence.		Section 21(2). The court may, if satisfied on the application of the prosecutor that any property which was at the time of the offence or of the accused's apprehension in his ownership or possession or under his control— (a) has been used for the purpose of committing, or facilitating the commission of any offence; (b) was intended for that purpose, make a suspended forfeiture order in respect of that property.
Prosecutor must intimate to court interest in property of someone other than accused. SFO shall name person having or suspecting to have interest in property.		Section 21(4). If the prosecutor knows or reasonably suspects he knows that someone other than the accused is the owner, or has an interest in the property to which the SFO relates, he shall intimate that fact to the court on making the application. The SFO shall then name the person having or suspecting to have interest in property. (If prosecutor becomes aware of interest after SFO made, he must intimate to court and can apply to vary SFO).
Facilitation.		Section 21(5). Facilitation under s 21 includes any steps taken to dispose of property or avoid apprehension or detection after the offence.
		Section 21(7), (8). Where a statute prohibits the forfeiture of property for offence for which accused convicted an SFO cannot be made. Where the statute specifies the property which may be subject to an SFO then other property cannot be forfeited.

Court may order compensation order to be paid off first.	Section 21(9). If SFO made along with compensation order court may order CO be paid off first from the sale of the property.
Property placed under control of clerk of court.	Section 21(11). Any property in respect of which SFO made shall be placed under the control of the clerk of the court until— (a) the order is recalled; or (b) the property is forfeited.
Property not forfeited right away:	*Note:* in general property is not forfeited immediately.
moveable ...	Section 24. Moveable property is generally forfeited 60 days after making SFO. If, however, it is perishable, dangerous, of no commercial value, or cannot be lawfully be sold, supplied or possessed, it shall be forfeited immediately. Heritable property is forfeited six months later.
heritable.	
	Section 23. If reasonable cause to believe property subject to SFO is at specified place or premises the court may grant warrant to search premises and seize property.
Person other than accused with interest in property: SFO shall be recalled unless prosecutor proves knowledge/acquiescence.	Section 25. If person other than accused satisfies court on the balance of probabilities that he is owner or has interest in property subject to SFO, it shall be recalled—unless the prosecutor proves beyond reasonable doubt that: (a) he knew or ought to have known property was used to facilitate the commission of the offence; and (b) the applicant failed to take reasonable steps to prevent this use. If applicant came to own property after commission of offence prosecutor must prove that applicant knew or ought to have known that the property was so used.
Even so, order may be recalled if excessive or inappropriate.	Section 25(3). Even if court satisfied applicant knew or should have known, the court may recall an SFO if it appears to the court in all the circumstances of the case that the SFO is excessive or inappropriate. (Forfeiture of motor vehicles: see s 33A of the Road Traffic Act 1988, under RTA. Note PC(S)A 1995 does not apply here).
Appeals.	Section 27(2). SFO appealable as if appeal against sentence.

Confiscation

The court has powers of confiscation for all offences on indictment and all those summary offences with a fine larger than level 5 on the standard scale and/or where more than 3 months imprisonment is available. Part I of the Proceeds of Crime (Scotland) Act 1995 extends to the Sheriff Court powers of confiscation for drug-trafficking offences. In cases of non-drug trafficking offences it is the <u>benefit</u> the accused gets from the offence which is confiscated, whereas with drug trafficking offences it is the <u>proceeds</u> of the drug trafficking which are confiscated. Court can make assumptions as to what constitutes benefit or proceeds (see below). The property itself does not have to be surrendered only its value plus interest. Confiscation orders may be postponed or varied and are appealable as if appeals against sentence.

COMMENTARY	CASE LAW	STATUTE LAW
		Proceeds of Crime (Scotland) Act 1995
		Non-drug trafficking offences:
Non-drug trafficking offences. It is the 'benefit' which is confiscated.		Section 1(4). The court may make a confiscation order against the accused only if it is satisfied beyond reasonable doubt by the Crown that he has benefited from the commission of the offence concerned.
'benefit'		Section 2(1). 'Benefited' means if in connection with commission of offence he has obtained, directly or indirectly, any property or other economic advantage. Court can make assumptions on the extent of benefit received unless the accused proves them to be incorrect on the balance of probabilities. The court may assume any benefit received since the date of the offence was received in connection with the offence, and that any expenditure in that period was paid out of such benefit.
Assumptions as to extent of benefit.		
		Section 2(4)–(6). Where confiscation order applied for in relation to two or more offences, or where the offender has a previous conviction for which a confiscation order would have been competent in the past six years, the court can assume that all benefits since first offence within the six years were received in connection with these offences and any expenditure was met out of these benefits. Again, the accused can disprove these assumptions on the balance of probabilities.

Order to make material available.

Section 18. Order to make material available. Where reasonable grounds to suspect that a person has received a benefit for which a confiscation order would be competent; it is in the public interest; and the material is not subject to legal privilege and is likely to be of substantial value to the investigation; the sheriff may grant an order allowing police access to the specified material to investigate the value of benefits received.

Drug trafficking offences:

Drug trafficking offences.

Section 1(5). The sum for confiscation shall be the amount not exceeding—
(a) what the court assesses to be the value of the proceeds of the person's drug trafficking; or
(b) amount which court satisfied might be realised at time of confiscation order albeit less than value of proceeds.

It is the 'proceeds' which are confiscated.

'proceeds'

Section 3(1)(a). Proceeds of drug trafficking include any payments or other rewards received by a person (whether before or after commencement of Act) in connection with drug trafficking carried on by him or another.

Section 3(1)(b). The value of the proceeds of drug trafficking is the aggregate of the values of the payments or other rewards (includes proceeds outwith Scotland).

Assumptions as to extent of proceeds.

Section 3(2). Court may assume that any property held by accused since conviction or in six years before his indictment/complaint are proceeds of drug trafficking free of any other interest and that expenditure since that date was met out these payments. Again, accused can disprove this on the balance of probabilities.

General:

Definitions of 'property'.

Property need not be surrendered.

Procedure.

Rowan, Petrs 1996 SCCR 887
Proceeds of Crime (Scotland) Act 1995, s 6(3). Confiscation order sought. Petitioner stated PC(S)A 1995, s 6(3) was applicable.
Held, not sufficient for petitioner merely to repeat words used in subsection. He must go further and specify or at least indicate basis for contending he satisfied requirements of PC(S)A 1995, s 6(3)(a)–(c). Unless he does so court may grant order declaring gift not implicative gift forming part of realisable property for purposes of confiscation order.

Sections 4-7 define property which constitutes a proceed or a benefit. Property need not be surrendered, only sum equivalent to value plus interest.

Section 9. Where a prosecutor applies for a confiscation order, he lodges with the clerk of court a statement assessing either the value of the accused's proceeds from drug trafficking or the benefit from the commission of the offence. This statement is also served on the accused. The court may require accused to indicate within such period as court may specify the extent to which he accepts each allegation and to indicate the basis for non-acceptance. If accused fails to respond he may be treated as accepting every allegation. Acceptance by accused of statement is conclusive proof. Accused can lodge statement which if prosecutor accepts shall be conclusive proof. If challenged, court must hold a hearing to consider the matters being challenged. (Parties can lodge a joint minute under CP(S)A 1995, s 256)

Appeals.

Postponement, variation.

HMA v Donnelly 1996 SCCR 904
Held, six-month time limit for postponing confiscation order (Proceeds of Crime (Scotland) Act 1995, s 10) has no application where hearing required under PC(S)A 1995, s 9(6) to consider challenge to allegation in prosecutor's (or for that matter defence's) statement, and no restriction on court's common law power to adjourn hearing where necessary in the interests of justice.

Confiscation orders appealable as if appeals against sentence. They may be postponed, varied or made up to six years after sentence: PC(S)A 1995, ss 10,11,13.

References: Renton and Brown, 23–72 to 23–120.

RESTRICTION OF LIBERTY ORDER

Court may make a Restriction of Liberty Order (ROLO) where offender 16 or over (and convicted of offence the sentence for which is not fixed by law) if it is the most appropriate disposal. Offender's consent is required. ROLO may restrict offender's movement for up to 12 hours a day in place specified and may run for up to 12 months. ROLO is a sentence for the purpose of appeal. Offender is monitored by person / device approved by the Secretary of State. ROLO can be made concurrent with probation order. ROLO can be reviewed on application of offender / person responsible for monitoring. If breach then ROLO may be varied or revoked, or a fine may be imposed. If revoked, court may dispose of offender as competent at time order made.

COMMENTARY	CASE LAW	STATUTE LAW
		Crime and Punishment (Scotland) Act 1997, s 5 inserts ss 245A–245H into Criminal Procedure (Scotland) Act 1995.
		Criminal Procedure (Scotland) Act 1995
Offender 16 or over.		Section 245A(1). Court can make ROLO on offender 16 or over (where sentence not fixed by law) if most appropriate disposal.
Not more than 12 hours a day.		Section 245A(2). ROLO may restrict offender's movement to place(s) specified but not for period(s) totalling more than 12 hours in one day.
Not longer than 12 months.		Section 245A(3). ROLO may be made up to 12 months.
Explanation of order.		Section 245A(4). Explanation to offender in ordinary language about order, consequences, reviews. Offender's consent required.
Copy of order.		Section 245A(5). Copy of order to offender and monitor.
		Section 245A(6). Court to consider information as to place of enforced presence and those likely to be affected by it.
Appeal.		Section 245A(7). ROLO is sentence for purpose of appeal.
Monitoring		Section 245A(11). No ROLO unless court satisfied compliance can be monitored as specified in order.
		Section 245B. Secretary of State to notify court of class of persons who may be monitors.
Remote monitoring		Section 245C. Court can require offender to wear device for remote monitoring.

Concurrent with probation order.

Section 245D. ROLO can be made concurrent with probation order if expedient with regards to circumstances such as nature of offence and character of offender.

Review: offender's consent required.

Section 245E. Offender/monitor may apply for review; offender' consent required.

Breach.

Section 245F. If appears to court offender has failed to comply without reasonable excuse court may fine, or revoke or vary order.

Disposal.

Section 245G. If ROLO revoked, court can dispose as competent at the time order made (having regard to time order in force).

Evidence from automatic statement from device sufficient.

Section 245H. Automatic statement from device of offender's movements accompanied by a signed certificate by nominated person that statement relates to offender shall be sufficient evidence, provided copy of statement served on offender prior to hearing and in any event if appears to court offender has insufficient notice court may adjourn.

SEX OFFENDER ORDER

The Crime and Disorder Act 1998, s 20, provides for sex offender orders, which prohibit the subject from doing anything described in the order. The applicant is the chief
constable and the action proceeds by way of summary application (civil procedure).
See the Crime and Disorder Act 1998 for details.
See Anti-social behaviour order (p 214 above) for details of offences in connection with
breach of both orders.

MISCELLANEOUS

HUMAN RIGHTS ACT 1998

The Human Rights Act 1998 gives effect to the European Convention on Human Rights. A court in determining a question in connection with a convention right must so far as relevant take into account any judgment of the European Court of Human Rights, opinion or decision of the Commission, and decision of the Committee of Ministers.

COMMENTARY	CASE LAW	STATUTE LAW
Act commences on 1 January 2000.		Human Rights Act 1998
		Section 1. HRA 1998 gives effect to the following rights: (a) arts 2 to 12 and 14 of the Convention; (b) arts 1 to 3 of the first Protocol; and (c) arts 1 and 2 of the Convention.
Court to take account (so far as relevant) of any judgment of ECHR.		Section 2. A court determining a question arising in connection with a convention right must (so far as relevant) take into account any judgment of the European Court of Human Rights, opinion or decision of the Commission, decision of the Committee of ministers.
Legislation to be read as compatible with Convention.		Section 3. So far as possible to do so, legislation must be read and given effect to in a way compatible with Convention rights, but this section does not affect the validity, continuing operation or enforcement of any incompatible legislation.
Declarator of incompatibility.		Sections 4, 5. A court may declare legislation incompatible with Convention but declarator has no effect on validity of legislation and is not binding on parties to the proceedings and Crown has right to intervene if court considering making such declarator.
		Section 4. If a court is satisfied a provision is incompatible with a Convention right it may make a declaration of incompatibility, but such declaration does not affect the validity, continuing operation or enforcement of the provision and is not binding on the parties to the proceedings in which it was made. (Declaratory power under HRA 1998, s 4 vested in High Court of Justiciary sitting as an appeal court.)

Public authorities.

Section 5. Where court is considering making a declaration of incompatibility the Crown is entitled to notice and on giving notice a minister is entitled to be joined as a party to the proceedings.

Public authorities:

Sections 6 to 9. Breach of Convention is unlawful but 'nothing in this Act creates a criminal offence': HRA 1998, s 7(8).

Section 6. It is unlawful for a public authority to act in a way which is incompatible with a Convention right unless the authority could not have acted differently as a result of legislation. Public authority includes a court or tribunal and any person certain of whose functions are of a public nature (not members of Parliament). An act includes a failure to act but does not include a failure to introduce legislation.

Section 7. Only a victim (or would be victim) of an unlawful act under HRA 1998, s 6 may bring proceedings or rely on the Convention rights. Proceedings under HRA 1998, s 7(1)(a) must be brought before the end of—
(a) one year beginning with the date on which the act complained of took place; or
(b) such longer period as court considers equitable having regard to all the circumstances, but that is subject to any rule imposing a stricter time limit in relation to the procedure in question.

Section 7(7). A person is a victim only if a victim for the purposes of article 34 of the Convention.

Section 7(8). Nothing in this Act [HRA 1998] creates a criminal offence.

Section 8. In relation to a court finding public authority acted (or proposed to act) unlawfully under HRA 1998 s 6, the court may grant such relief or remedy, or make such order, within its powers as it considers just and appropriate. Damages may be awarded where the court is satisfied it is necessary to afford just satisfaction to person in whose favour it is made.

Judicial acts.

Section 9. Proceedings where claimed a judicial act is unlawful in terms of HRA 1998, s 7(1)(a) may only be brought by exercising a right of appeal, on petition for judicial review or as rules may prescribe.

Amending legislation.

Section 10. Minister can by order amend legislation to remove the incompatibility after there has been a declaration of incompatibility (and no appeal in those proceedings) or in response to a judgment of the European Court made after coming into force of this section.

Existing human rights.

Section 11. A person's reliance on a Convention right does not restrict any other right conferred on him by UK law.

Section 12. Where court considering whether to grant relief which may affect the exercise of the Convention right to freedom of expression then no relief is to be granted unless respondent present or represented or all practicable steps taken to notify respondent or compelling reasons why he should not be notified.
No relief to restrain publication before trial unless court satisfied that applicant likely to establish that publication should not be allowed. Court must have regard to the extent to which the material has or is about to become available to public or extent to which it would be in public interest to publish and any relevant privacy code.

Section 12(5). In this section 'relief' includes any remedy or order than in criminal proceedings.

Section 14. UK has designated derogation from art 5(3) of the Convention—set out in HRA 1998, Sch 3, Pt I. To be extended every five years, otherwise ceases to have effect: HRA 1998, s 16.

Section 15. UK has designated reservation to art 2 of the first Protocol of the Convention—set out in HRA 1998, Sch 3, Pt II. To be reviewed every five years: HRA 1998, s 17.

Section 19. A minister must before second reading of bill make a statement to effect in his view either bill is compatible with Convention rights or he is unable to say so but government wishes to proceed with Bill.

Articles of the Convention.

Human Rights Act 1998, Sch 1: The Articles of the Convention

Right to life.

Art 2. Right to life.

Art 2.1. Everyone's right to life shall be protected by law. No one shall be deprived of his life intentionally save in the execution of a sentence of a court following his conviction of a crime for which the penalty is provided by law.

Art 2.2. Right to life not contravened where deprivation of life results from the use of force which is no more than absolutely necessary:
(a) in defence of any person from unlawful violence;
(b) to effect a lawful arrest or prevent the escape of a person lawfully detained;
(c) in action lawfully taken for the purpose of quelling a riot or insurrection.

Freedom from torture.

Art 3. No one shall be subjected to torture or to inhuman or degrading treatment or punishment.

Prohibition of slavery and forced labour.

Art 4. Prohibition of slavery and forced labour.

Art 4.1. No one shall be held in slavery or servitude.

Art 4.2. No one shall be required to perform forced or compulsory labour (does not include work as part of detention or on conditional release, military service or civil equivalent, service exacted in emergency, or any work forming part of normal civic obligations).

Right to liberty and security.

Art 5. Right to liberty and security.

Art 5.1. Everyone has the right to liberty and security of person. No one shall be deprived of his liberty save in the following cases and in accordance with a procedure prescribed by law, inter alia:
(a) the lawful detention of a person after conviction by a competent court;
(c) the lawful arrest or detention of a person on reasonable suspicion of having committed an offence or when it is reasonably considered necessary to prevent his committing an offence or fleeing having done so.

Art 5.2. Everyone who is arrested shall be informed promptly, in language which he understands, of the reasons for his arrest and of any charge against him.

Art 5.3 (see derogation, HRA 1998, Sch 3, Pt I). Everyone arrested or detained in accordance with the provisions of paragraph 1(c) shall be brought promptly before a judge and shall be entitled to trial within a reasonable time or to release pending trial. Release may be conditioned by guarantees to appear at trial.

Art 5.4. Everyone who is deprived of his liberty at arrest or detention shall be entitled to take proceedings by which the lawfulness of his detention shall be decided speedily by a court and his release ordered if the detention is not lawful.

Right to a fair trial.

Art 6. Right to a fair trial.

Pullar v UK 1996 SCCR 755
Juror was employee of prosecution witness but sheriff not alerted until after conviction, clerk of court had known prior to this time.
European Court *held* by majority there had been no contravention of Convention, art 6 since no evidence that juror actually prejudiced in favour of this witness nor evidence that objective observer would infer such prejudice and safeguards since one of 15 jurors.

Art 6.1. In determination of any criminal charge against him, everyone is entitled to a fair and public hearing within a reasonable time. Judgment shall be pronounced publicly, but the press and public may be excluded from all or part of the trial in the interests of morals, public order or national security in a democratic society; where the interests of juveniles or the protection of the private life of the parties so require; or to the extent strictly necessary in the opinion of the court in special circumstances where publicity would prejudice the interests of justice.

John Murray v UK (Feb 8, 1996) Reports of Judgments and Decisions 1997

Accused charged in Northern Ireland with aiding unlawful detention of a prisoner, he was silent during questioning and did not give evidence at trial. In a Diplock court, accused convicted, and judge said inference had been drawn from failure to explain his actions.

ECHR *held* by majority right to silence (Convention, art 6) was not absolute and it would be decided on a case by case basis looking at the weight given to inference but no violation here. Note should be taken of the fact the court gave weight to the fact the inference was made by a judge as opposed to a jury and the trial took place in a terrorist setting. May be different if jury trial and prosecution relying on inferences to a large degree.

Saunders v UK (Dec 17, 1996) Reports of Judgments and Decisions 1996

Saunders compelled under company law statute to answer questions of DTI inspectors and these were relied on in trial. Crown argued these were mainly exculpatory.

ECHR *held* Convention, art 6(1) violated and that the right not to self incriminate could not reasonably be confined only to remarks which are directly incriminating.

Gregory v UK (1998) 25 EHRR 577

Judge given note saying 'Jury showing racial overtones, one member to be excused', but judge never excused.

Held, 8 to 1, no violation of Convention, art 6(1), since direction by judge for jury to put aside prejudice was sufficient to ensure fair trial.

Dougan v UK 1997 SCCR 57

Delay. D failed to appear for trial in 1981 (for attempted murder of wife). Non-appearance warrant not handed to police until November 1984 and warrant issued for arrest. In 1991 Fiscal replied to letter from accused in USA saying no proceedings against him but check with police. Warrant executed in 1992 and convicted of assault and failure to appear. D never appealed when his plea in bar of trial repelled.

Held by Commission and Council of Ministers that due to poor administration by Fiscal and giving wrong advice and failing to notify the police the 'reasonable time' provided for by Convention, art 6(1) exceeded. Also held D had exhausted all domestic remedies because this requirement extended only to remedies likely to be effective and no prospect of successful appeal against unsuccessful plea in bar of trial.

Campbell v UK Application No 12323/86 July 13 1988 57 DR 148

Commission stated handcuffing of prisoner to prison officer during appeal proceedings did not breach Convention, art 6(1) and security considerations could justify interference with rights of prisoners.

Presumption of innocence.

Ukak v HMA 1998 SCCR 517
Convention, art 5(2) and 6(3)(a). Turkish Kurd arrested and charged without interpreter. He spoke no English. Presence of interpreter at interview, judicial examination and trial (where same interpreter for Crown and defence).
Held, arrest, detention and interview not unlawful or unfair and complaints that he thought interpreter agent of police (and therefore suspicious) were devoid of merit.

Benham v UK (June 10, 1996) Reports of Judgments and Decisions 1996
Civil action against B for non-payment of poll tax: given advice under legal aid but not representation. ECHR *held* Convention, art 6(3)(b) breached as classified action as criminal since custodial sentence available and B entitled to free legal representation.

X v UK Application No 9285/78, Oct 9 1978 52 DR 244
Legal aid—no right to choose representative: Convention, art 6(3)(c).
Note: following *Granger* (1990) 12 EHRR 460, where Convention, art 6 breached by denying legal aid at appeal stage, law changed and no 'open door' right of appeal, leave to appeal is now required which if granted will bring with it free representation.

Art 6.2. Everyone charged with a criminal offence shall be presumed innocent until proved guilty according to law.

Art 6.3. Everyone charged with a criminal offence has the following minimum rights:
(a) to be informed promptly, in detail, of the nature and cause of the accusation against him;
(b) to have adequate time and facilities for the preparation of his defence;
(c) to defend himself in person or through legal assistance of his own choosing or, if he has not sufficient means to pay for legal assistance, to be given it free when the interests of justice so require;
(d) to examine or have examined witnesses against him and to obtain the attendance and examination of witnesses on his behalf under the same conditions as the witnesses against him.

No punishment without law.

Art 7. No punishment without law.

Handyside v UK No 5493/72 17 YB 228
Argued offence of obscenity under Obscene Publications Act 1959–64 so imprecise that it might be applied without limit and breach Convention, art 7. Commission stated requirement of certainty did not require solid facts constituting crime to be set out in statute and a general definition for the courts to apply would suffice.

Art 7.1 No one shall be guilty of a criminal offence if act or omission did not constitute a criminal offence under national or international law at the time when it was committed. Nor shall a heavier penalty be imposed than the one that was applicable at the time when the offence was committed.

Art 7.2. This article shall not prejudice the trial of any person for acts or omissions which at the time when committed was criminal according to the general principles of law recognised by civilised nations.

Right to respect for private and family life.

Art 8. Right to respect for private and family life.

Campbell v UK (1993) 15 EHRR 137
Prison authorities interfered with prisoner's correspondence with solicitor.
Held, 8 to 1, that Convention, art 8 breached and only when authorities believe a letter has an illicit enclosure which normal means of detection have failed to disclose should a letter be opened but not read and with suitable guarantees such as opening letter in presence of prisoner.
Note: decision led to change in standing orders.

Art 8.1. Everyone has the right to respect for his private and family life, his home and his correspondence.

Art 8.2. There shall be no interference by a public authority with the exercise of this right except such as in accordance with the law and is necessary in a democratic society in the interests of national security, public safety or the economic well being of the country, for the prevention of disorder or crime, for the protection of health or morals, or for the protection of rights and freedom of others.

Freedom of religion.	*BBC Scotland, McDonald, Rodgers and Donald v UK* App No 34324/96 23 October 1997	Art 9. Freedom of thought, conscience and religion.
Freedom of expression.	Appeal from decision of *nobile officium* of High Court to postpone 'Frontline Scotland' programme on prisoner assaults by guards since distinct risk that evidence of prison doctor would be taken as testimony to be given great credibility by potential jurors. European Court said breach of Convention, art 10 unless it falls within art 10(2) ie prescribed by law in pursuance of a legitimate aim and was necessary in a democratic society.	Art 10. Freedom of expression. Art 10.1. Everyone has the right to freedom of expression. This right shall include freedom to hold opinions and receive and impart information and ideas without interference by public authority and regardless of frontiers.

Held, grounds for *nobile officium* sufficiently precise to be prescribed by law and postponement justified to ensure fair trial as not urgent (BBC never wanted to postpone it because it was last in series and would have to wait to Autumn for rescheduling). Held by 1st chamber application unanimously inadmissible.
(See *Muir v BBC* 1996 SCCR 584 for *nobile officium* case, contempt of court.)

Art 10.2. The exercise of these freedoms may be subject to such restrictions as prescribed by law and are necessary in a democratic society in the interests of national security, public safety, for the prevention of disorder or crime, for the protection of health or morals, for the protection of the reputation or rights of others, for preventing the disclosure of information received in confidence.

Freedom of assembly.

Art 11. Freedom of assembly and association.
Everyone has the right to freedom of peaceful assembly and to freedom of association with others. Again, this can be restricted as provided by law and necessary in a democratic society in the interests of national security etc.

Right to marry.

Art 12. The right to marry.

Prohibition of discrimination.

Sutherland v UK Report of the Commission (July 1, 1997)
Commission found the difference in age of consent for heterosexual and homosexual sex in UK was a violation of Convention, art 8 and art 14.
Note: The Sexual Offences (Amendment) Bill contains plans to equalise the age of consent.

Art 14. Prohibition of discrimination.
These rights shall be secured without discrimination on any ground such as sex, race, colour etc.

The First Protocol

Art 1. Protection of property; right to education (reservation, see HRA 1998, Sch 3, Part II: State to respect philosophical and religious convictions of parents in education of child. This is accepted by UK only so far as compatible with the provision of efficient instruction and training, and the avoidance of unreasonable public expenditure); right to free elections.

The Sixth Protocol

Art 1. Abolition of the death penalty.
Art 2. Death penalty in time of war.

Derogation from art 5(3).

HRA 1998, Sch 3, Pt I: derogation from art 5(3). On grounds of terrorism in Northern Ireland and the Prevention of Terrorism legislation which enables detention in right of arrest, for up to 48 hours where constable suspects person guilty of terrorist offence, and further detention without charge for up to five days where Secretary of State extends the detention period. The UK Government required derogation after 1989 case of *Brogan and Others* (1989) II EHRR 117.

In this case, the ECHR held that even the shortest of four periods of detention (four days and six hours), breached time permitted by art 5(3), and also that there had been violation of art 5(5) in case of each applicant.

From 1 November 1998 Protocol No. 1 comes into effect and does away with Commission and Court and replaces it with a full-time court sitting in Strasbourg.

CHILDREN'S HEARINGS

I Applications to sheriff for finding under Children (Scotland) Act 1995, s 68

COMMENTARY	CASE LAW	STATUTE LAW
Applies only to child of eight years or over.	*Merrim v S* 1987 SLT 193 Sheriff dismissed application by reporter to sheriff on grounds that s 32(2)(g) of SW(S)A 1968 had no application to persons of non-age.	*Note:* Criminal Procedure (Scotland) Act 1995, s 41: non-age provision. Social Work (Scotland) Act 1968
Jurisdiction—children's hearing and sheriff.	*L v McGregor* 1980 SLT 17 *Held* (2nd Div, Ct of Session) that the reporter has a discretion to make application to any sheriff, at least within the area of the reporter's jurisdiction.	Children (Scotland) Act 1995, s 68(3)(a): jurisdiction. This provides that the sheriff in whose area alleged criminal offence would be prosecuted has jurisdiction. In all other cases appropriate to apply to sheriff court situated in local authority area within which children's hearing took place.
Application to sheriff—time limit.	*H v Mearns* 1974 SC 152; 1974 SLT 184 *Held* (2nd Div, Ct of Session): a hearing is incompetent if outwith the statutory 28 days allowed for the lodging of an application to the sheriff.	C(S)A 1995, s 68(2)
Second proceedings brought by reporter because of intervening strike.	*McGregor v L* 1983 SLT (Sh Ct) 7 *Held* that the reporter was not barred from bringing proceedings five months after his first instructions to apply because of intervening strike of sheriff court staff.	
Continuation by sheriff.	*H v Mearns* 1974 SC 152; 1974 SLT 184 *Held* (2nd Div, Ct of Session) that provisions re continuation of hearing by sheriff applied only where initial hearing had actually begun.	Act of Sederunt (Child Care and Maintenance Rules) 1997, SI 1997/291, r 3.49.
Amendments.		SI 1997/291, r 3.48. Sheriff may at any time, on application of either party or on his own motion, allow amendment of grounds of referral.
Grounds disposed of previously (not *res judicata*).	*McGregor v D* 1981 SLT (Notes) 97 *Held* (2nd Div, Ct of Session) that sheriff was bound to hear all the evidence which reporter proposed to tender in relation to a referral, even if that evidence had been led in relation to other grounds disposed of previously. See also: *Kennedy v S* 1986 SLT 679	Grounds disposed of previously (not *res judicata*). These cases decided on express statutory authority requiring sheriff to hear evidence: see SI 1997/291, r 3.47. Norrie states therefore this authority not supportive of general proposition that grounds disposed of previously not *res judicata*: otherwise it would mean the reporter seeking a review of a children's hearing decision which he had no legitimate interest to do so. However, it is appropriate if there is enough new material to make it a new case.
Grounds of referral—incorrect reference to statutory provision in statement of grounds of referral.	*McGregor v A* 1982 SLT 45 Circumstances in which held (2nd Div, Ct of Session) that technically defective statutory reference did not invalidate referral when meaning clear.	
Summary procedure—prosecution of child—consent of Lord Advocate may be given by general directions.	*M v Dean* 1974 SLT 229 *Held* (2nd Div, Ct of Session) that general directions given by Lord Advocate, which did not appear on face of complaint, sufficient to comply with s 31(1) of SW(S)A 1968.	Social Work (Scotland) Act 1968, s 31(1) (preserved by C(S)A 1995, s 105(5), Sch 5).

Proof of grounds for referral.	*McGregor v H* 1983 SLT 626 *Held* (1st Div, Ct of Session) that ground for referral established in one application may be sufficiently proved in subsequent applications on same common factual basis by production of certified copy interlocutor.	
Consideration of referral on alternative 'offence' grounds.	*McGregor v A* 1982 SLT 45 *Held* (2nd Div, Ct of Session) that Act of Sederunt (Social Work) (Sheriff Court Procedure Rules) 1971, SI 1971/92, r 10 permits—but does not require—sheriff to make an alternative finding on the facts, where offence alleged in original ground of referral was unproved, and the facts prove that another offence has been committed.	SI 1997/291, r 3.50
Change of circumstances to be considered in application to sheriff for finding—evidential weight of unsworn statement to sheriff—duty of sheriff when new matter suddenly disclosed.	*Kennedy v B* 1973 SLT 38 *Held* (2nd Div, Ct of Session) that in reaching his decision sheriff had to take into account (1) change of circumstances of family in period of time between decision of hearing and date of proof, and (2) that sheriff was entitled to give weight to unsworn statement. *Observed* that when faced with a 'surprise disclosure' sheriff should consider adjourning to allow other side chance to reply.	
Decision—whether founded on the established grounds of referral.	*K v Finlayson* 1974 SLT (Sh Ct) 51 *Held* that when case is remitted back to children's hearing after finding by sheriff, children's hearing should base its decision on information laid before sheriff and not on additional information not available to sheriff: observations re what constitutes adequate 'reasons' stated by hearing.	C(S)A 1995, s 68(10)(a): grounds found established. Sheriff shall remit the case to reporter to arrange for children's hearing to consider and determine the case. *Note:* C(S)A 1995, s 68(10)(b) in addition may order child to be kept in place of safety if required. C(S)A 1995, s 68(9): grounds not established. Sheriff shall dismiss the application, discharge referral to children's hearing and recall any order under this Act which relates to child in respect of those grounds. *Note:* SI 1997/291, r 3.50: sheriff can find another offence established. *Note:* C(S)A 1995, s 85. If grounds of referral not made out but evidence establishes other grounds of referral, sheriff can remit case under C(S)A 1995, s 68(10) to reporter to arrange children's hearing on these grounds. (C(S)A 1995, s 85(6)(a) only where none of original grounds established.)
Grounds of referral—cannot petition *nobile officium* asking sheriff to reconsider.	*R, Petr* 1993 SLT 910 Parent petitioned *nobile officium* asking for Court of Session to order sheriff to consider anew whether grounds of referral made out (since new evidence as child retracted allegations of father's abuse). *Held*, petition incompetent as to allow would usurp SW(S)A 1968 by allowing procedure to reconsider grounds of referral at any stage. See also: *H, Petr* 1997 SLT 3	

II Appeals against decision of children's hearing

COMMENTARY	CASE LAW	STATUTE LAW
Time limit for lodging appeal.	*S, Appellants* 1979 SLT (Sh Ct) 37 *Held* that time for appeal must be computed to include date of children's hearing whose decision is being appealed against. *Kennedy v H* 1988 SLT 586 Discretion to extend time limit only available to a prospective appellant if he had right to appeal within time limits prescribed in Social Work (Scotland) Act 1968, s 49. But contrast: *Tudhope v Lawson* 1983 SCCR 435 (Sh Ct)	C(S)A 1995, s 51(1)(a)
Meaning of 'decision' of a children's hearing.	*H v McGregor* 1973 SLT 110 *Held*, that a 'decision' for the purposes of an appeal under SW(S)A 1968, s 49(1) is a decision by a children's hearing as to the final disposal of the referral to the hearing.	C(S)A 1995, s 51(1)(a)
Change of circumstances between hearings.	*D v Sinclair* 1973 SLT (Sh Ct) 47 *Held* that two-month interval between hearings long enough to allow circumstances to change materially and this should be taken into consideration when final decision being made. *Observed* that sheriff should not allow appeal merely because he thought another disposal preferable, but only if satisfied there had been flaw in procedure or proper consideration not given to some factor.	

III Evidence

COMMENTARY	CASE LAW	STATUTE LAW
Hearing before sheriff—nature of proceedings.	*McGregor v T* 1975 SC 14; 1975 SLT 76 *Held* (1st Div, Ct of Session) that proceedings before sheriff (on application by reporter under SW(S)A 1968, s 42) are judicial, but not criminal proceedings, and therefore normal rules of evidence, as regards competence and compellability of witnesses apply. See also: *Costanda v M* 1997 SLT 1396 Per LP Rodger: 'It is a case where the child is being charged with criminal conduct and nothing else. It thus passes the limit beyond which proof by normal criminal standard is necessary.' SW(S)A 1968, s 42(6). Sheriff shall apply standard of proof in criminal procedure where charge of criminal conduct: ground referred to in C(S)A 1995, s 52(2)(i). In all other cases civil standard applies: see *B v Kennedy* 1987 SLT 765. *P v Kennedy* 1995 SLT 476 If the ground of referral is not that of an offence (C(S)A 1995, s 52(2)(i)), then it is not appropriate to direct in terms of criminal standard of proof.	There is no provision requiring relevant person to attend. Children (Scotland) Act 1995, s 68(4). Relevant person and child entitled to be legally represented by person other than legally qualified (ie reporter). C(S)A 1995, s 68(4). Child has right and obligation to attend hearing before sheriff. C(S)A 1995, s 68(5)(b). Sheriff may relieve child of obligation if satisfied detrimental to child's interests, if application involves scheduled offence by someone other than child. C(S)A 1995, s 68(5)(a). Sheriff must also be satisfied attendance not necessary for just hearing of application.

Civil Evidence (Scotland) Act 1988 applies except where ground of referral is child committed an offence, in which case proof is beyond reasonable doubt: Children (Scotland) Act 1995, s 68(3)(b). Otherwise, no corroboration required; CE(S)A 1988, s 6: hearsay allowed. See *L v L* 1996 SLT 767: child must be admissible at date of proof.

C(S)A 1995, s 68(8). Sheriff can dispense with hearing of evidence as to whether ground established and is entitled to deem ground established. (Where child and parent accept ground of referral sheriff obliged to dispense with hearing). May dispense if parent accepts grounds and child could not understand explanation of grounds.

Competency and compellability of relevant person.

McGregor v T 1975 SC 14; 1975 SLT 76
Held (1st Div, Ct of Session) that parents of children involved in proceedings under Social Work (Scotland) Act 1968 are competent and compellable witnesses.
Observed that when objection taken sheriff should normally allow evidence subject to relevance and competency.

S v Lynch 1997 SLT 1377
L (father of illegitimate daughters) had no right of representation as no charge or control over daughters at relevant time and not within definition of parent or guardian at time of hearing.

McMichael v UK (Ser A No 307-B, 24 February 1995)
Held, exclusion of unmarried fathers from children's hearings was justifiable.

Unsworn statement—weight of evidence.

Kennedy v B 1973 SLT 38
Held (2nd Div, Ct of Session) that unsworn statement of child's parent entitled to have some weight given to it, if accepted. (See above under I.)

L v L 1996 SLT 767
Lord Hamilton *held*, inter alia, direct oral evidence of extra-judicial statement of child not admissible under s 2(1) of the Civil Evidence (Scotland) Act 1988 unless direct evidence of such matter was admissible at proof.

Identification and corroboration.

D v Kennedy 1974 SLT 168
Held (2nd Div, Ct of Session) that evidence given about identification and corroboration had to be specific.

Confidentiality.

A v G 1996 SCLR 787 (Sh Ct)
Held, social work records not confidential in sense that person might prohibit disclosure to a party having a legitimate interest to argue in relation to a child.

Proof of previous decisions by production of certified copy documents.	*McGregor v H* 1983 SLT 626 *Held* (1st Div, Ct of Session) that in subsequent application concerning another child in same family, certified copies of the sheriff's decision in earlier case sufficiently proved existence of common ground of referral. (See also below, and above under I.)	
Offences under Sch 1, Criminal Procedure (Scotland) Act 1995.	*McGregor v K* 1982 SLT 293 *Held* (2nd Div, Ct of Session) that when child referred under SW(S)A 1968, s 32(2)(d), it is not necessary to specify person who is alleged to have committed offence against child in terms of CP(S)A 1975. *S v Kennedy* 1996 SLT 1087 Scheduled offences committed outwith Scotland could found the basis of referral to a children's hearing.	Criminal Procedure (Scotland) Act 1995, Sch 1 Children (Scotland) Act 1995, s 52(2)(d)
Re 'Membership of household' in terms of C(S)A 1995, s 52(2)(e).	*McGregor v H* 1983 SLT 626 *Held* (1st Div, Ct of Session) that test to be applied is membership of household, not whether child is, at relevant time, living in same household as victim of relevant offence. (See also above.)	C(S)A 1995, s 52(2)(e)
'Likely to cause unnecessary suffering'— proper test includes whole facts.	*M v McGregor* 1982 SLT 41 *Held* (2nd Div, Ct of Session) that in reaching his decision, sheriff must consider whole facts of the case. Circumstances in which appellate court held that sheriff not entitled to hold grounds established. Observations of sheriff tending to 'pre-empt the disposal of the case by the children's hearing' *disapproved*.	C(S)A 1995, s 52(2)(c)
'Likely lack of parental care'— whether competent ground for referral.	*McGregor v L* 1981 SLT 194 *Held* (2nd Div, Ct of Session) that 'likely lack of parental care' was a competent ground under SW(S)A 1968. Circumstances in which inference of likely lack of parental care entitled to be drawn from parents' previous mode of life, even although child had never been in parents' care. *D v Kelly* 1995 SLT 1220 *Held*, sheriff erred by failing to identify impairment, establish a causal link between parent's regime and lack of care, look at prospective parental care and individual circumstances of each child. *Observed*, where parents through no fault of their own (accident/illness) rendered incapable of caring properly for children, criteria might be met even though no blame attached to parents. *M v Kennedy* 1995 SLT 123 *Observed*, inter alia, a parent's acceptance of ground in respect of one child not sufficient proof of the facts in subsequent referral of another child on the same grounds.	C(S)A 1995, s 52(2)(c)

IV   Assumption of parental rights

COMMENTARY	CASE LAW	STATUTE LAW
		Children (Scotland) Act 1995, ss 86–89
		Section 86(1). On application of the local authority the sheriff may make a Parental Responsibility Order (PRO) transferring to them the appropriate parental rights and responsibilities relating to the child (only during such period as the order remains in force).
		Section 86(3). 'Appropriate' parental rights are all parental rights and responsibilities, excluding right to agree or decline to agree to making of adoption order or freeing for adoption.
A v B and C 1971 SC (HL) 129 Adoption Act 1958. Question of whether parent unreasonably withholding consent to adoption. Per Lord Reid: 'The test is an objective test—would a reasonable parent have withheld consent?' *Central Regional Council v B* 1985 SLT 413 Meaning of 'persistently failed without reasonable excuse to fulfil parental responsibilities'. Per Lord Brand: 'I think [persistently] connotes consistent and repeated behaviour which need not be wilful.'		Section 86(2). PRO shall not be made unless the sheriff is satisfied that the relevant person either: (a) agrees unconditionally that the order be made; or (b) is a person who— (i) cannot be found, is not known, or is incapable of giving agreement; (ii) is withholding such agreement unreasonably; (iii) has persistently failed without reasonable cause to fulfil responsibility to safeguard and promote the child's health, development and welfare or if the child is living with him, the responsibility to maintain personal relations and direct contact with the child on a regular basis; or (iv) has seriously ill-treated the child, whose reintegration into the same household is for that or other reasons unlikely.
		Section 86(4). Relevant person under C(S)A 1995, s 86 is person who is parent or for the time being has parental rights in relation to the child.
		Section 86(5). Sheriff may in PRO impose such conditions as he considers appropriate and he may vary or discharge such order on the application of the local authority, child, any person who immediately before making the order is a relevant person, or any other person claiming an interest.

Miscellaneous

Section 86(6). A PRO shall if not first discharged by sheriff terminate on occurrence of any of the following—
(a) child attains 18 years;
(b) child becomes subject to—
(i) adoption order;
(ii) order freeing for adoption;
(c) order is made for return of child under Child Abduction and Custody Act 1985;
(d) a decision, other than a decision mentioned in s 25(2) of said Act of 1985 (decisions relating to rights of access) is registered with respect to him under s 16 of that Act.

Section 87(2). Even if PRO local authority may allow child to reside with parent, guardian, relative or friend where it appears to the local authority that to do so would benefit child.

Section 87(4). In course of application for PRO a reporting officer and curator ad litem may be appointed.

Section 88. Parental contact.

Section 88(2). Where PRO in force the child shall be allowed reasonable contact by the appropriate authority with—
(a) each person who immediately before the PRO is made is a relevant person; and
(b) where, immediately before that order was made—
(i) a residence order or contact order was in force with respect to the child, the person in whose favour the residence order or contact order was made;
(ii) a person was entitled to have the child residing with him under a court order, that person.

Section 88(3). On application to sheriff by child, local authority or by any person with an interest, the sheriff may make such orders as he considers appropriate as to contact, if any, between child and person specified in order.

Section 88(4). Sheriff may make order under C(S)A 1995, s 88(3) even if no application.

Section 88(5). An order under C(S)A 1995, s 88 may impose such conditions as the sheriff considers appropriate, and he may vary or discharge it on application of child, authority, or any person with an interest.

Section 88(6). An order under C(S)A 1995, s 88 shall if not first discharged by sheriff, terminate when the PRO to which it relates does.

See section 89 for offences in relation to PROs.

V Supervision order made by children's hearing—condition of residence

COMMENTARY	CASE LAW	STATUTE LAW
Residential condition prevails over contrary decision by court re custody.	*Grant v Grampian Regional Council* (May 1983, unreported) *Held* (Sh Ct) that a residential condition of supervision order made by children's hearing in favour of one party could not be overridden by any court making custody order in favour of another party.	Children (Scotland) Act 1995, s 70(3), (4)
'Place of supervision'—precise specification required.	*R v Children's Hearing for the Borders Region* 1984 SLT 65 *Held* (2nd Div, Ct of Session) that 'place' (where child under supervision to reside) had to be narrowly construed and that therefore children's hearing acted ultra vires by including in supervision requirement a condition that child 'to reside in a pre-adoptive home chosen by local authority'. Hearing's action also in contravention of ss 29(1) and 57(2) of Adoption Act 1958.	C(S)A 1995, s 70(3), (4)

VI Extension of local authority care orders

COMMENTARY	CASE LAW	STATUTE LAW
Extension of warrants.	*Humphries, Petr* 1982 SLT 481 *Held* (1st Div, Ct of Session) that extension of warrants (authorising two children who were in care, to be kept by foster parents) via *nobile officium* not contrary to the intention of SW(S)A 1968; in the instant case the children's father was awaiting trial for the murder of their sibling.	Children (Scotland) Act 1995, s 66(1). Allows child to be kept in a place of safety for a maximum period of 22 days but if risk to child remains **warrant** may be continued. C(S)A 1995, s 67(1). Reporter can apply to sheriff for a warrant to keep child where he is after warrant (granted and continued by children's hearing) has expired. *Note*: Norrie, p 173: 'appears sheriff can grant as many warrants for further detention as he thinks fit' therefore no need to apply to the *nobile officium*.

VII   Other orders

COMMENTARY	CASE LAW	STATUTE LAW
		Children (Scotland) Act 1995
Child Protection Orders.		Sections 57–61. CPO, granted by sheriff, can last until eighth working day after implementation and is subject to review(s).
		Section 60(1). Unless CPO implemented within 24 hours it ceases. Children's hearing comes in when CPO ends. CPOs replace safety orders. (See Norrie, ch 15 and Appendix 1 for details.)
Child Assessment Orders.		Section 55. CAO may be granted to assess physical or emotional well-being of child.
Exclusion Orders.		Sections 76–80. EO may be granted to exclude a named person from child's home.
Section 16 Principles.		Section 16. Overarching principles which children's hearing and courts must apply: (1) welfare of child is paramount consideration; (2) child to be given opportunity to express views and views to be regarded so far as practicable; (3) order not to be made unless considered it would be better for child that order made than none at all.

References: in general, see Kearney *Children's Hearings and the Sheriff Court*; Norrie *Children's Hearings in Scotland*.

BIBLIOGRAPHY

Publications referred to in the text
Alison, A.   I *Principles of the Criminal Law of Scotland* (1832).
Alison, A.   II *Practice of the Criminal Law of Scotland* (1833).
Ashworth, A.   *The European Convention on Human Rights* [1997] Crim LR 461.
Bovey, K.   *Misuse of Drugs* (1986).
Dickson, B. (ed).   *Human Rights and European Convention* (1997). (See chapter four on Scotland and ECHR by Jim Murdoch.)
Gane, C. H. W. and Stoddart, C. N.   *A Casebook on Scottish Criminal Law* (2nd edn, 1988).
Gordon, G. H.   *The Criminal Law of Scotland* (2nd edn, 1978, with second supplement, 1992).
Harris, D. J., O'Boyle, M. and Warbrick, C.   *Law of ECHR* (1995).
Hume, D.   *Commentaries on the Law of Scotland Respecting Crimes* (with supplement by B. R. Bell, in two volumes, 4th edn, 1844).
Kearney, B.   *Children's Hearings and the Sheriff Court* (1987).
McCall Smith, R. A. A. and Sheldon, D.   *Scots Criminal Law* (2nd edn, 1997).
Macdonald, Sir J. H. A.   *A Practical Treatise on the Criminal Law of Scotland* (5th edn, 1948).
Murdoch, J. L.   'The Civic Government Act and Public Processions' (1984) *Scolag* 97, 144.
Norrie, K.   *Children's Hearings in Scotland* (1997).
Renton and Brown   *Criminal Procedure according to the Law of Scotland* (by G. H. Gordon, Looseleaf, 1993).
Shiels, R. S.   *Controlled Drugs* (2nd edn, 1997).
Williams, G.   *Criminal Law* (2nd edn, 1961).
Wheatley, J.   *Road Traffic Law in Scotland* (2nd edn, 1993).

Books for additional reference
Archbold   *Pleadings, Evidence and Practice in Criminal Cases* (43rd edn, 1988).
Dickson, W. G.   *A Treatise on the Law of Evidence in Scotland* (two volumes, 1887).
Field, D.   *Law of Evidence in Scotland* (1988).
Gane, C. H. W. and Stoddart, C. N.   *Criminal Procedure in Scotland: Cases and Materials* (1988).
Harper, J. R.   *A Practitioner's Guide to the Criminal Courts* (1985).
Lewis, W. J.   *Manual of the Law of Evidence in Scotland* (1925).
Macphail, I. D.   *A Revised Version of a Research Paper on the Law of Evidence in Scotland* (1987).
Nicholson, C. G. B.   *Sentencing: The Law and Practice in Scotland* (2nd edn, 1992).
Walker, A. and Walker, N.   *The Law of Evidence in Scotland* (1964, reprinted 1980).
Wilkinson, A. B.   *The Scottish Law of Evidence* (1986).
Wilkinson's Road Traffic Offences   (P. Halnan and J. Spencer, eds, two volumes, 13th edn, 1987).

Index